*Richard Austin's*

# WESTCOUNTRY ANIMAL MAGIC

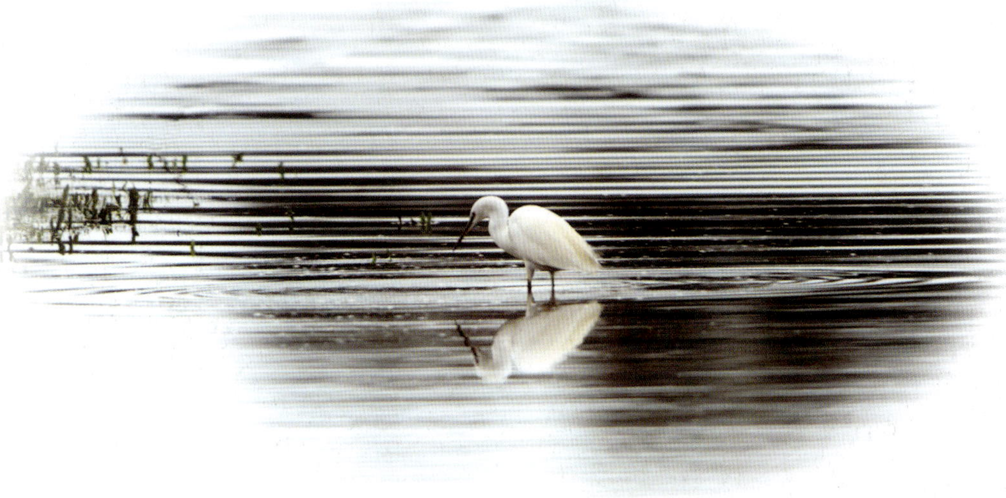

HALSGROVE

First published in Great Britain in 2002



**Title page photograph:** Reflections on the water attracted me to the Little Egret fishing on the flooded fields at Topsham.



**British Library Cataloguing-in-Publication Data**
A CIP record for this title is available from the British Library

ISBN 1 84114 184 4

HALSGROVE

Halsgrove House
Lower Moor Way
Tiverton, Devon EX16 6SS
Tel: 01884 243242
Fax: 01884 243325
email: sales@halsgrove.com
website: www.halsgrove.com

Printed and bound in Italy by
Centro Grafico Ambrosiano

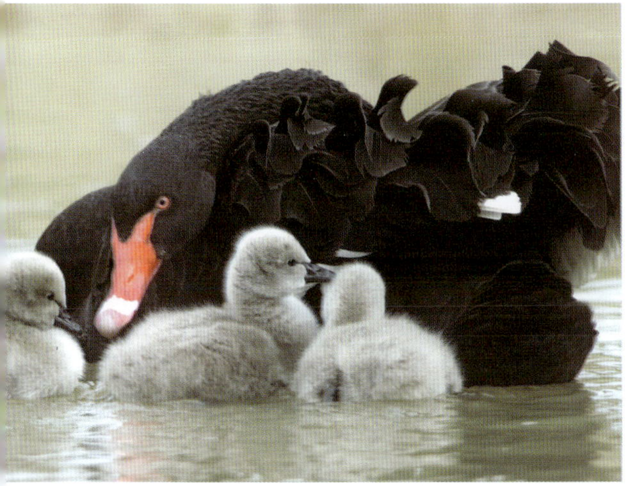

The male Black Swan is one of the most bad tempered and aggressive birds I have ever met, especially when there are cygnets around, a blow from one of their wings hurts, believe me I know from first-hand knowledge. This family made the news because they were hatched in North Devon in December.

I've spent many hours at the Abbotsbury Swannery waiting for cygnets to pop up through their mother's feathers. There can't be many baby birds as cute as newly-hatched cygnets and photographing them is always a challenge, as the cygnet emerged through the pure white feathers of his mother he began using his natural instincts and started to preen himself just like his mother.

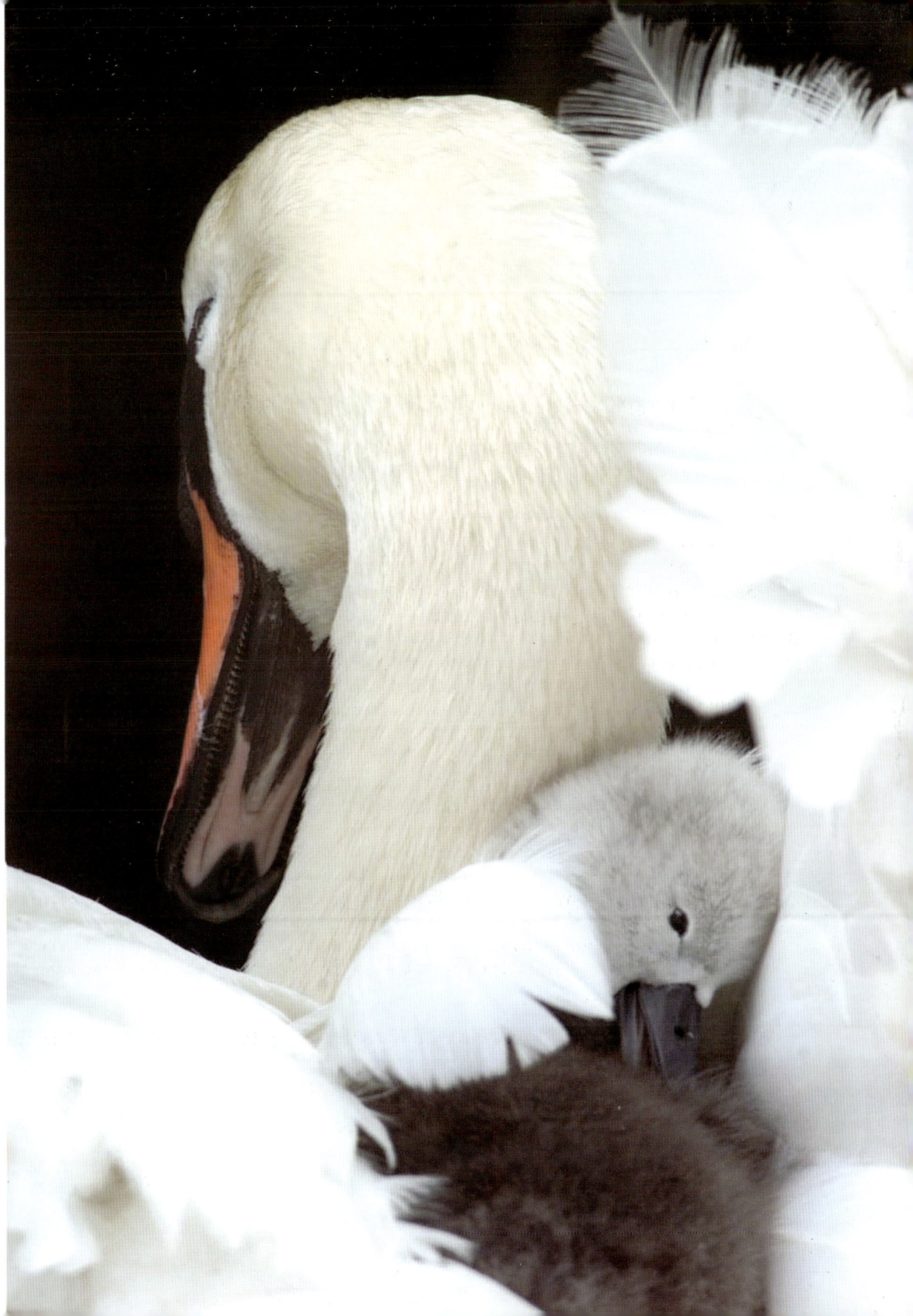

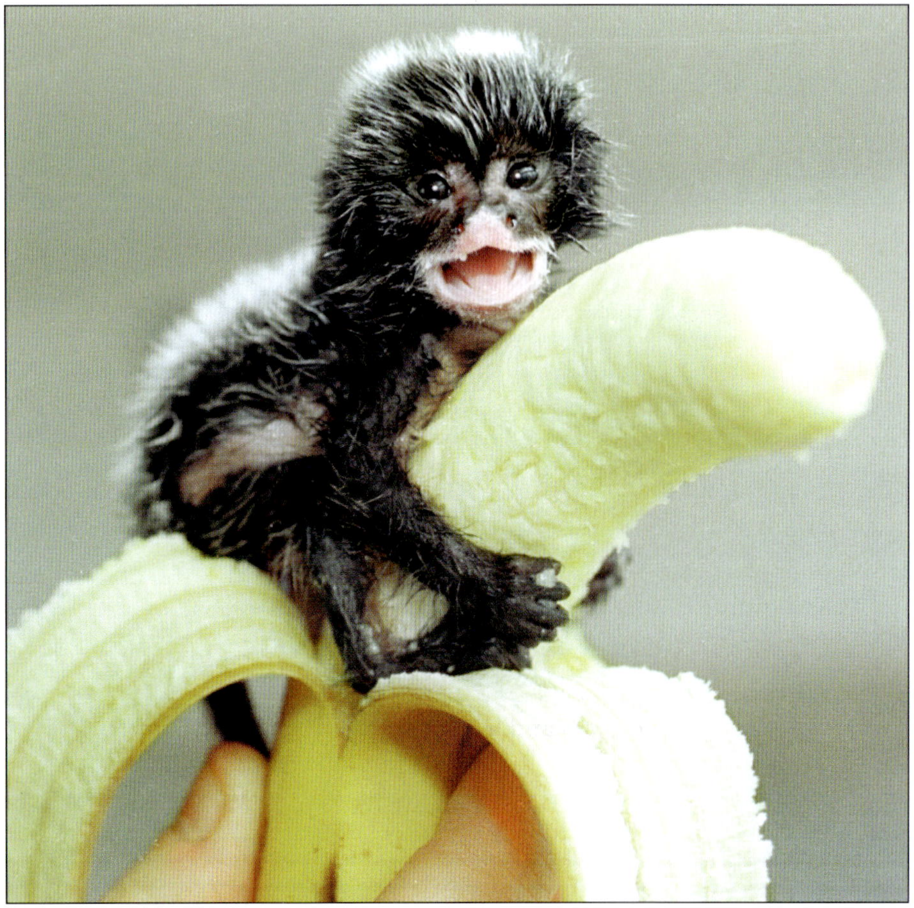

The future of this little monkey was in serious doubt when her mother rejected her and her life was in the balance. The story of her struggle being brought up by human kindness hit the newspapers and to illustrate the size and vulnerability of the little fighter I persuaded her to grasp the banana – but I had to warm up the banana in the microwave before she would hold it...

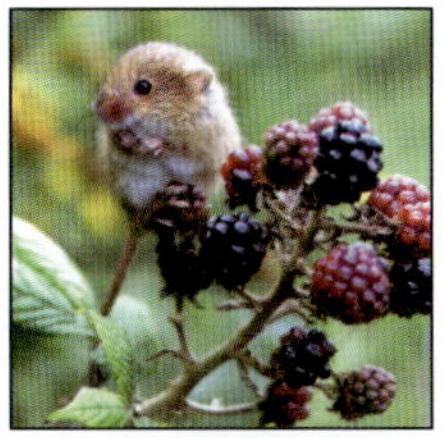

# INTRODUCTION

Newspaper photographers are expected to reach a certain level of professional excellence in many different fields of the art which includes news, sport, features, fashion, advertising, landscape and animal photography.

This book features just one aspect of a fascinating job which allows me as a photographer to take a peek into a multitude of different subjects, professions and livelihoods.

The photographs reflect a part of my life as an on-the-road press photographer working in the Westcountry, much of the time for the *Western Morning News*.

Most of the pictures have a story to tell, sometimes tragic sometimes funny and sometimes just a picture that rests easy on the eye.

I didn't start out to publish a book of animal pictures, the number of images have just crept up over the years and producing a book seemed inevitable.

The pictures are in no special order which reflects the way I work in not knowing from day to day what delights or disasters are lurking just around the corner.

The book is a celebration of the many species of animals and birds throughout the region and of the people who care so passionately for them.

Richard Austin

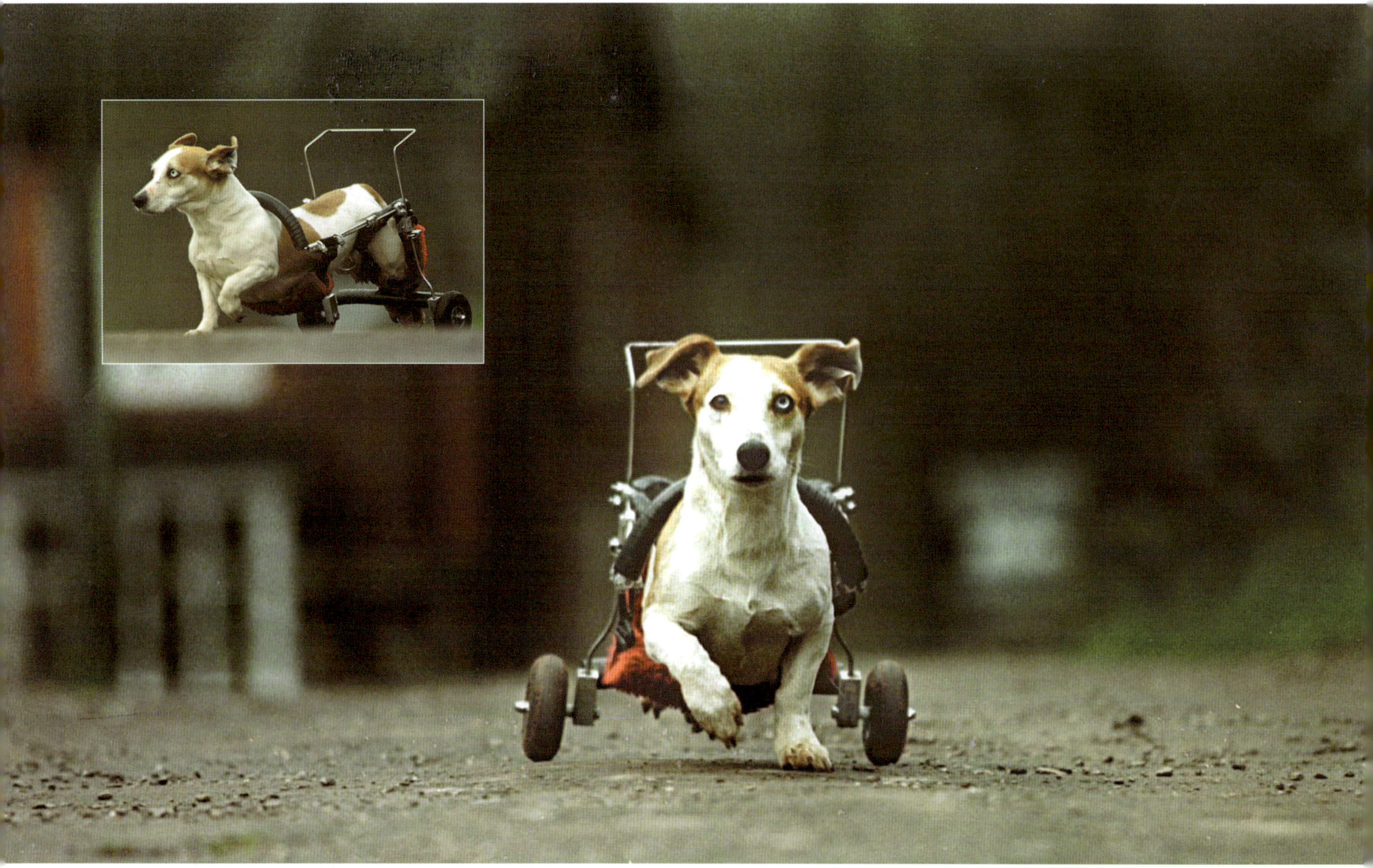

Chimba the terrier is without doubt one of the bravest little dogs I have ever met. Seriously injured after an horrific farming accident after she had fallen asleep in a hayfield, she was sucked in at one end of a bailing machine and spat out at the other end. Her injuries have left her back legs paralysed but quicker than Michael Schumacker around the farmyard on her custom-built trolly.

Three baby birds all being brought up by human kindness. The Dunnock, Goldfinch and Blue Tit all made it back into the wild after spending their first few weeks eating cat food off the bristles of an artist's paint brush.

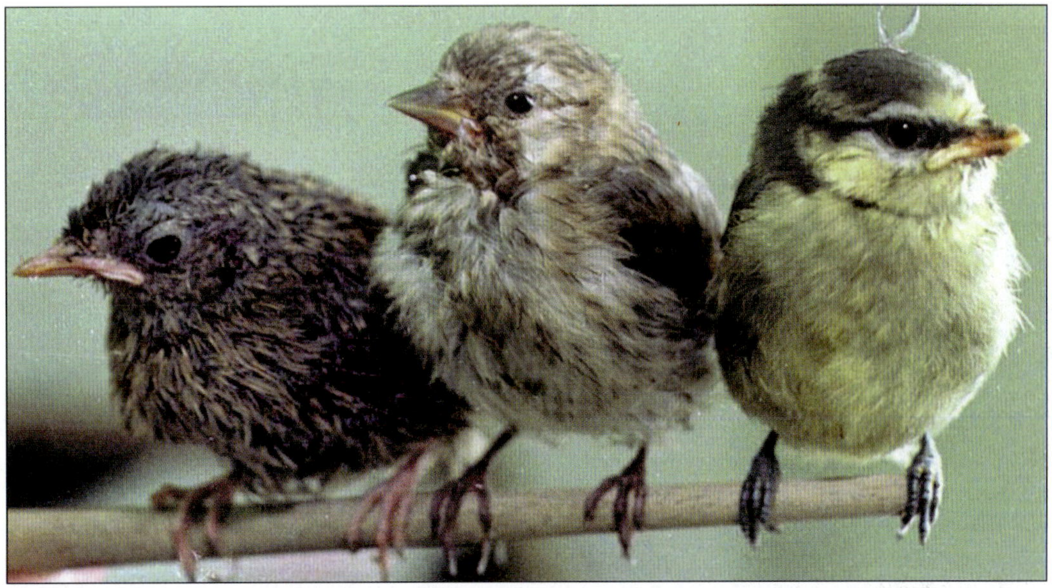

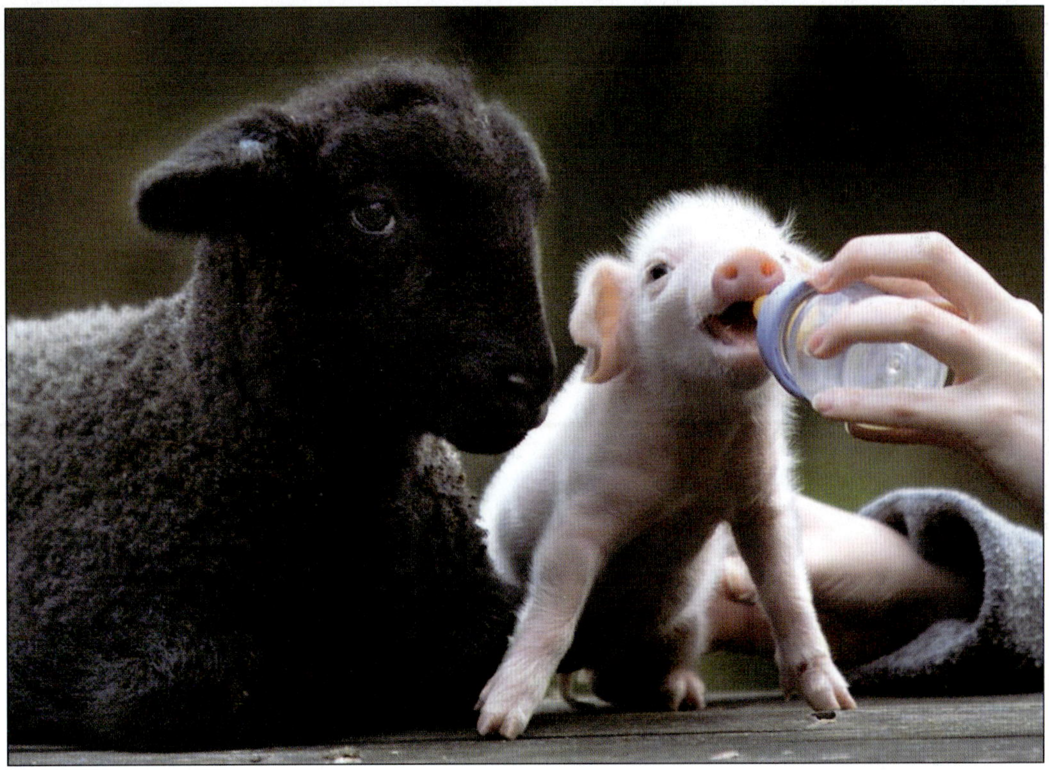

Farming casualties like the piglet and black lamb became best friends at Secret World Animal Sanctuary; at lunch time it was a question of 'Wait your turn' as the bottle of milk arrived from the animal kitchen.

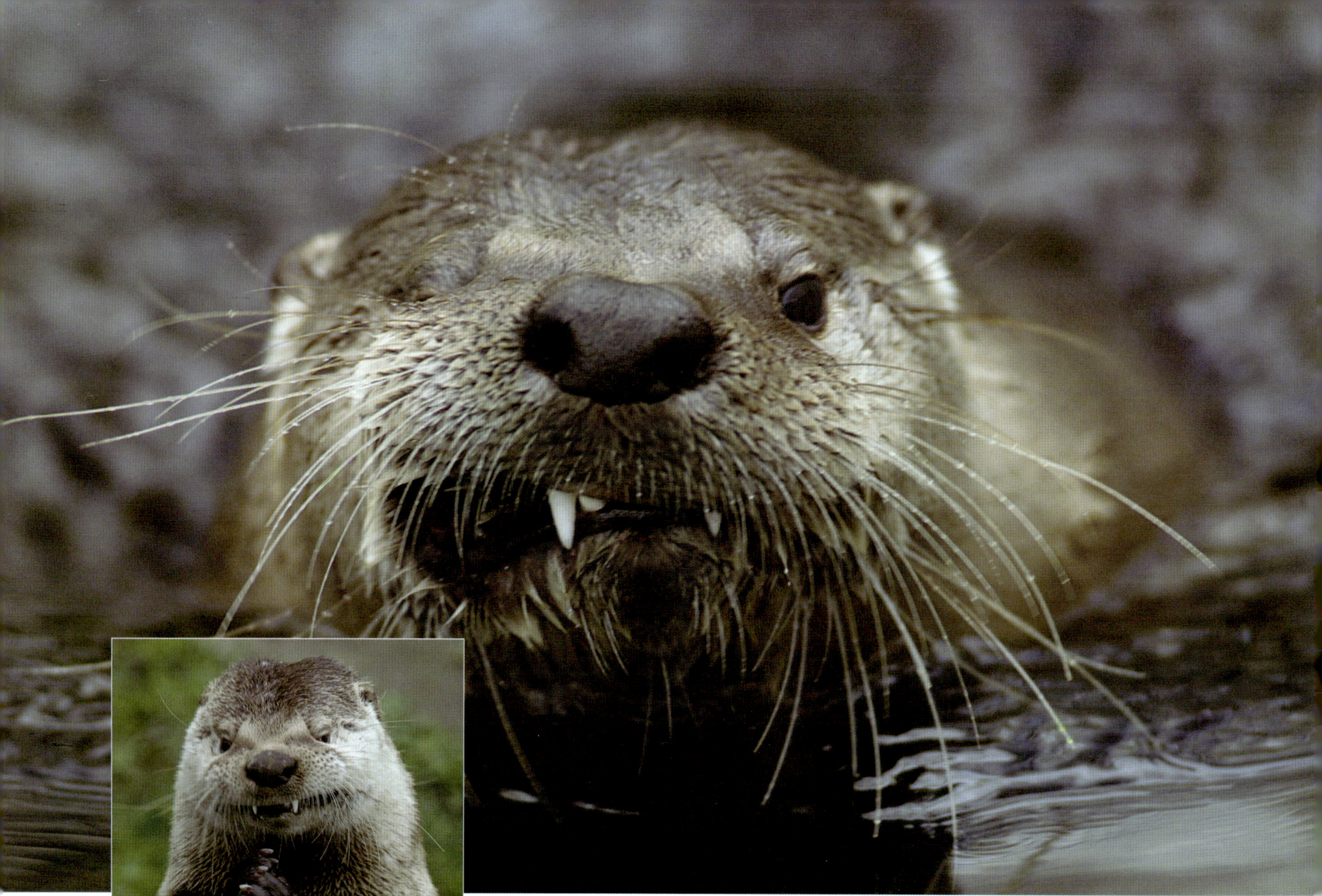

Everybody loves otters and they don't come more lovable than the otters at the Buckfastleigh Butterfly Farm and Otter Sanctuary. These North American otters pull all sorts of faces at feeding time. As one of them began saying a prayer for more fish, his friend was chewing on a tough piece of trout and pulling all sorts of funny faces as he struggled to get it down.

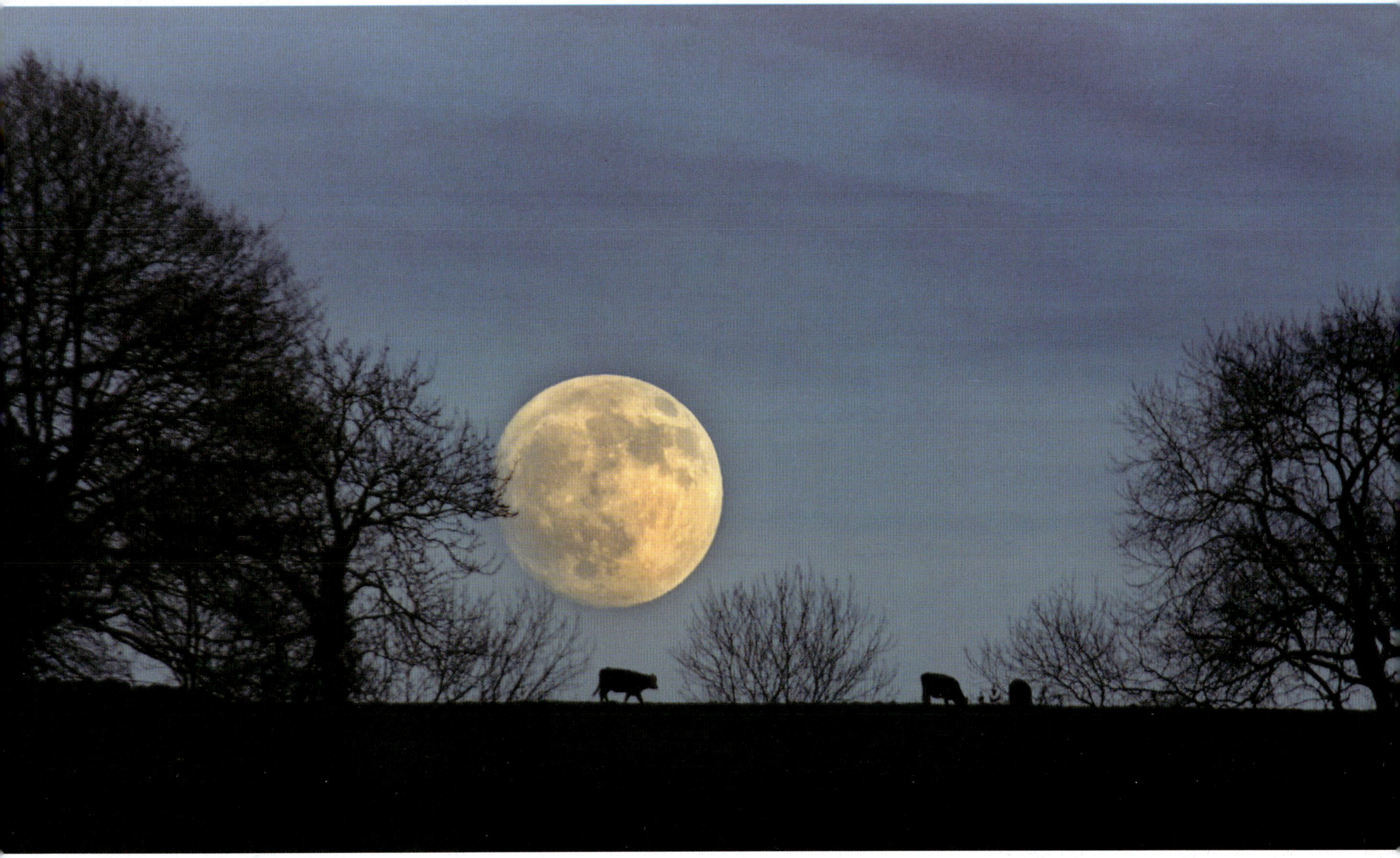

Driving around the Westcountry day after day can sometimes have its advantages – just like the day the full moon appeared at dusk over the hill at Wilmington near Honiton as the cows drifted across the skyline. Having your camera on the passenger seat is an advantage; I was very surprised just how quickly the moon moves across the sky.

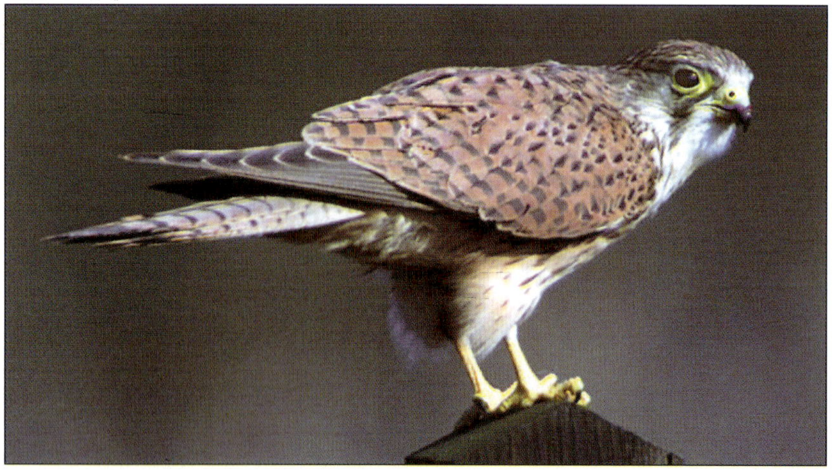

Every press photographer deserves a bit of luck now and again. I was sent to Dawlish Warren Nature Reserve to photograph its wildlife for a two-page feature and as I entered the reserve I came face to face with a Kestrel eating a field mouse on top of the nature-reserve sign – a great start to the assignment.

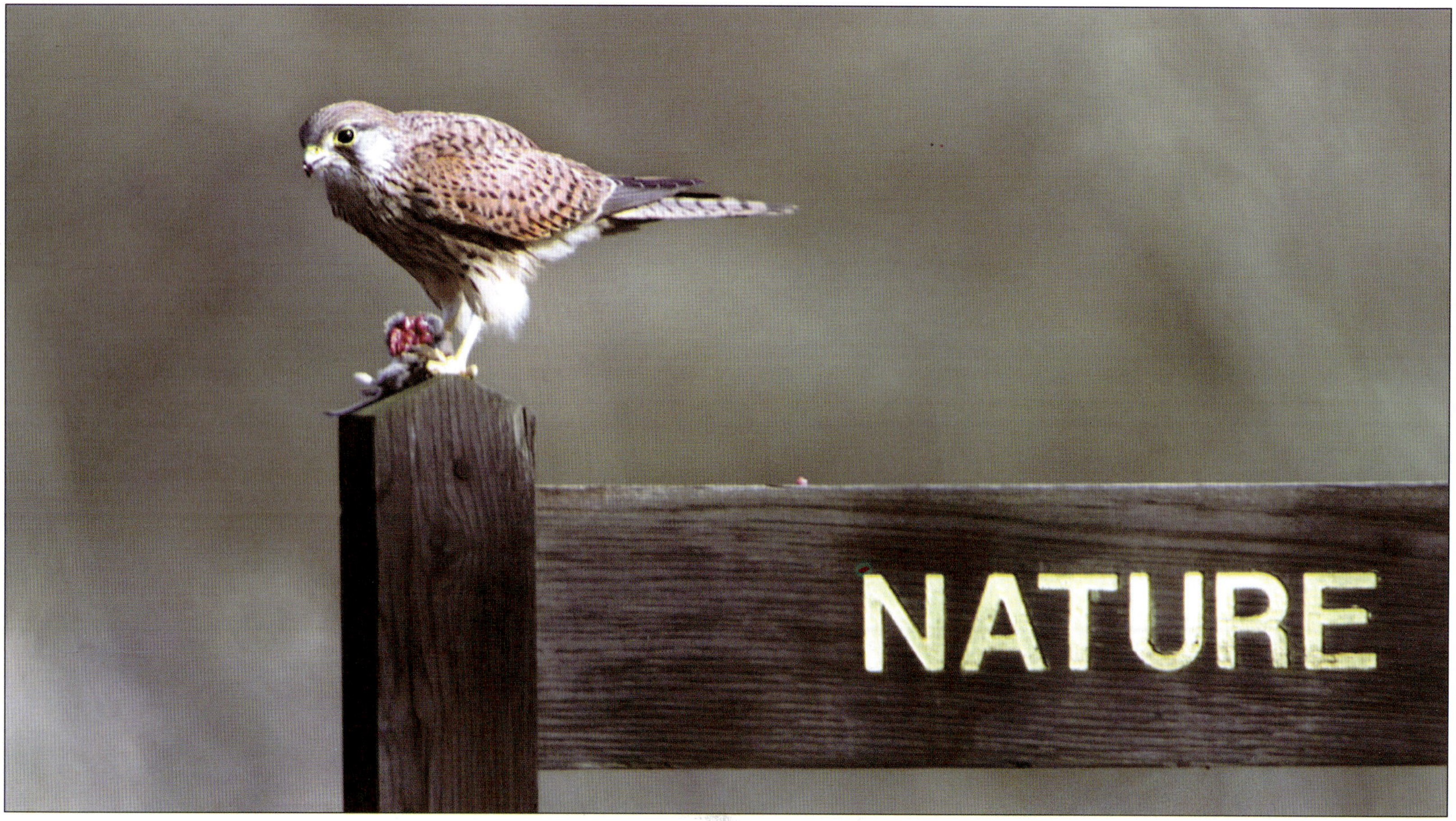

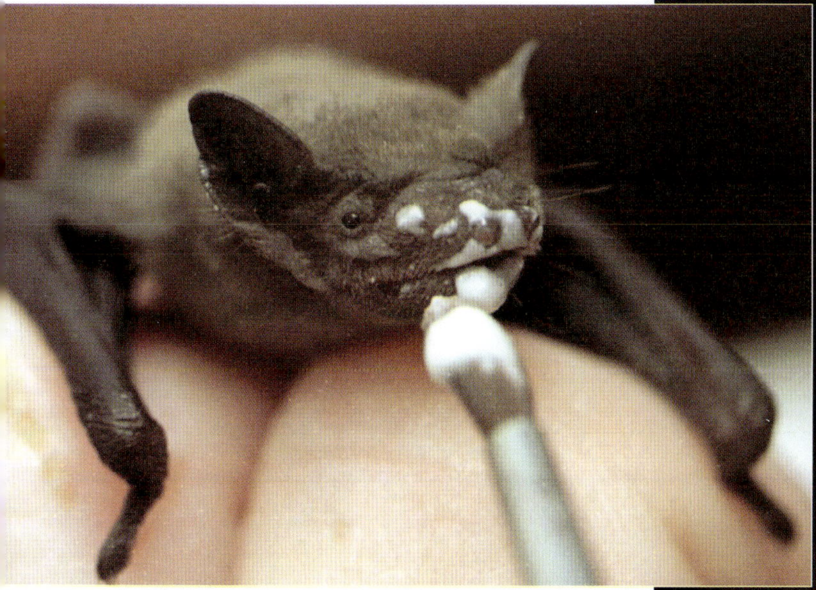

Brave Nikki Hawkins wanted to draw attention to the plight of orphaned and injured bats and the fact that the girls at Secret World Animal Sanctuary look after the flying mice during the day by keeping them under their sweat shirts clinging to their bras. Apparently the bats feel assured through warmth and being able to listen to a heart beat all day. Any fellas out there wanting to come back as a bat in their next life – join the queue.

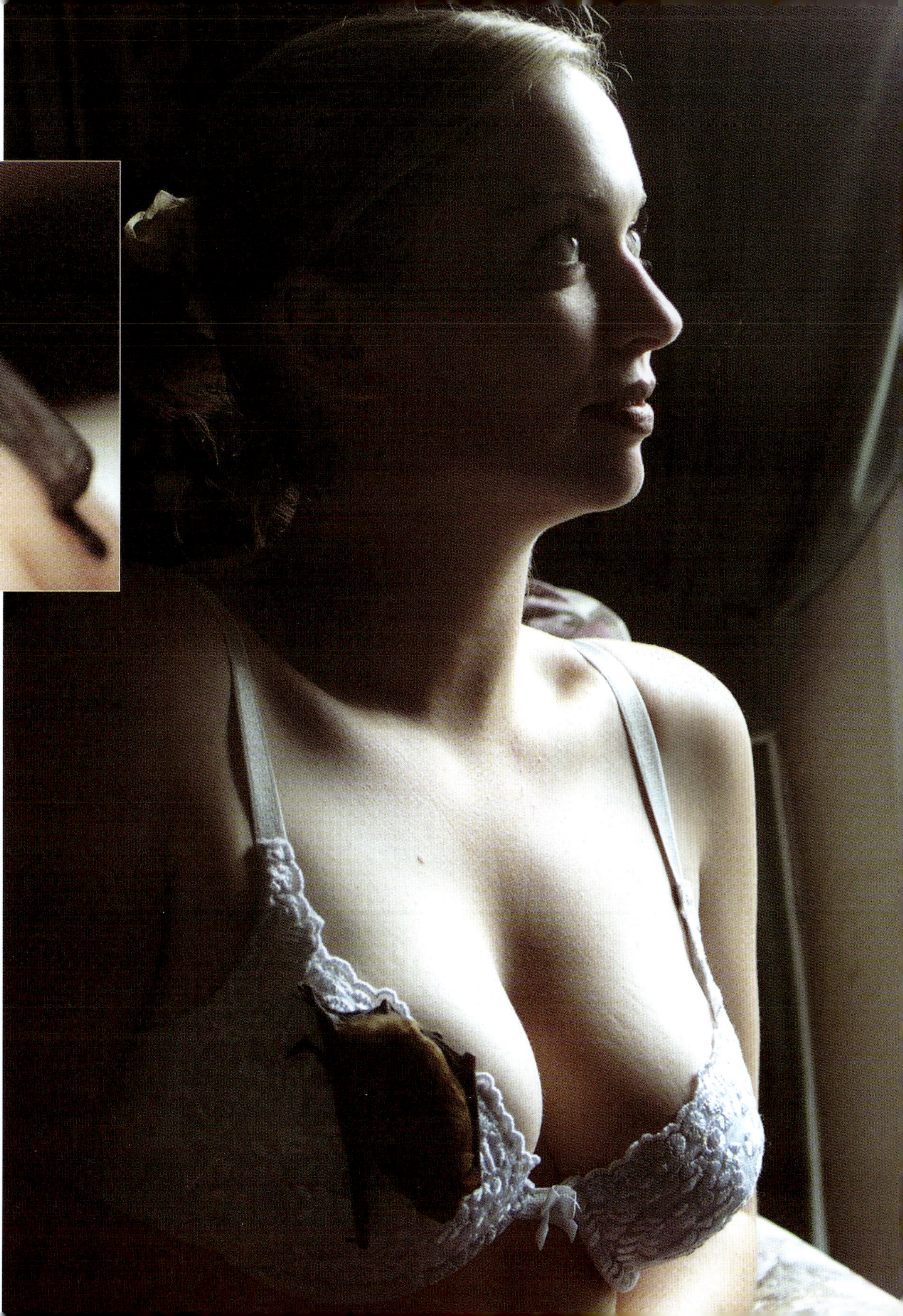

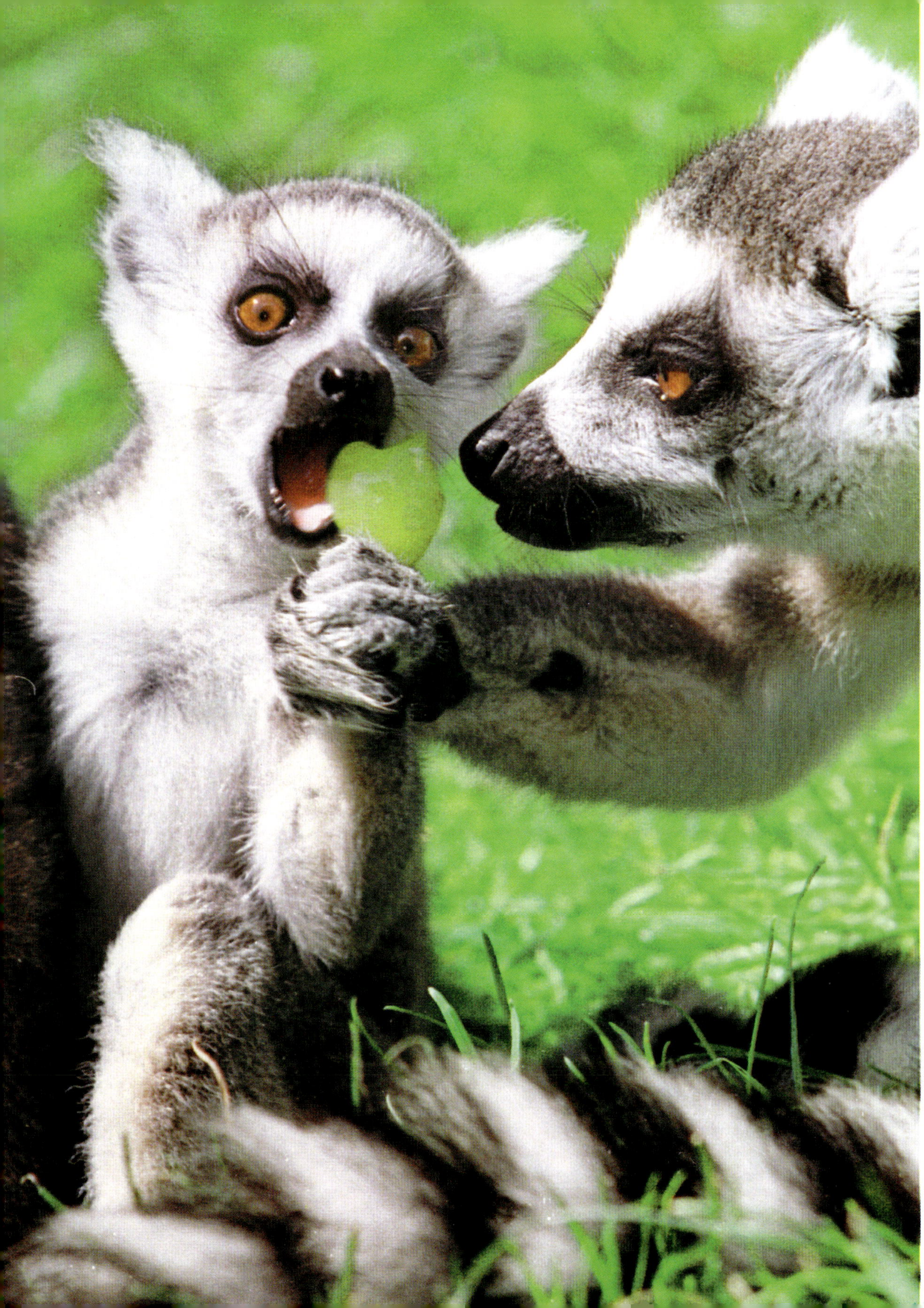

Descriptive words for Ring Tailed Lemurs include cheeky, intelligent and downright funny; here motherly love did not extend to letting her offspring eat the last grape.

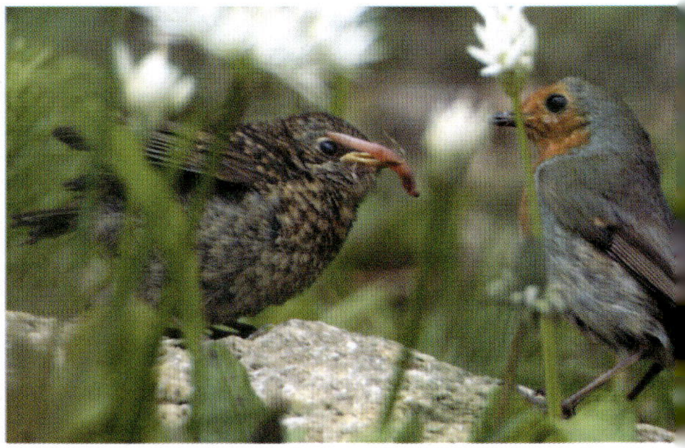

How the parent Robins know where the babies are once they have flown the nest is a small miracle, the fact is that they do know where they are and spend all the daylight hours feeding them.

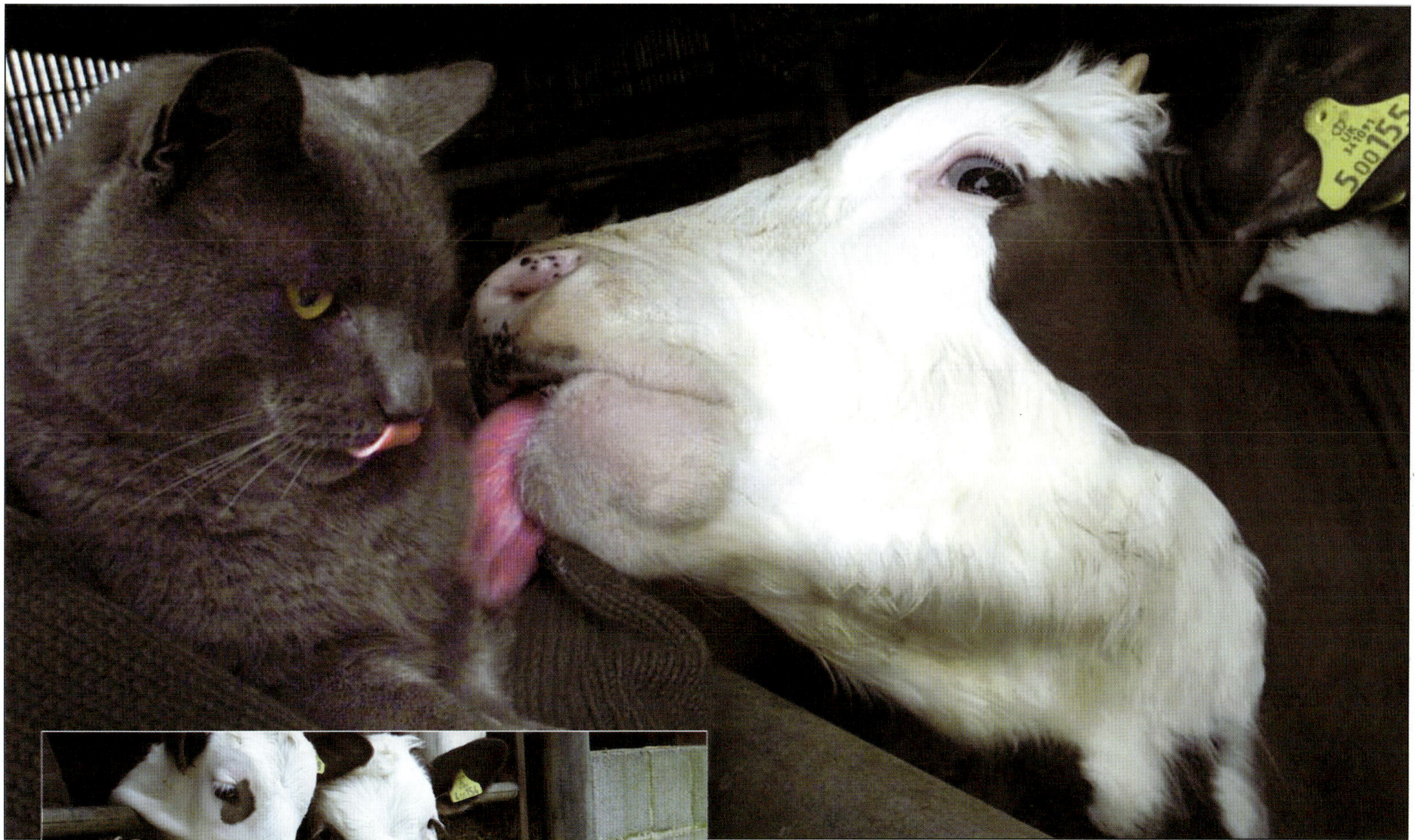

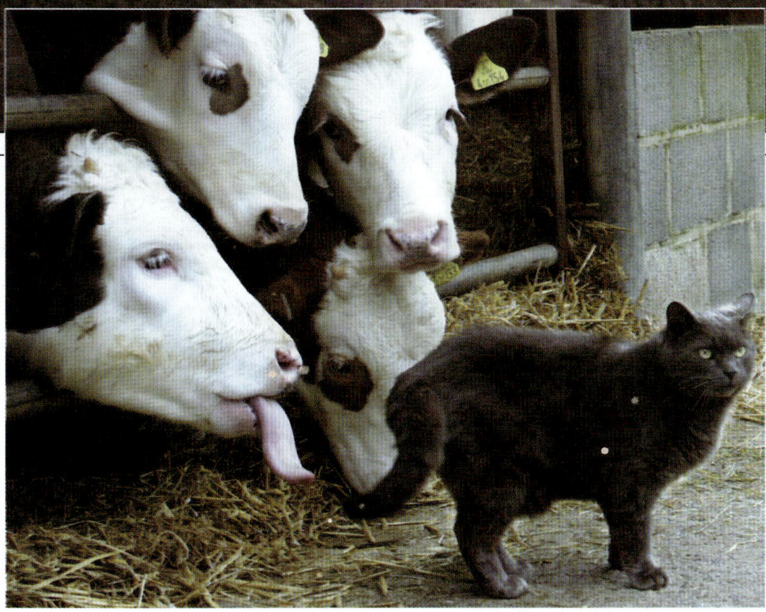

Farm cats have a special purpose on the farm keeping rats and mice numbers down, this tom-cat often stands still for the calves to lick him clean.

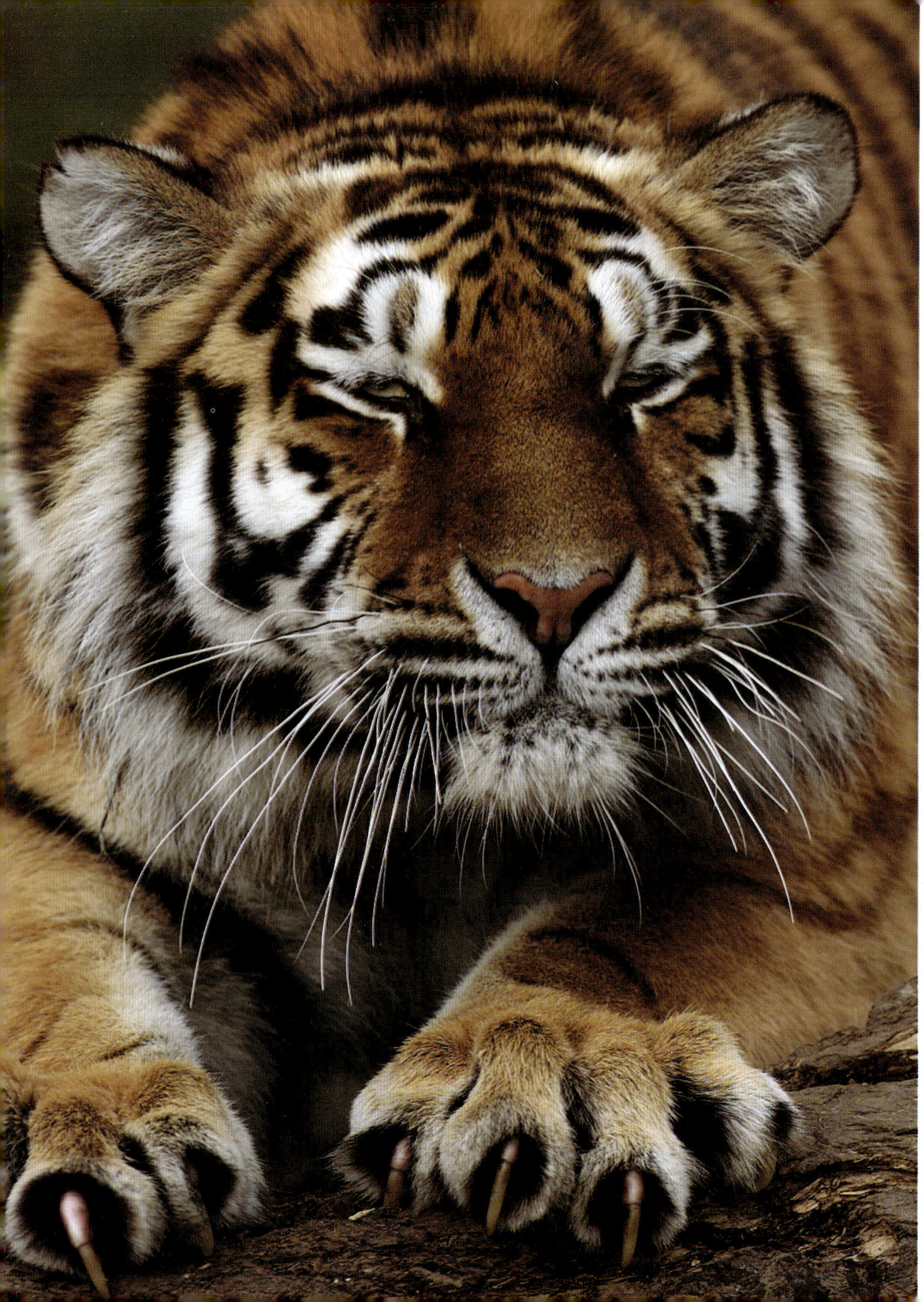

Siberian Tigers are the biggest cats in the world and when one of them shows off his gigantic claws as he stretches in the morning – people sit up and take notice.

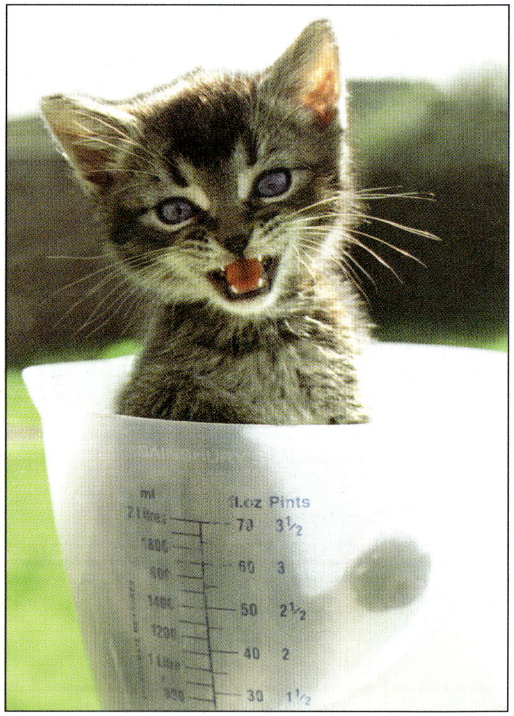


Pint-sized kitten seeks new home, another way of showing how small the little kitten is in a newspaper picture – needless to say that he found a new home the very same day as publication.

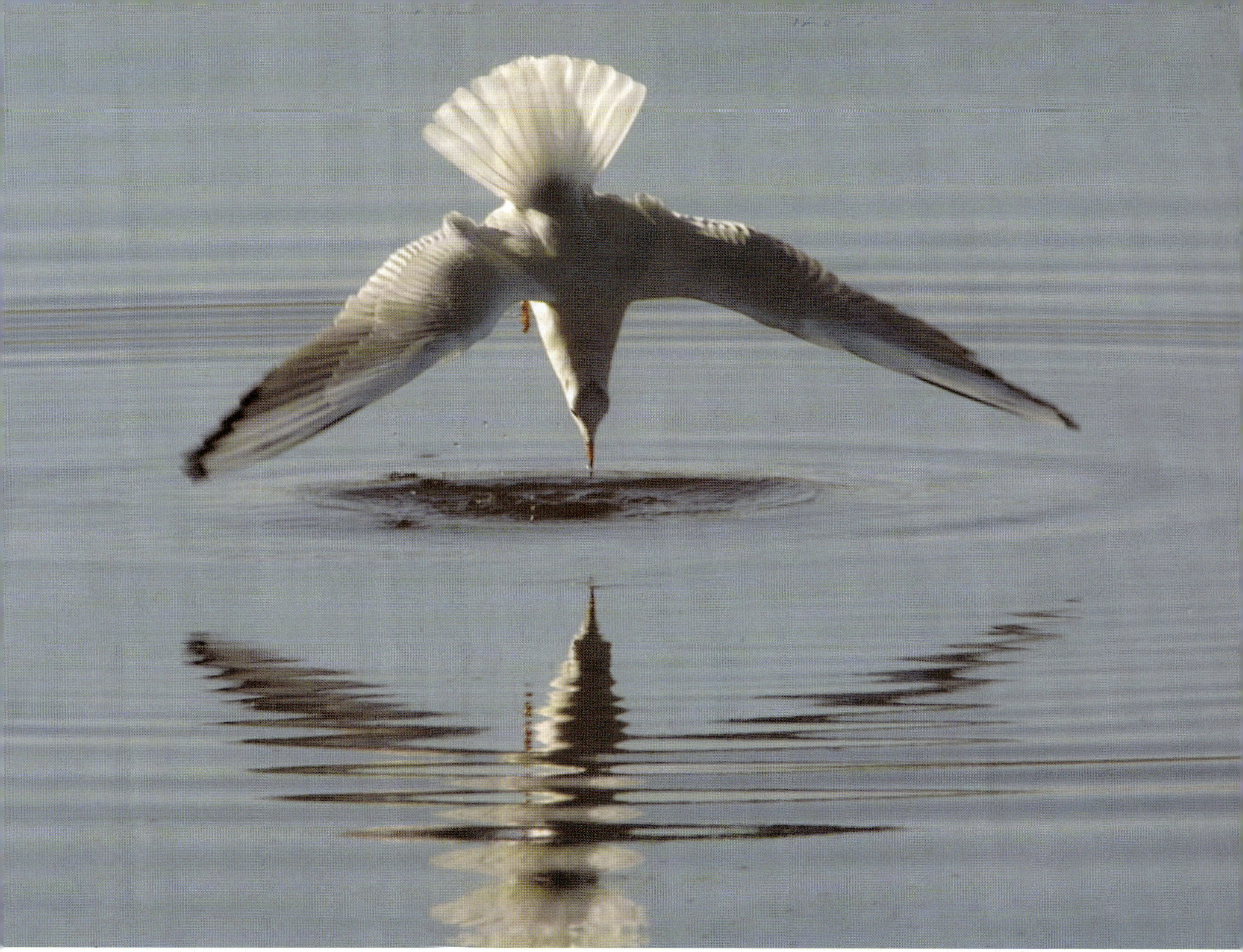

Once in a while all the waiting and planning pays off. I had watched the Blackheaded Gulls sitting in the water ducking their heads under catching small shrimps on the River Axe for quite a few months. They had developed a little trick for catching their food when the shrimps were just a little too deep, two flaps of their wings would lift them just enough out of the water to dive down those extra few inches. The success of the picture depended on the light and the stillness of the water for the reflection and the angle of the bird; on this day all things came together.

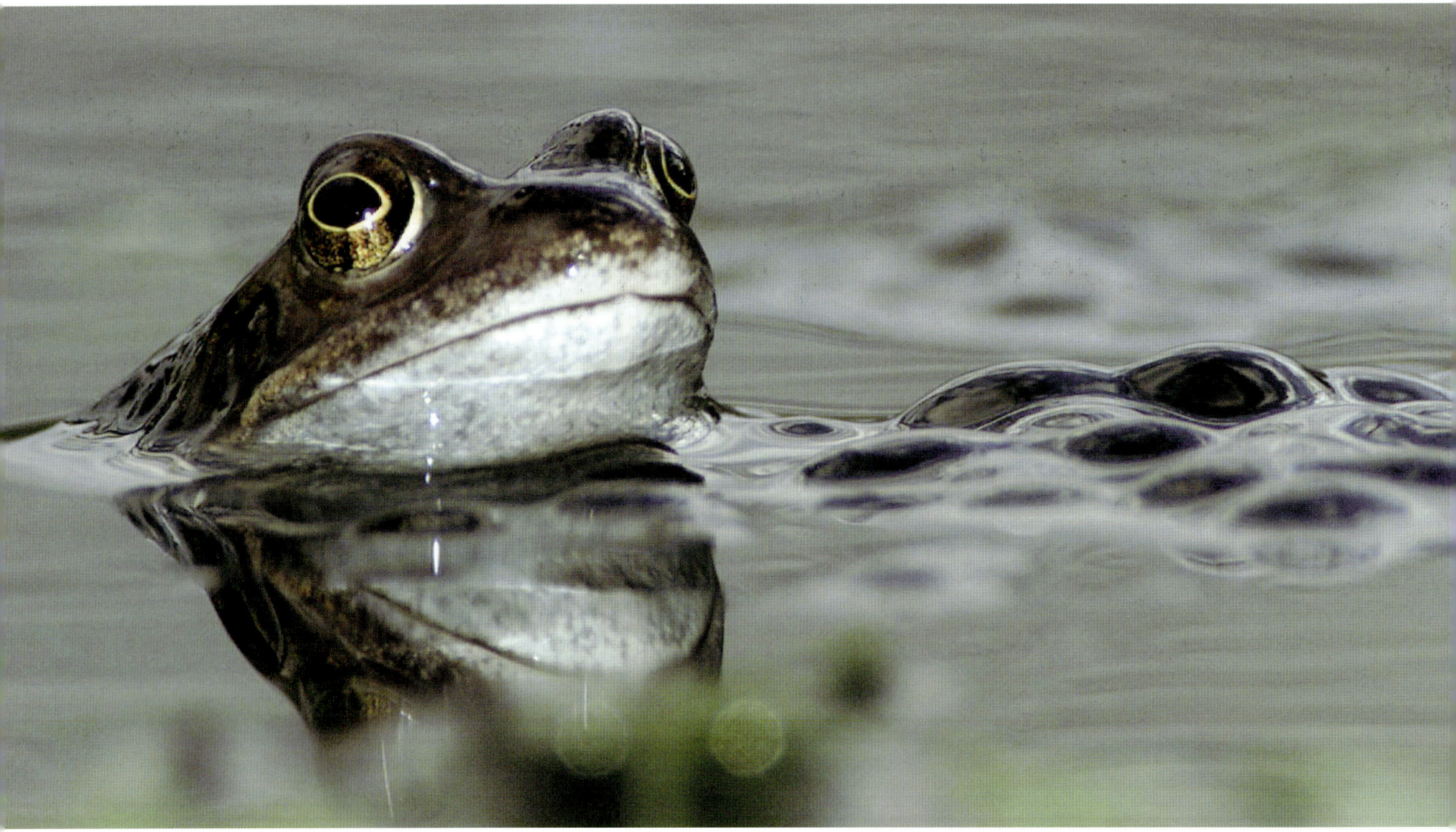

The first British frog in the wild I have ever photographed and it wasn't easy... A call from Sampford Shrubs near Tiverton told me that the male frogs were very active in the pond because the females were producing ample amounts of spawn. As the frogs are shy and very timid I ended up crawling along on my belly with a big lens that weighed a ton. I was covered in mud and soaking wet but to my amazement the frogs were attracted to my flashgun, every time the flash went off the frogs moved closer to me making it a little easier to bag a quality picture. What really made the day was listening to the frogs croaking which was another first for me.

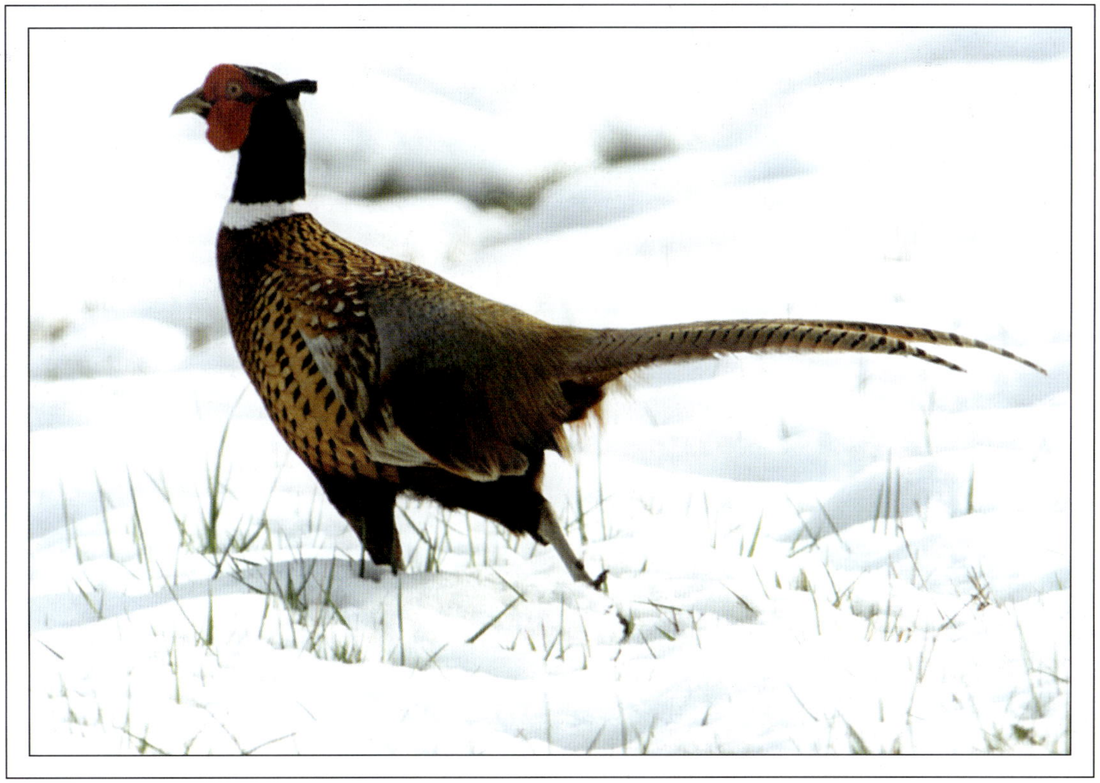

The pheasant in the snow on the Blackdown Hills,
shot from the car window as he raced across the snow.

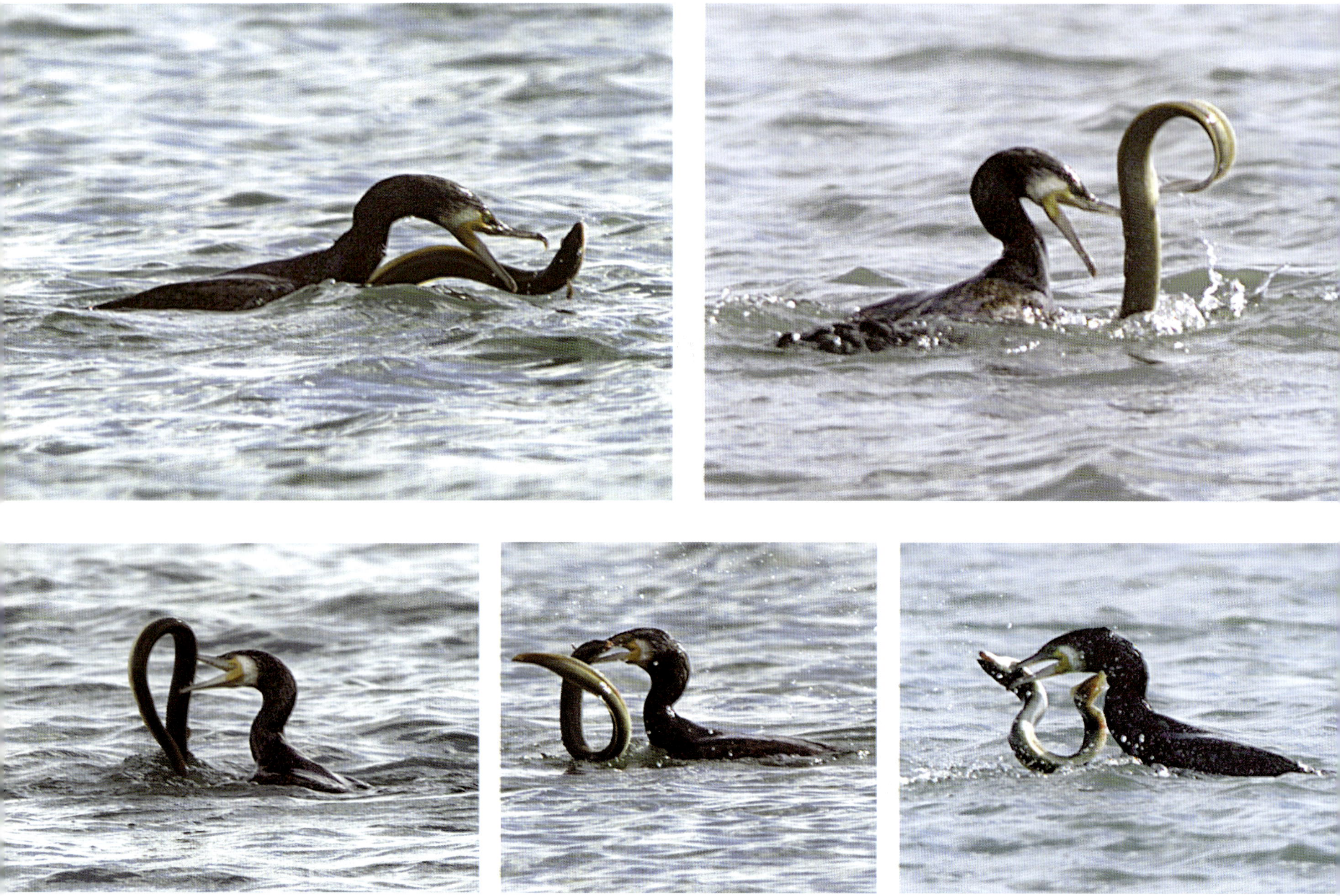

Loud explosions in the sky at Lyme Regis means the lifeboat is about to be launched and perhaps a newspaper story is in the making. As I stood on the cobb wall waiting for the lifeboat to be launched I noticed the cormorant who was about 50m from the shore and realising he was fighting with an eel, I ran to the beach and witnessed a great battle of life and death – the cormorant won of course but not before the eel escaped three times.

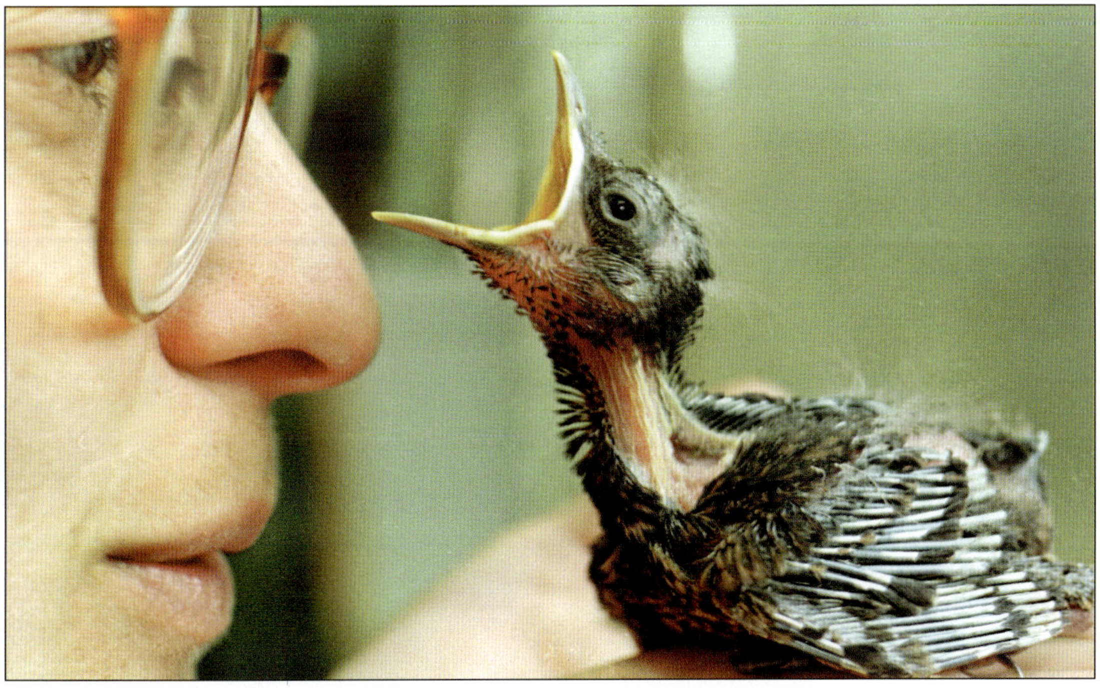

Fledgling birds spend most of their first few weeks on auto-pilot, the slightest movement in front of them and they open their mouths and swallow whether or not it's an animal-care assistant or a baby squirrel.

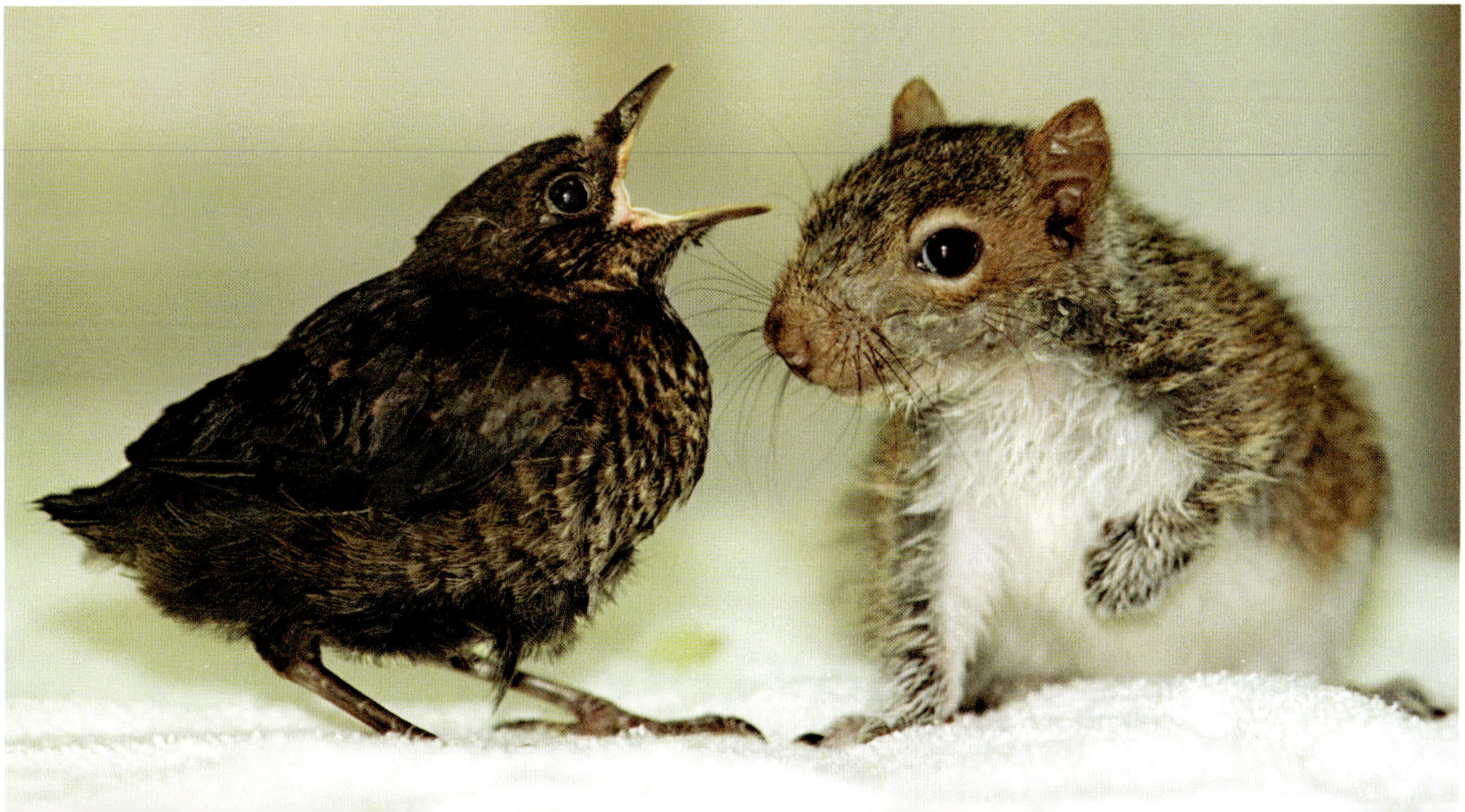

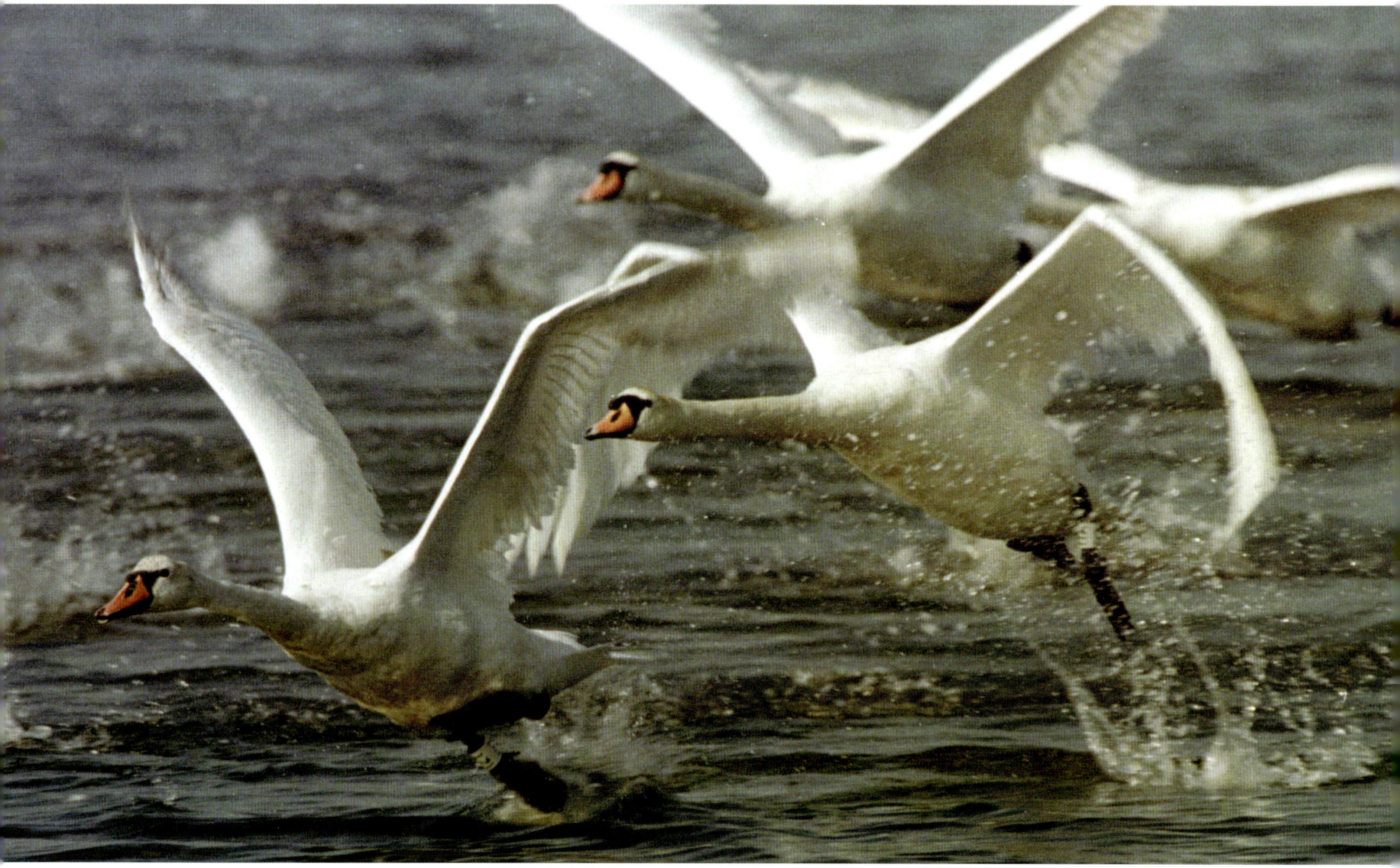

The light was just right as a group of swans took off from the lagoon at Abbotsbury, the birds take a little while to get airborne but when they are up – what a sight!

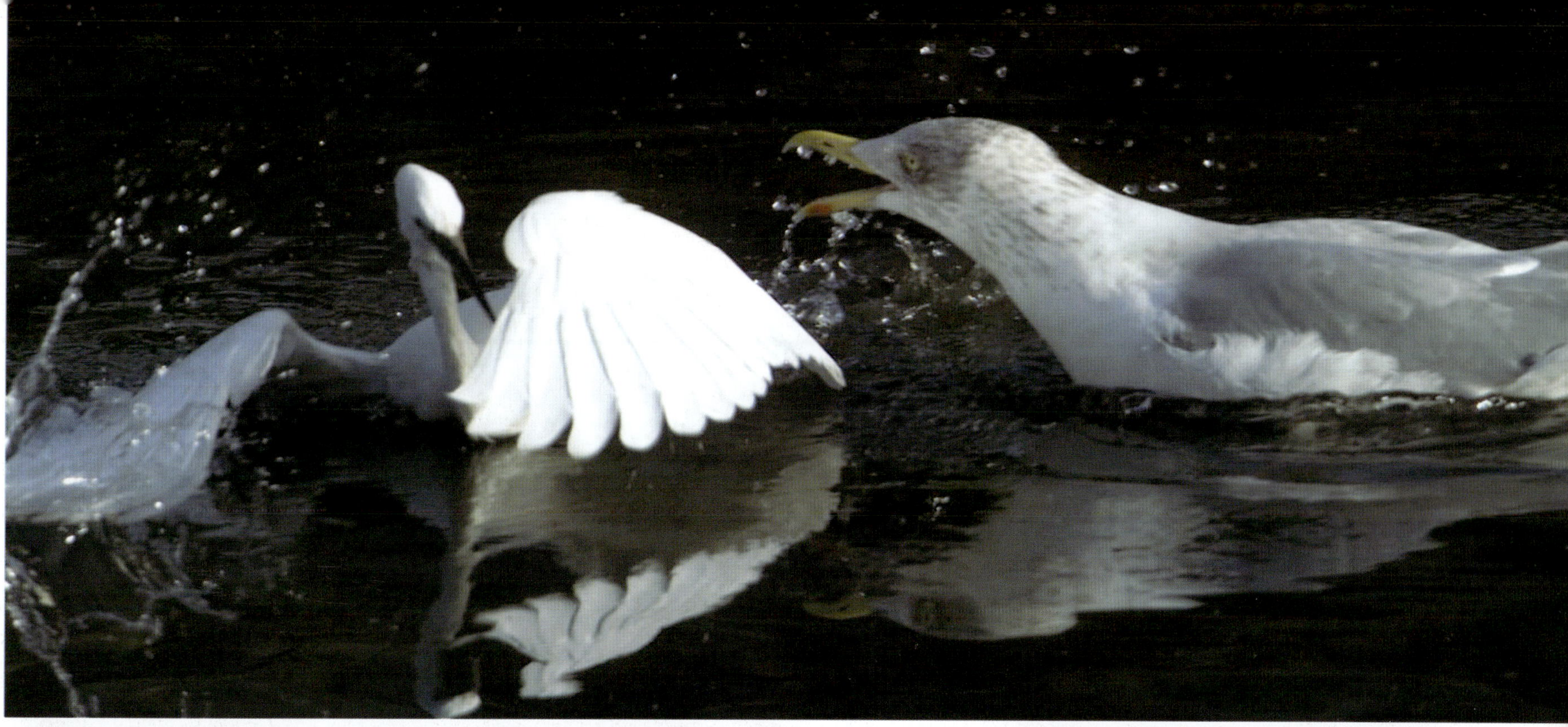

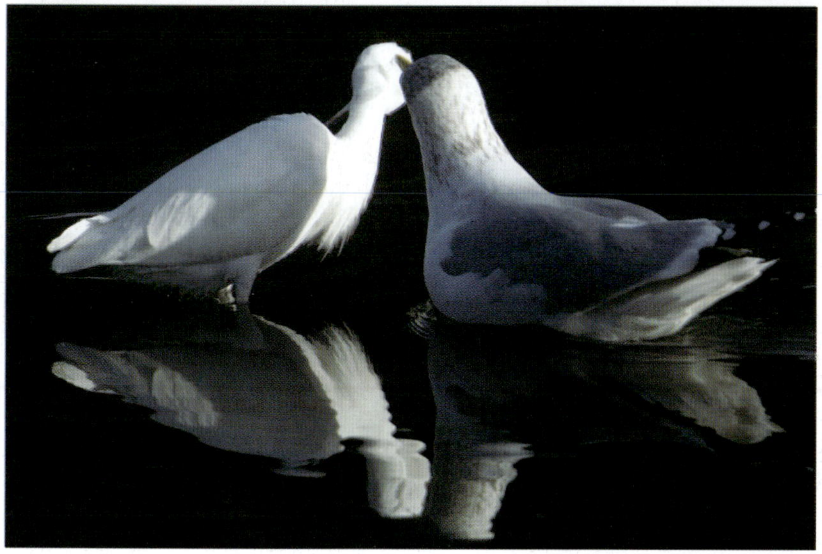

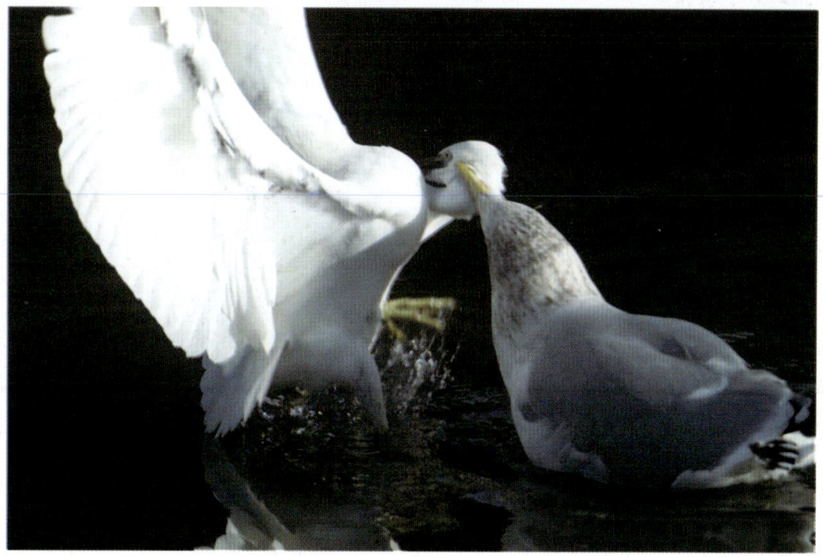

Herring Gulls come in for a lot of stick in the Westcountry and on this occasion
I caught one of them red-handed pitching into a Little Egret at Kingsbridge.
Had the gull not been disturbed the egret would have been in big trouble.

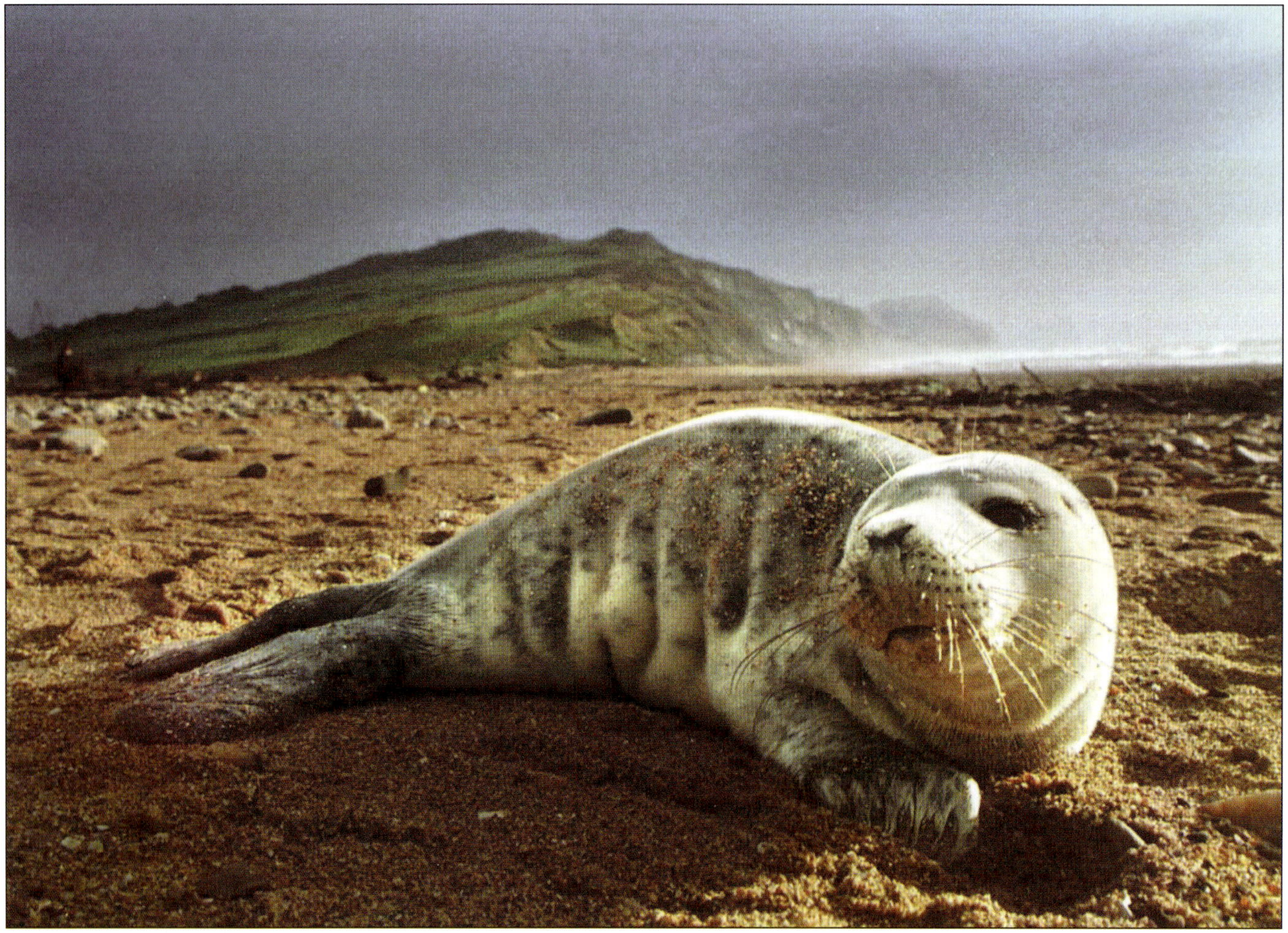

In rough seas grey seals are often separated from their mothers. This one was resting up on Charmouth beach, the RSPCA waited for quite a while to see if the mother was waiting around just off shore – she wasn't and the little one was caught and taken to the RSPCA Wildlife Unit at West Hatch near Taunton. He was released a few weeks later in good weather.

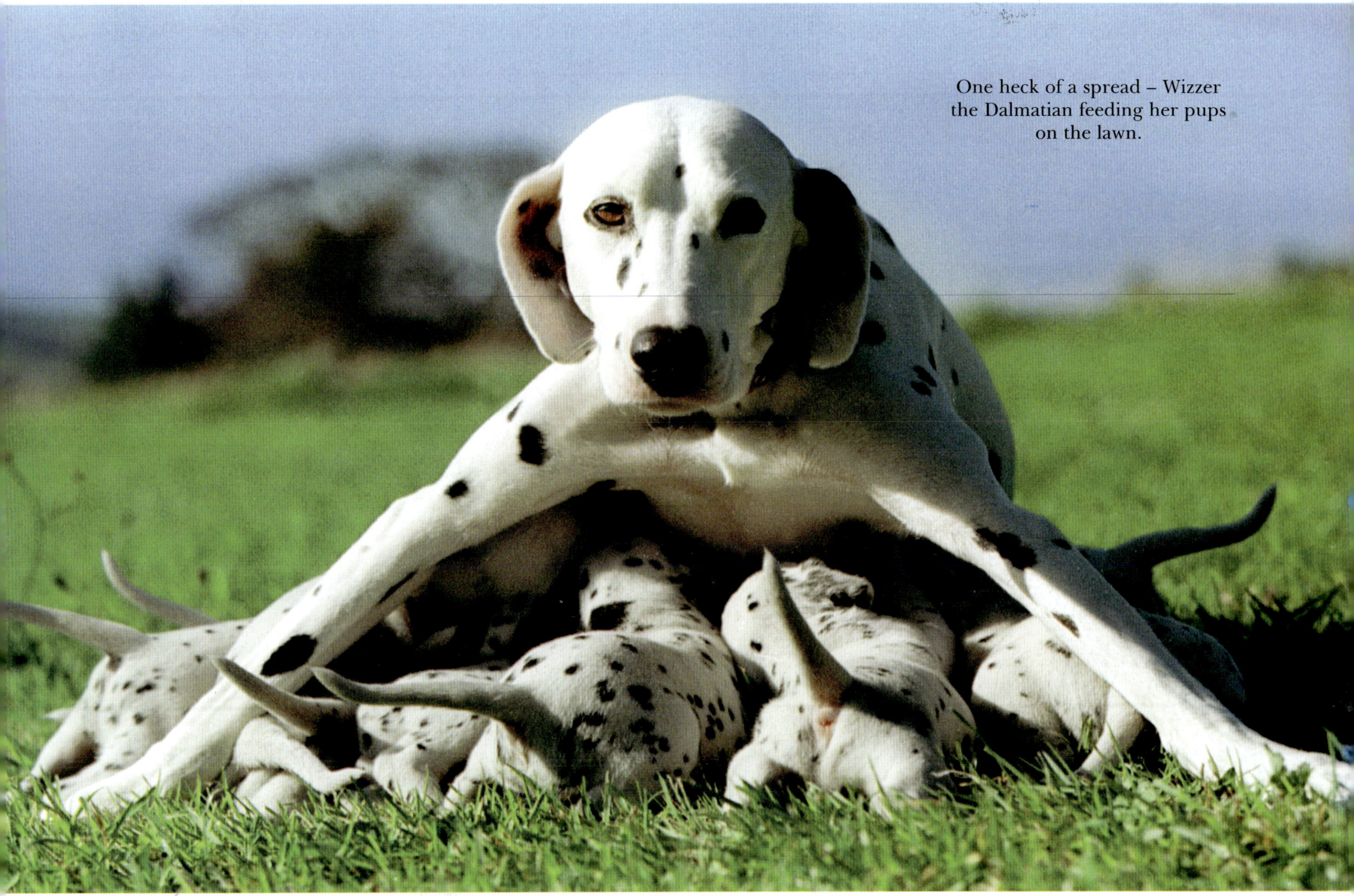

One heck of a spread – Wizzer the Dalmatian feeding her pups on the lawn.

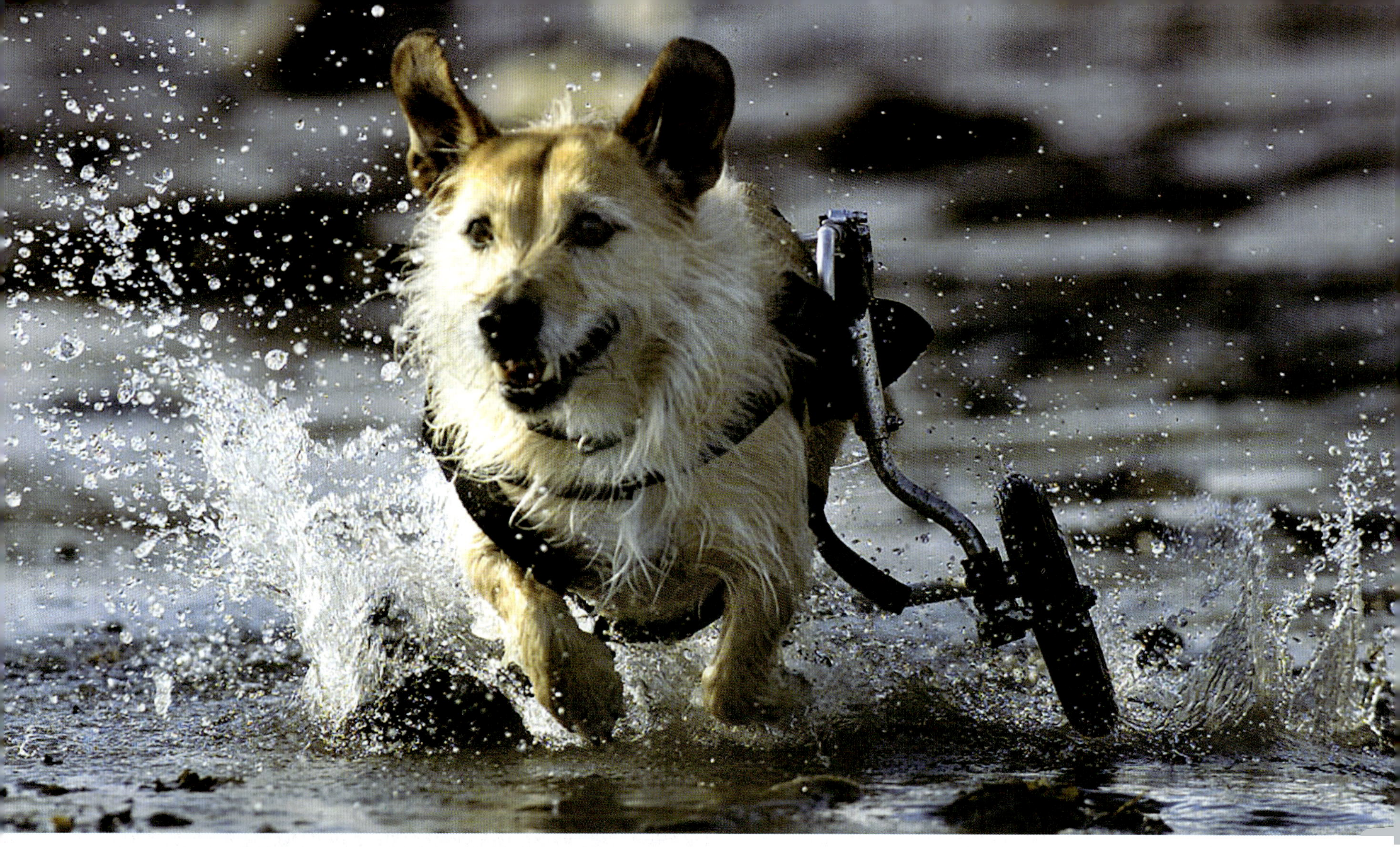

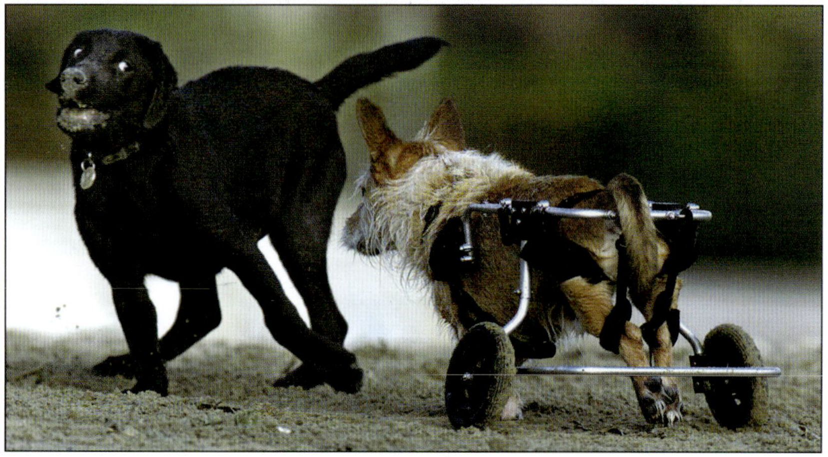

Tragic Biggles fell off the sofa and seriously damaged his spine in a freak accident leaving his back legs useless. His devoted owners bought him a state-of-the-art trolley and it transformed his life. He chases sticks into the sea and will soon let other dogs know who is still at the top of the pecking order – especially Labrador pups.

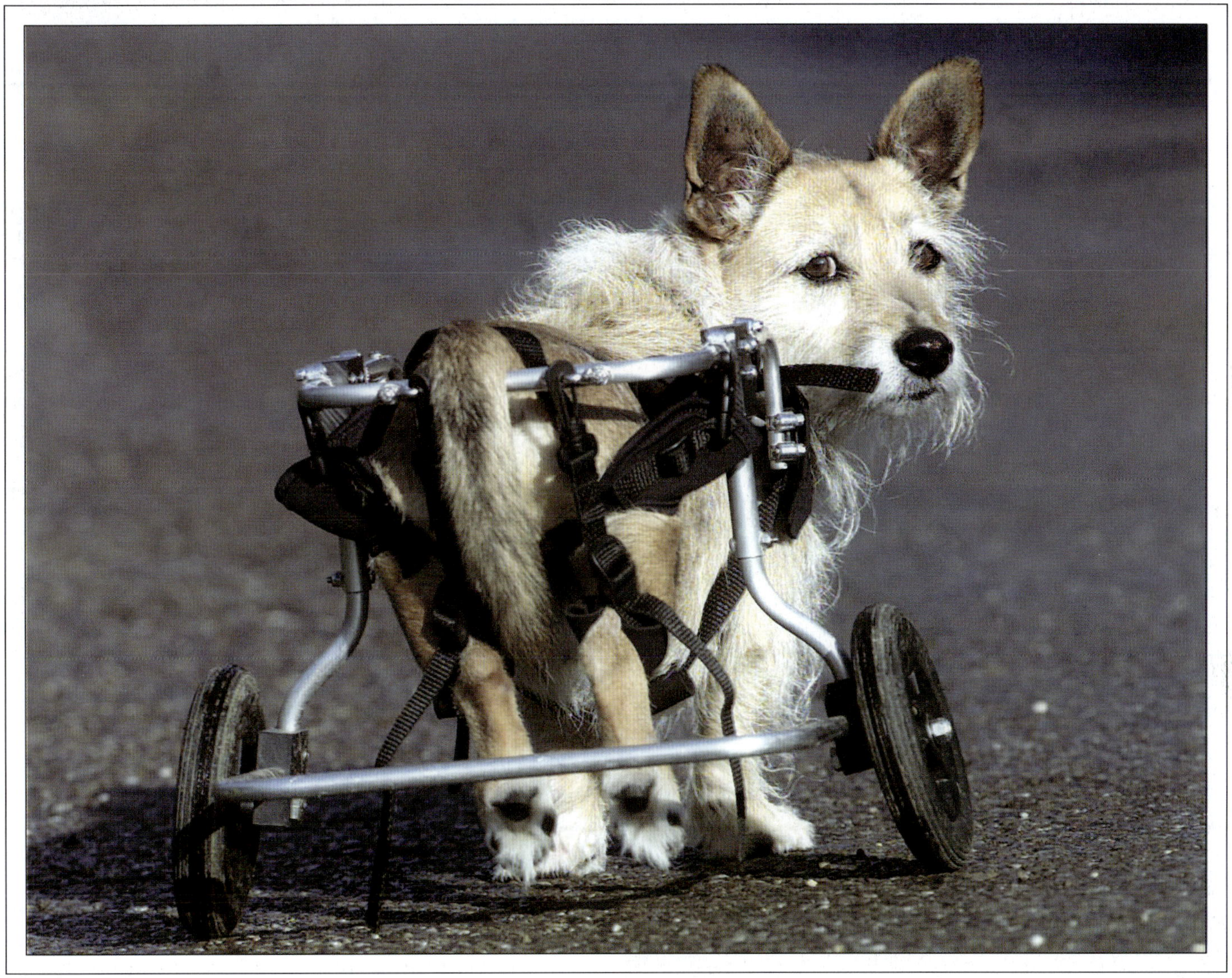

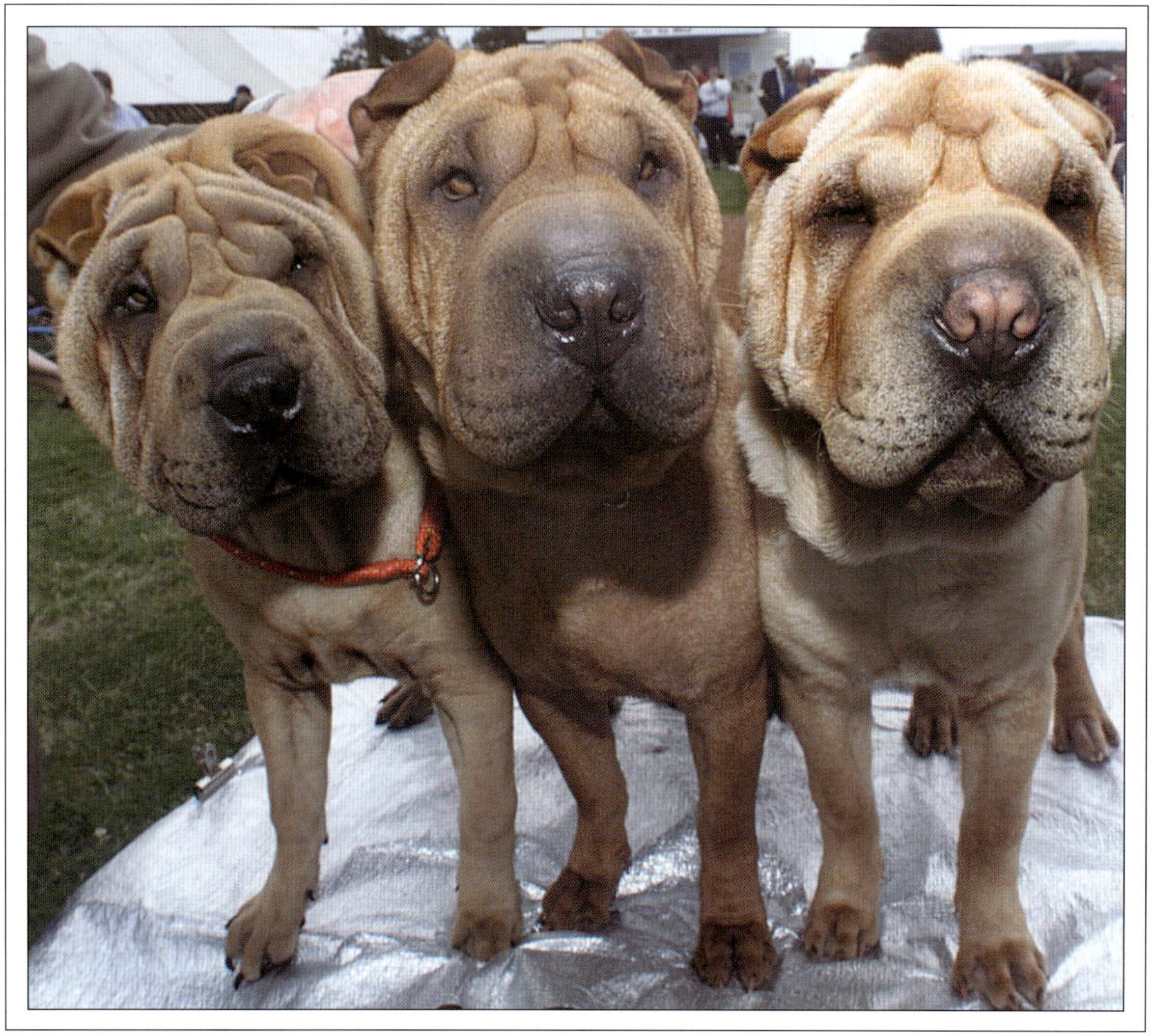

The three Chow Pei puppies looked like they had enough furry coat left over to make another half-dozen dogs.

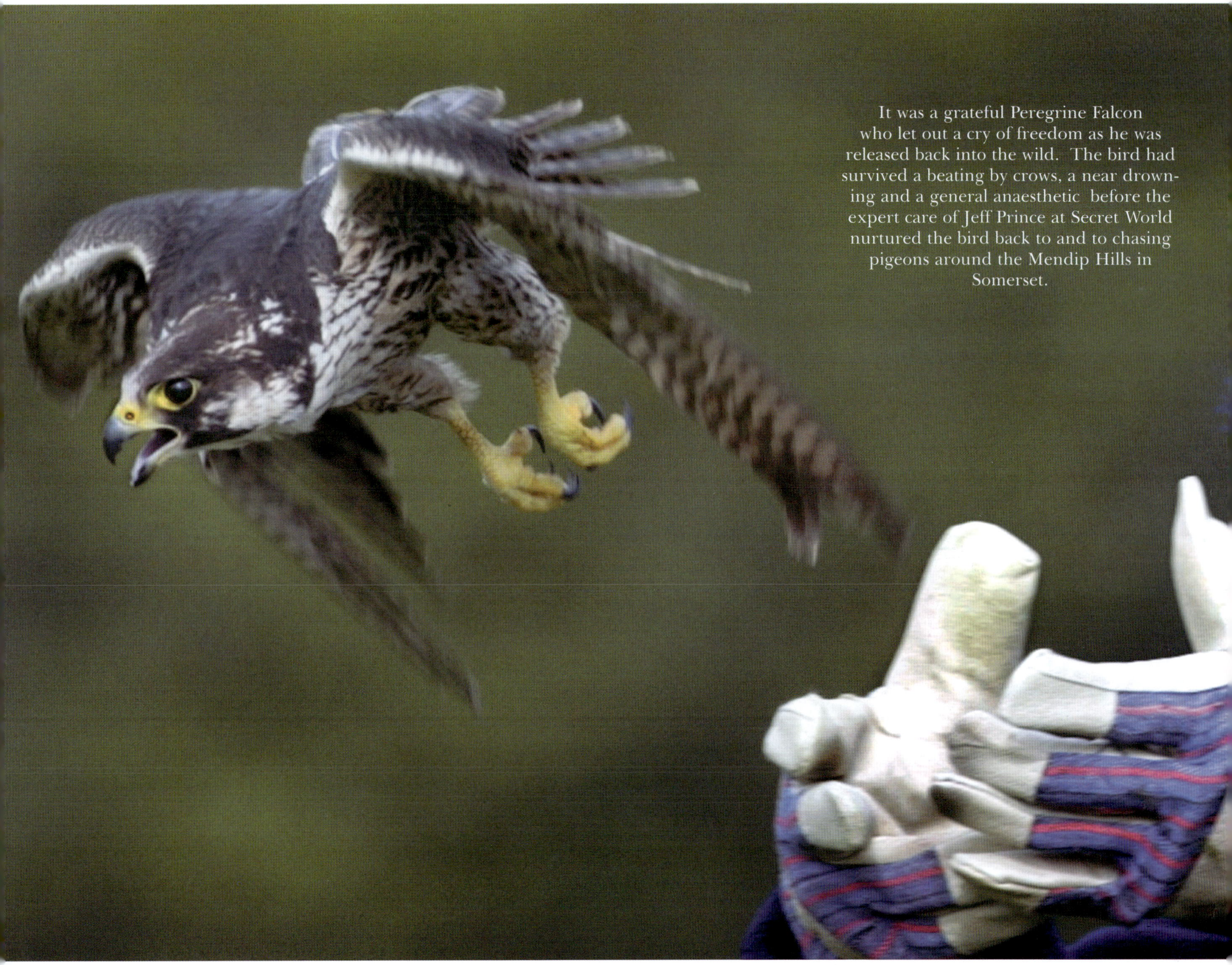

It was a grateful Peregrine Falcon who let out a cry of freedom as he was released back into the wild. The bird had survived a beating by crows, a near drowning and a general anaesthetic before the expert care of Jeff Prince at Secret World nurtured the bird back to and to chasing pigeons around the Mendip Hills in Somerset.

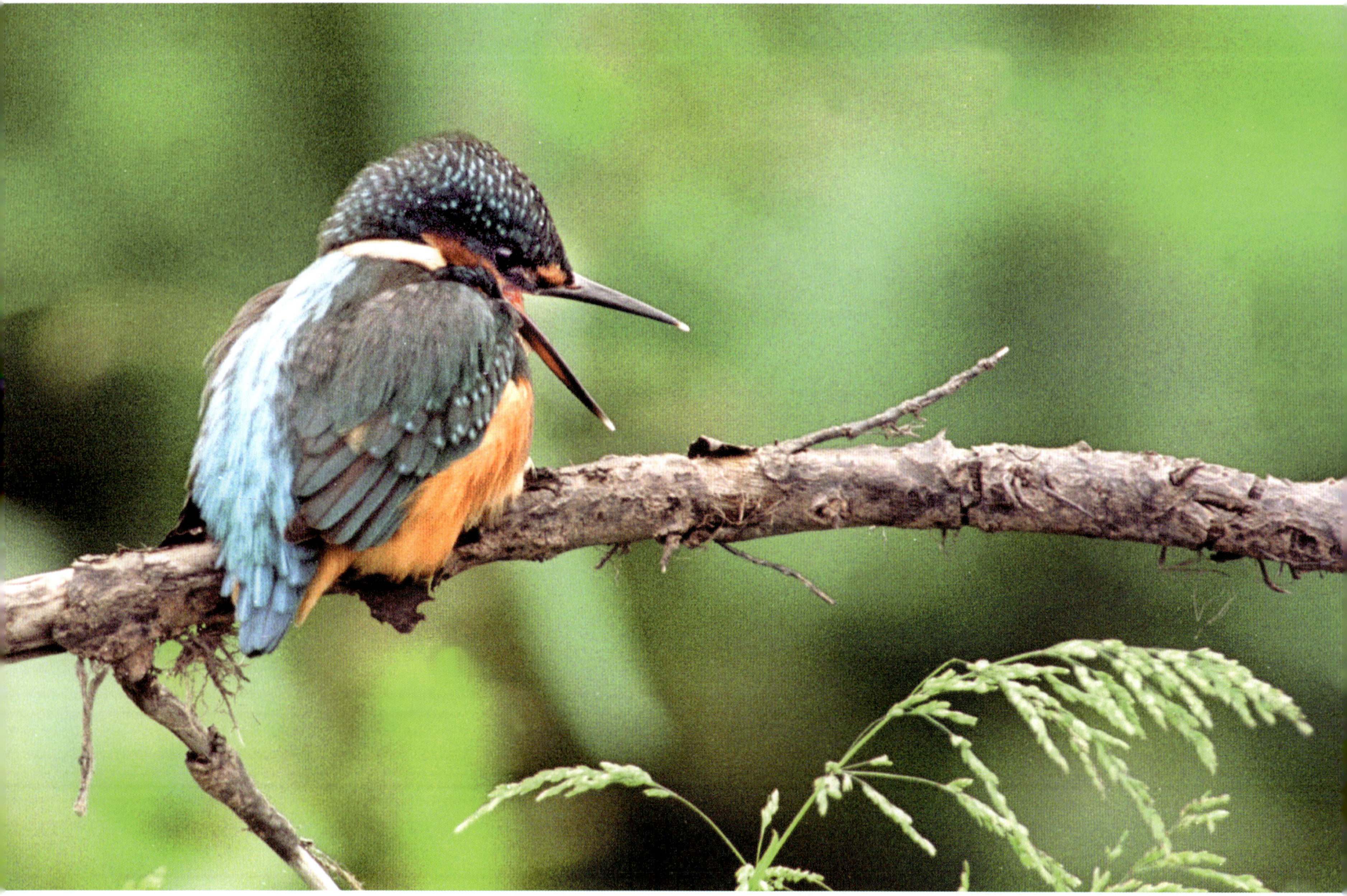

They say that the Kingfisher is the most colourful bird in Europe and I quite agree. A call from farmer William Pickard in Bow alerted me to the bird fishing for dragonfly nymphs on his large pond – it was a quiet news day so I spent about five hours with the bird who seemed to accept my presence, in fact he was so close to me at one time that I could have patted him on his head. I made no attempt to hide and made no sudden movements and it worked a treat.

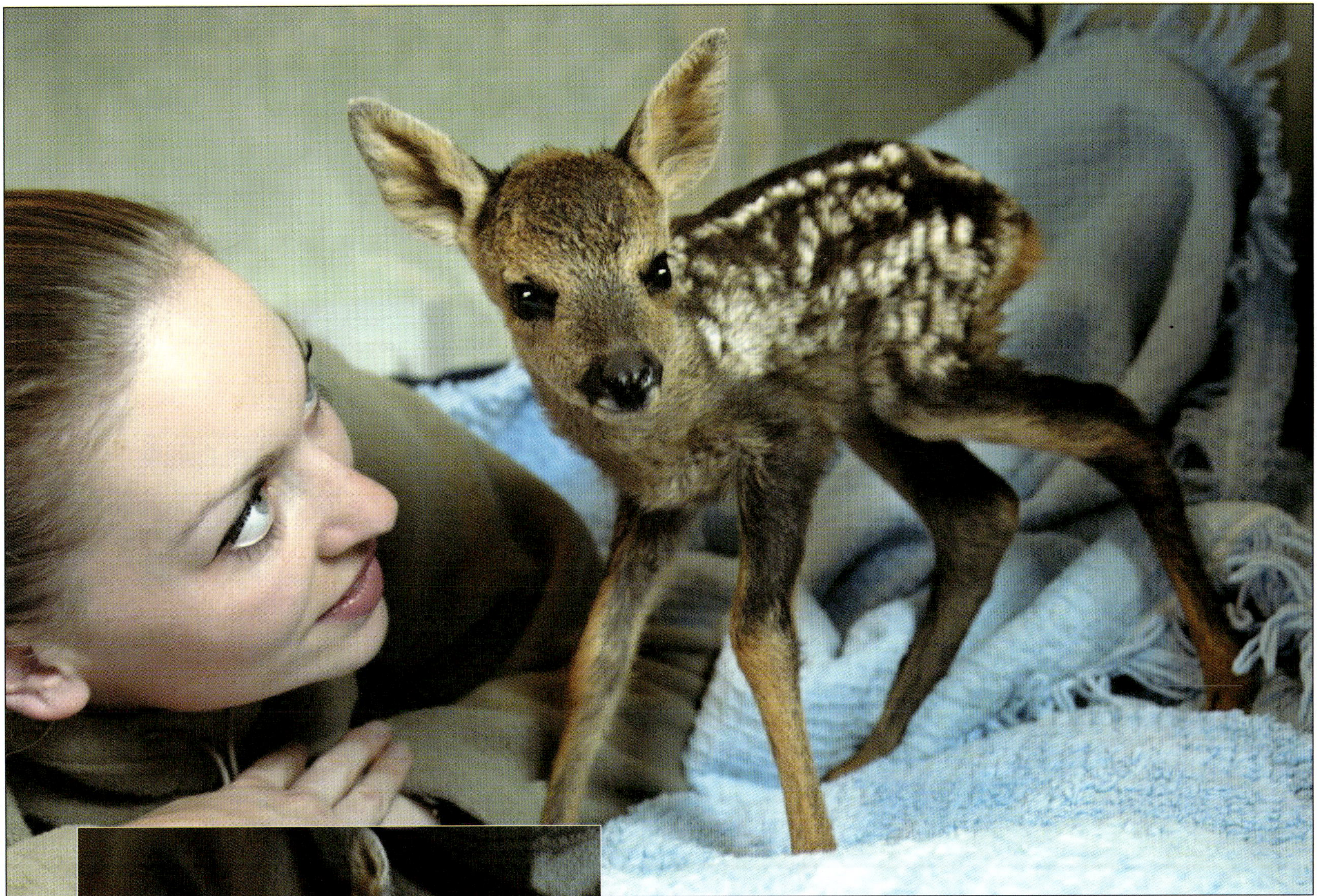

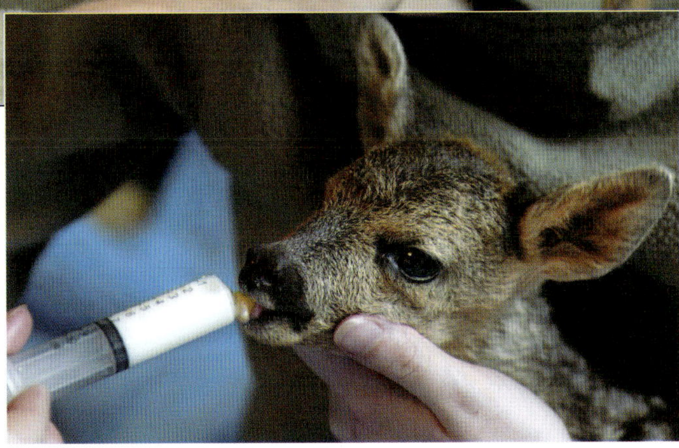

With round-the-clock care at Secret World Animal Sanctuary, Nikki Hawkins did everything she could to keep this tiny day-old female roe deer fawn alive – sadly she didn't make it. Nikki told me that raising very young roe deer fawns is very difficult and a large percentage do not make it.

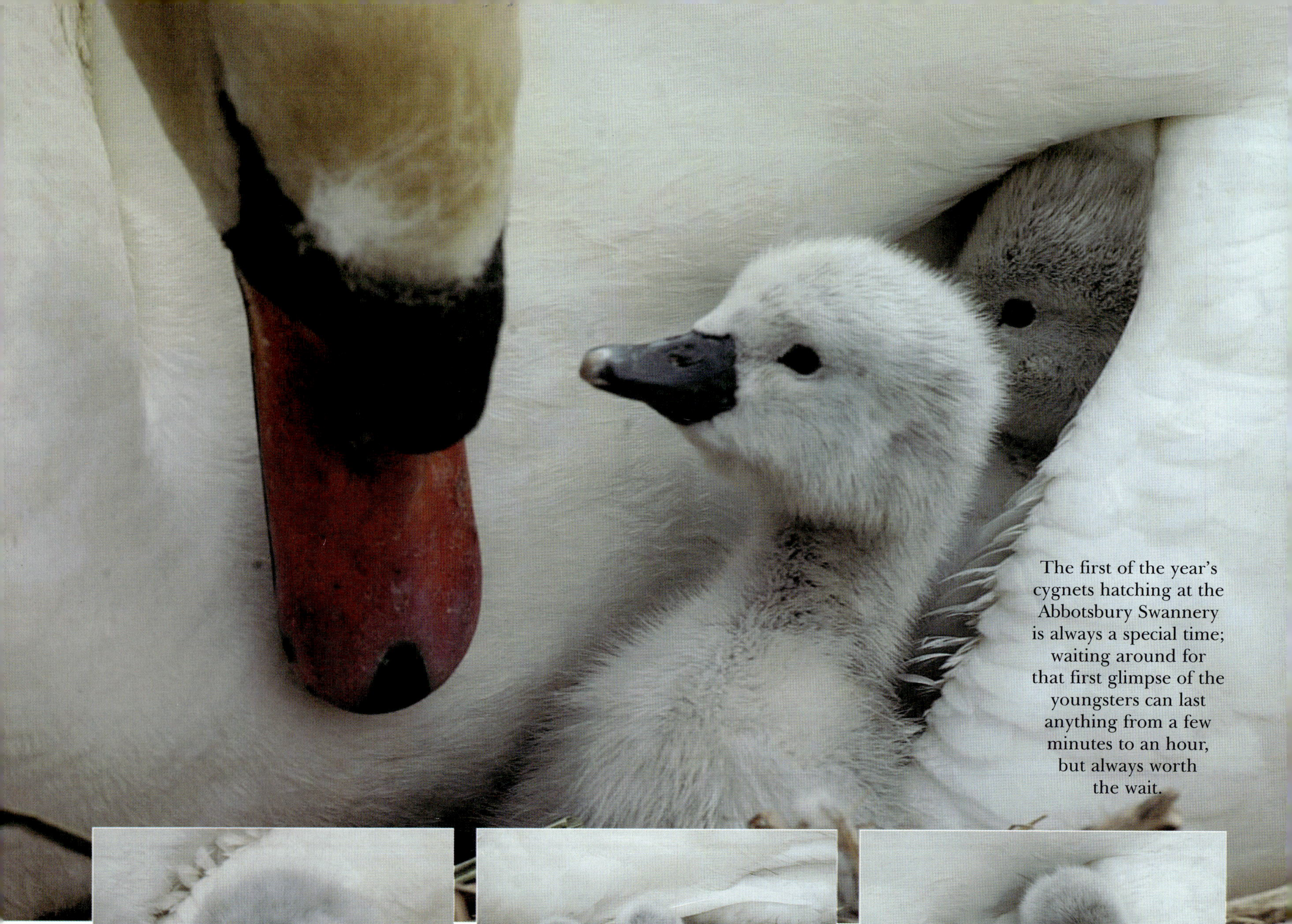

The first of the year's cygnets hatching at the Abbotsbury Swannery is always a special time; waiting around for that first glimpse of the youngsters can last anything from a few minutes to an hour, but always worth the wait.

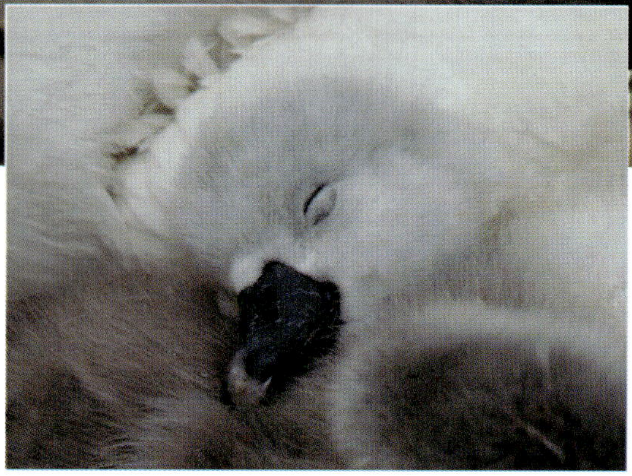

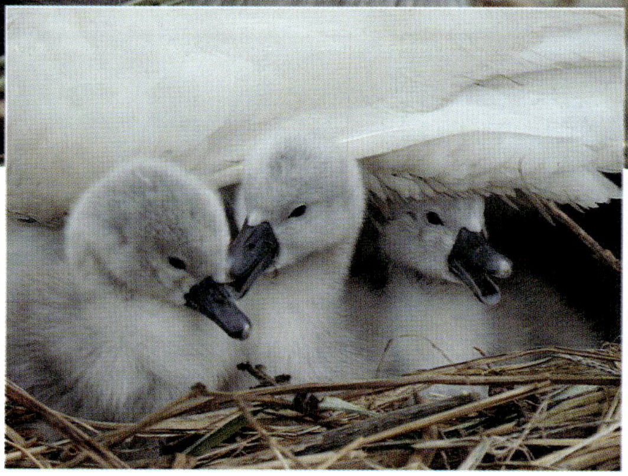

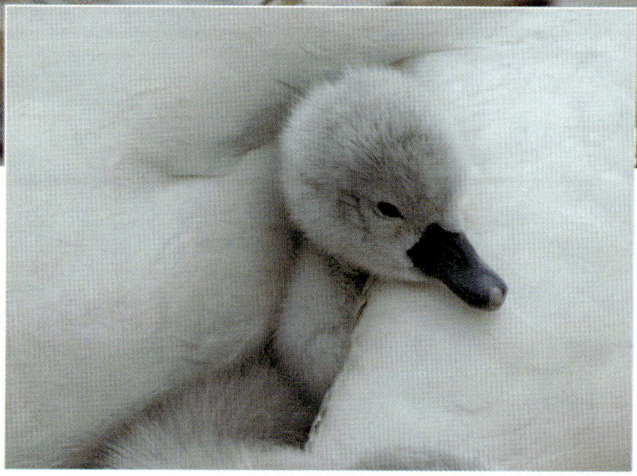

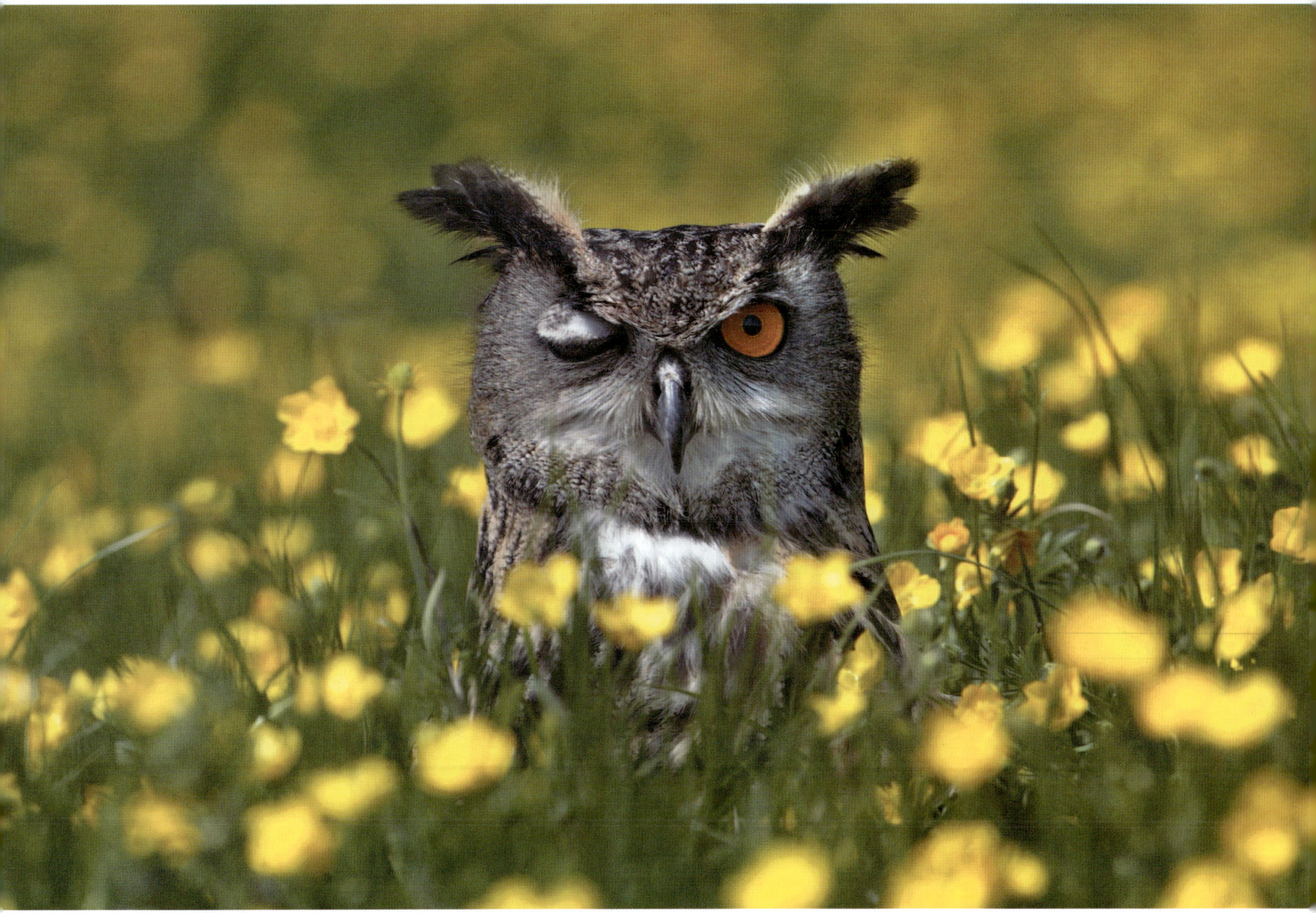

The world's biggest owl is the European Eagle Owl and they don't come much more spectacular than 'Eddie', the tame bird who winked at the camera as he rested in a field of buttercups.

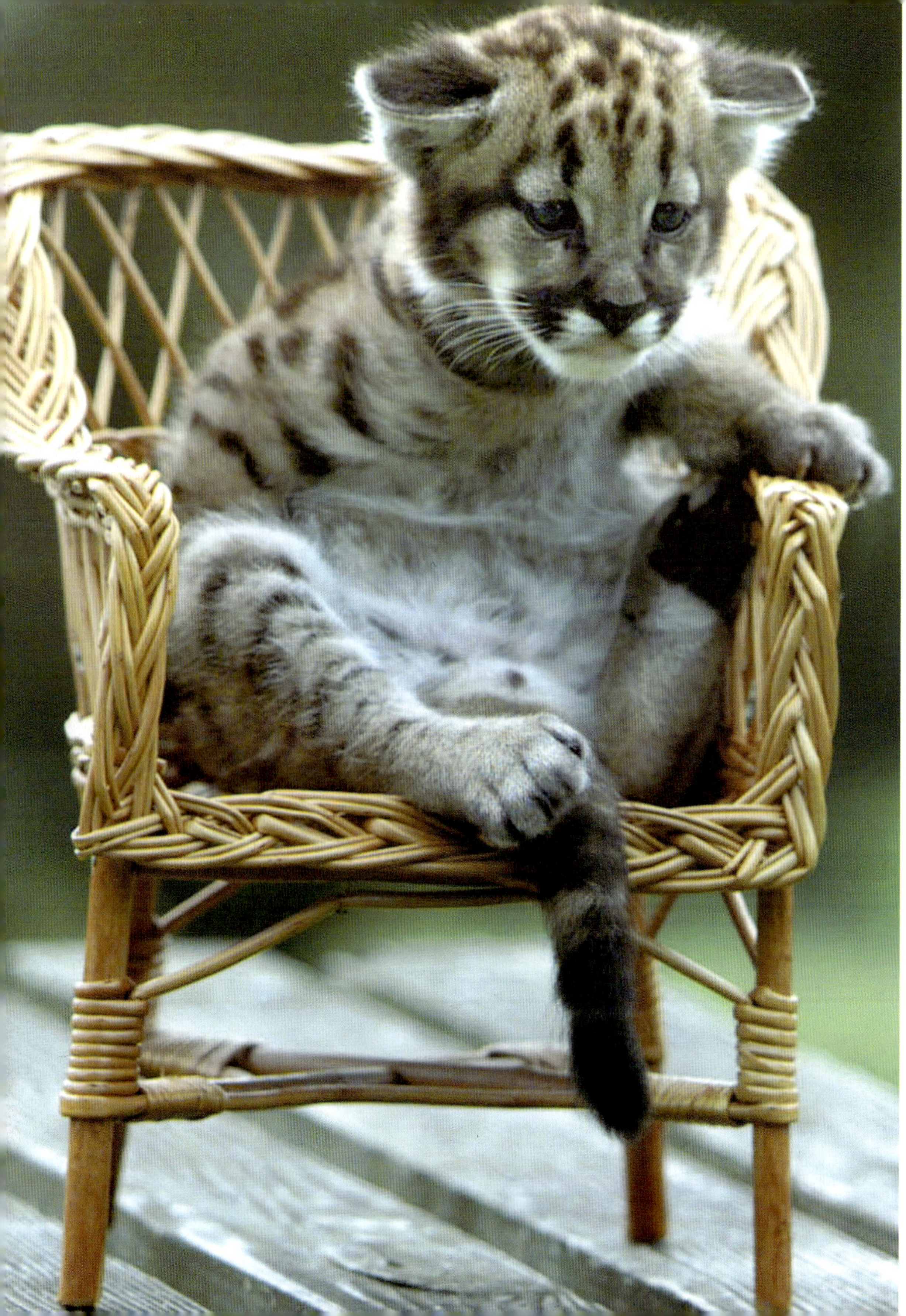

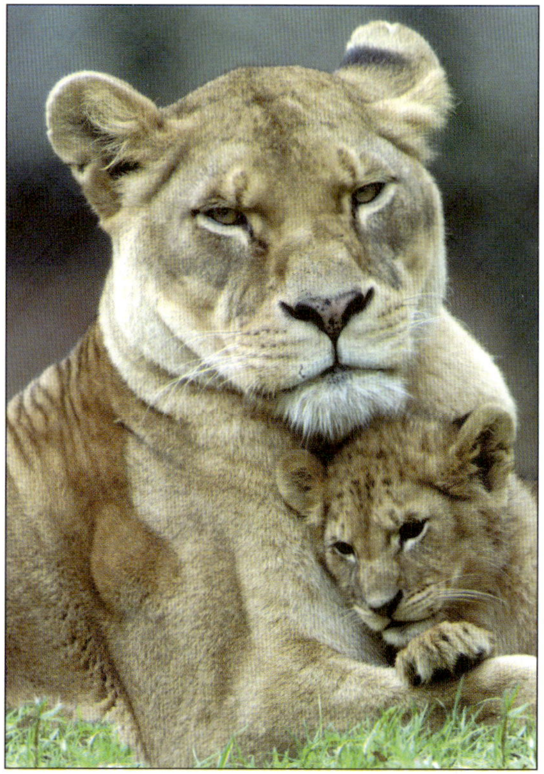

Big cats at the Dartmoor Wildlife Park...
a hand-reared Puma cub plays in
a basket chair whilst a lioness gets
close to her cub.

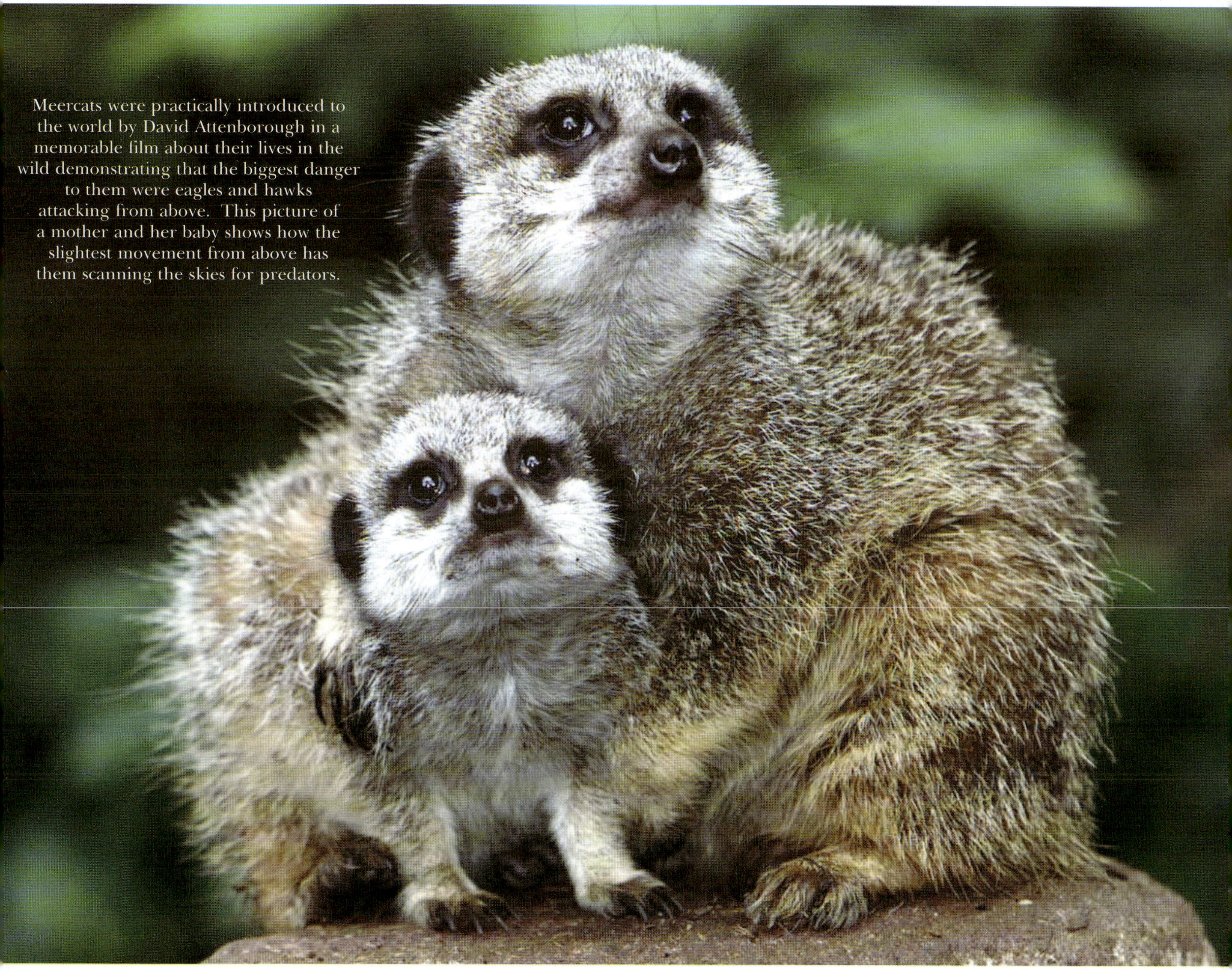

Meercats were practically introduced to the world by David Attenborough in a memorable film about their lives in the wild demonstrating that the biggest danger to them were eagles and hawks attacking from above. This picture of a mother and her baby shows how the slightest movement from above has them scanning the skies for predators.

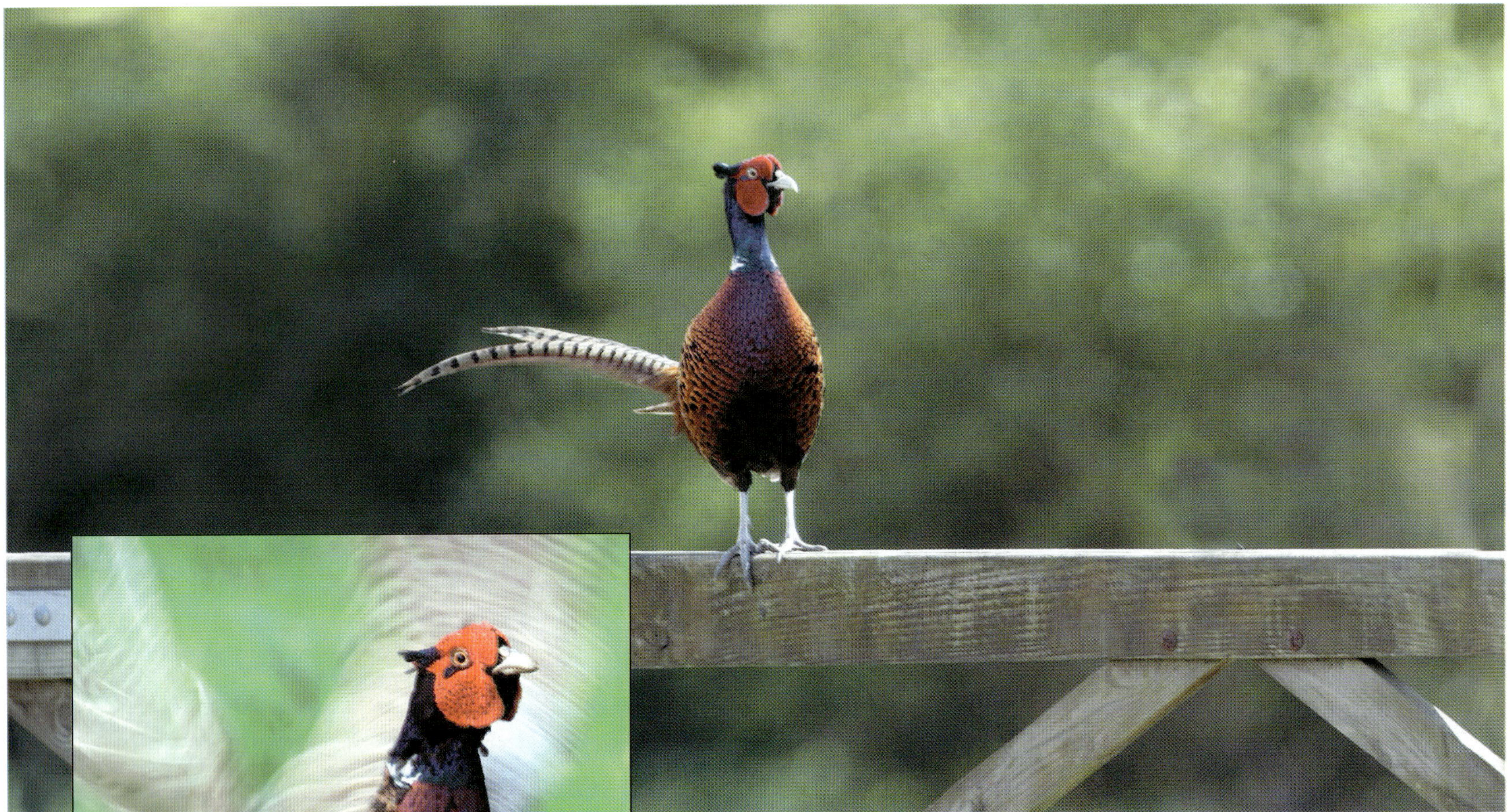

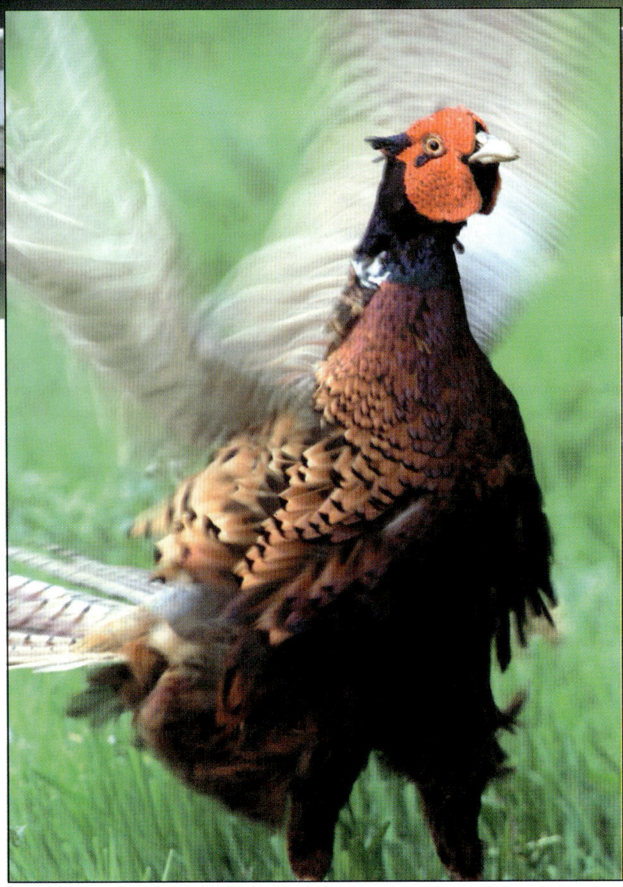

A cock pheasant in his full 'show-off' plumage comes a close second to the Kingfisher when it comes to brilliance of colour. Sadly the brightness of their feathers does not apply to their brains, there are nearly as many pheasants squashed on the roads as there are hedgehogs and badgers.

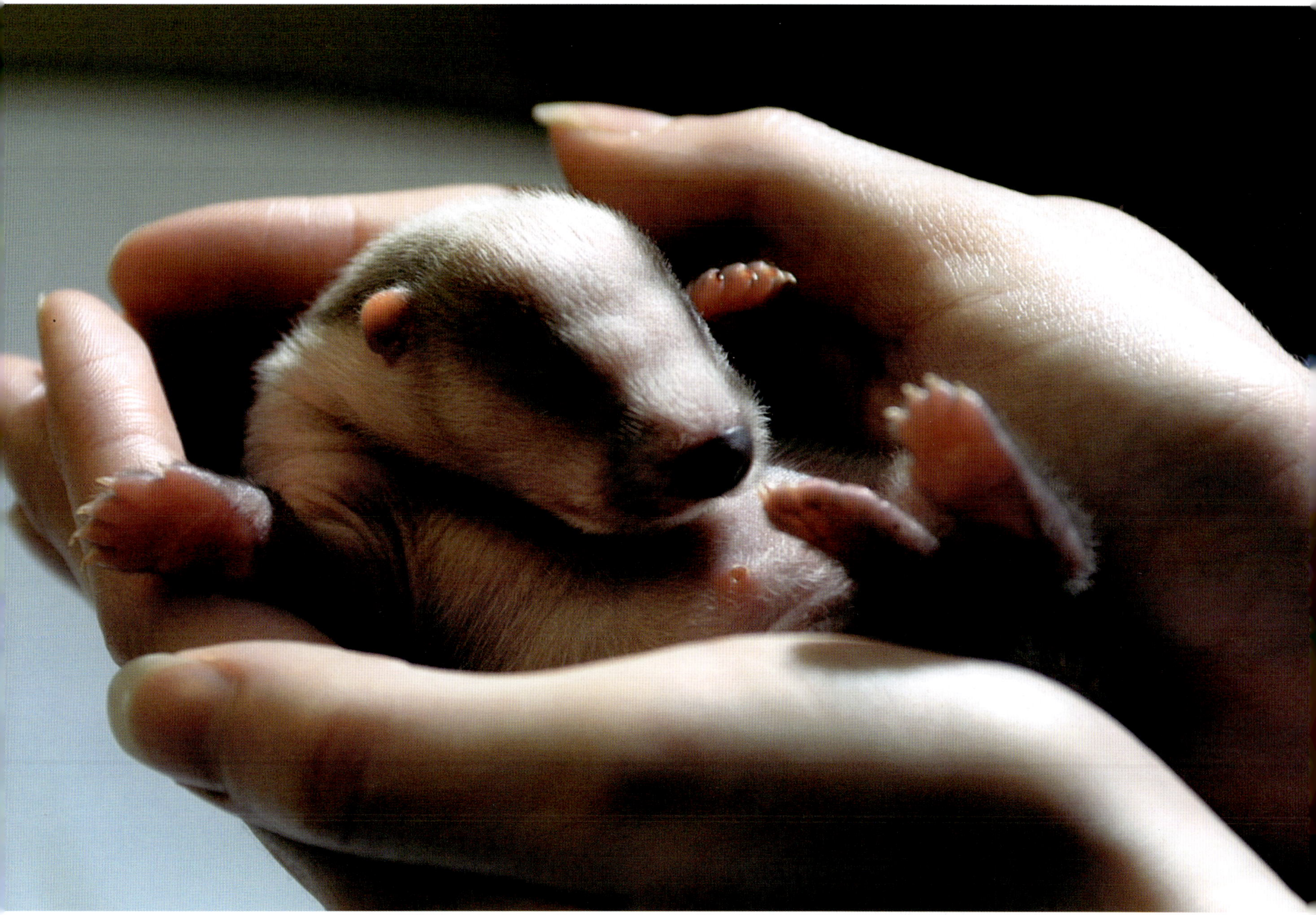

A tiny little badger having a tough time at the start of his life. Human skill and kindness by Pauline Kidner and her team at Secret World Animal Rescue have been responsible for bringing up hundreds of young badgers that have been successfully returned to the wild.

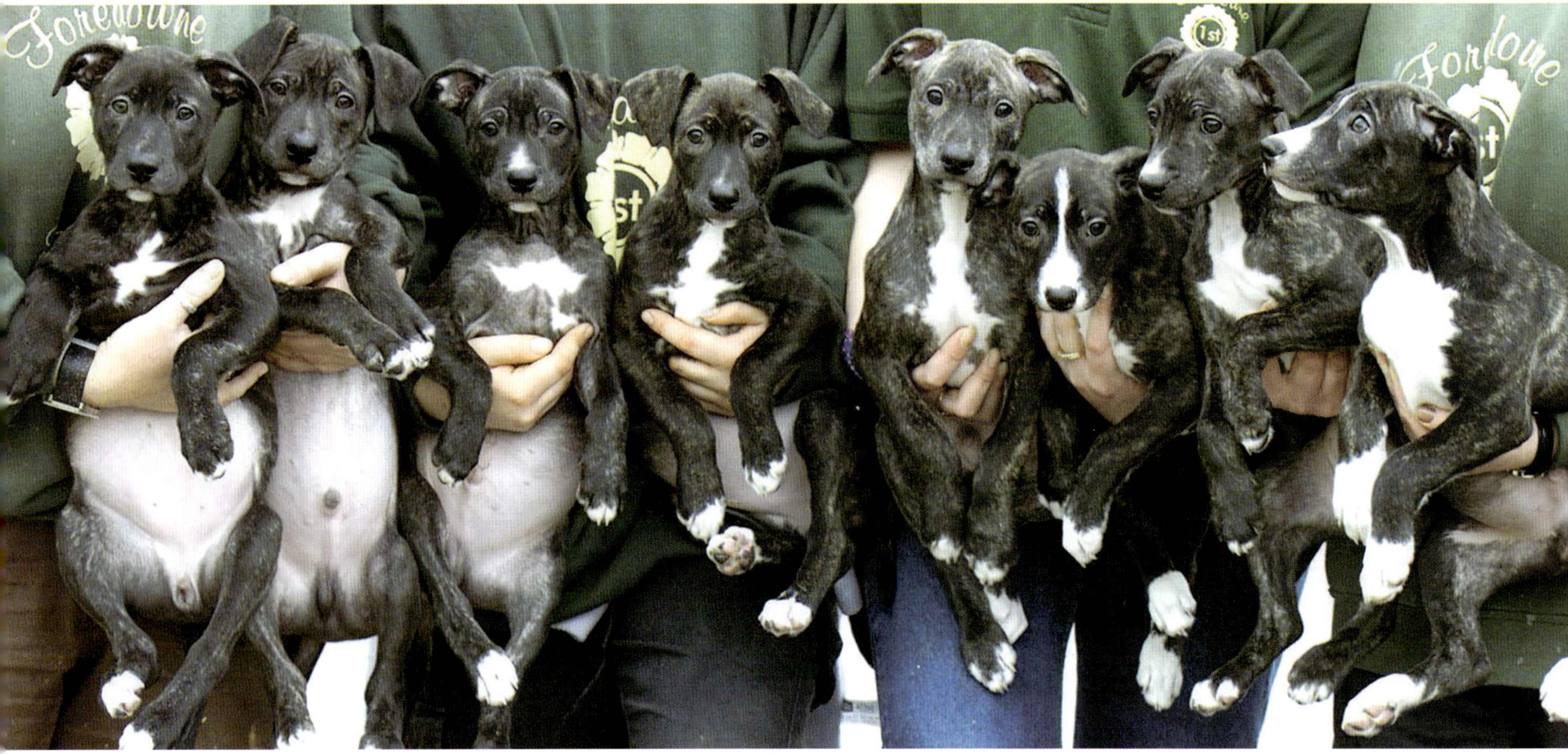


Eight puppies all from the same litter and very difficult to photograph successfully. The plan was to grab their attention and get their ears to stand up which meant my making a selection of silly noises. All the pups needed homes so it was important for the pups to look most appealing.

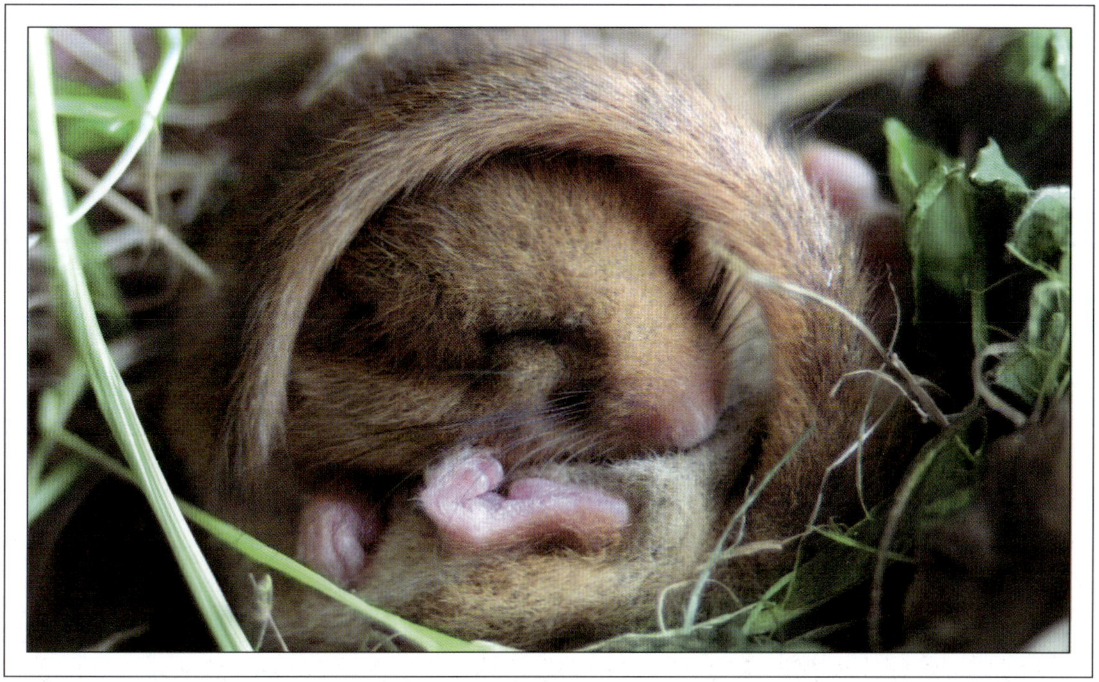

Dormice when fast asleep look so cuddly. This picture was taken at Paignton Zoo where they have a breeding programme enabling dormice to be put into areas in the UK where they no longer exist. The mice are very well looked after during hibernation with a constant temperature playing a very important role.

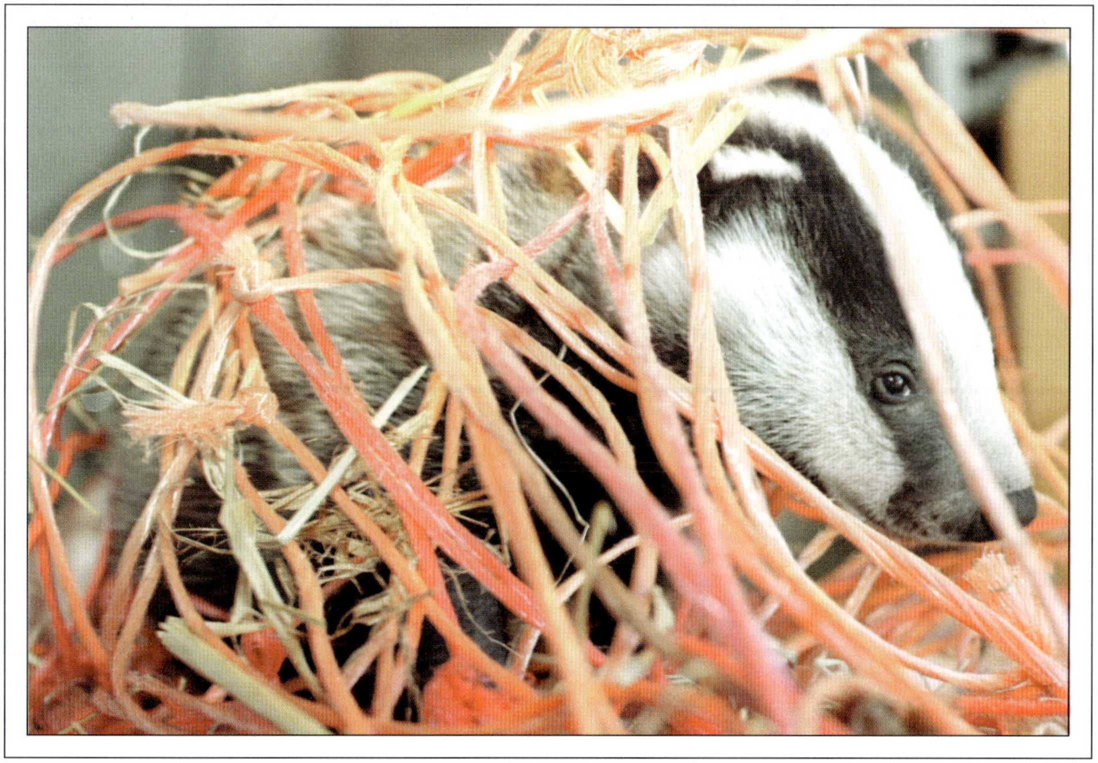

The fortunate badger cub was a lone survivor when he and his brother were thrown out of the sett by accident when their mother changed the bedding. The mother had taken the bundle of discarded baler twine down into her sett as fresh bedding, the cubs became tangled and ended up on the outside when the bedding was changed. Sadly only one cub was found alive but still entangled.

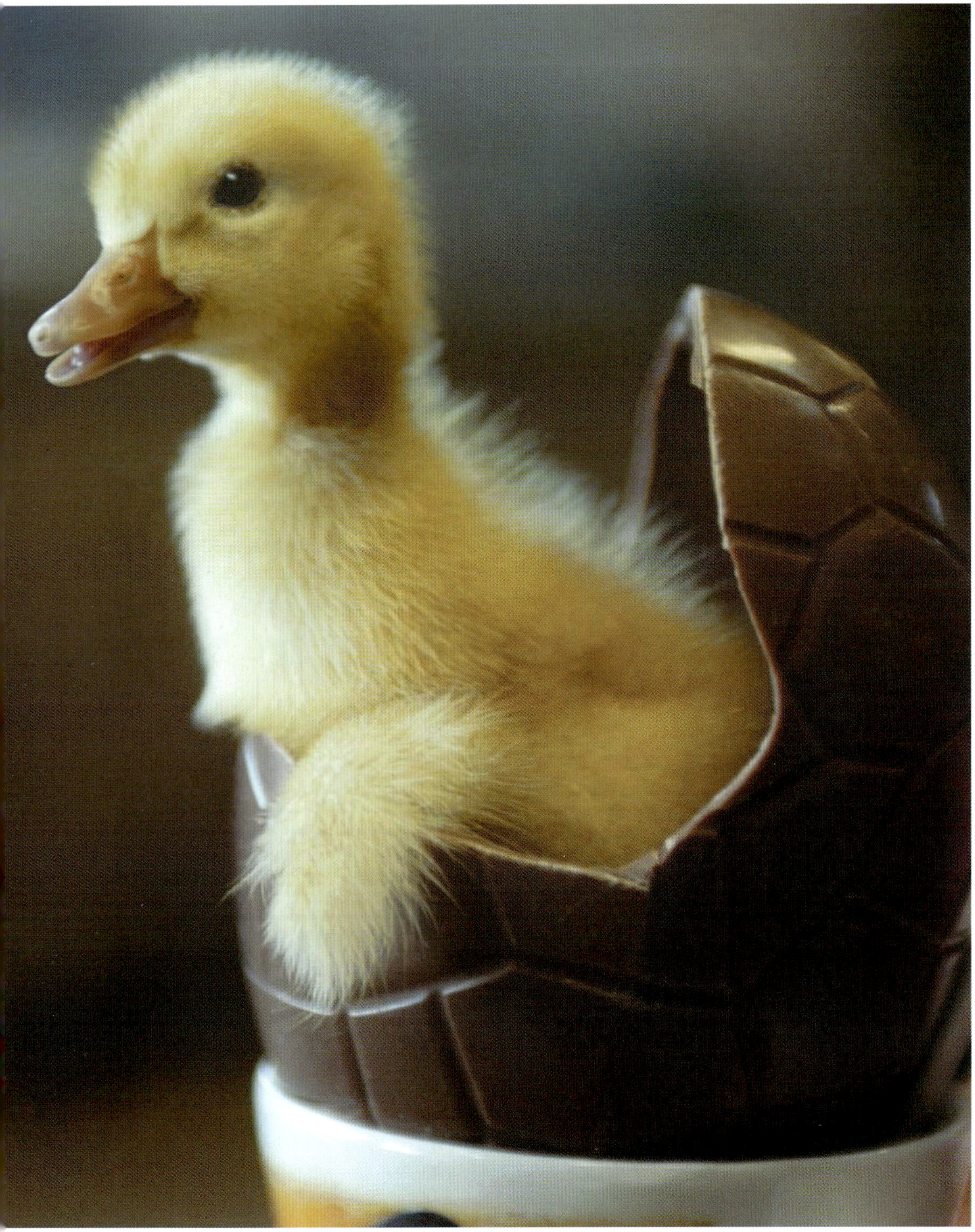

Easter time at Pennywell Farm and things go a lot better with shell for the baby squirrel who didn't care where he took a rest in the wildlife hospital unit at Secret World.

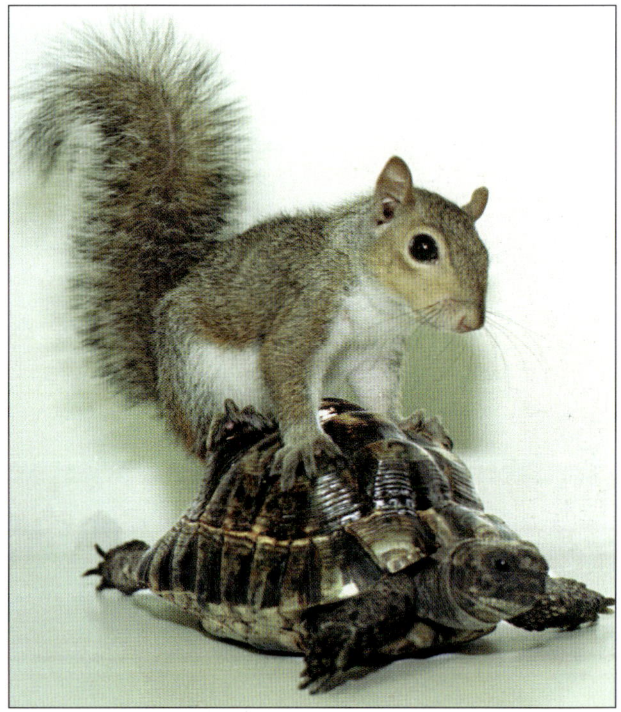

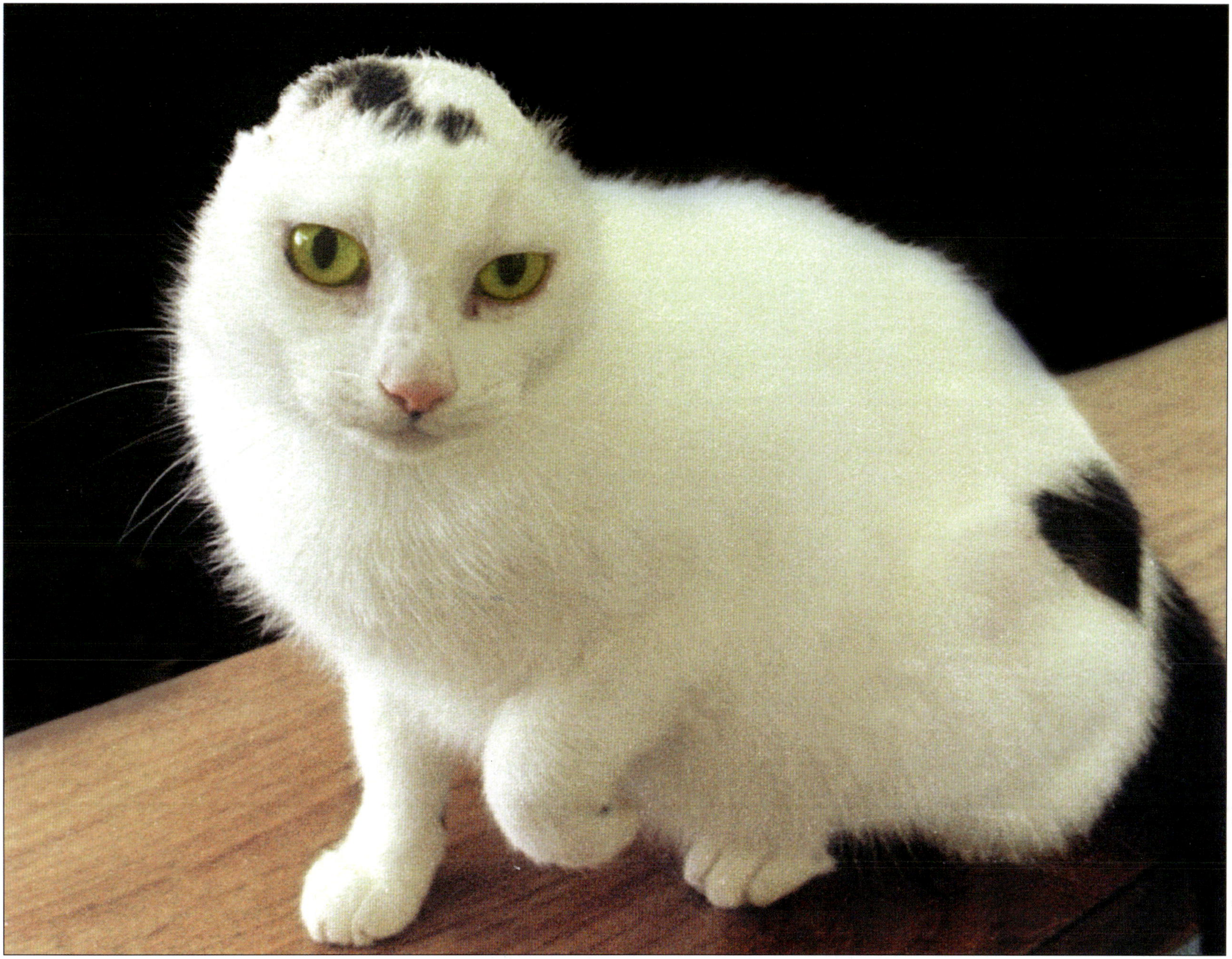

Skin cancer caused this lovely cat to lose her ears and her home. After press publicity a new home was found for her at a local hospice as the hospital cat.

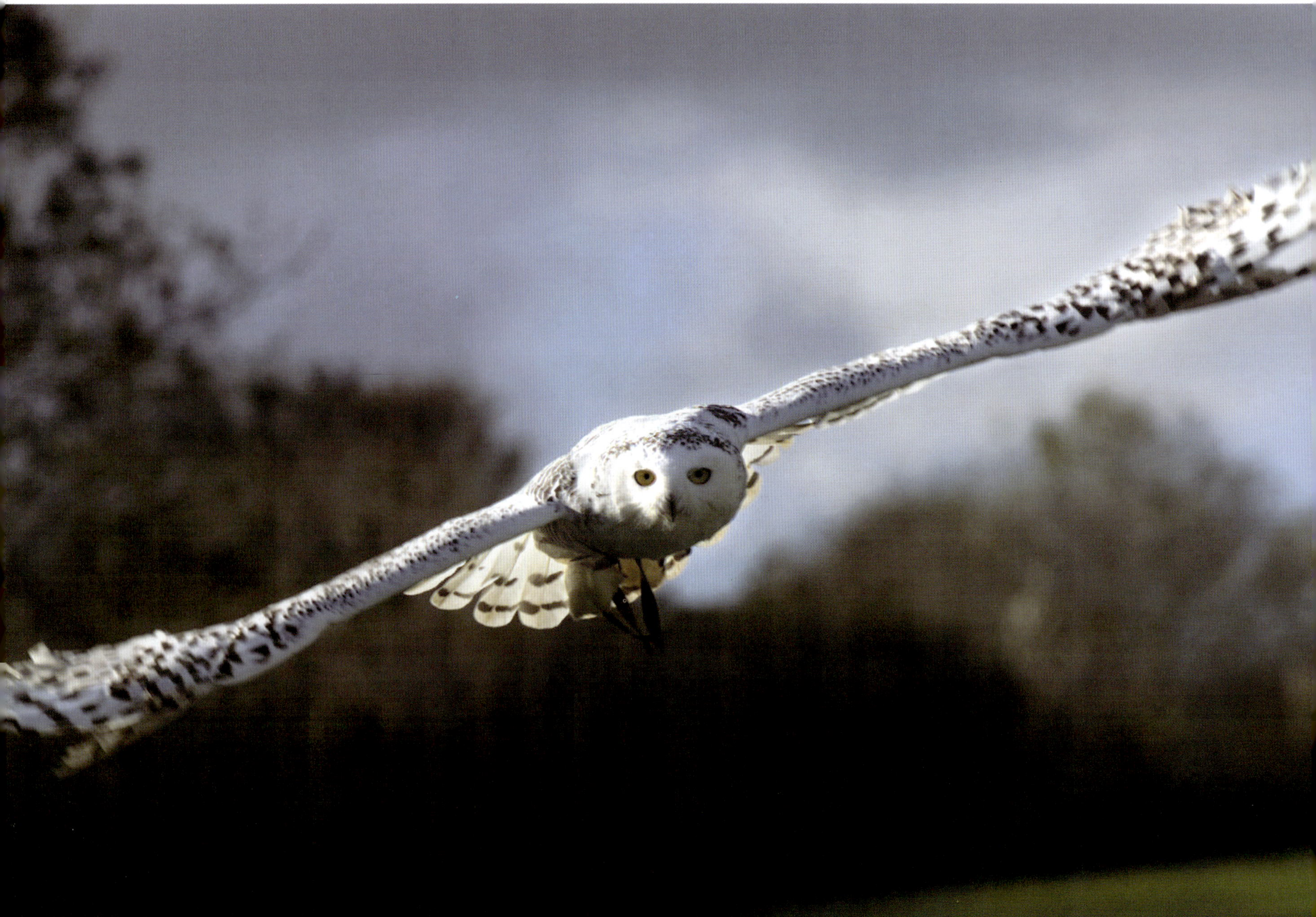

Photo call for the tame barn owl to publicise the setting up of barn-owl nesting boxes in farm outbuildings throughout Devon. In the meantime the Harry Potter blockbuster movie has rekindled the public's interest in owls – especially snowy owls – as pictured.

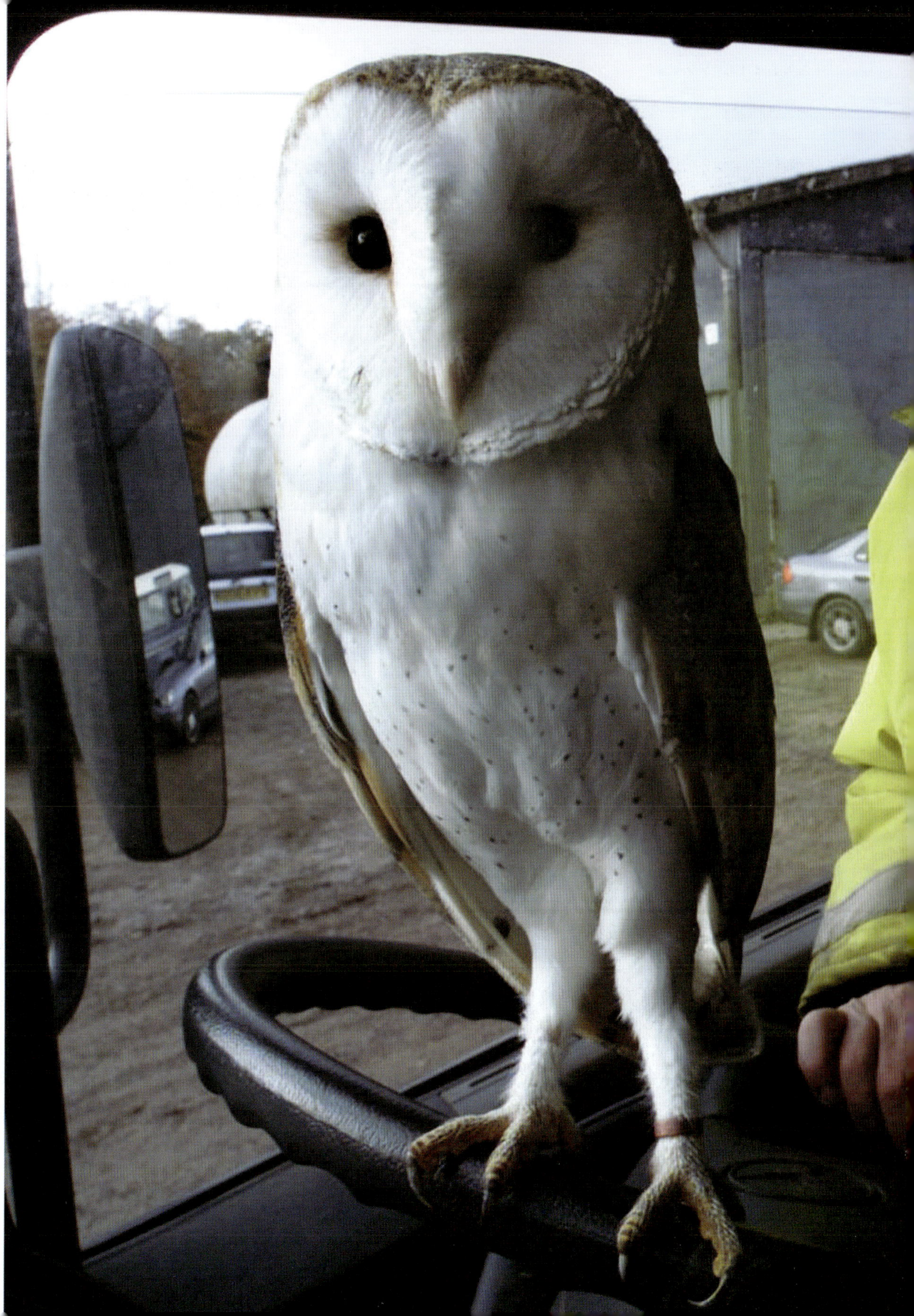

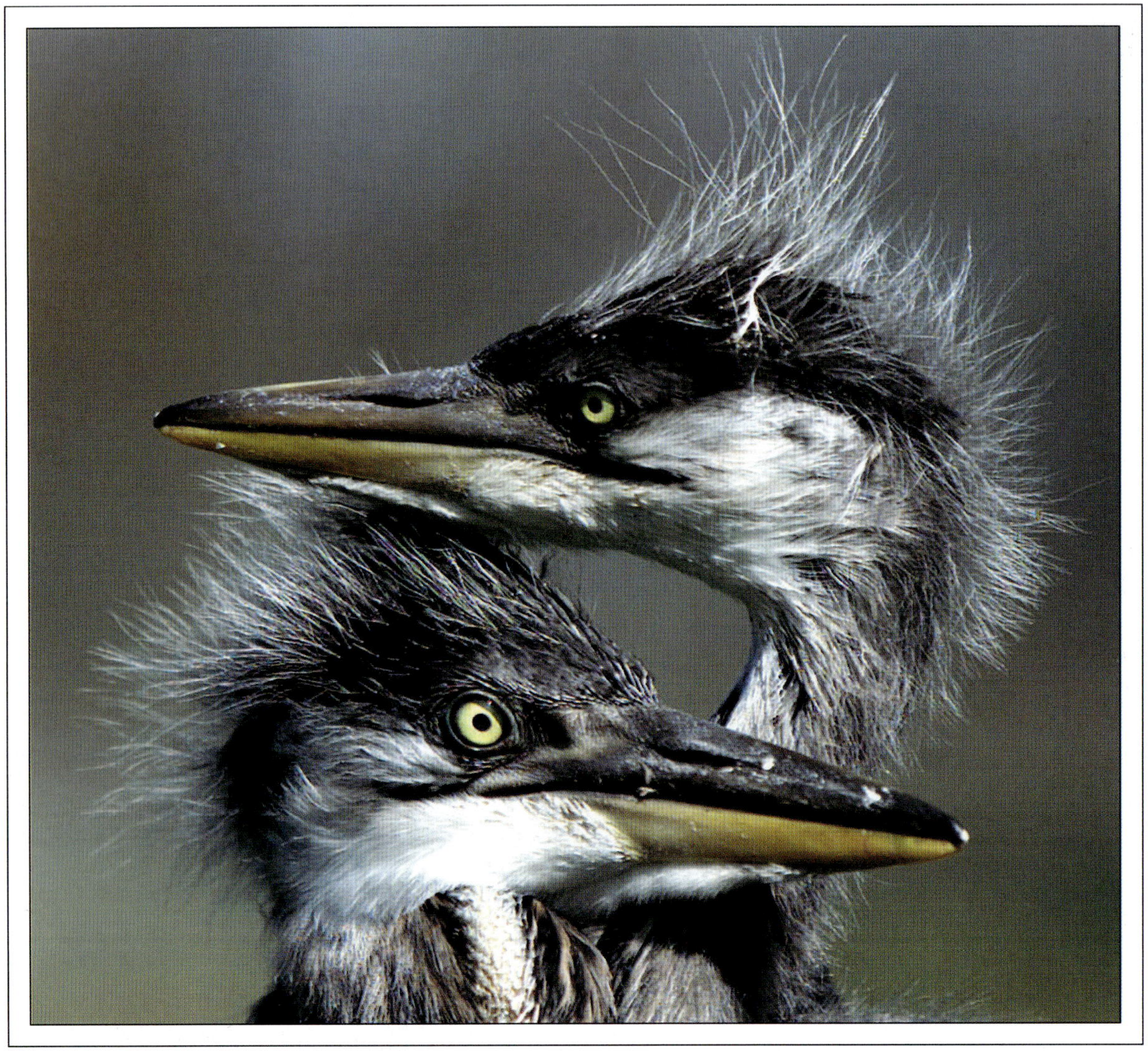

Double-take of two young herons being looked after at the Dartmoor Wildlife Park.

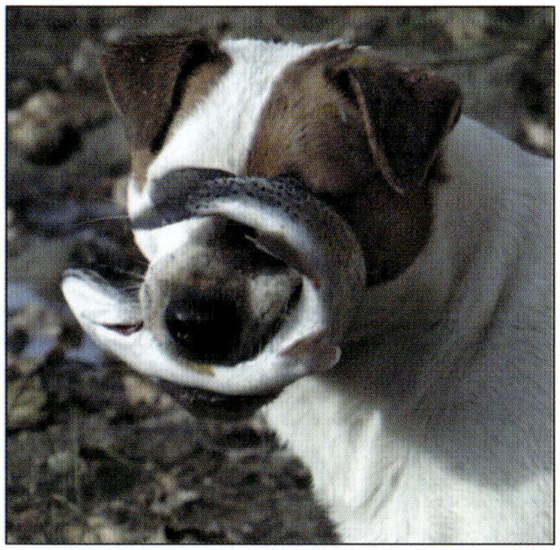

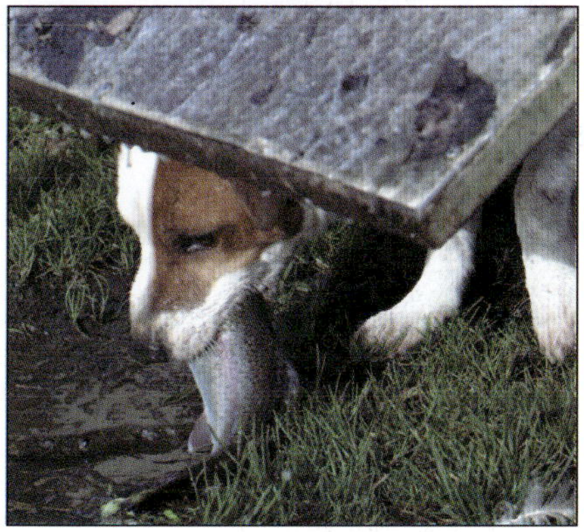

A call from the picture desk sent me to a local trout farm near Dartington where reports had come in of a young Osprey seen catching fish in the trout ponds. As it was a quiet day I spent several wasted hours waiting for the bird who did not show up. I returned the following day after a call from the trout-farm owner and found the magnificent Osprey sitting in the tree but not fishing; he took off several times sizing up the trout but declined to dip his feet in the water. To my astonishment the owner's Jack Russell dog snatched a trout from the edge of the water and ate it – at least I managed to get one animal with a fish in its mouth, even if it wasn't the right one.

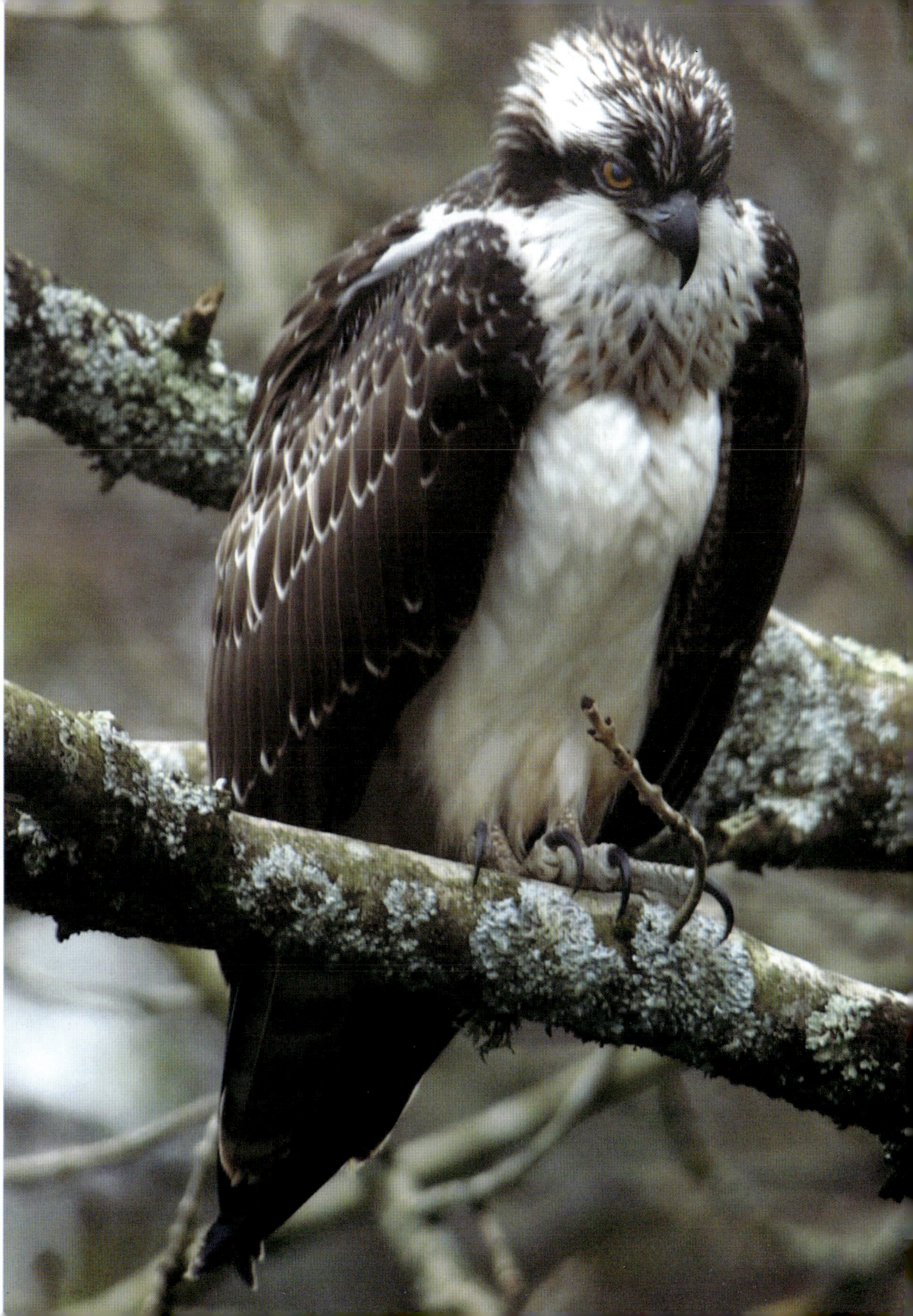

Best friends and inseparable – the Great Dane and Jack Russell who live on a horse stud were a fascinating pair to watch with hardly a cross word between them.

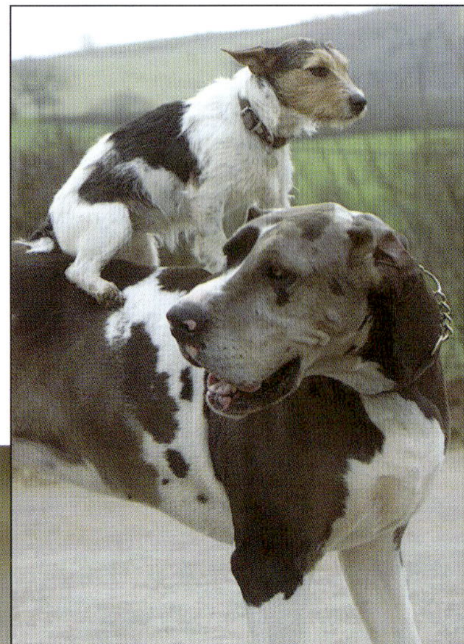

It was hard to imagine that in just a few weeks these little swallows would be flying across continents and oceans and the following year making their way back to sunny Devon. One unfortunate pair of swallows built their nest on top of a garage-door hinge in Bow near Crediton, disaster struck when the householder opened the door and the nest fell down. The horrified but industrious person found an old cooking sieve and nailed it to the wall, the swallows carried on as if nothing had happened.

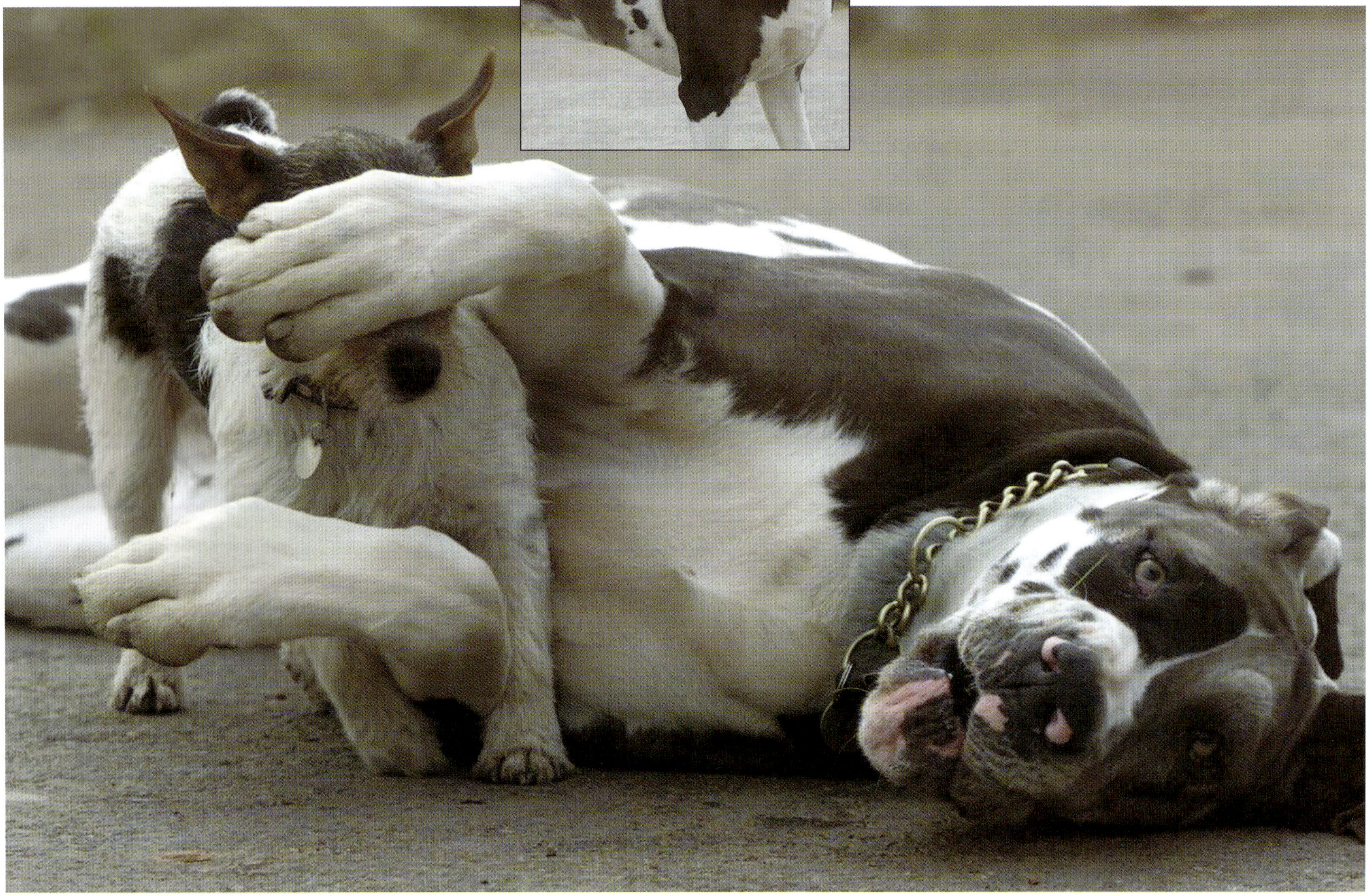

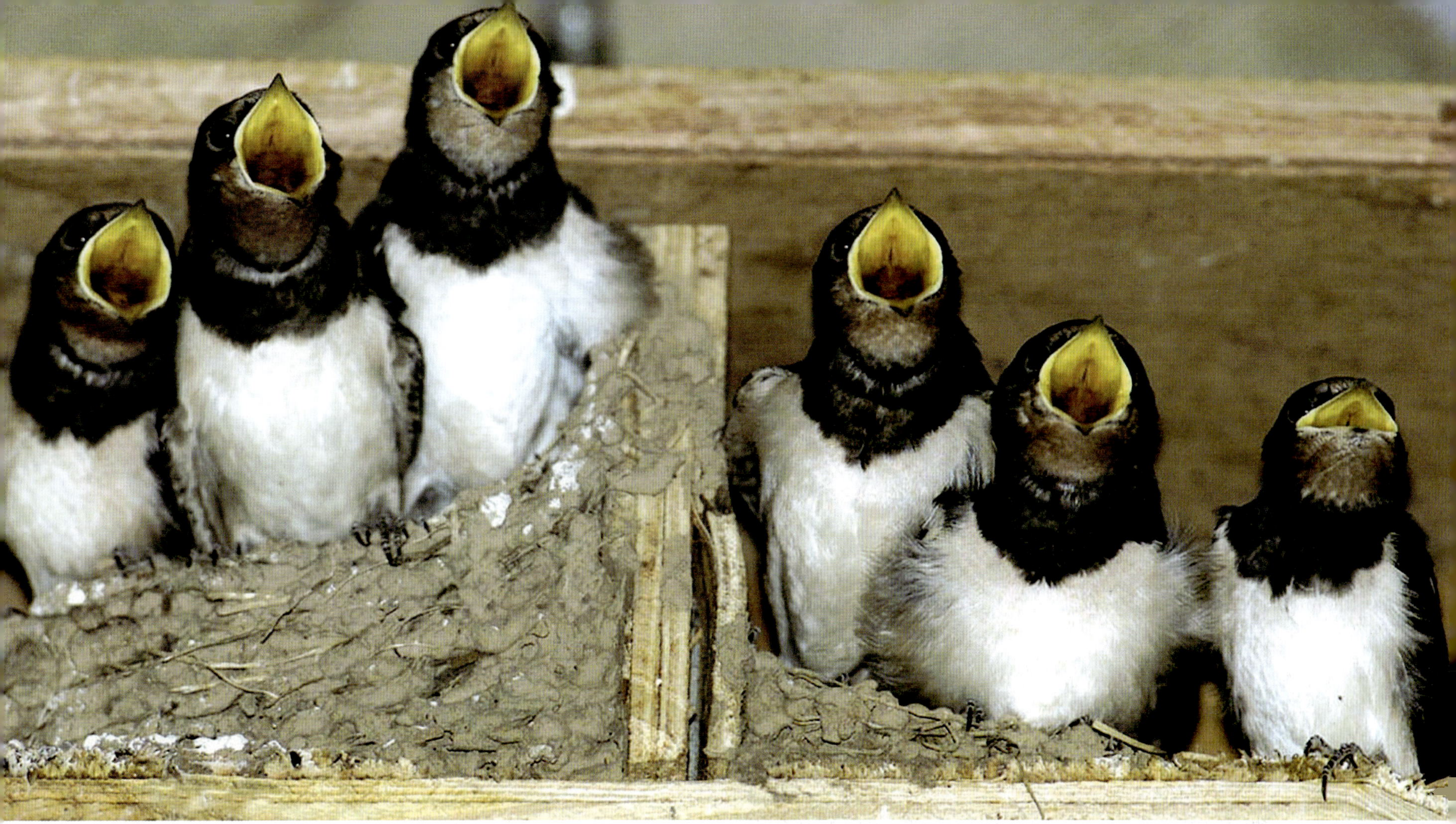

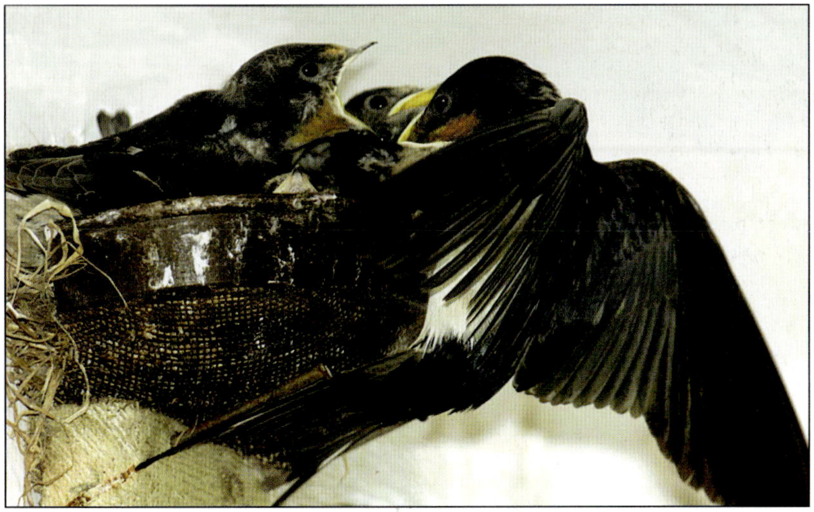

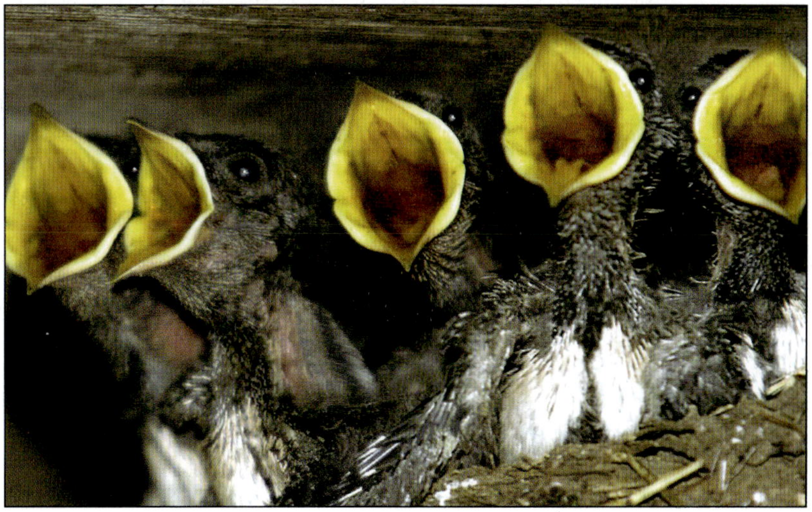

The answer is NO he didn't... Any number of people asked me if the Jaguar cub caught the cockerell he was stalking but the truth is that the cub was as scared of the cockerel as the big bird was of the cub. By using the telephoto lens the unusual pair look closer together than they actually are.

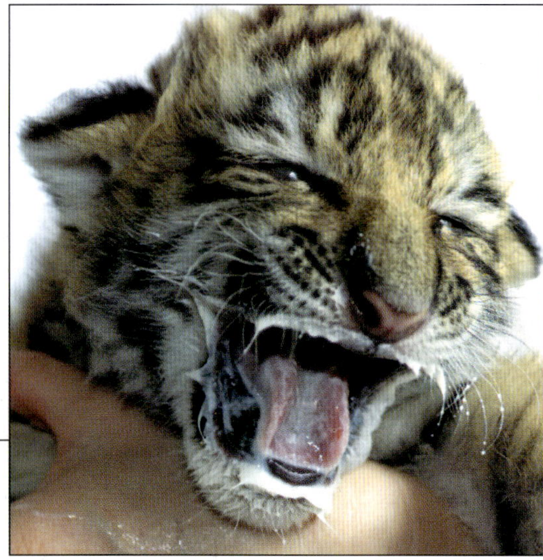

Just like the little baby that he is, the Siberian Tiger cub mews for more milk – if only he would lick his lips he would probably gather up another half-pint stuck to his fur.

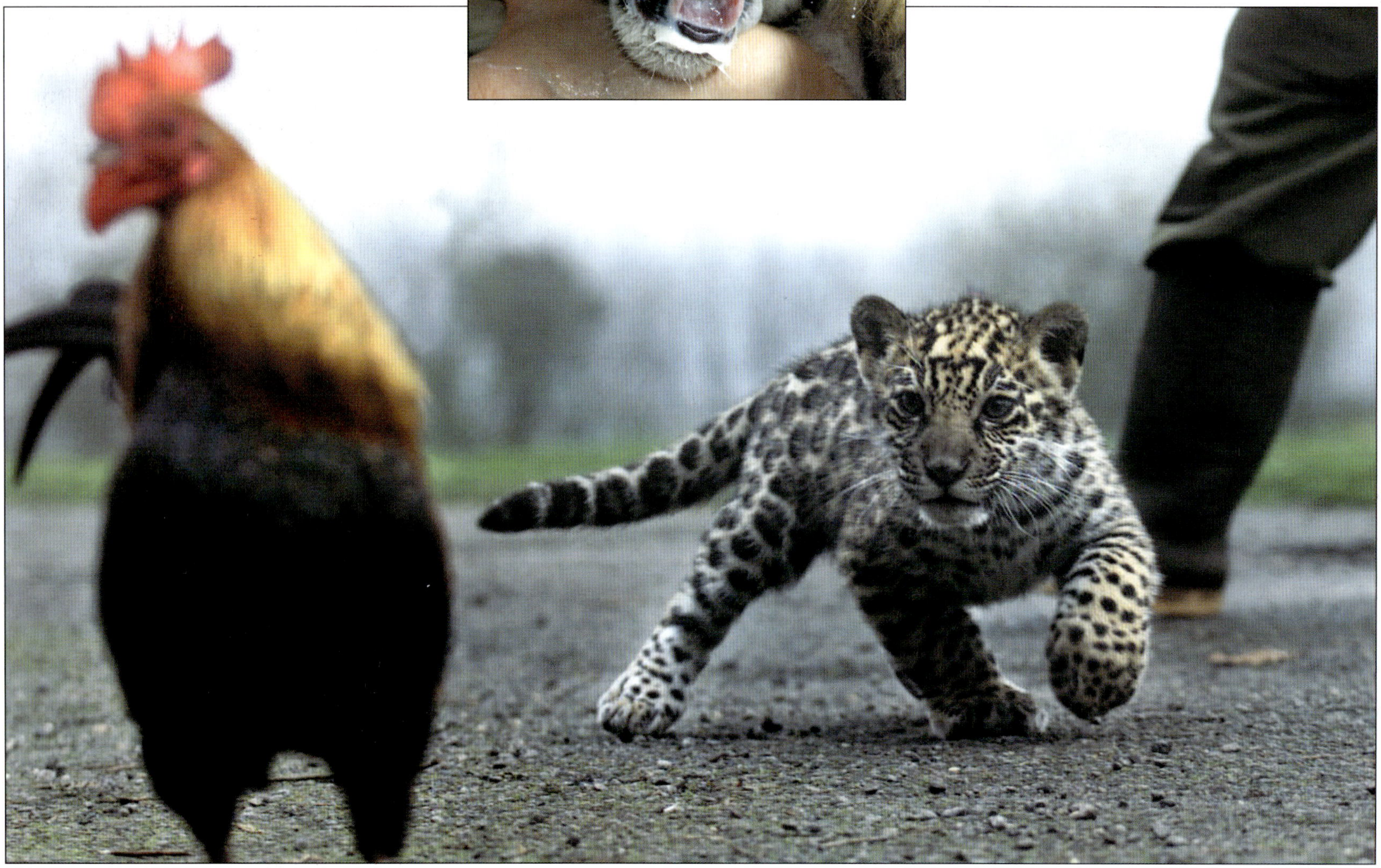

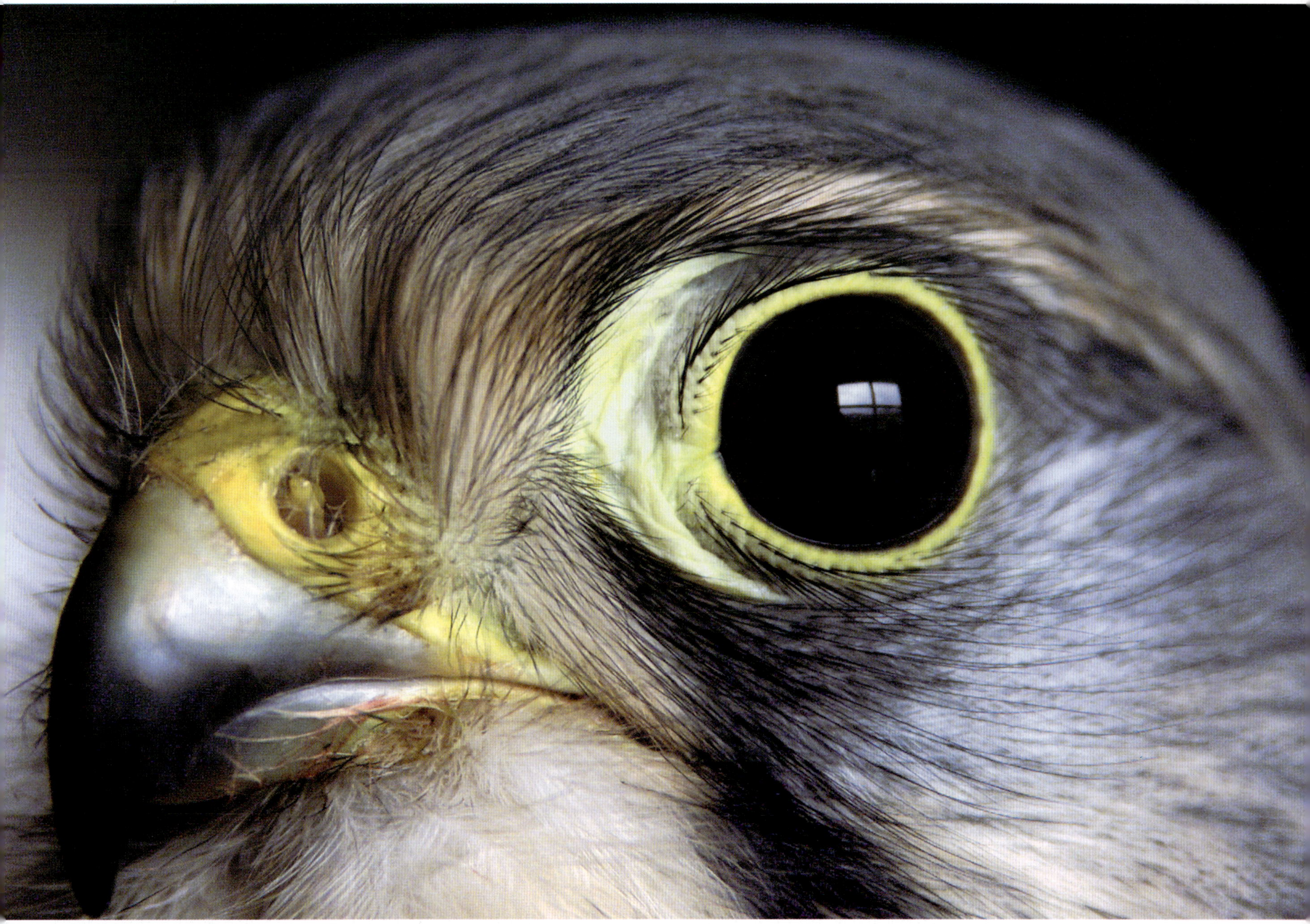

A close-up picture of the eye of the Kestrel, which I am told is the biggest eye in proportion to its body size of any of Britain's birds of prey. Looking at the bird's head through a macro lens was an incredible experience, the detail of the bird's skin, feathers and around his eyes surprised me.

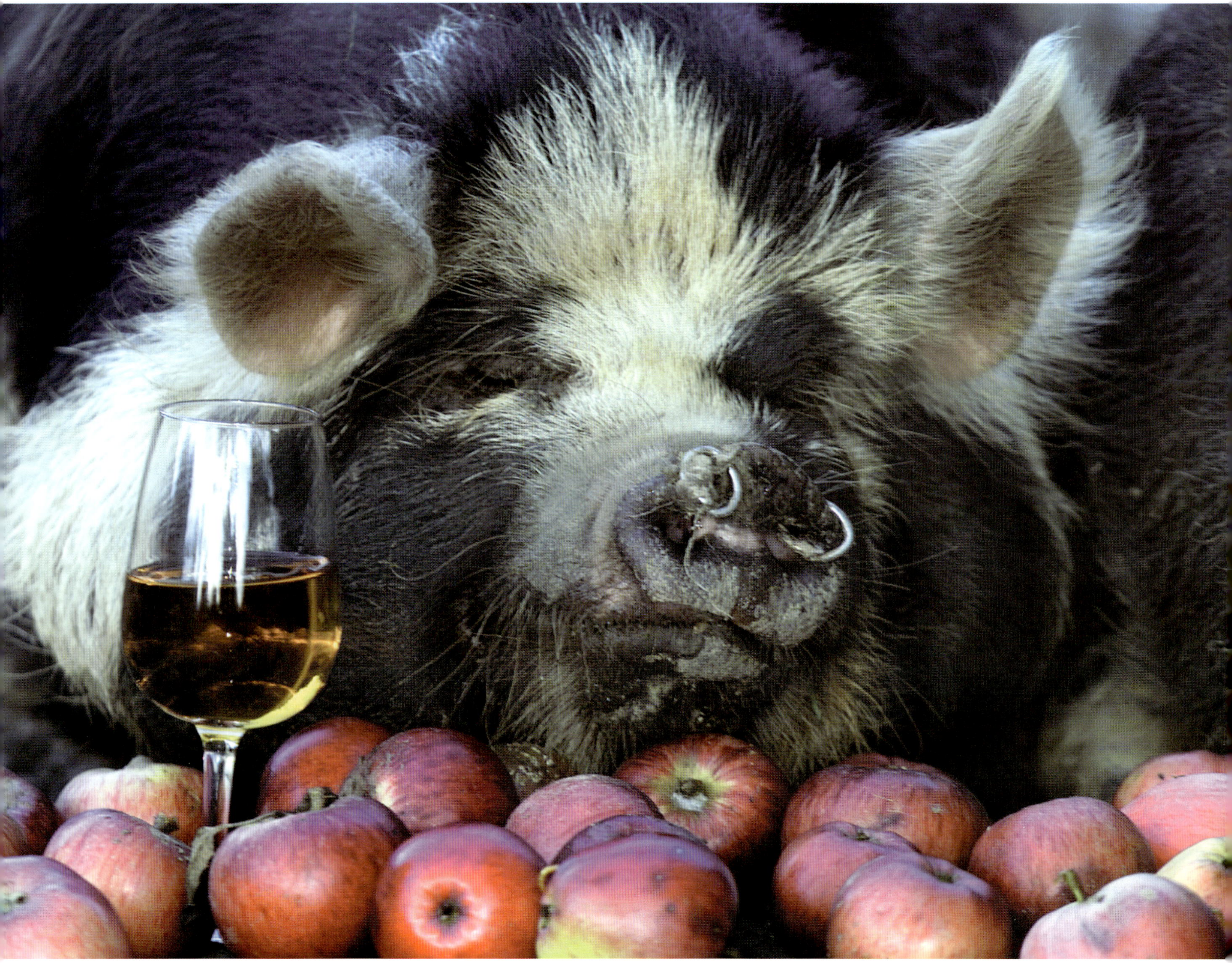

I couldn't resist setting up this picture of the drunken Kune Kune pig at Julian Temperley's cider distillery in Somerset. I had been commissioned to photograph the apple-rich orchards for a farming feature when I came across the sleeping beauty who had eaten too many fallen apples. The glass of cider brandy we brought out for the picture shoot complemented the snoring pig who didn't bat an eyelid all the time I was photographing him.

When mum decides to lie down – the bar is open and it's first come, first served.

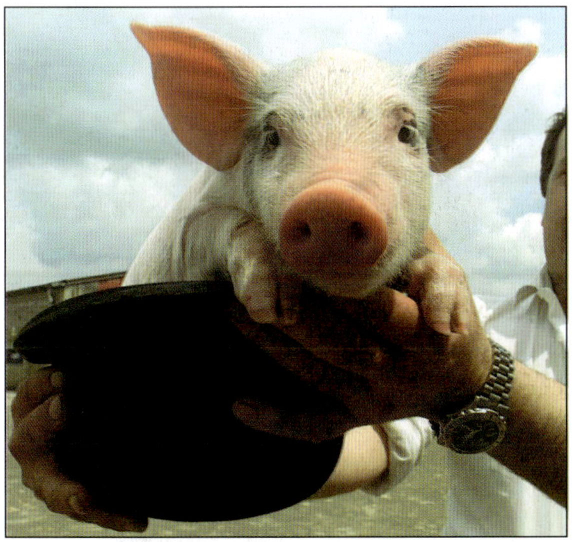

This little piggy was not at the market he was at the Royal Bath & West Show.

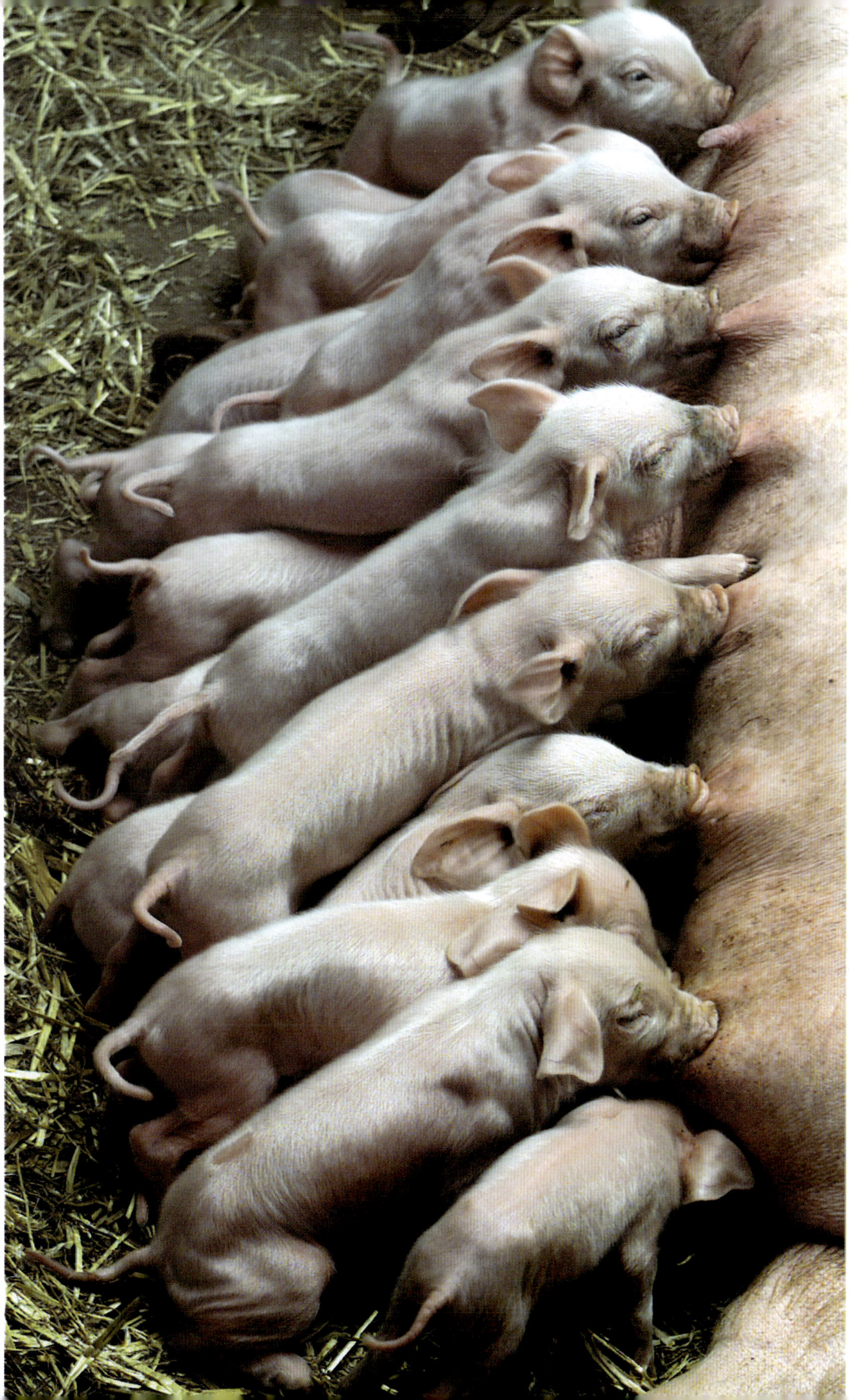

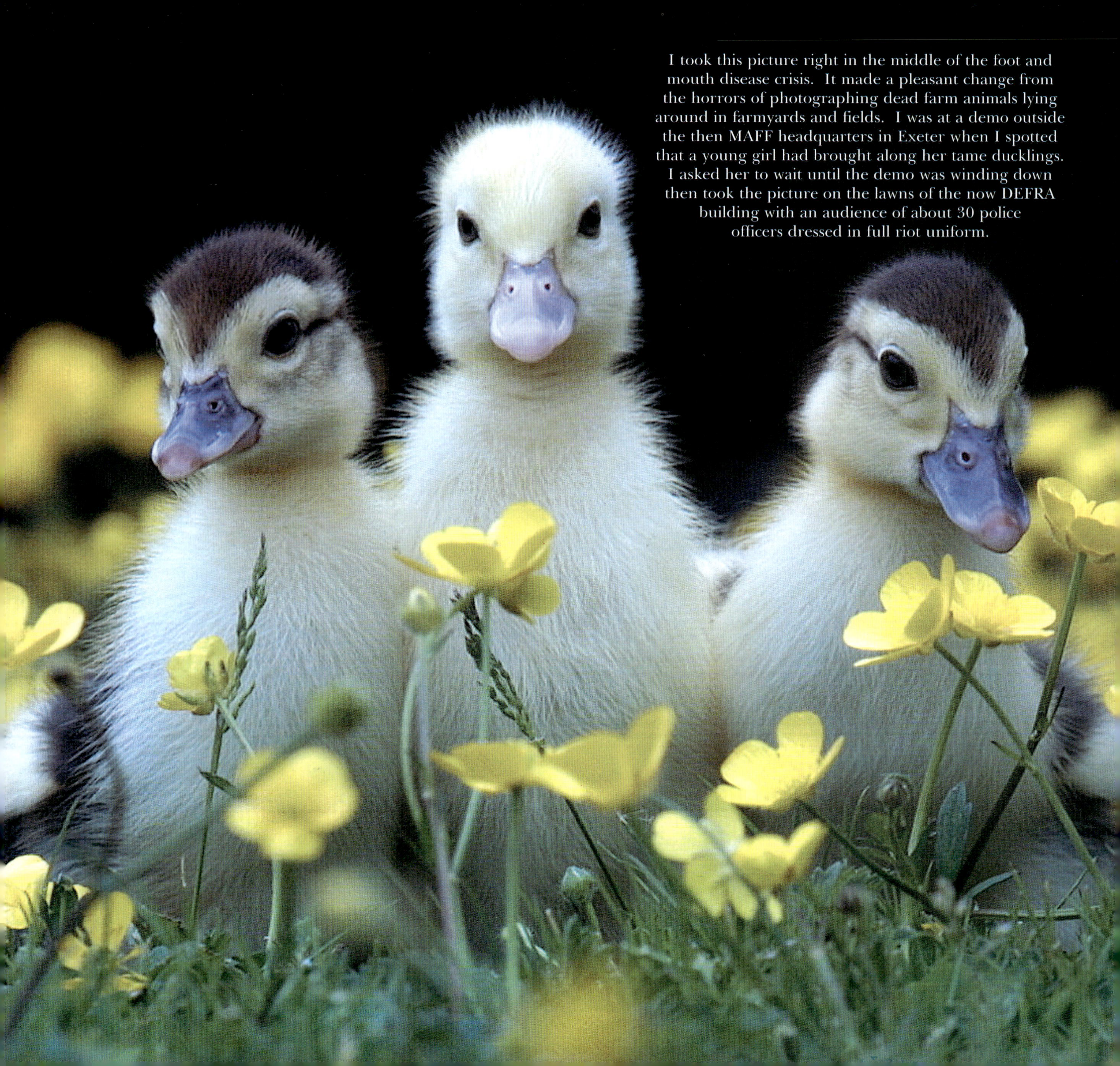

I took this picture right in the middle of the foot and mouth disease crisis. It made a pleasant change from the horrors of photographing dead farm animals lying around in farmyards and fields. I was at a demo outside the then MAFF headquarters in Exeter when I spotted that a young girl had brought along her tame ducklings. I asked her to wait until the demo was winding down then took the picture on the lawns of the now DEFRA building with an audience of about 30 police officers dressed in full riot uniform.

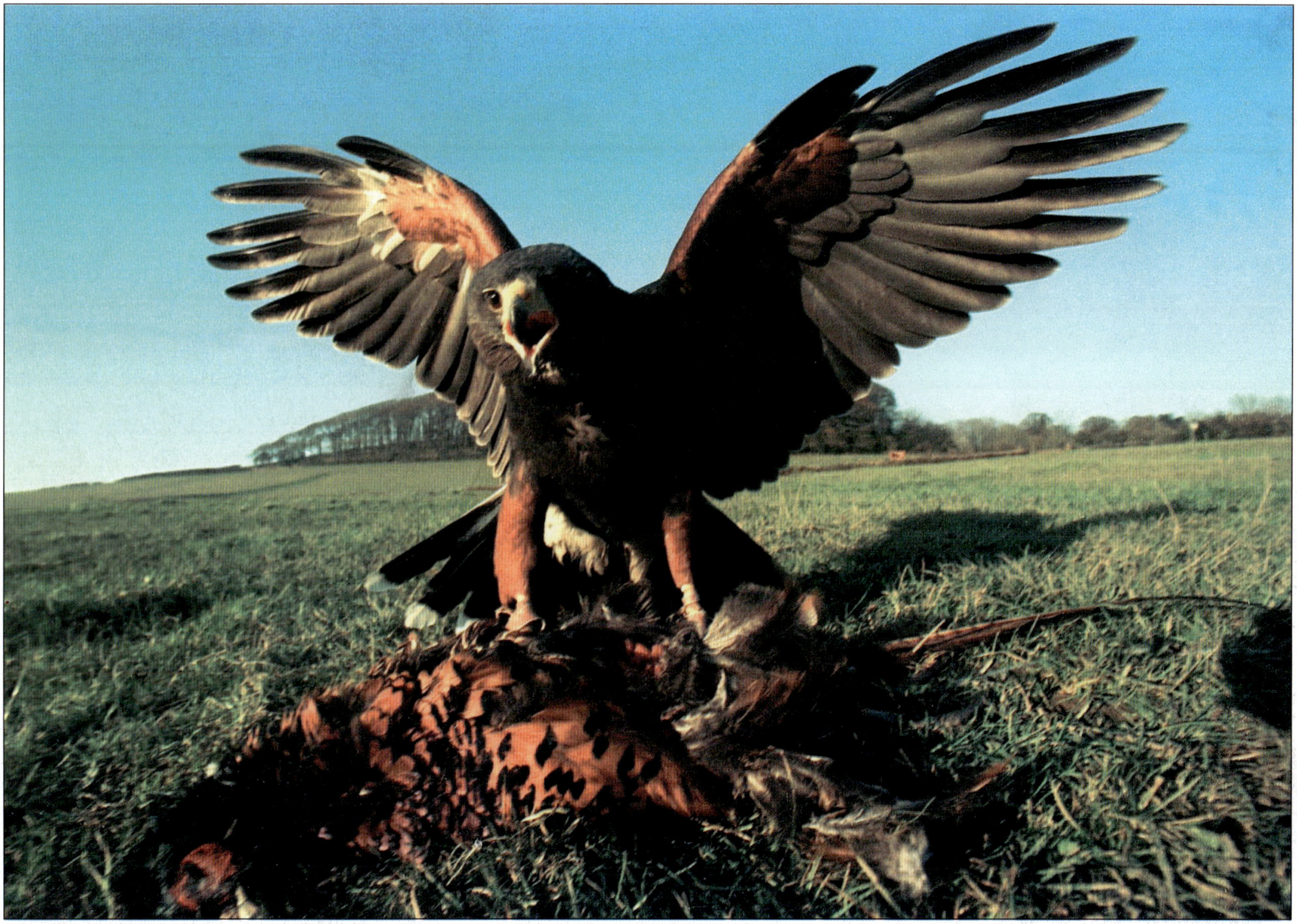

I purchased the dead pheasant from the local game butchers for an assignment to photograph 'Hawking' known as the ancient sport of kings. The story was that the National Trust had allowed Hawking to start up again after being banned for a long period. New DNA testing techniques could now detect if wild birds were being used in the sport and this satisfied the Trust. As I lay on the ground at eye level with the bird who had claimed the pheasant as its own, he went for me as I tried to pull the prey closer with the bird still on it – this action bagged the best picture of the day for me.

I have Rosemary Willets to thank for making a lifetime's dream come true. Even seeing an Osprey would have been a first for me, but to actually photograph this magnificent bird with a fish in its talons flying over my head within ten minutes of encountering it was out of this world. Water droplets fell on me from the bird as the Osprey glided off the River Axe at Axmouth and up into the trees to eat his easily-caught mullet. The bird stayed for four weeks in late-October 1999 but the best pictures were within the first few days. As an on-call press photographer it was difficult to spend too much time on the River Axe but I grabbed as many chances as I could before the mighty bird flew back to Africa.

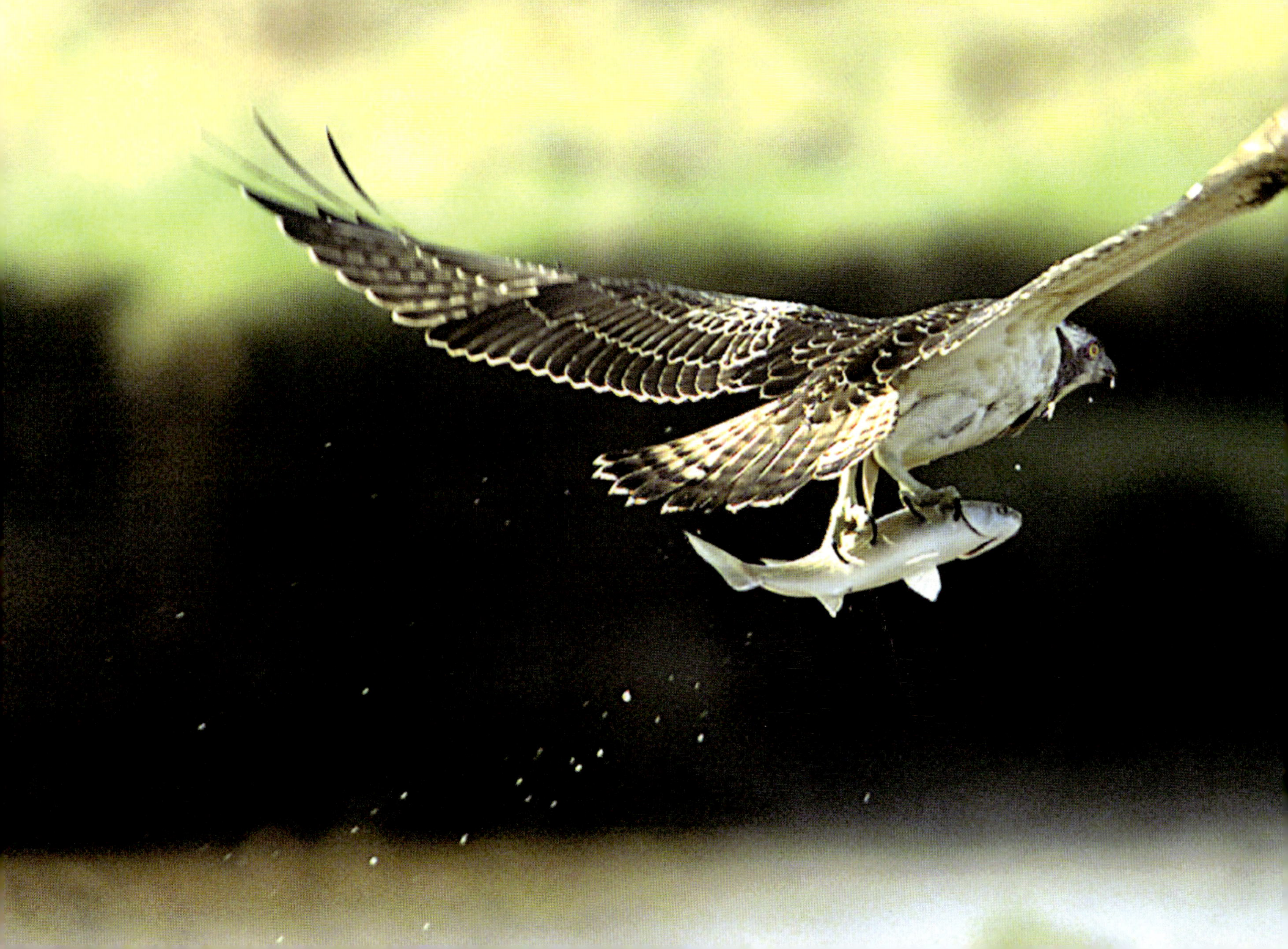

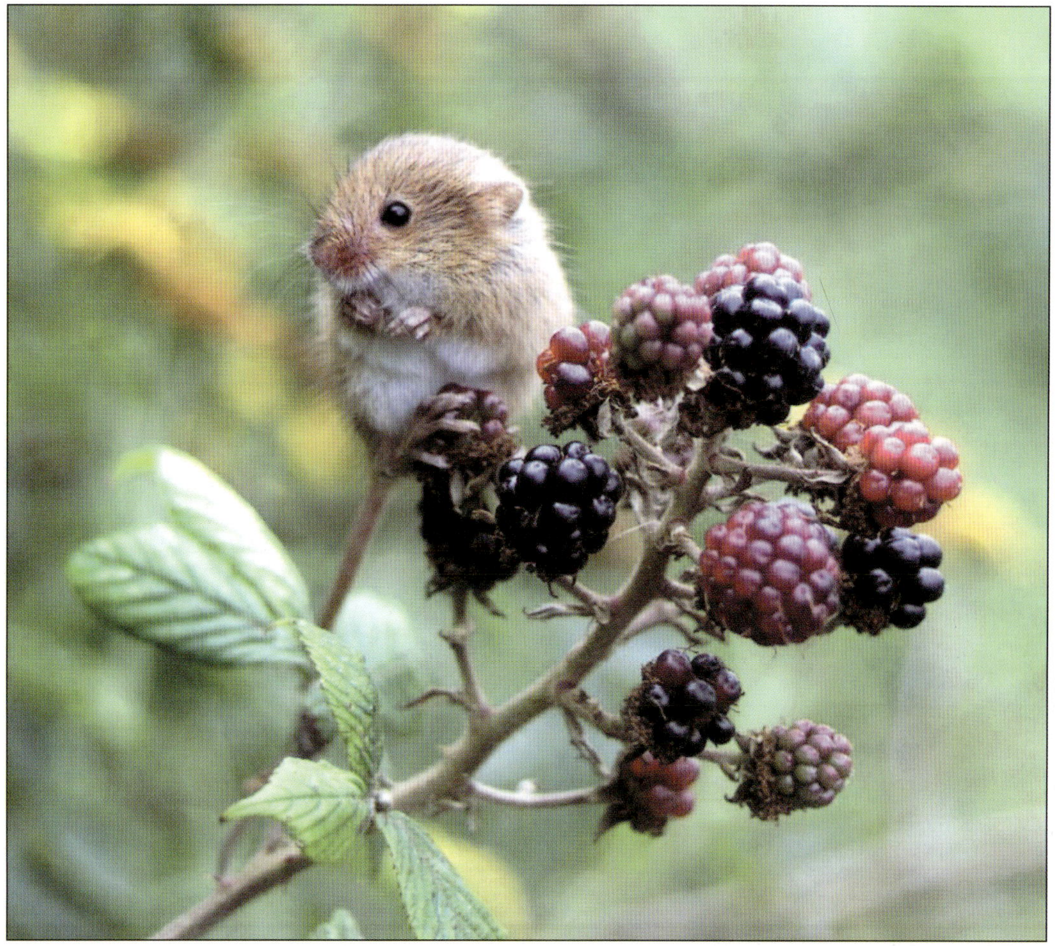

Harvest mice are one of the country's rarest and smallest rodents and Secret World in Somerset have a very worthwhile breeding programme introducing several of them back into the countryside. This picture shows that even in the event of being granted freedom, the cheeky mouse decided to clean itself on a blackberry bramble before calmly wandering off into the hedge in the Somerset countryside.

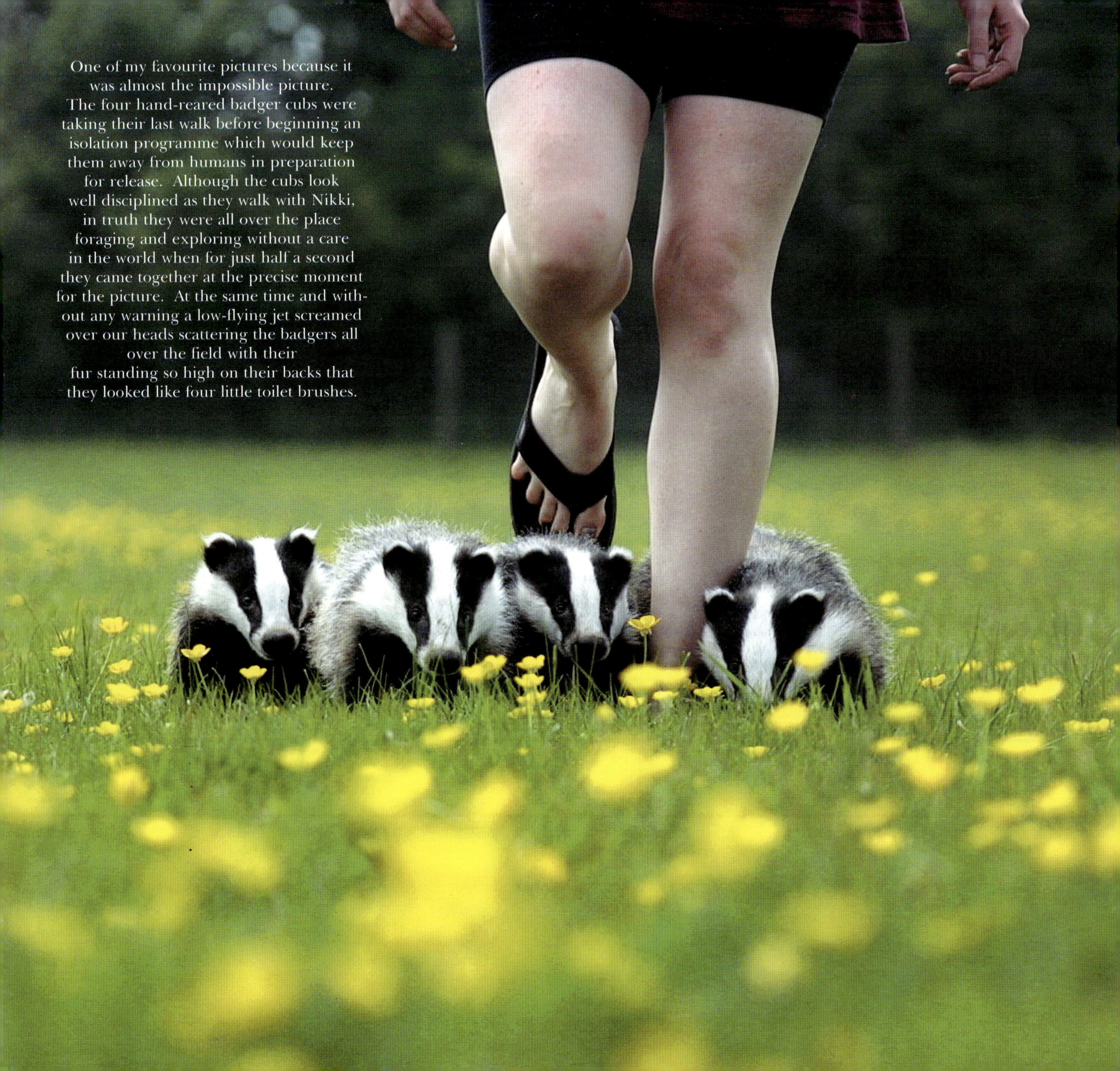

One of my favourite pictures because it was almost the impossible picture. The four hand-reared badger cubs were taking their last walk before beginning an isolation programme which would keep them away from humans in preparation for release. Although the cubs look well disciplined as they walk with Nikki, in truth they were all over the place foraging and exploring without a care in the world when for just half a second they came together at the precise moment for the picture. At the same time and without any warning a low-flying jet screamed over our heads scattering the badgers all over the field with their fur standing so high on their backs that they looked like four little toilet brushes.

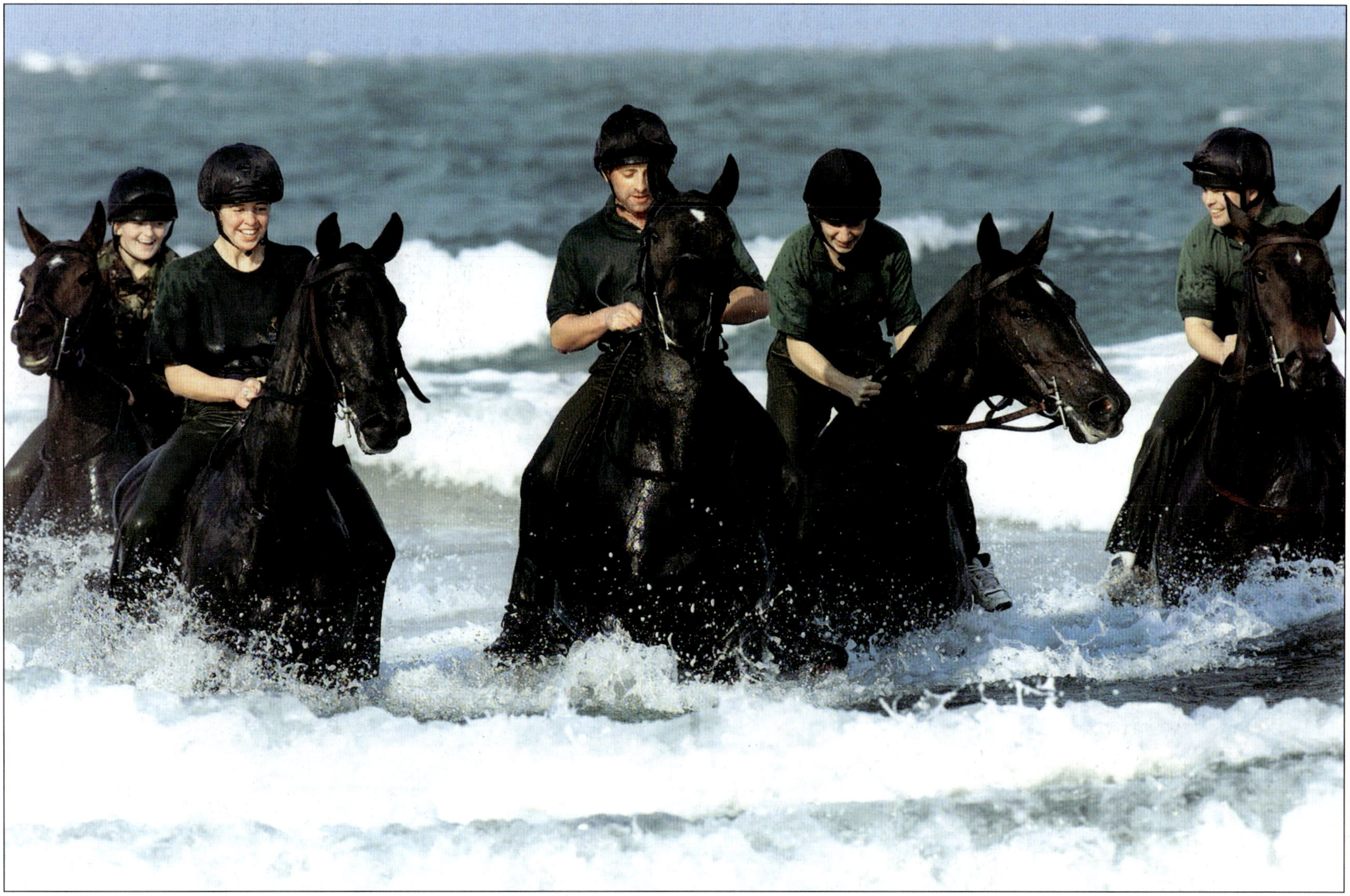

When the King's Troop go on holiday from smoggy London they take the horses with them to the sandy beaches of North Devon. Not all the horses venture into the sea, some are frightened to death of the waves, but what a sight it is to see them galloping across the vast sands of the North Devon coast.

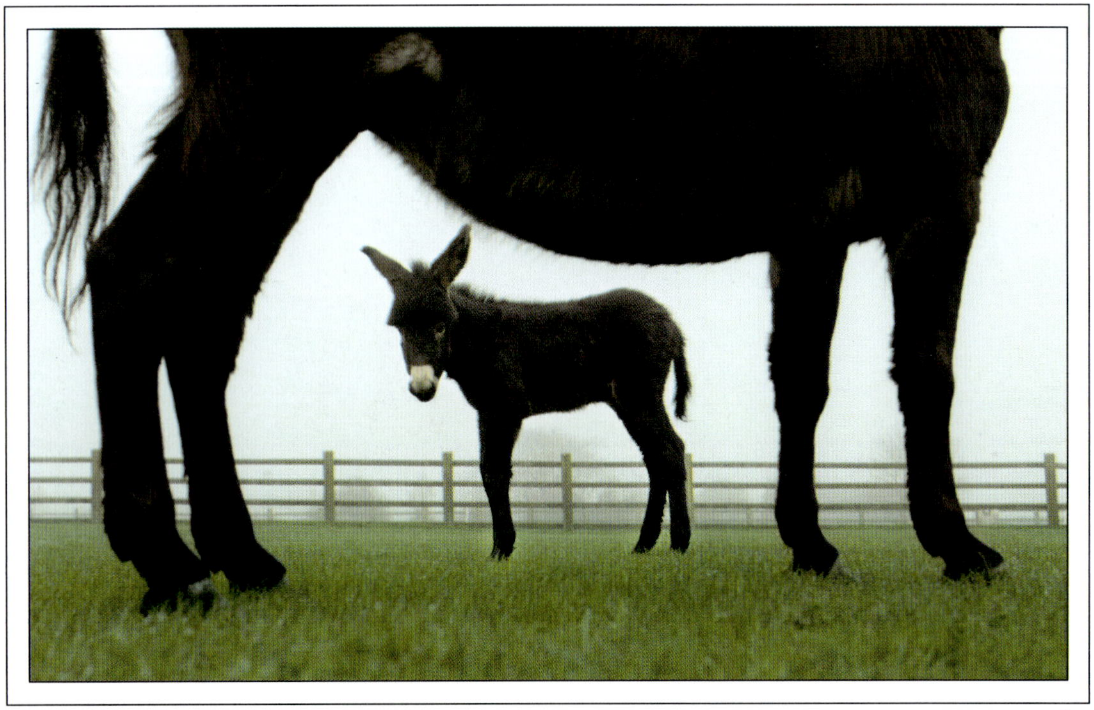

A different view of the newborn baby donkey from beneath his mother's belly at the Sidmouth Donkey Sanctuary.

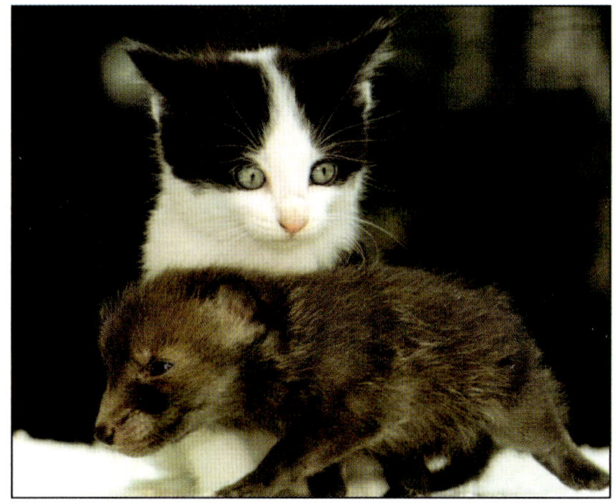

An unusual picture of a fox cub being brought up by a broody cat with a family of kittens.

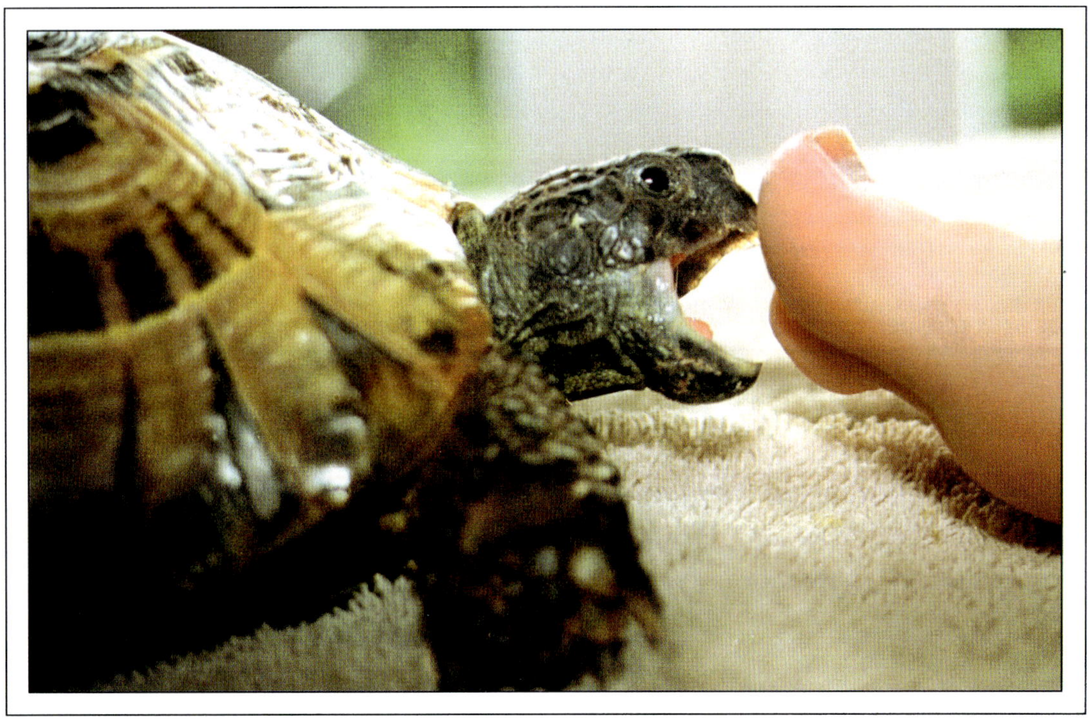

*Western Morning News* reporter Colin Bradley found out the hard way just how sharp a tortoise bite can be when he fell asleep in front of the 'telly' and woke up with a tortoise hanging from his big toe.

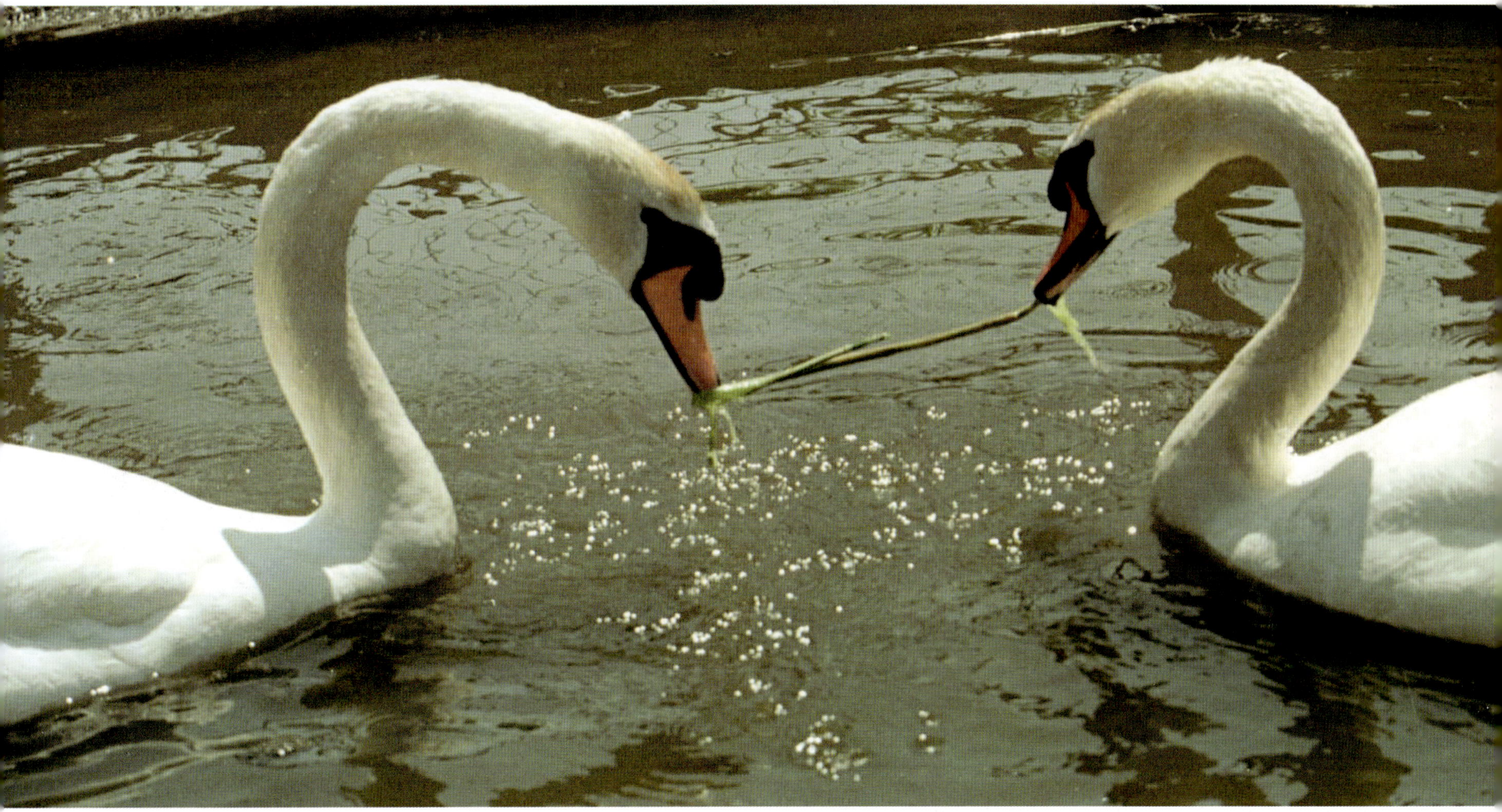

This pair of swans caused a media stir when they were outed as being gay. The pair of male swans had built a nest together at the Abbotsbury Swannery in Dorset and my brief was to capture a moment of tenderness between them. Four painfully boring hours later I threw a strand of long grass into their pond and to my great delight they each picked up an end and that was good enough for me.

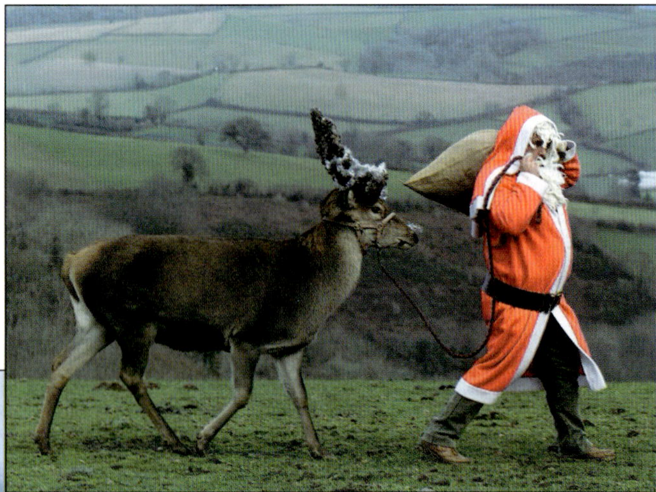

One of the funniest things I have seen in many years was when Rudolph the Randy Red-nosed Reindeer tried it on with Father Christmas who was in fact Devon farmer Richard Haddock, the former chairman of the Devon NFU. As I was doubled up with laughter I'll never forget Richard shouting from underneath Randy Rudolph, 'If this goes in the paper, you're dead.'

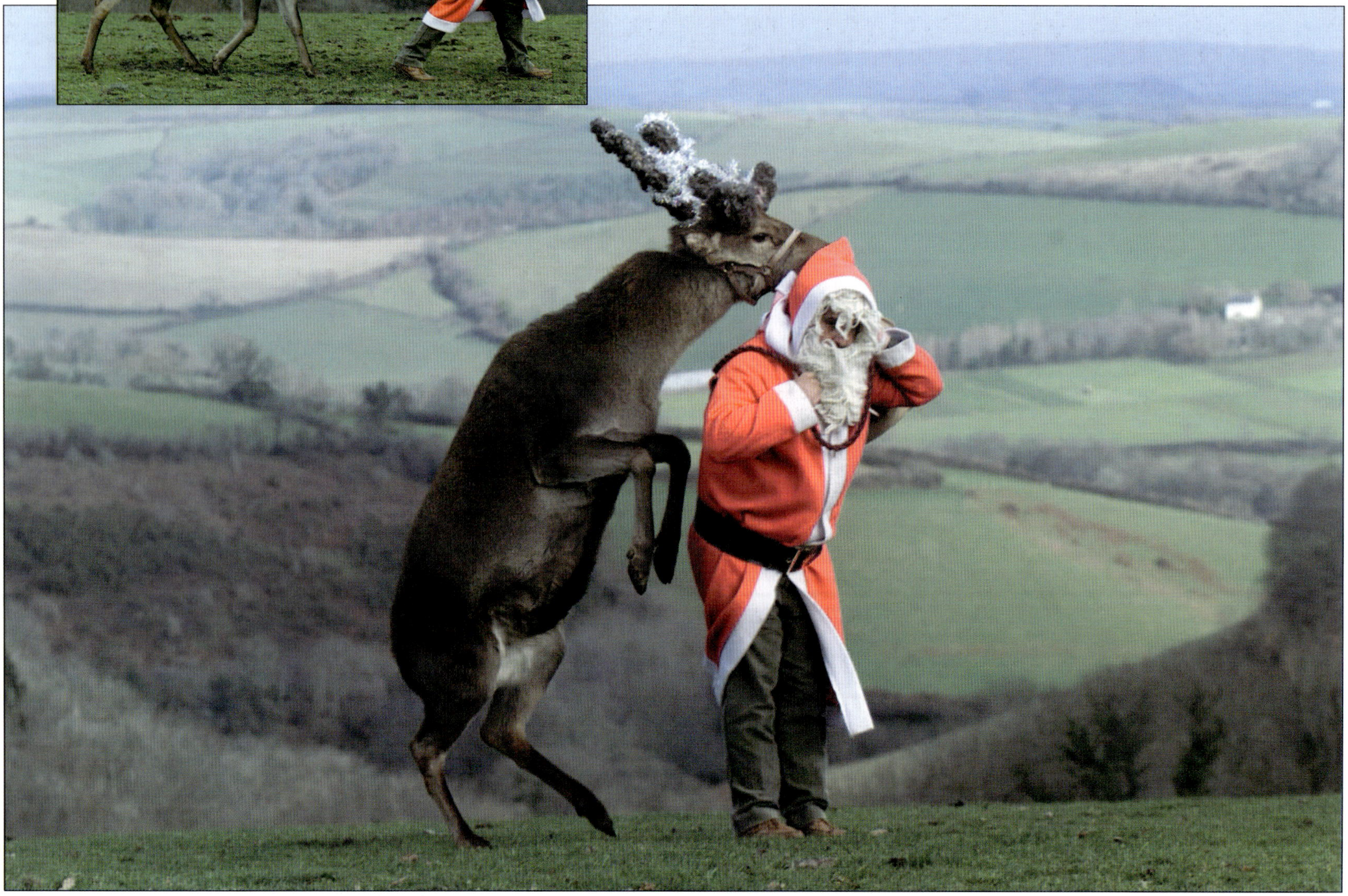

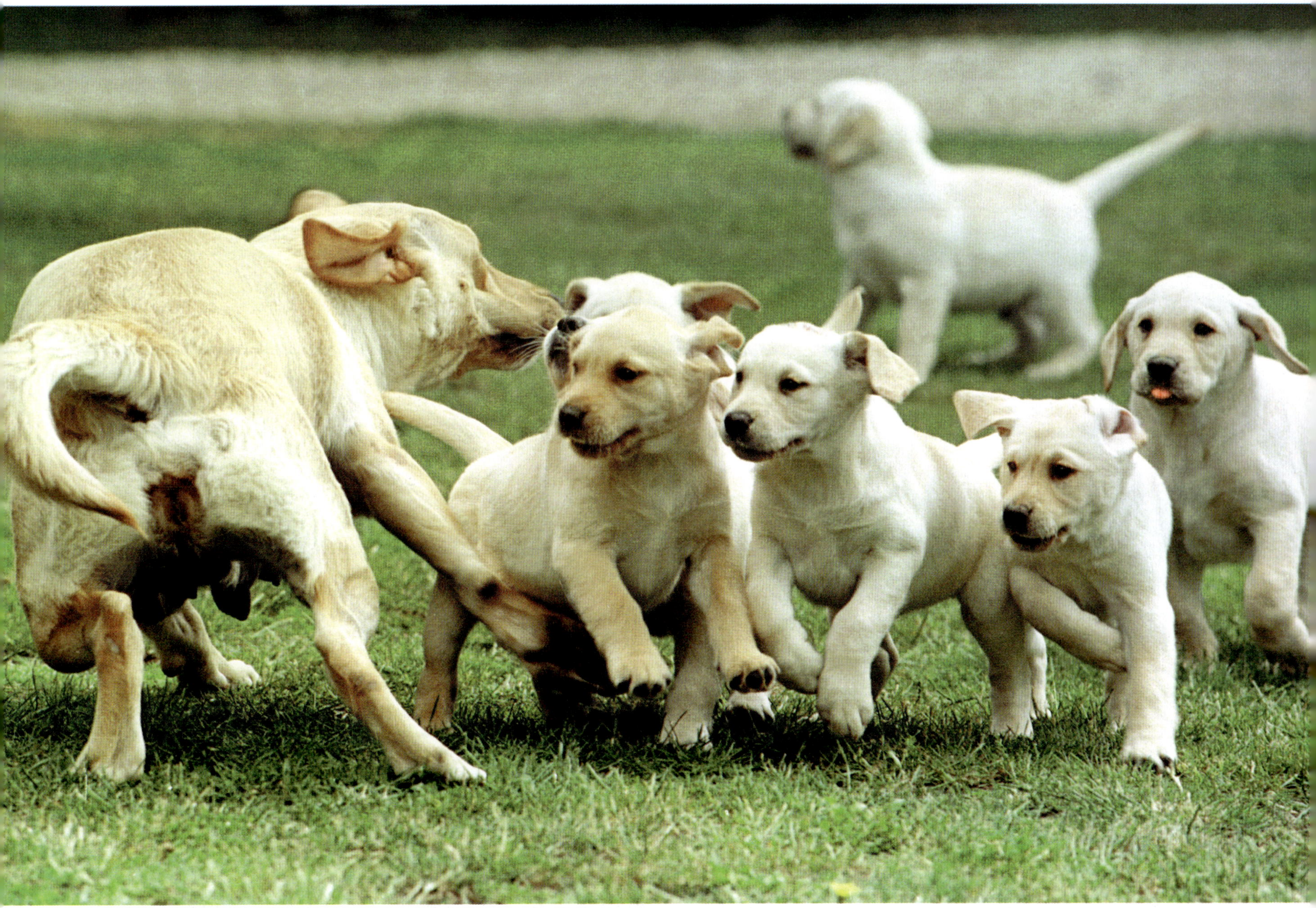

With more than half a dozen pups to feed, the Labrador bitch found time to play with her pups on her owner's lawn.

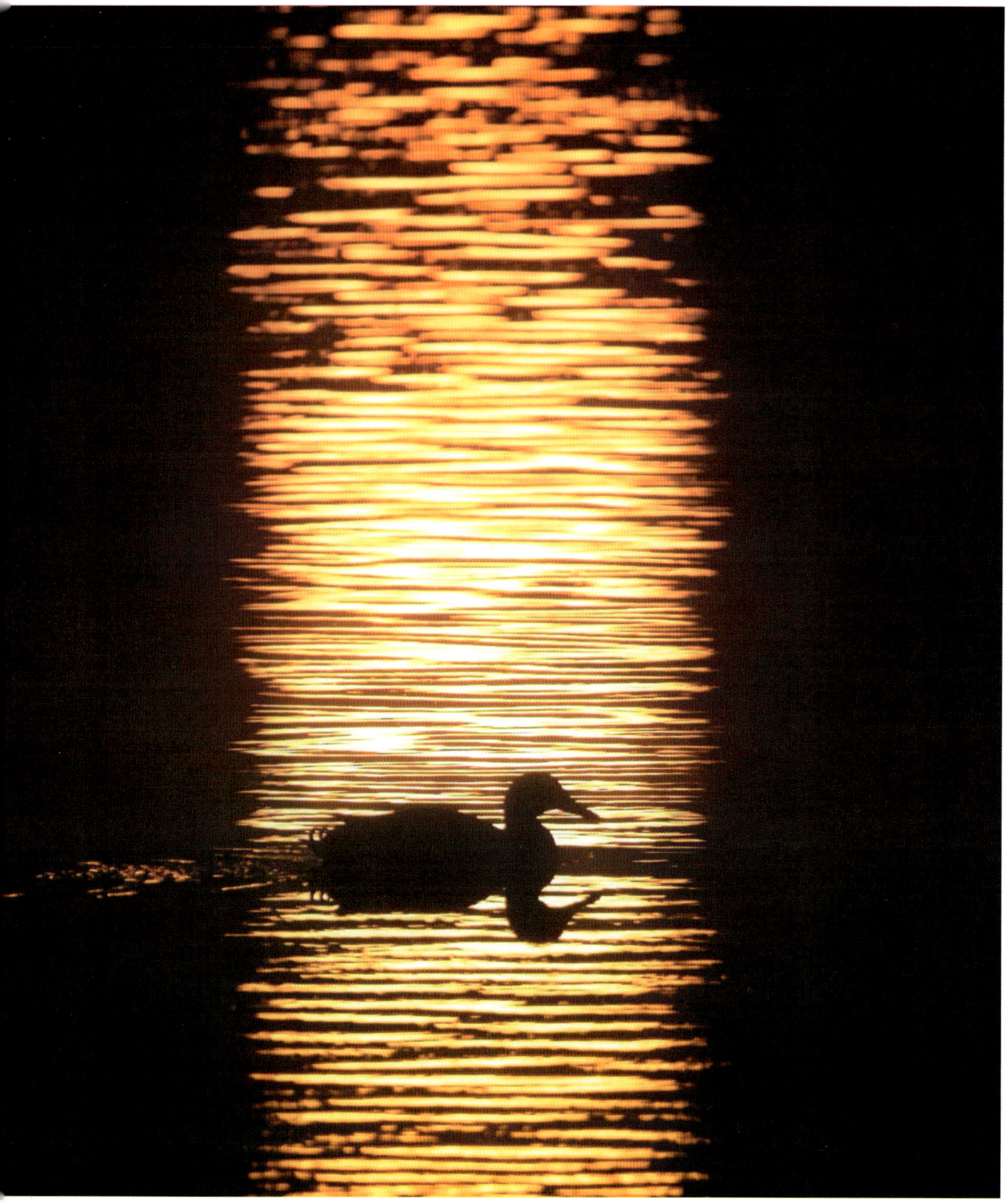

In the setting sun on the River Axe at Axmouth a mallard duck drifts up stream at the end of the day making a stark contrast to the shimmering water.

Orphaned hedgehogs are a common sight in many Westcountry wildlife hospitals; some just need plenty of tender loving care, others suffer from such crazy things as sunburn, hence the little one being treated with a special cream.

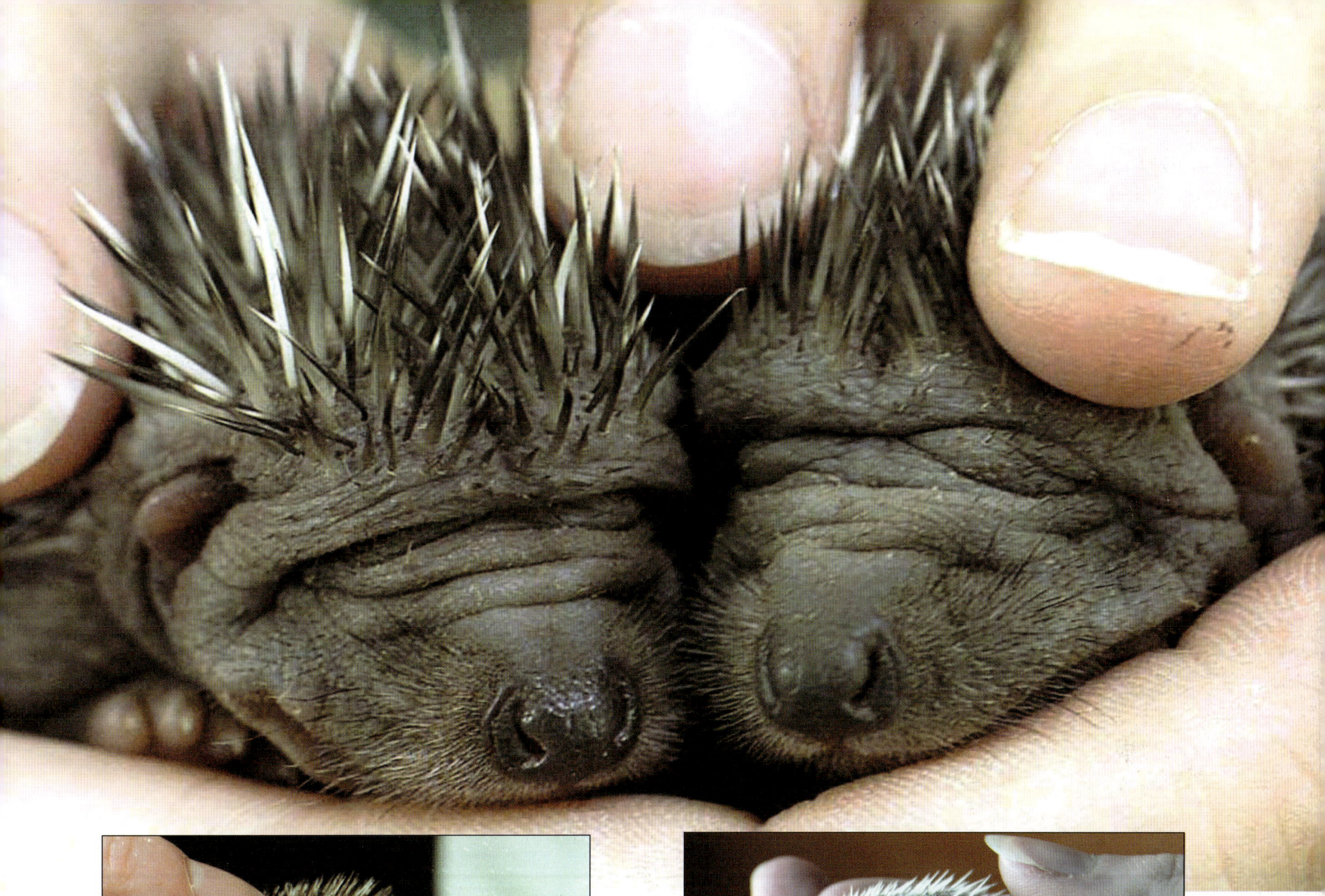

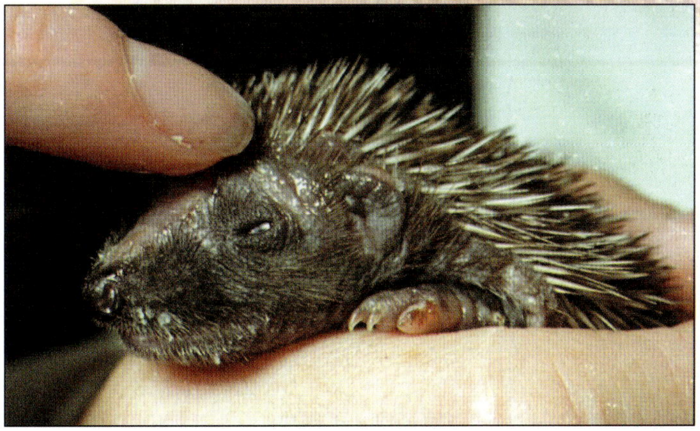

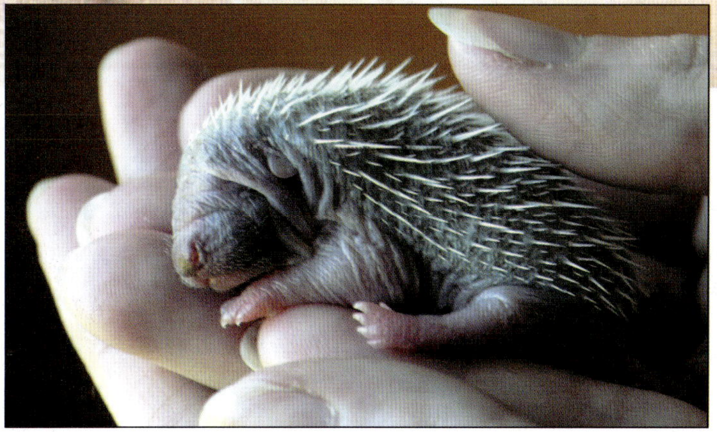

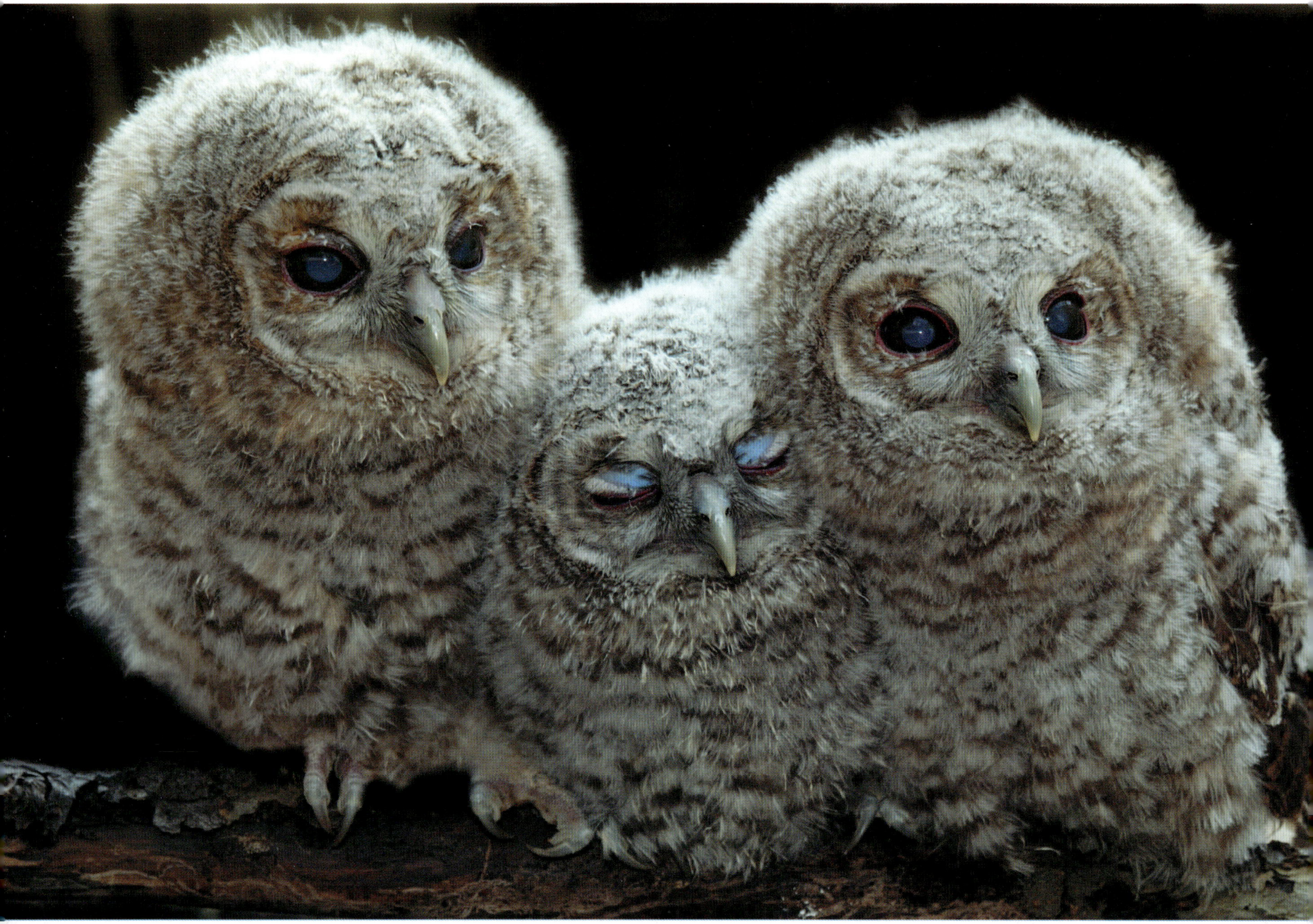

A trio of fluffy tawny owls, the victims of an accidental cutting down of their nesting tree which left them exposed to the elements. Young tawny owls have the most amazing eyes and look as if they have just come out of make-up with red eye-liner and pale blue eyelids.

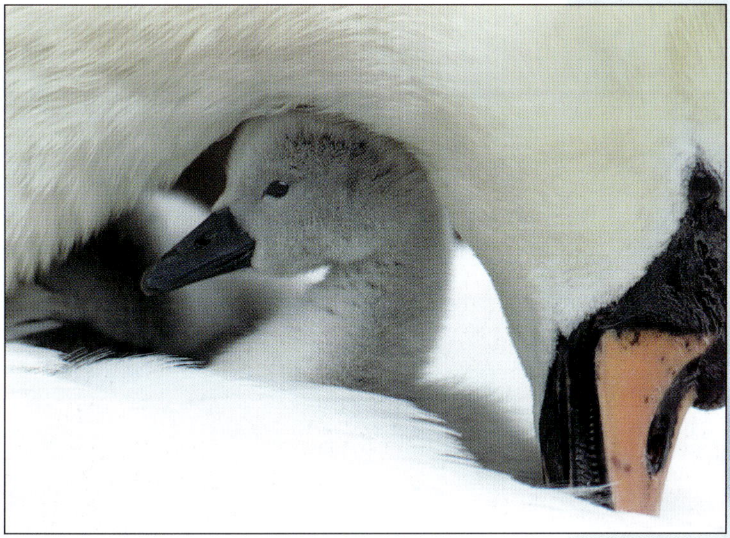

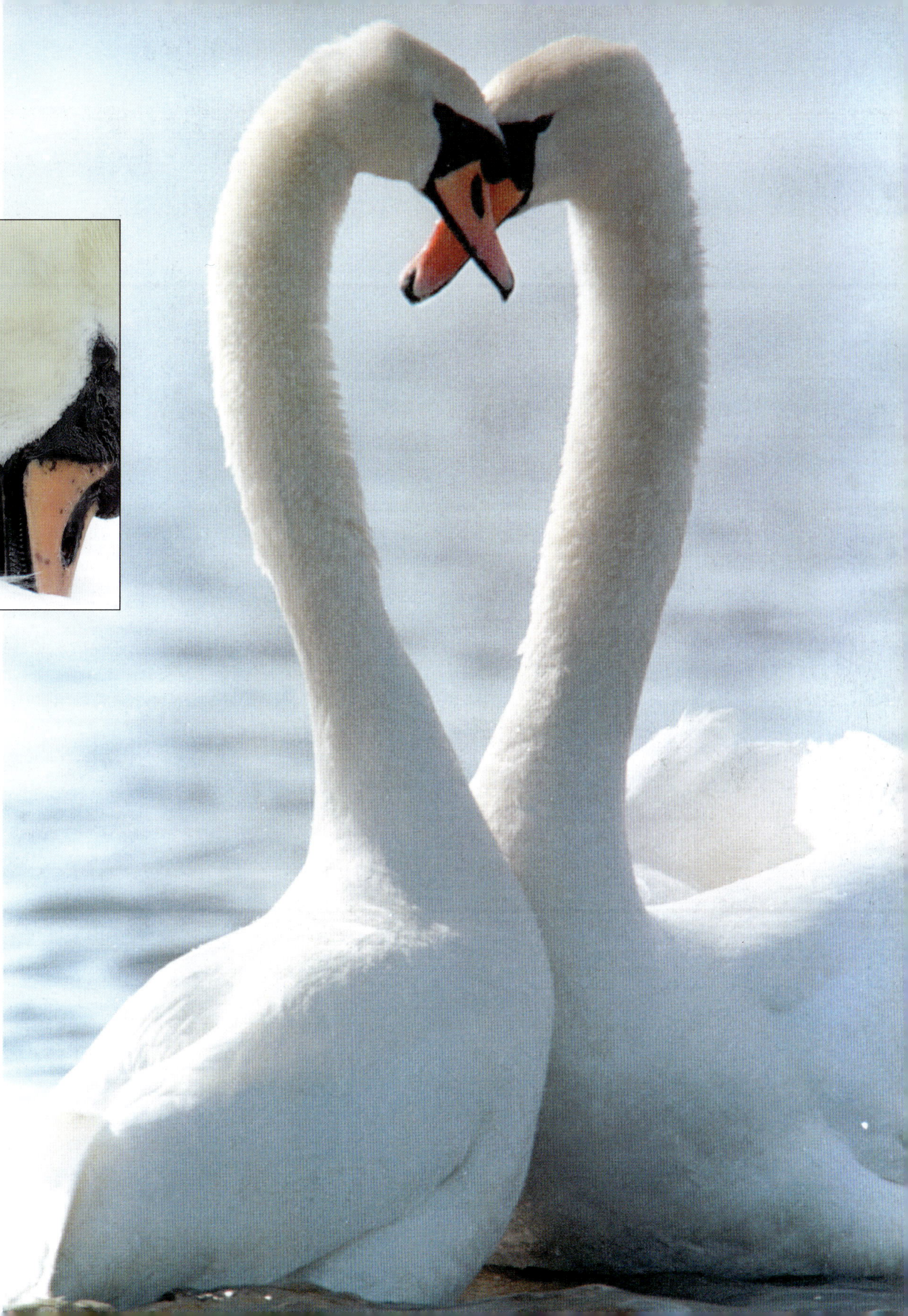

Beautiful swans at the Abbotsbury Swannery in Dorset, to me they are amongst the most beautiful birds in the world. Swans are unique, in the water they are graceful, elegant, aggressive and in total control, out of the water the birds are clumsy and vulnerable. As parents they will defend the cygnets with their lives and that of any would-be aggressor. In the early-spring males and females can be seen indulging in the annual courtship dance in which the two make the perfect heart shape as they snuggle up close.

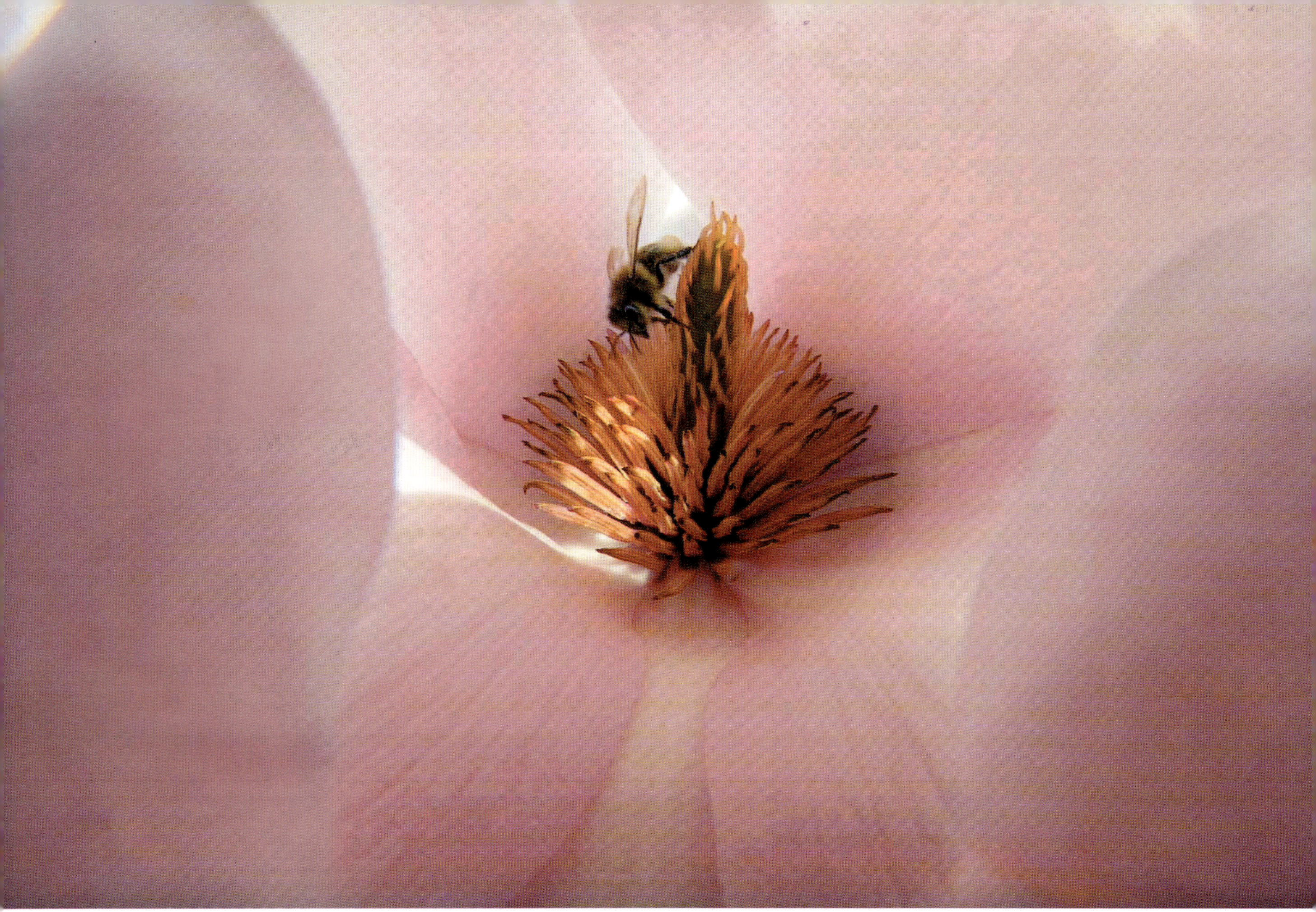

Each year the early-spring weather is gauged on how early the Magnolia trees spring into flower. Magnolias have huge flowers in pinks and whites, the display of Magnolias in the splendid gardens of Sir John Quick near Crediton are second to none. So the bee collecting pollen inside the giant flower was too tempting, perspective of size was achieved by the size of the busy bee against the huge petals of the flower.

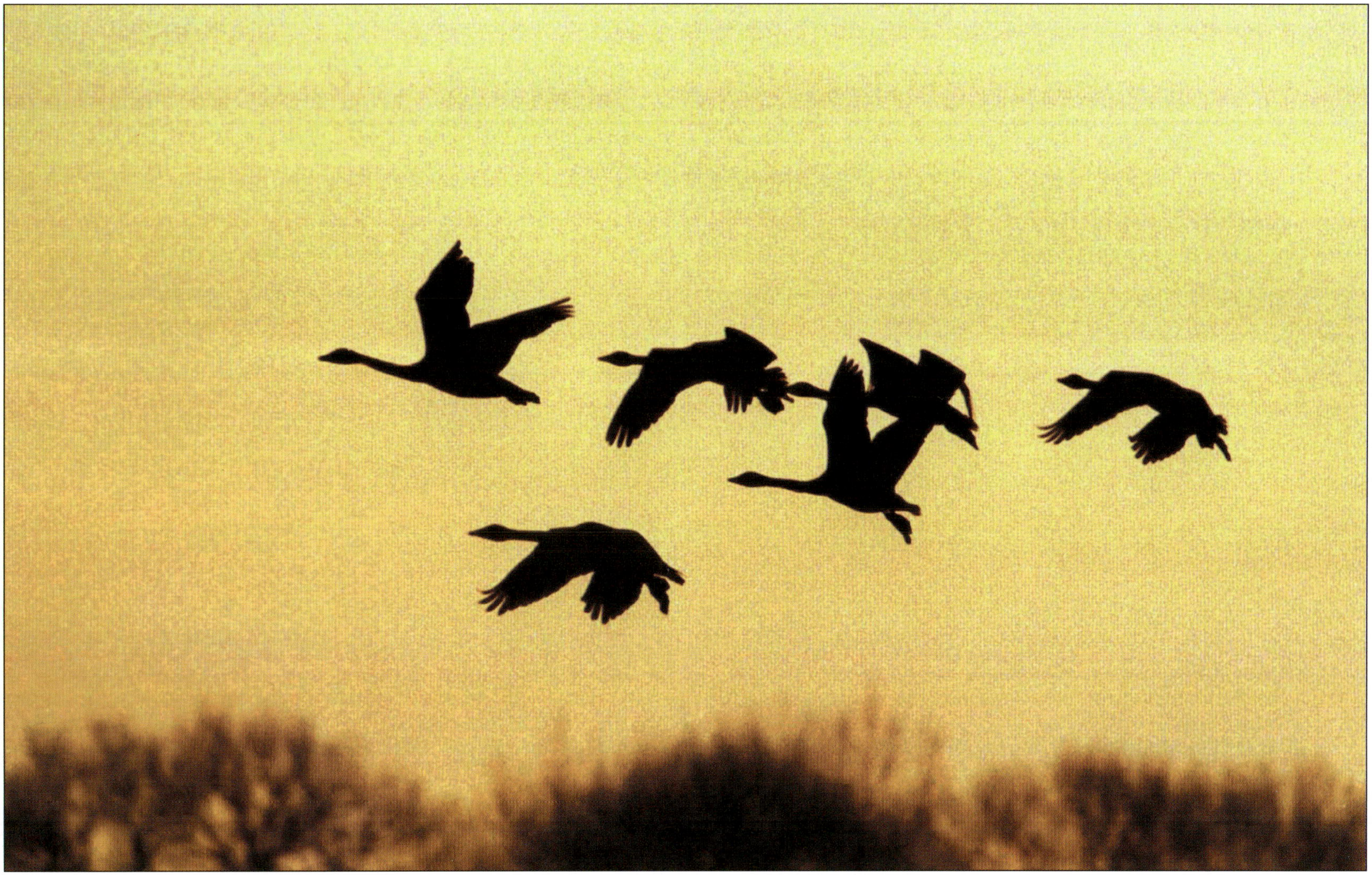

Berwick swans can be seen on the Somerset Levels and I was lucky enough to photograph six of them flying off into the winter's sunset near Burrow Bridge.

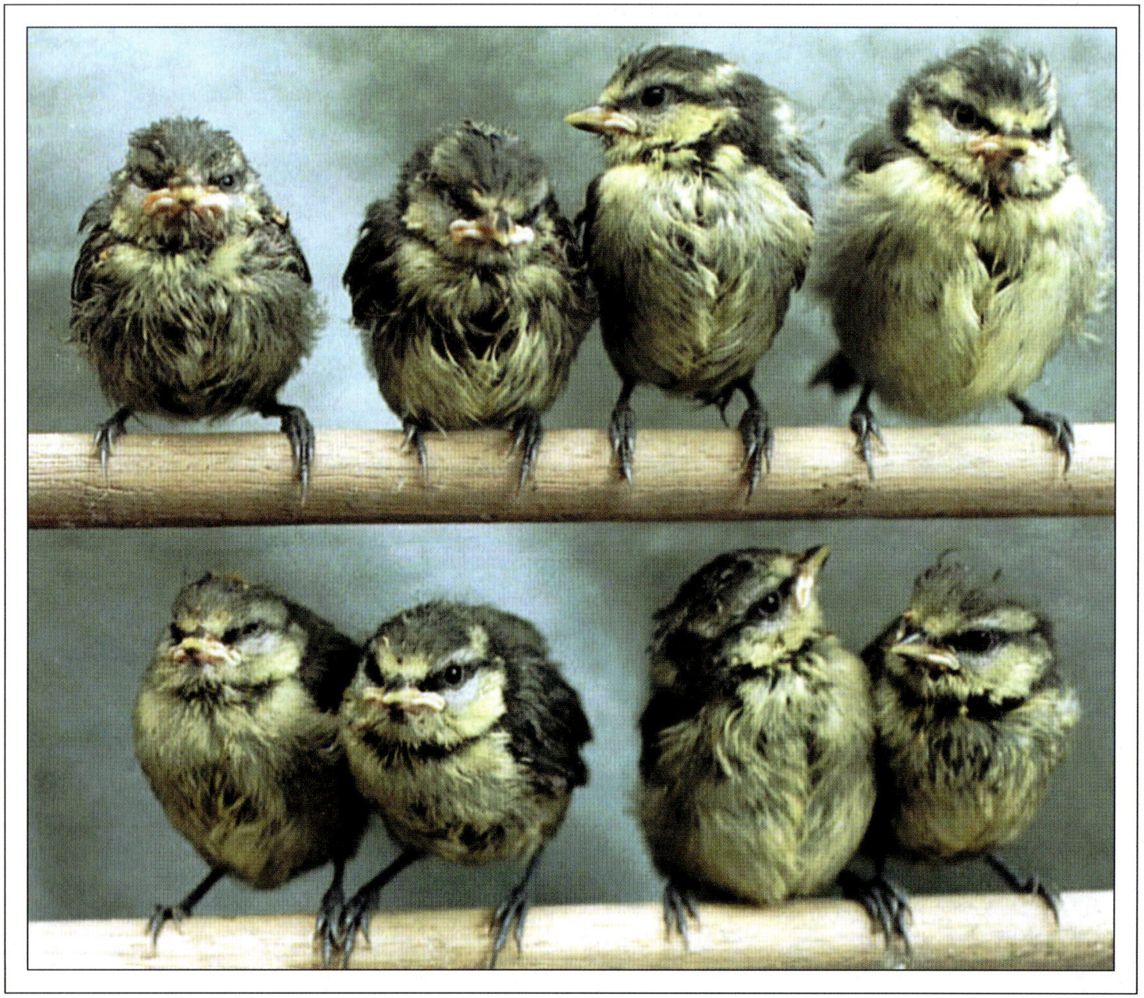

In University Challenge Bamber Gasgoine used to line up his teams in a way similar to these orphaned Blue Tits waiting to be fed inside the RSPCA wildlife unit at West Hatch.

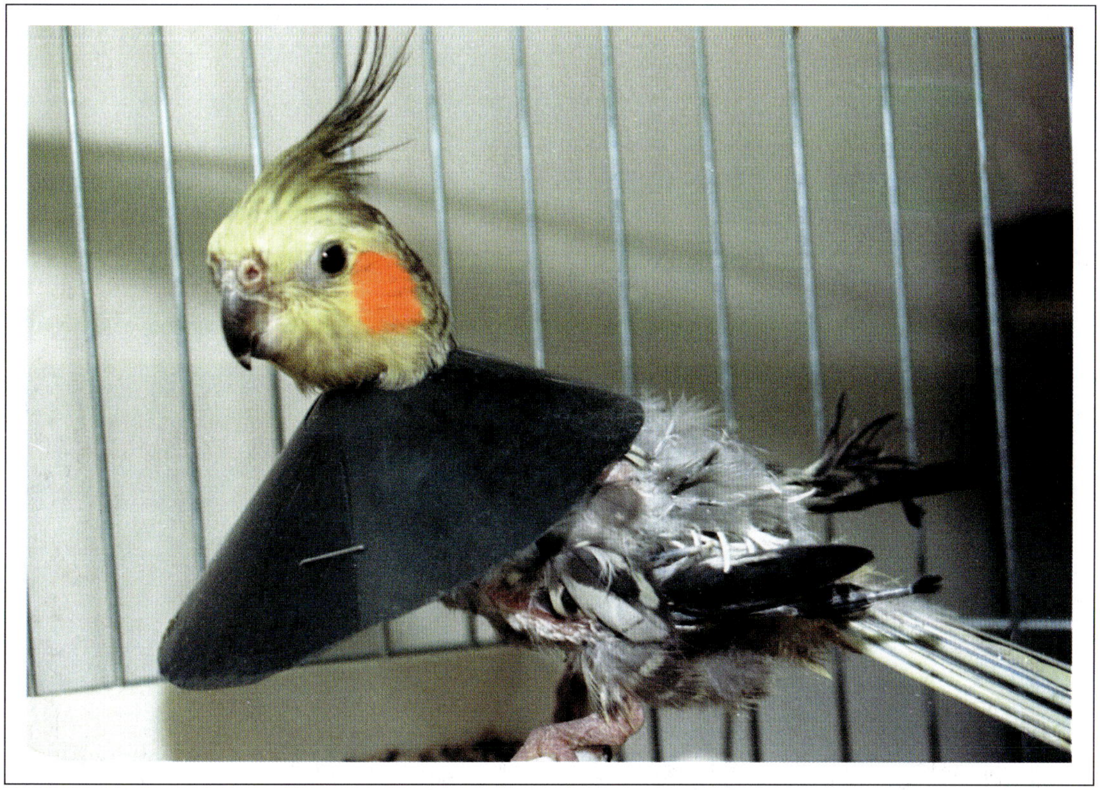

It was the bright idea of an industrious Somerset vet who in true 'Blue Peter' fashion selected the one he'd made earlier and fitted a home-made self-protection hood from an old piece of plastic to the parakeet which stopped him from pulling any more of his feathers out.

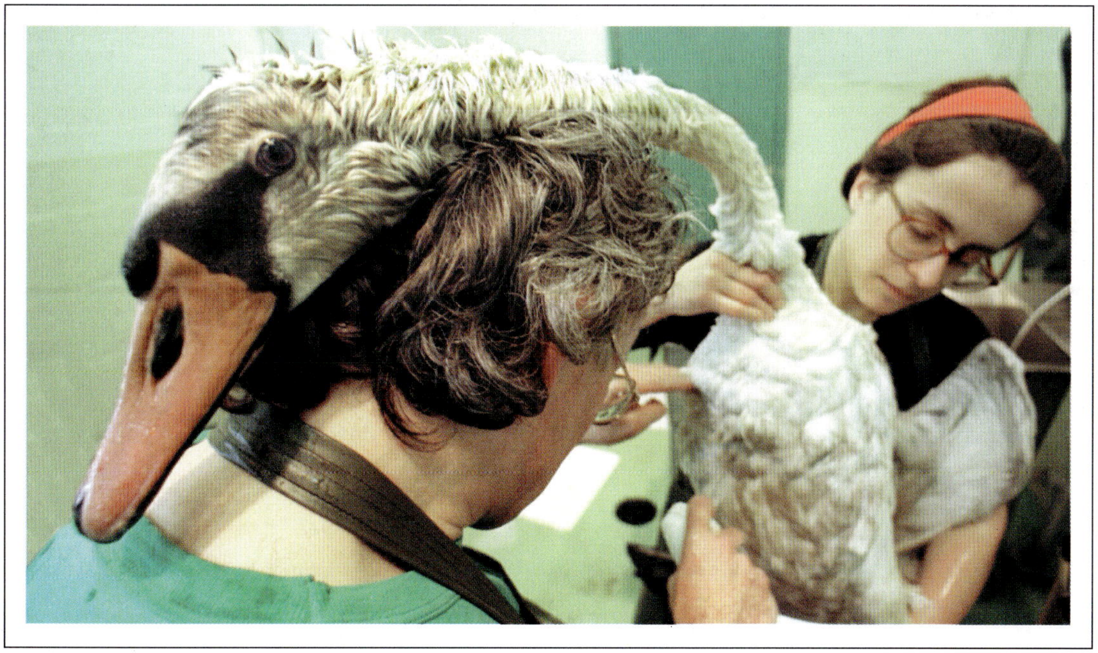

RSPCA wildlife staff are responsible for saving thousands of lives at their West Hatch unit near Taunton, none more so than the annual influx of badly-oiled birds which need a lot of time and effort spent on cleaning oil-matted feathers. Seeing this swan being treated for oil contamination was heart-breaking, this proud bird just gave up and accepted his fate as he rested on top of his rescuer's head.

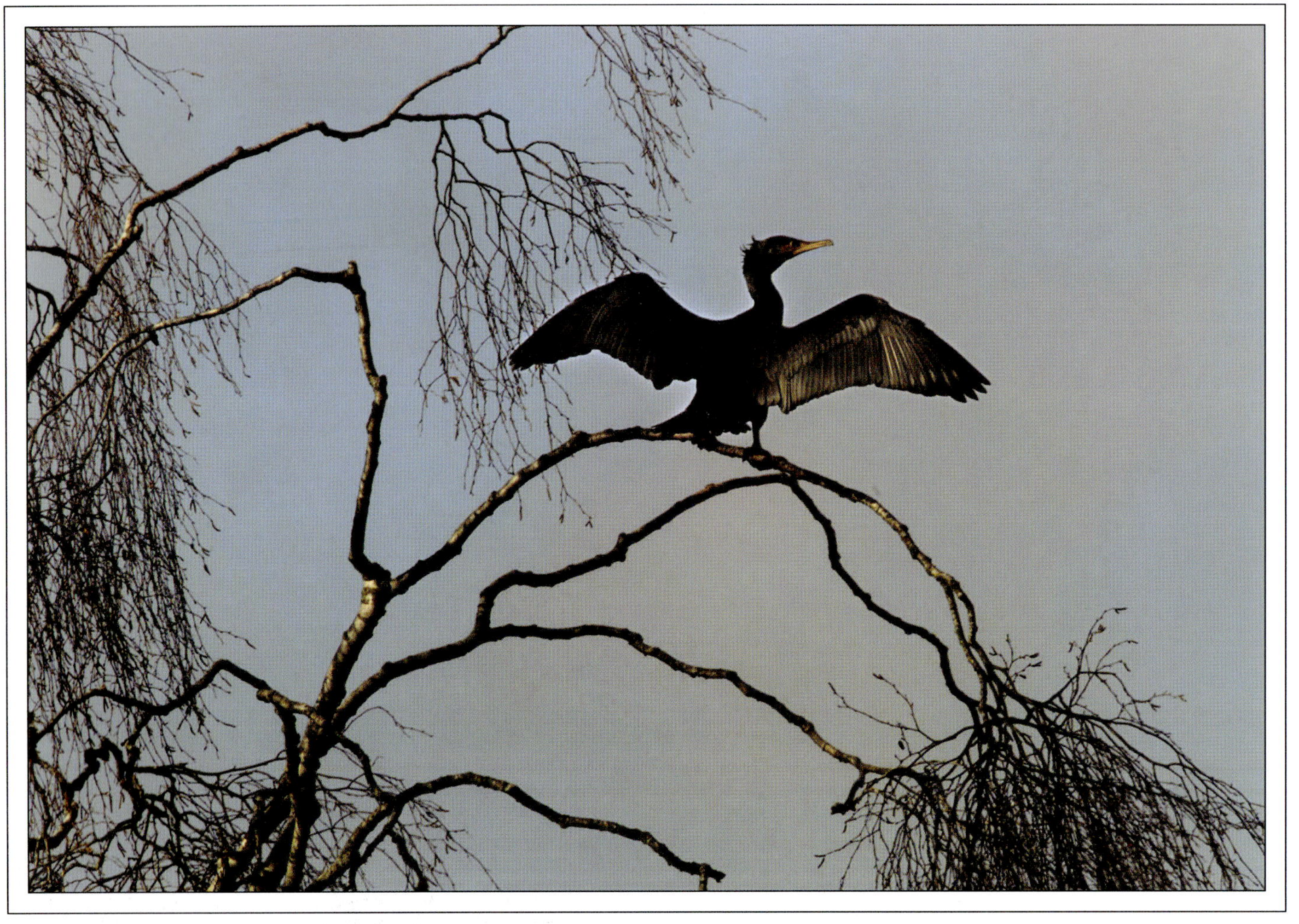

Drying wings over Stover Country Park near Newton Abbot,
the familiar sight of the outstretched wings of the Cormorant.

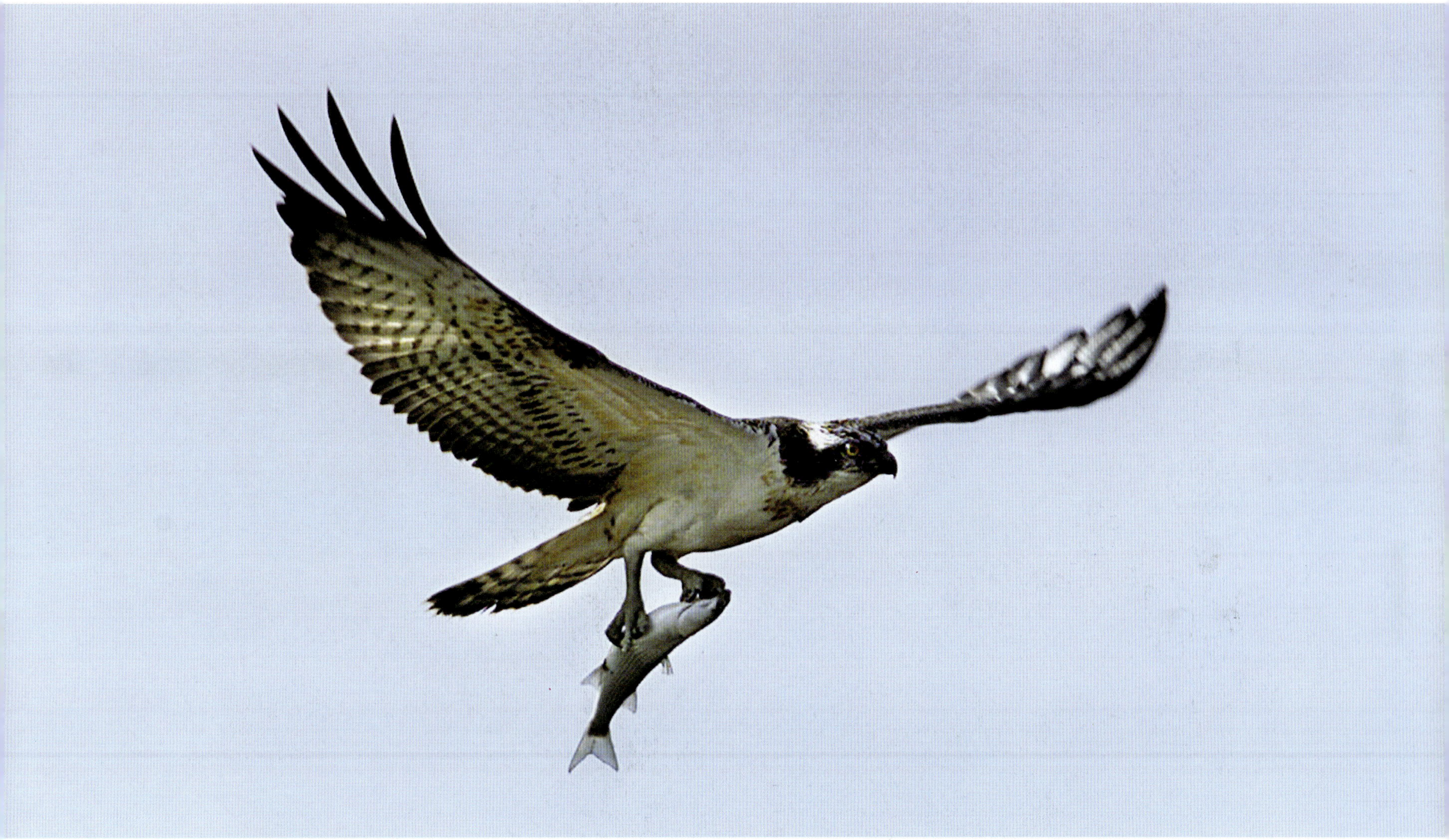

My old friend, the River Axe Osprey, who did me a favour when he flew over my head with a fish within ten minutes of my arrival at the river bank giving me a front-page picture for the following day.

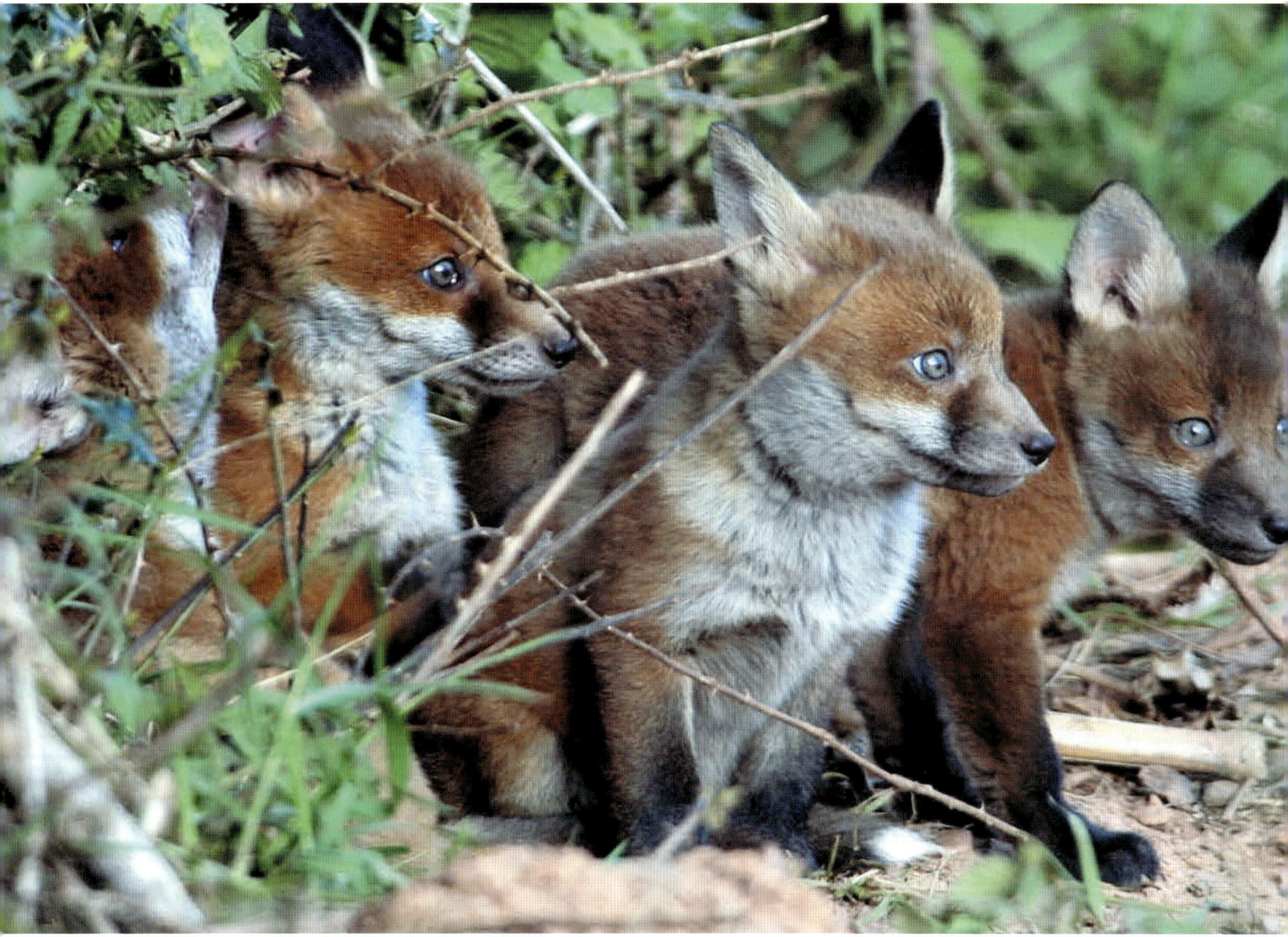

Three of seven wild fox cubs in one family wait for the vixen to return with the next rabbit in a field in Bradninch.

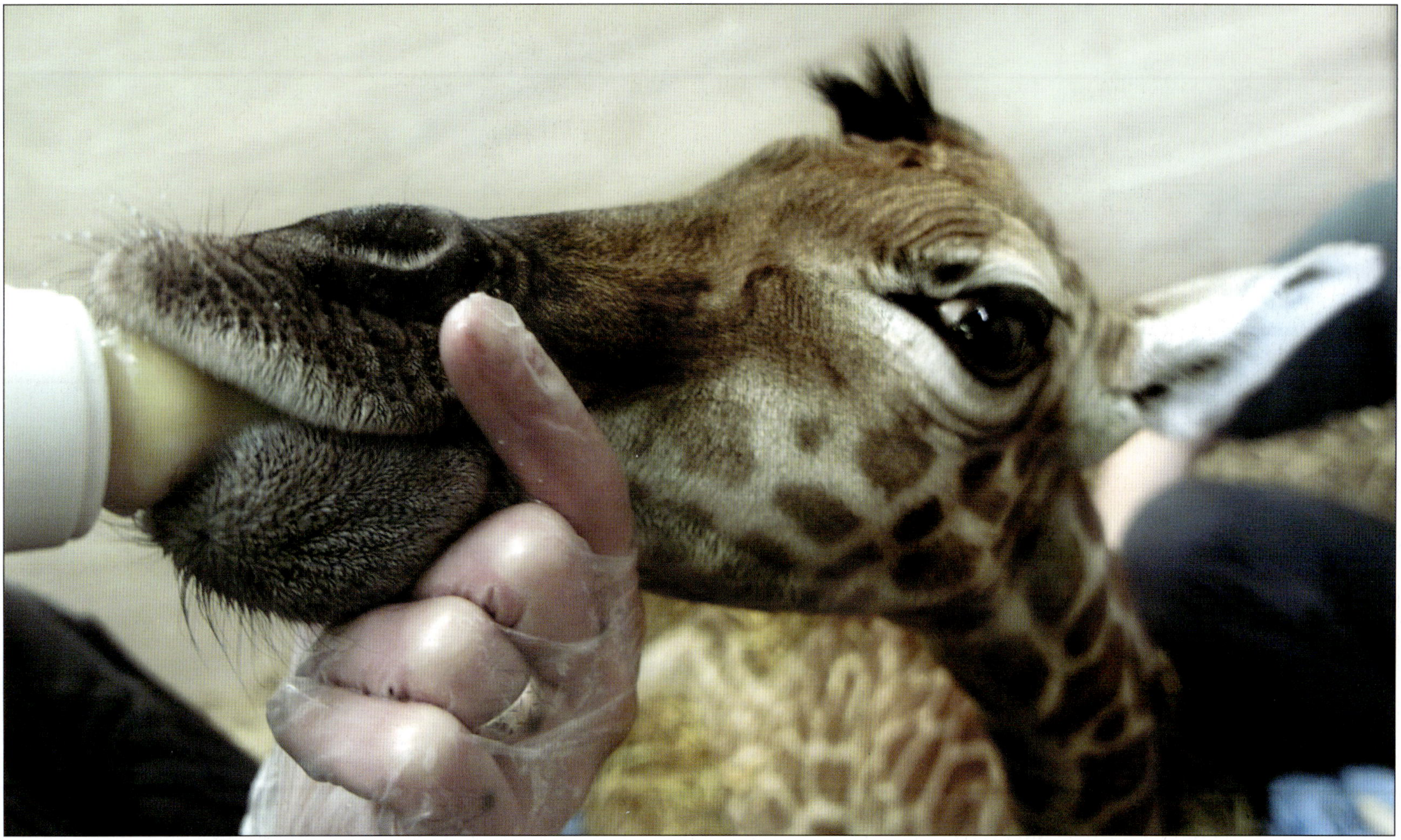

All abandoned babies have to be bottle-fed even if they are a long-legged baby giraffe. This little fella wasn't easy to bottle-feed and kept falling asleep instead of sucking, but staff at Paignton Zoo have bags of patience and saw the little giraffe through his first few weeks on planet earth.

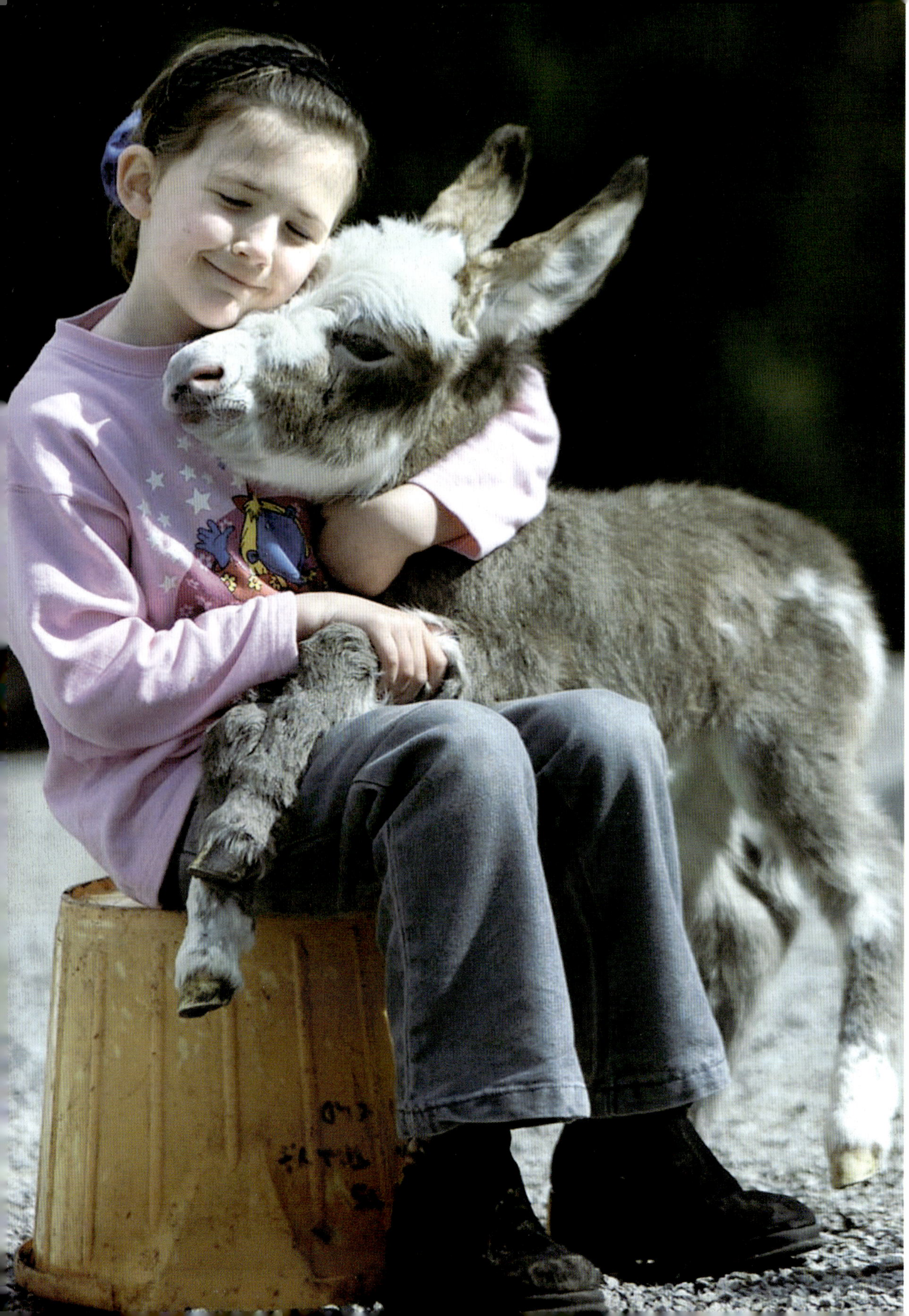

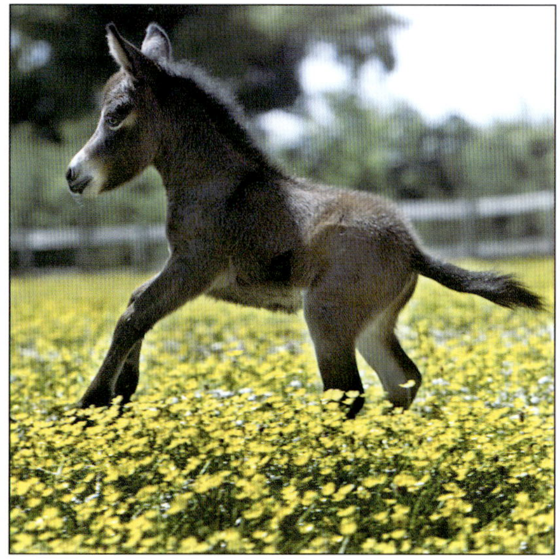

Believed to be the first ever Mini Mule born anywhere, a cross between a miniature pony and a miniature donkey, the lively foal was a fine sight darting around a paddock full of buttercups at the Miniature Pony Centre near Moretonhampstead on Dartmoor.

The expression on the little girl's face says it all as she cuddles Topsy Turvy, the donkey foal, although the two were placed in position for a newspaper picture, the young lady's reaction was perfectly natural.

Nikki Hawkins of Secret World knows her baby otter's body language and is ready when, just like a human baby, they nod off to sleep at the drop of a hood.

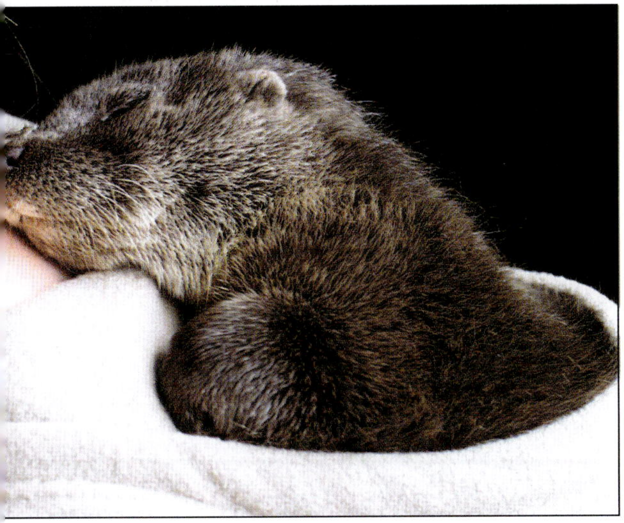

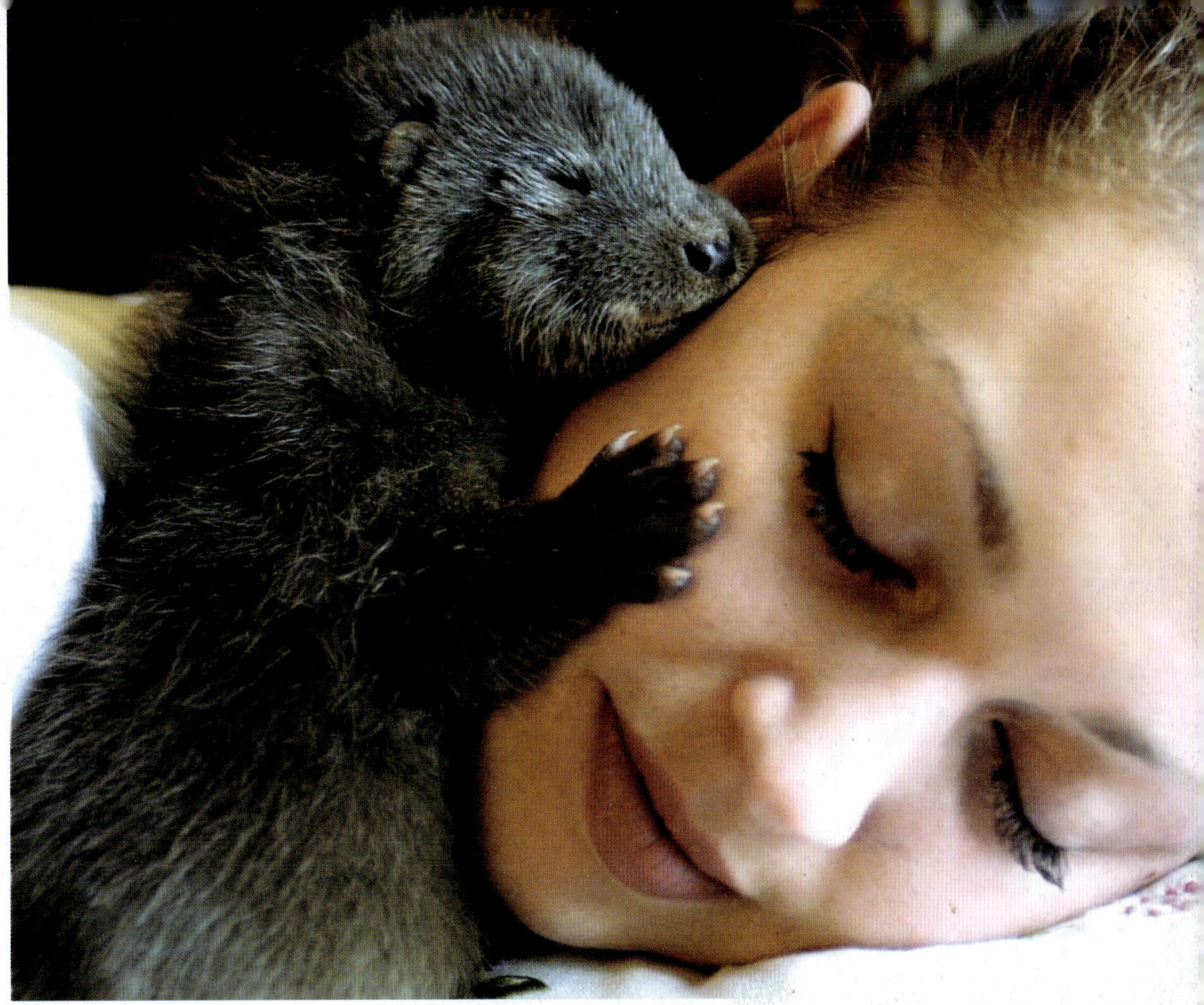

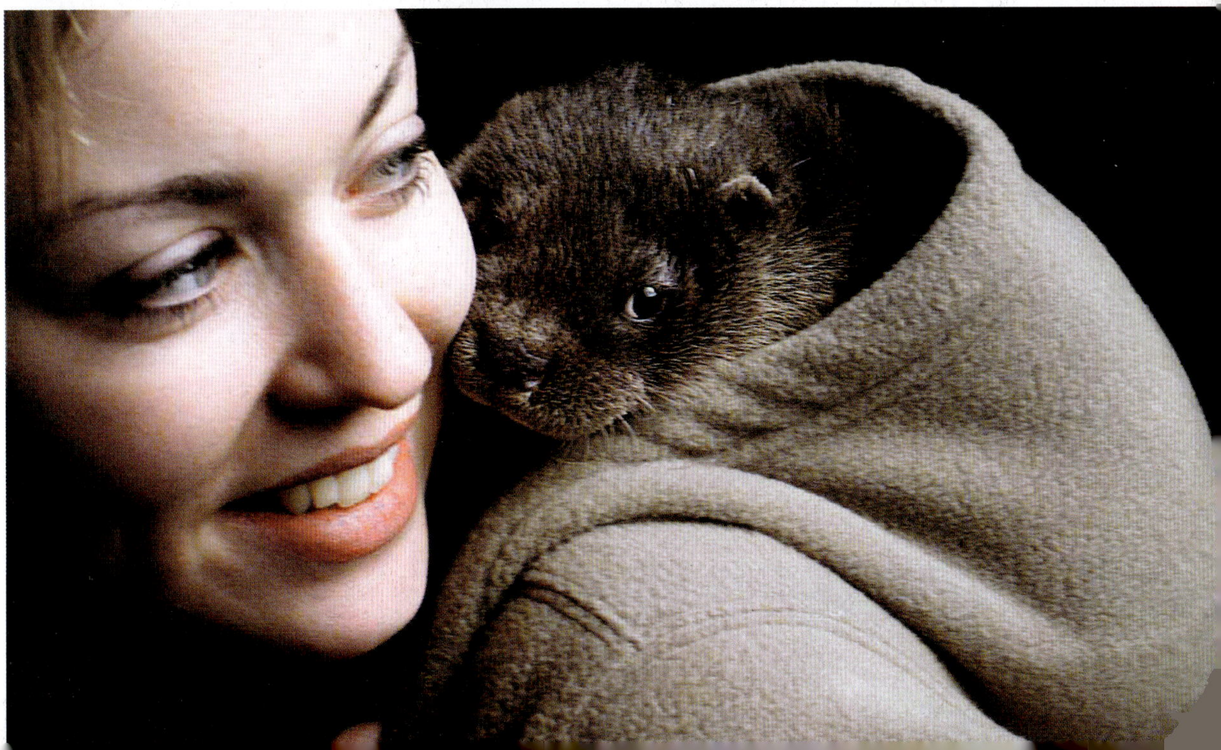

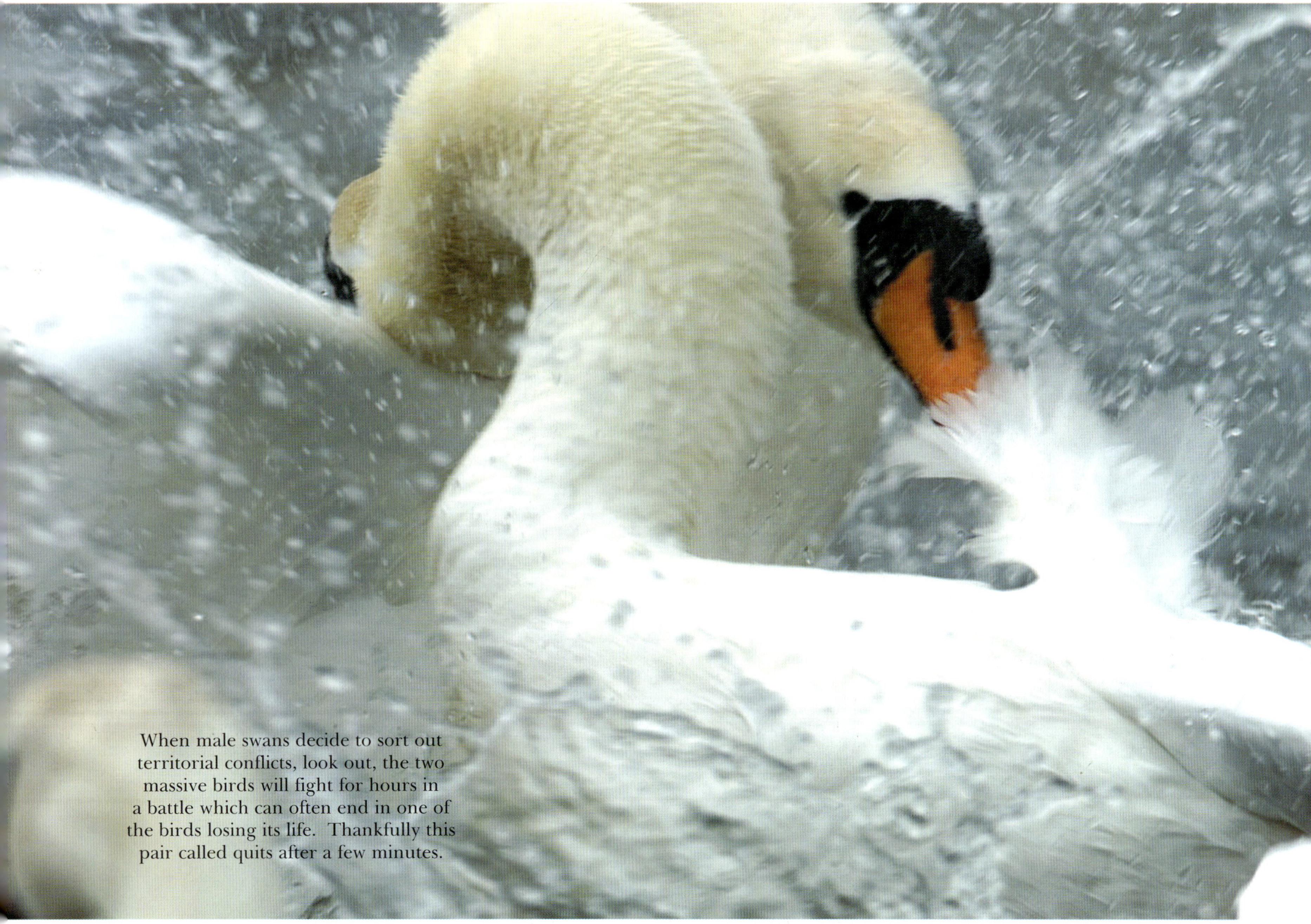

When male swans decide to sort out territorial conflicts, look out, the two massive birds will fight for hours in a battle which can often end in one of the birds losing its life. Thankfully this pair called quits after a few minutes.

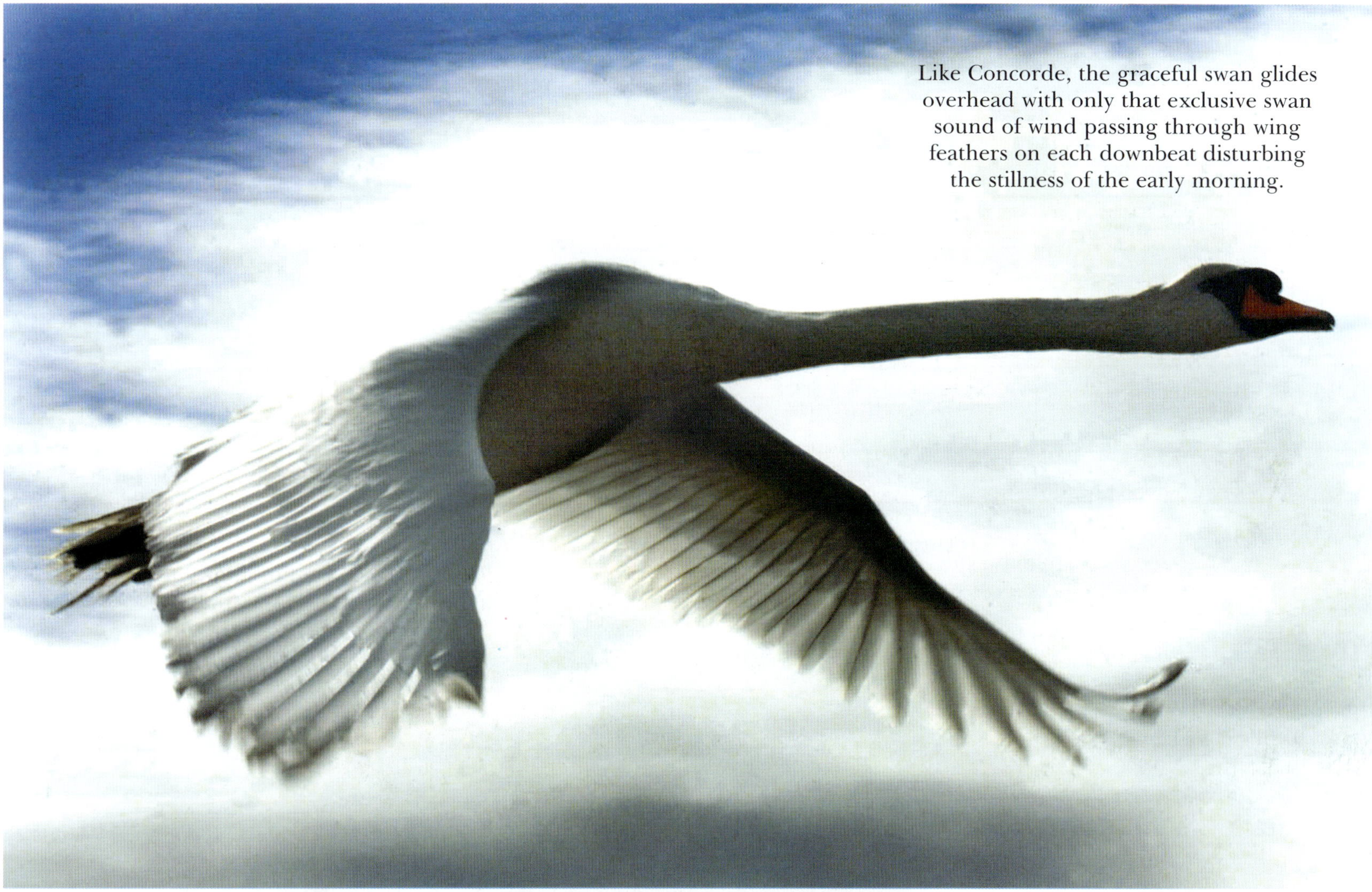

Like Concorde, the graceful swan glides overhead with only that exclusive swan sound of wind passing through wing feathers on each downbeat disturbing the stillness of the early morning.

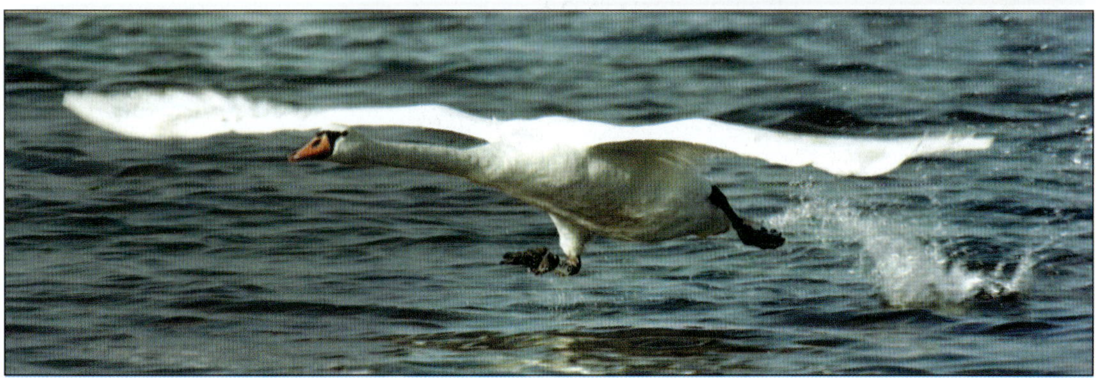

The picture of the swan trying to take off on a windless morning reminds me of a Hollywood cartoon I once saw. Without any wind assistance the swan seemed to run on the water for ages before eventually taking off.

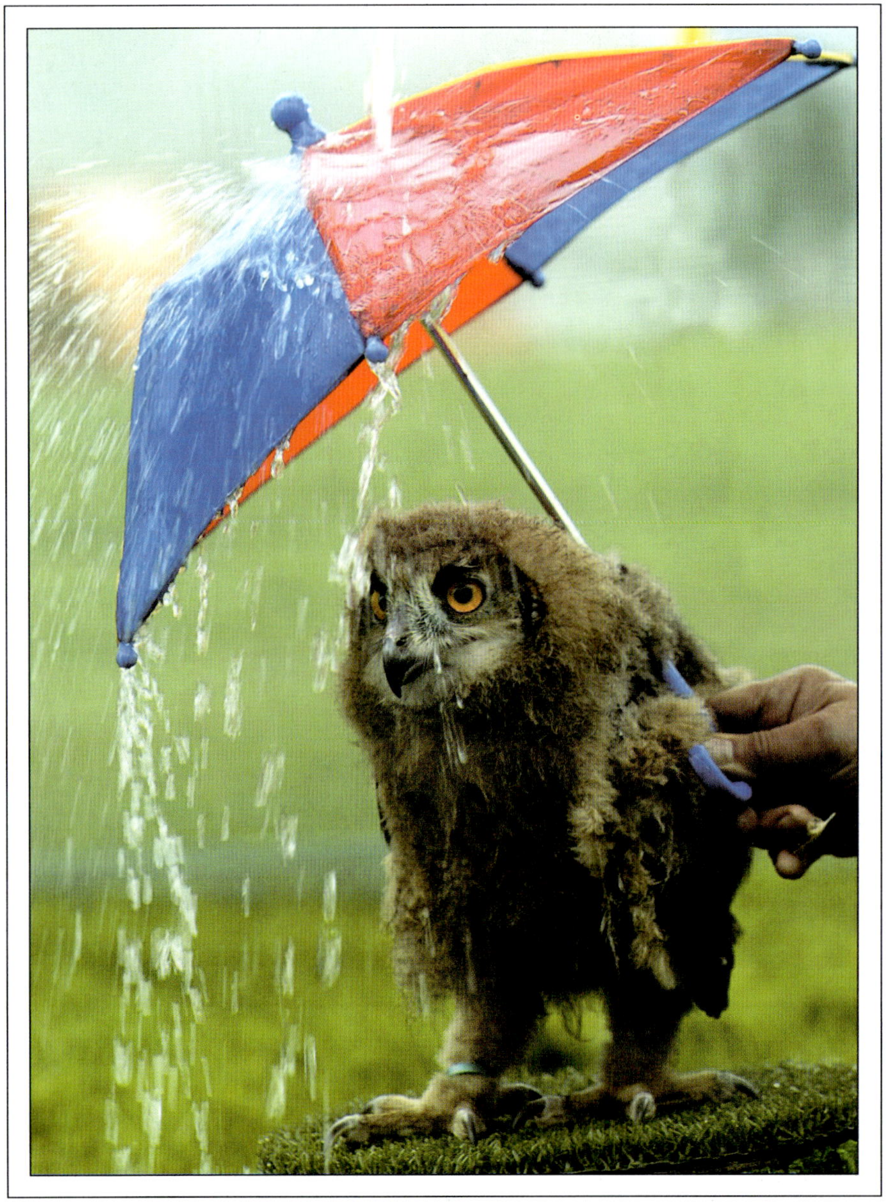

The weather was a talking point at the Devon County Show and the small umbrella came in handy, keeping the baby eagle owl dry.

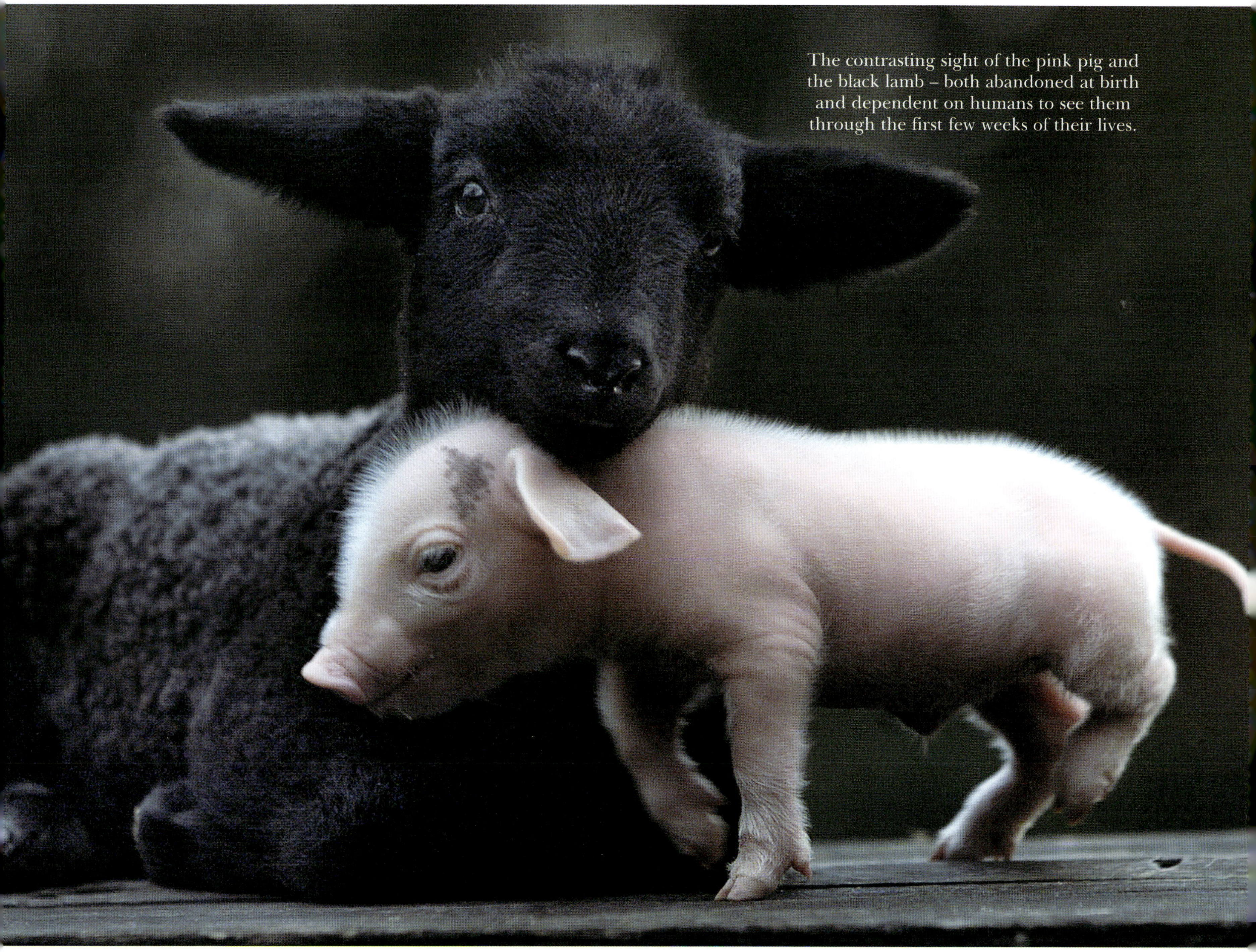

The contrasting sight of the pink pig and the black lamb – both abandoned at birth and dependent on humans to see them through the first few weeks of their lives.

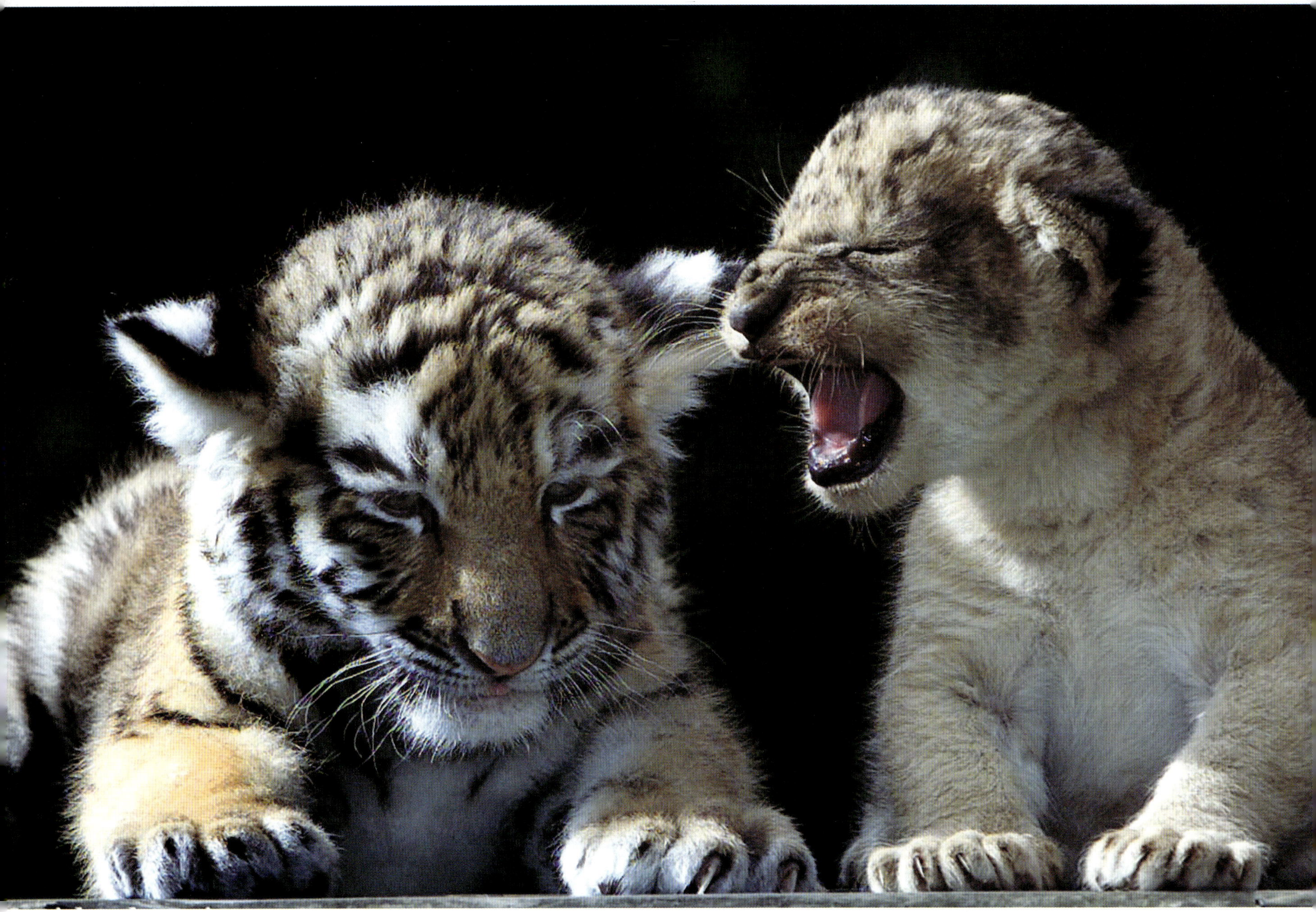

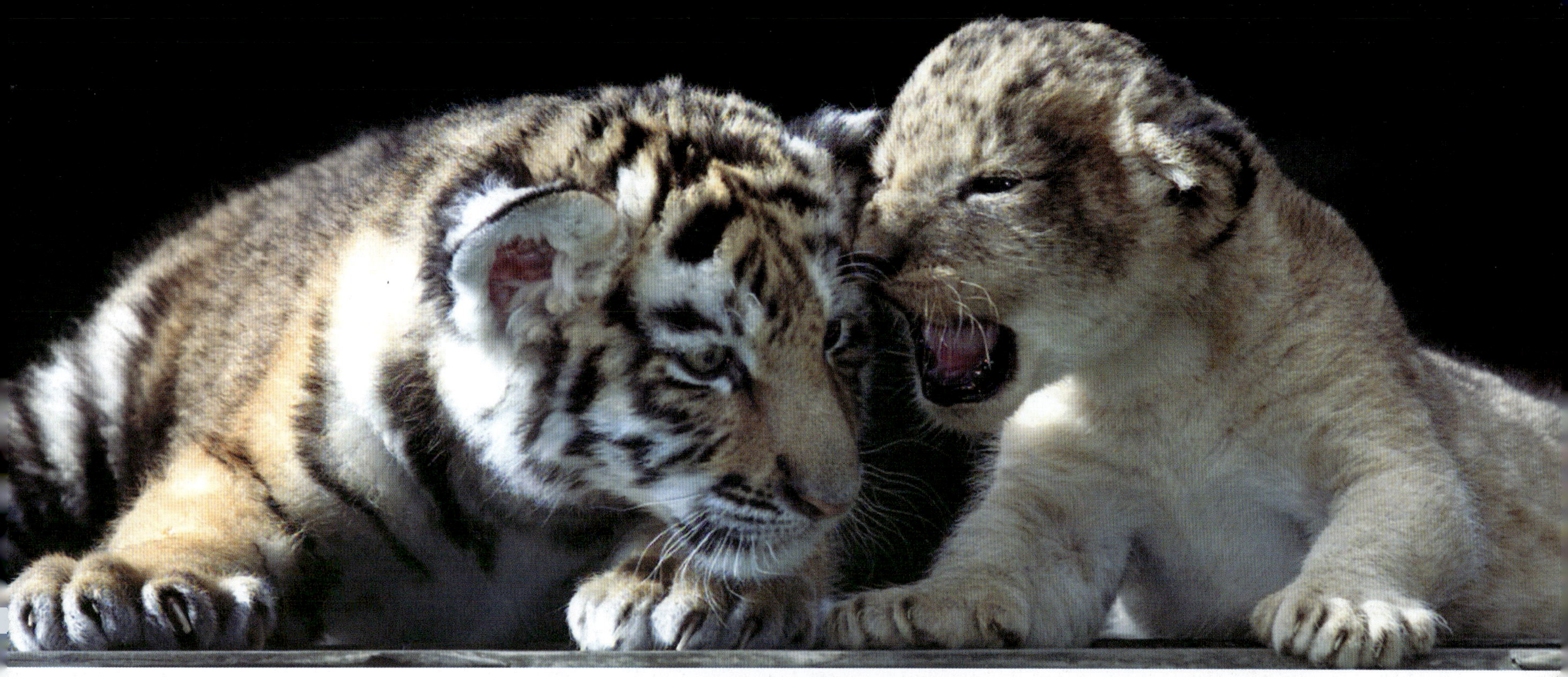

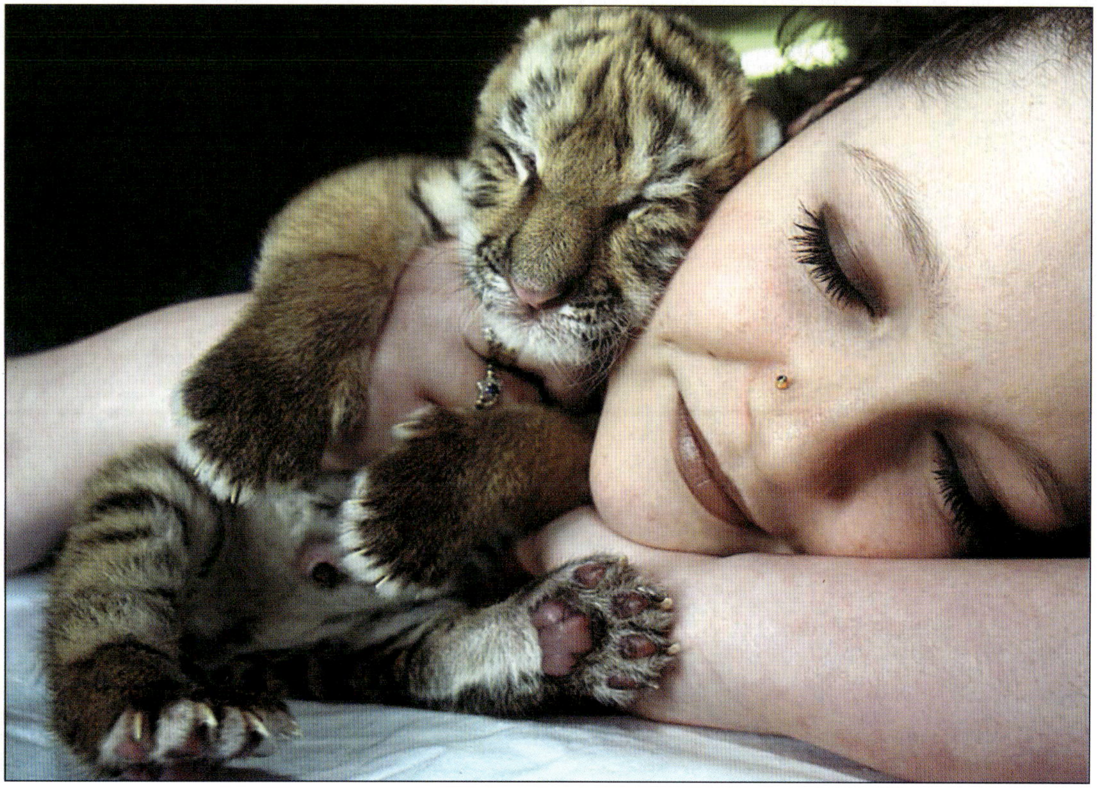

Never the twain shall meet in the wild, but the lion and tiger cubs at Dartmoor Wildlife Park near Plymouth get on well with each other.

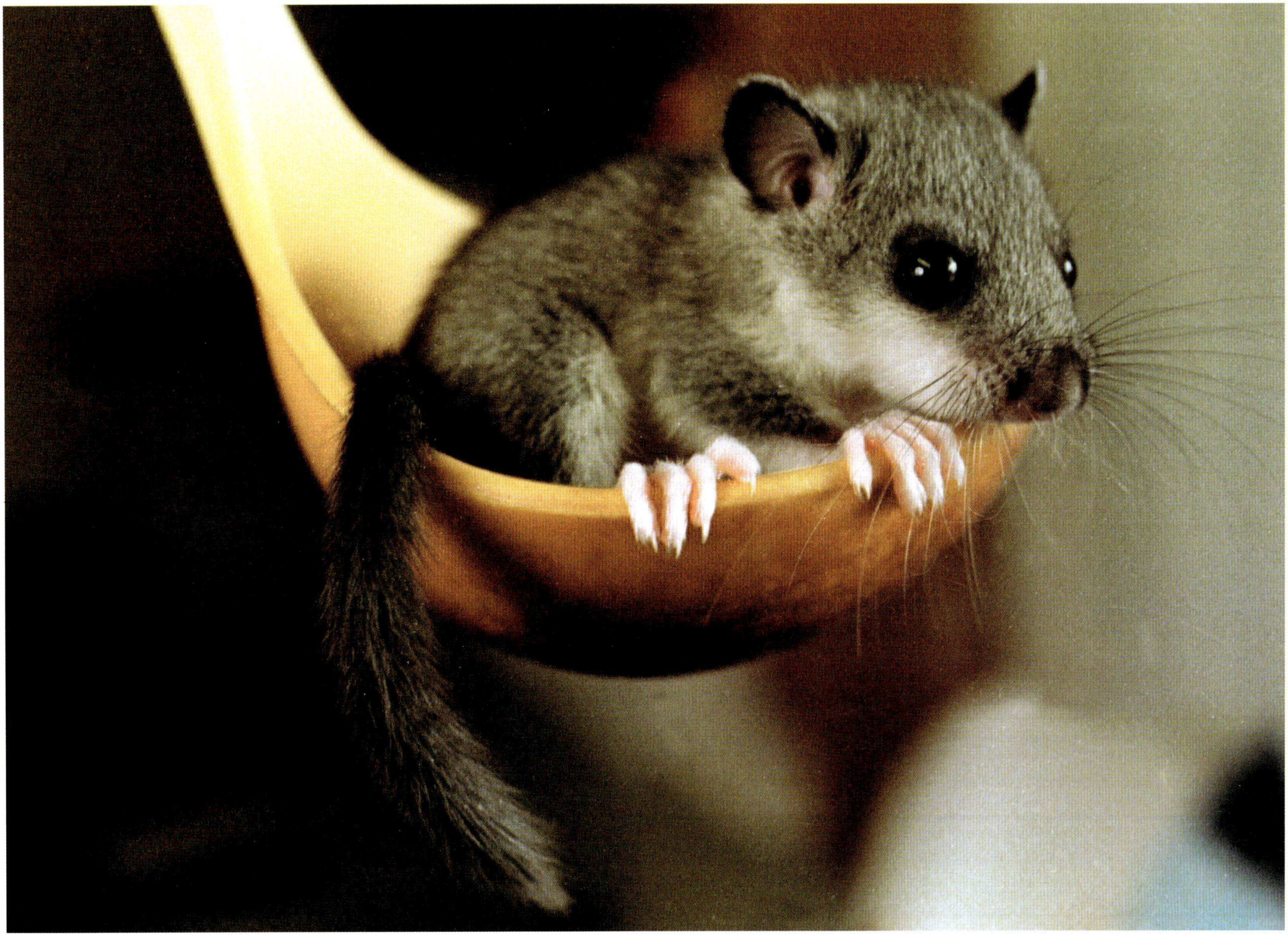

To illustrate a story about the little-known edible dormouse and how they were introduced to this country by the Romans who used to eat them as a delicacy. I placed this tame little mouse in a wooden soup ladle much to the anger of one reader who wrote to the paper complaining that I'd had the little guy under hot studio lights all day… he was as tame as somebody's pet hamster and was as happy as Larry sitting in the ladle.

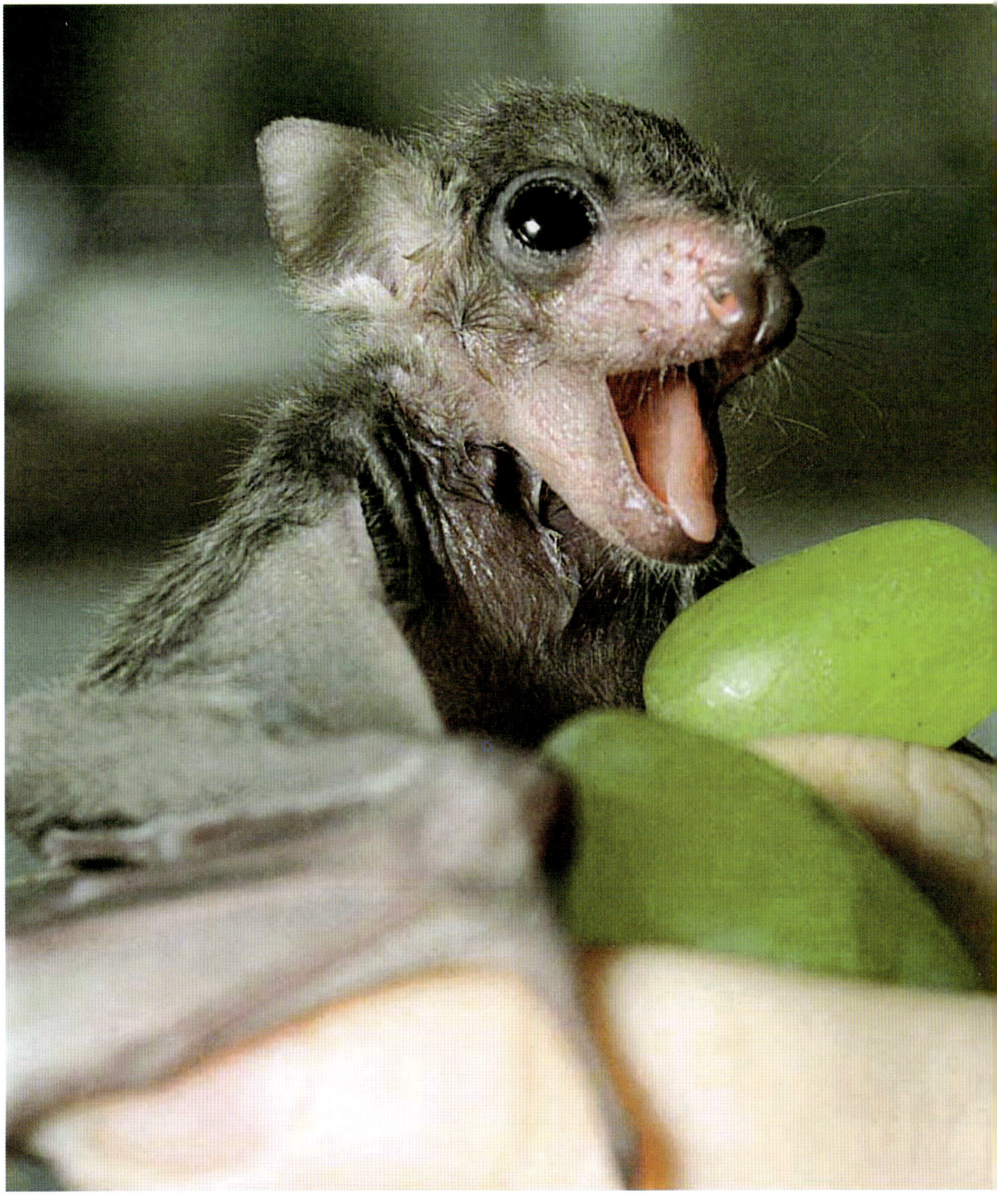

A symbolic picture of a stoat in the caring hands of animal rescuers and the ET look-a-like baby fruit bat making a fine pair as they shared the animal hospital wards.

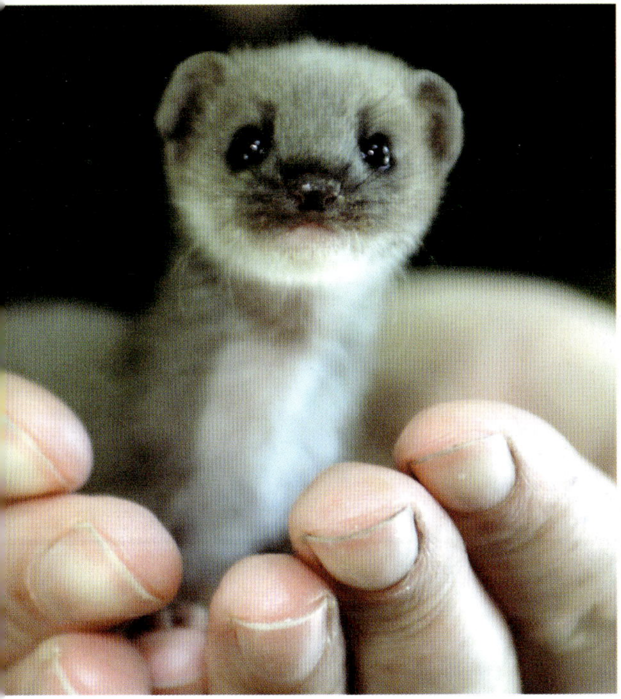

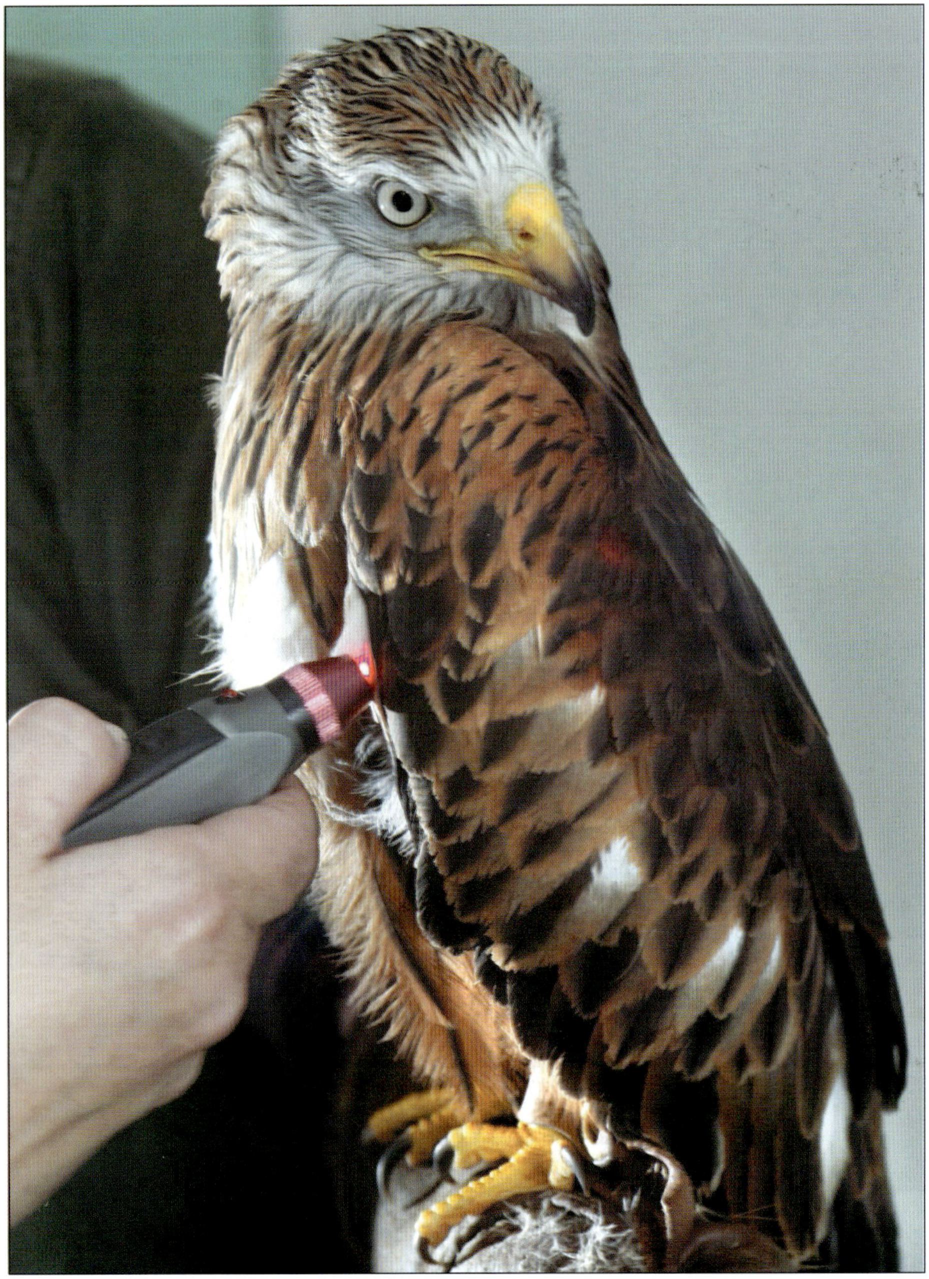

Red Kites are stunning birds, the plumage is striking and they are a very rare sight in the skies of England. However this bird owned by Karen Andriunas had to undergo infra-red light treatment on damaged wing feathers. The treatment was a delicate process as the bird was a little nervous of the process.

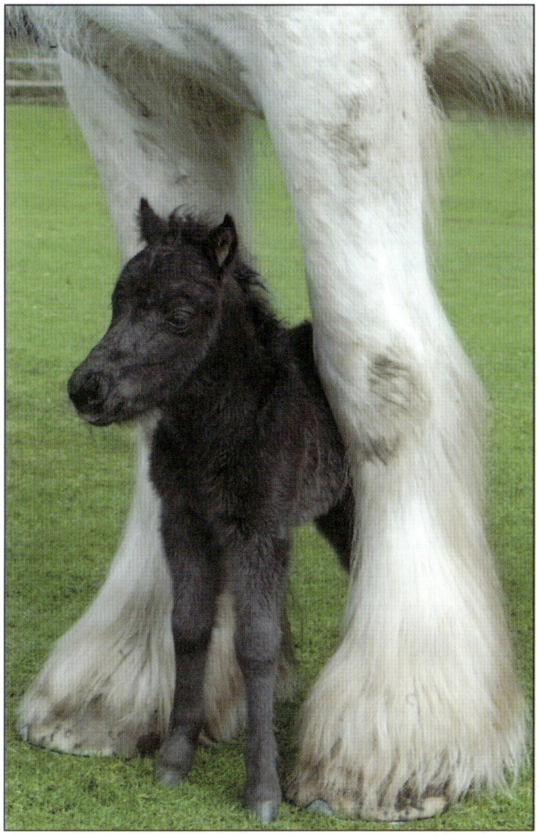

The legs of a Shire horse illustrated perfectly how small and vulnerable miniature pony foals are as they mix with other horses in the paddock.

Baby miniature donkey foals with a white face, pink nose and a pale grey coat are not that common, and when it comes to cuteness Topsy Turvy gets 10 out of 10 as he cuts a dash across the paddock at the Miniature Pony Centre on Dartmoor.

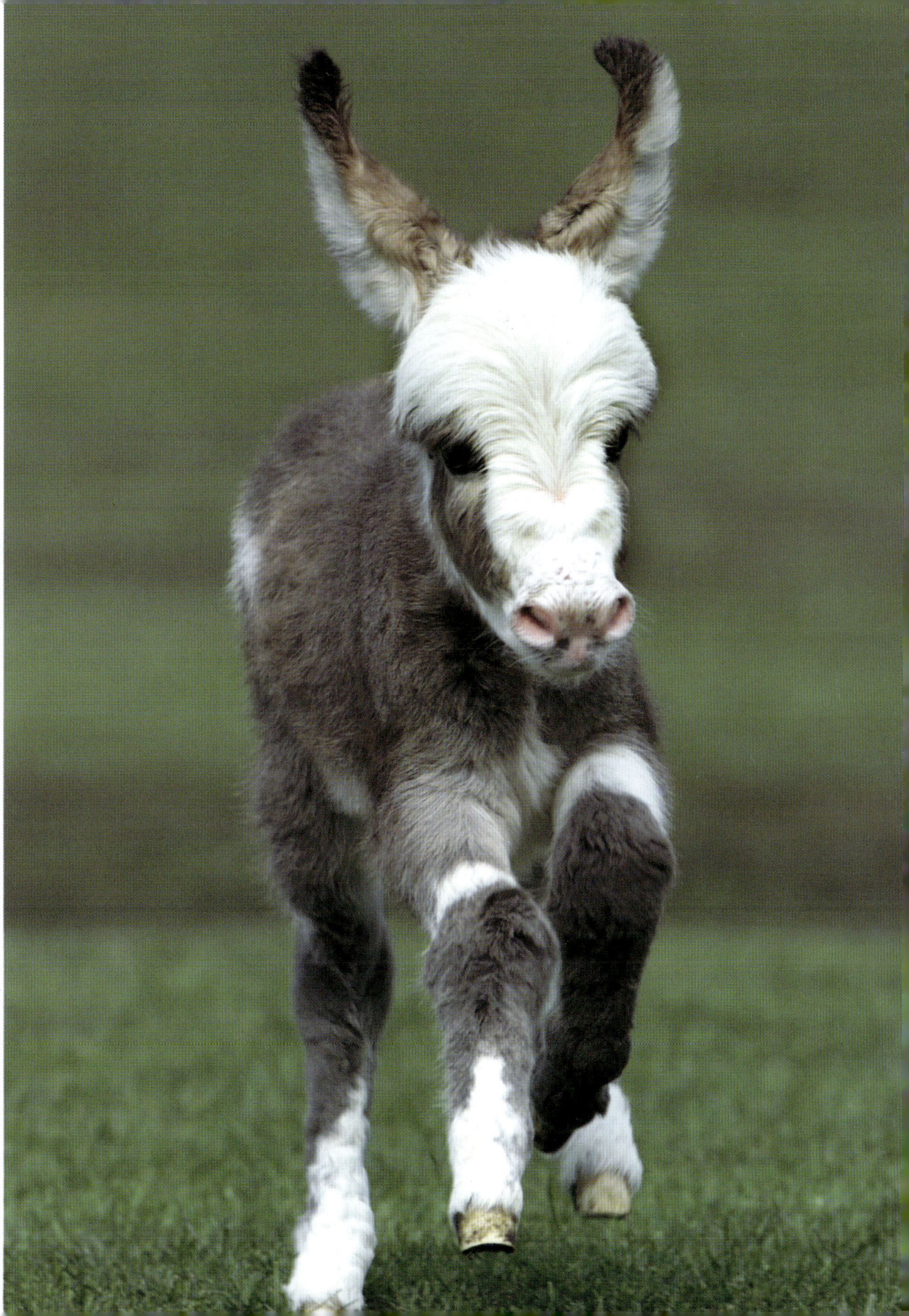

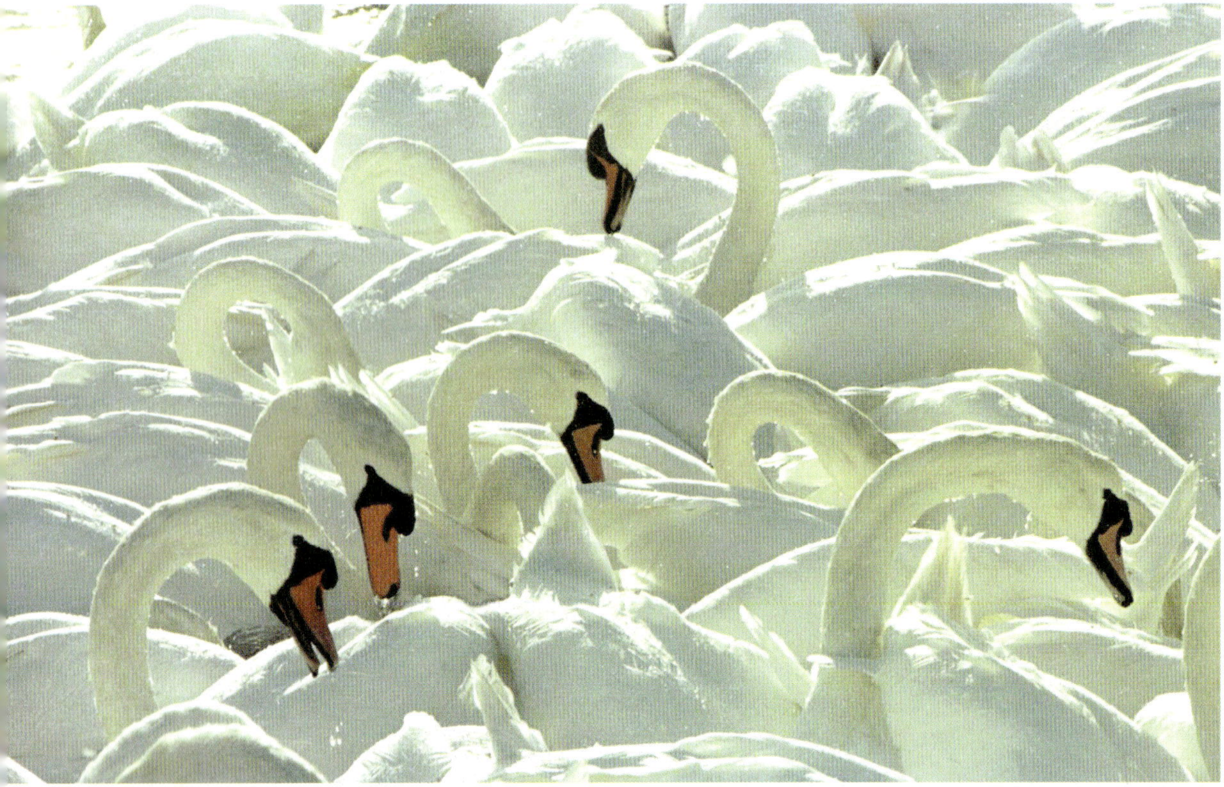

The 600-plus wild Mute Swans at the Abbotsbury Swannery are a rare sight in the UK and one could say the whole of Europe if not the world. With the morning sun on their backs the mass of swans at feeding time is spectacular and gives a great opportunity for unusual photographs.

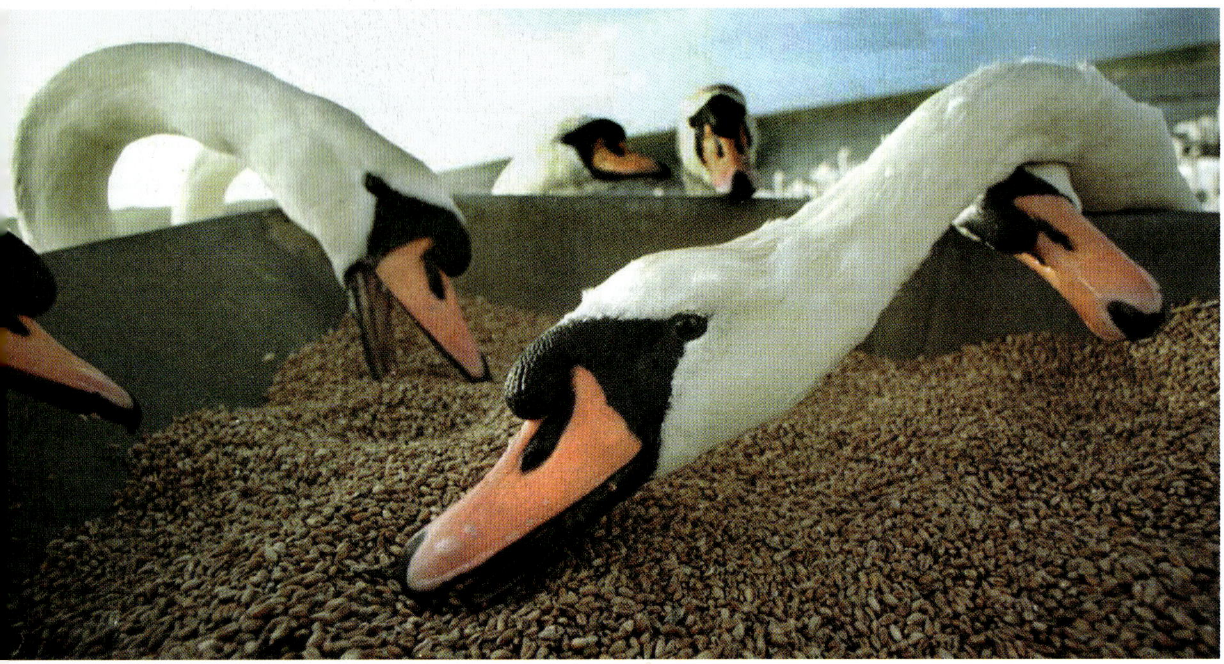

Mute Swans at Abbotsbury are quick learners and the swans have learned how to sneak a quick mouthful of corn from the wheelbarrow before feeding time.

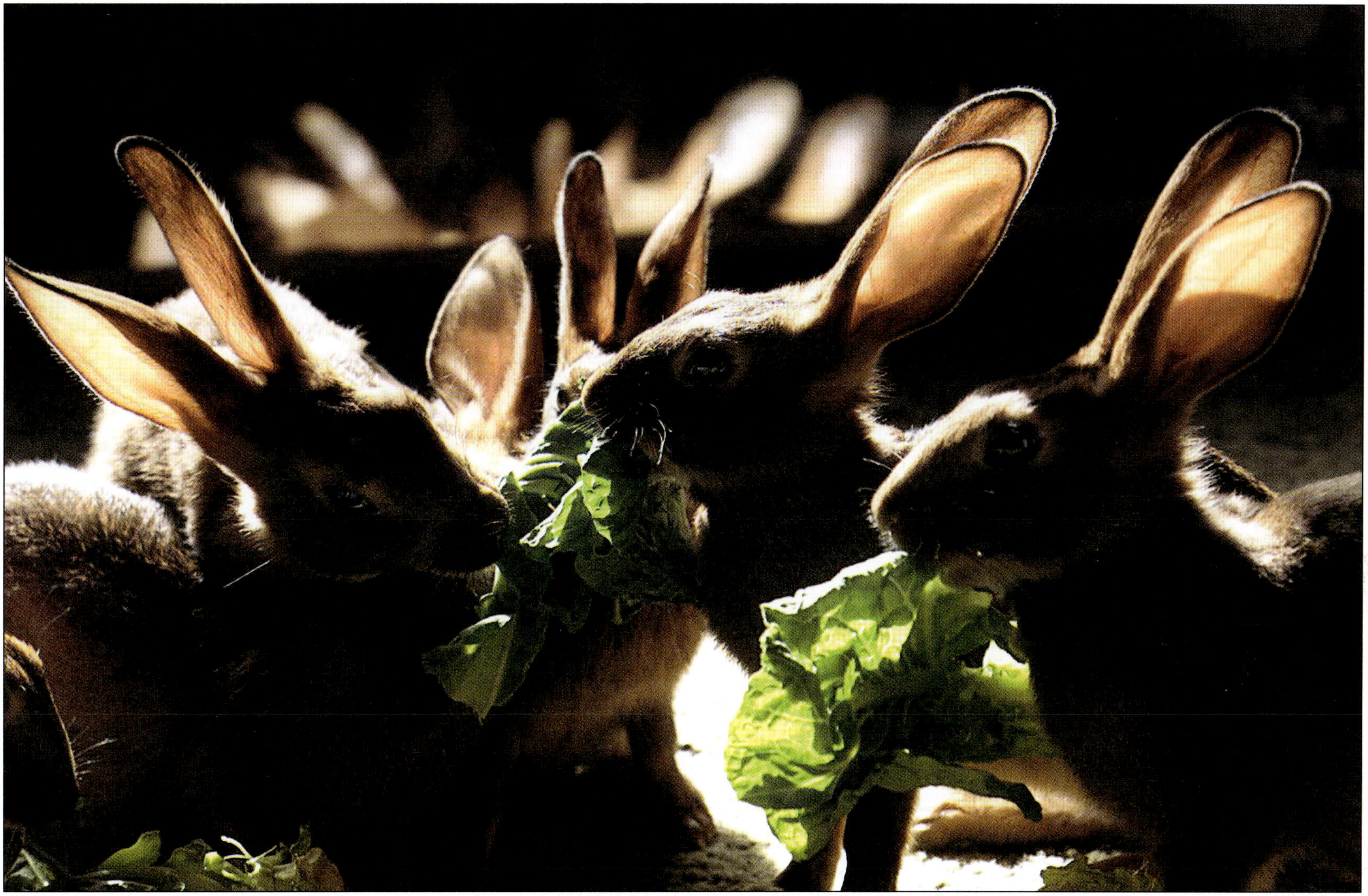

I was sent out to photograph a family of Belgian Hares living in the front room of a house in South Devon. Their owner sprinkled a few lettuce leaves on the carpet and the family began to feed as the sunlight beamed through the window causing their ears to appear transparent. On the floor behind them was a full-length mirror lying on its side which added to the lighting effects of the picture.

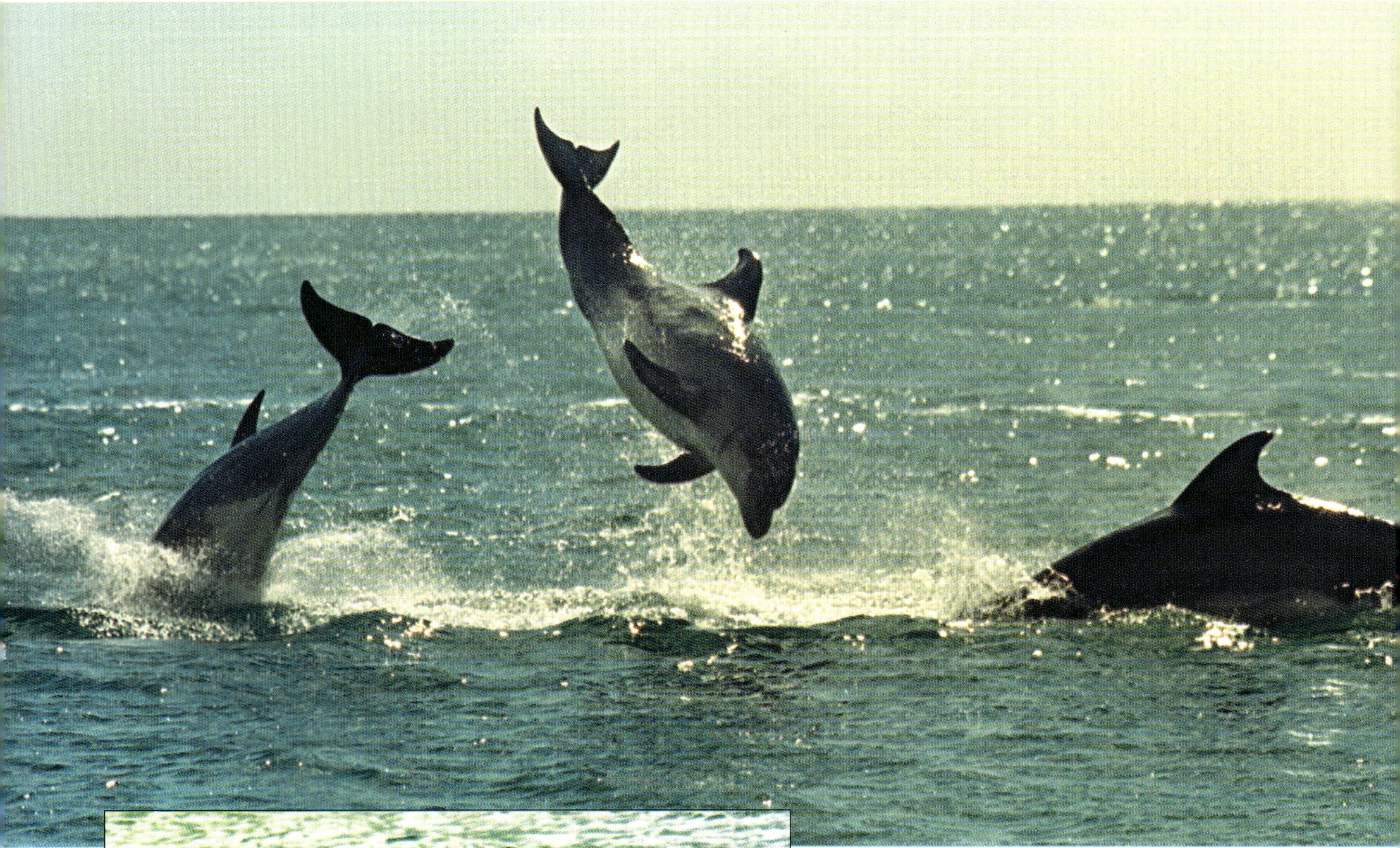

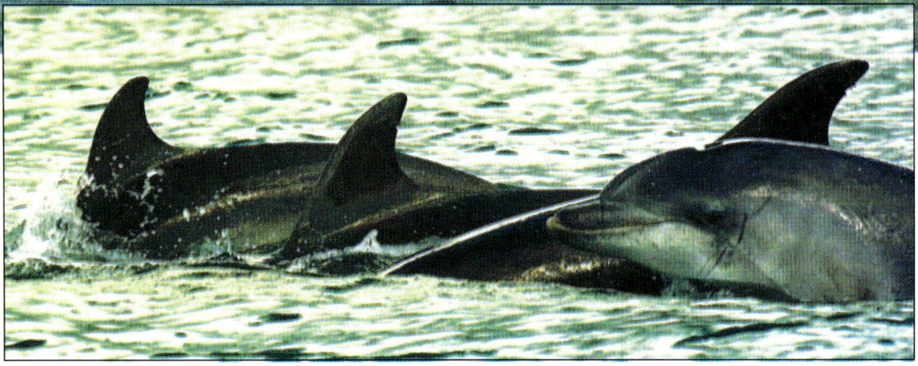

During the Easter weekend of 1998 a family of Bottle-nosed dolphins arrived at Lyme Regis and stayed all summer. Little did we know at the time that this was a very rare occasion and a lot of people, both local and holiday makers grasped the occasion and witnessed these beautiful intelligent animals at play in Lyme Bay. They have returned briefly but not for a whole summer and many people have special memories of the summer of 1998.

There must be thousands of healthy badgers out there running around our countryside all with a common denominator – Pauline Kidner. Pauline founded Secret World and over the years her knowledge of badgers from tiny day-old cubs to full-grown casualties is second to none. These pictures show what happens many times a day during the spring as cub after cub, all with a different tale of woe, arrive at her Somerset sanctuary.

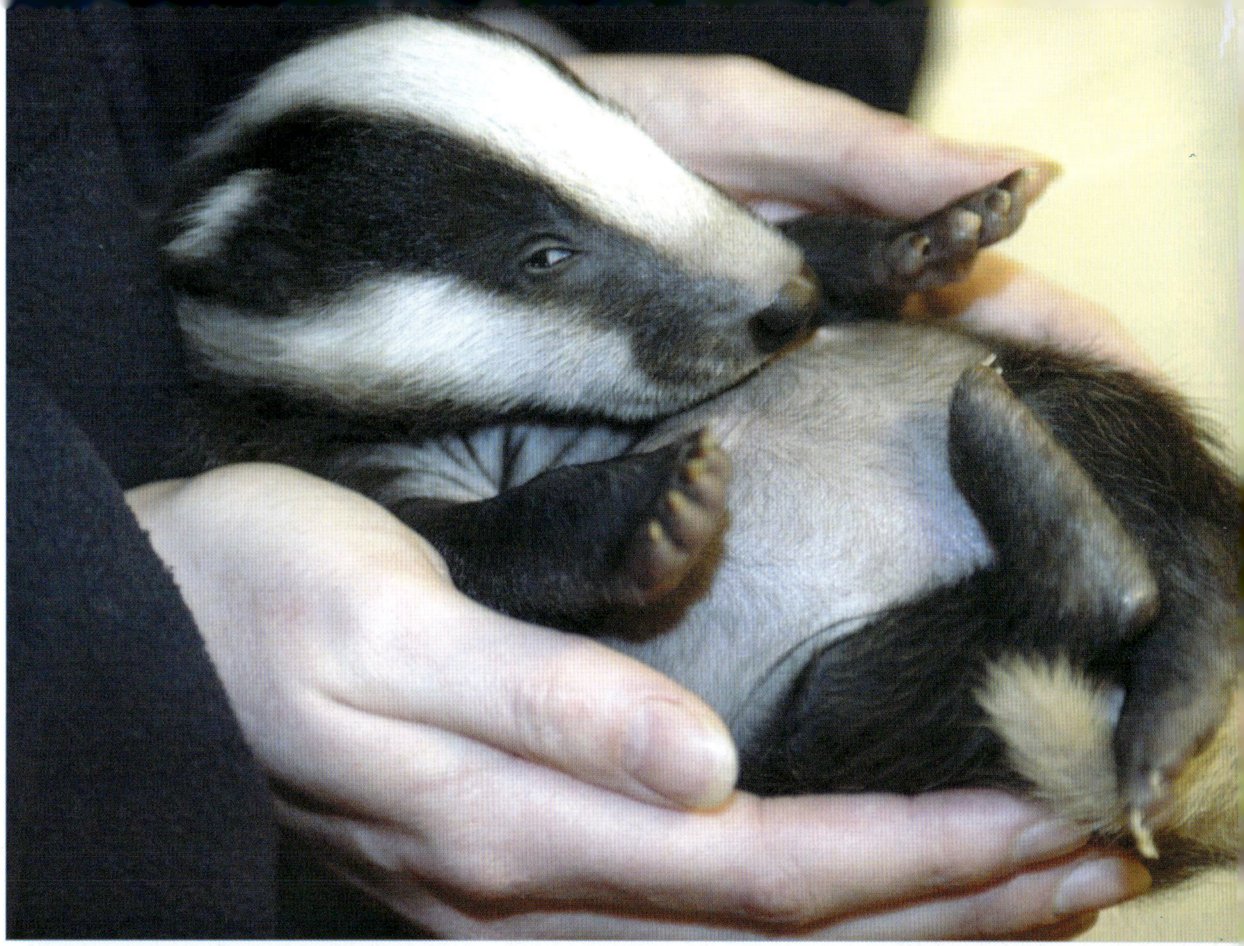

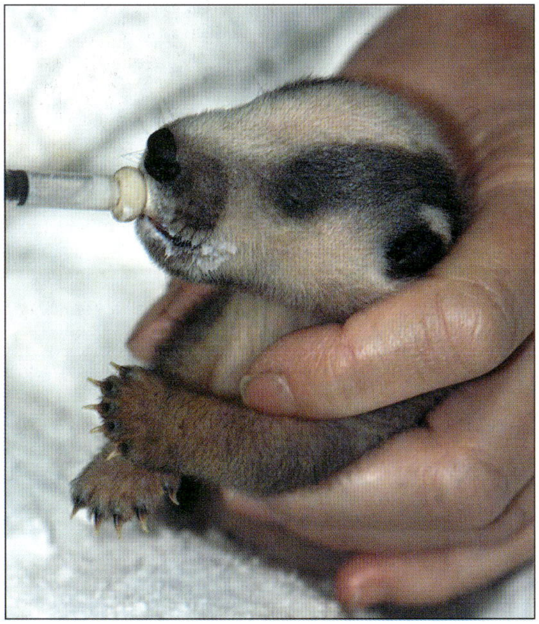

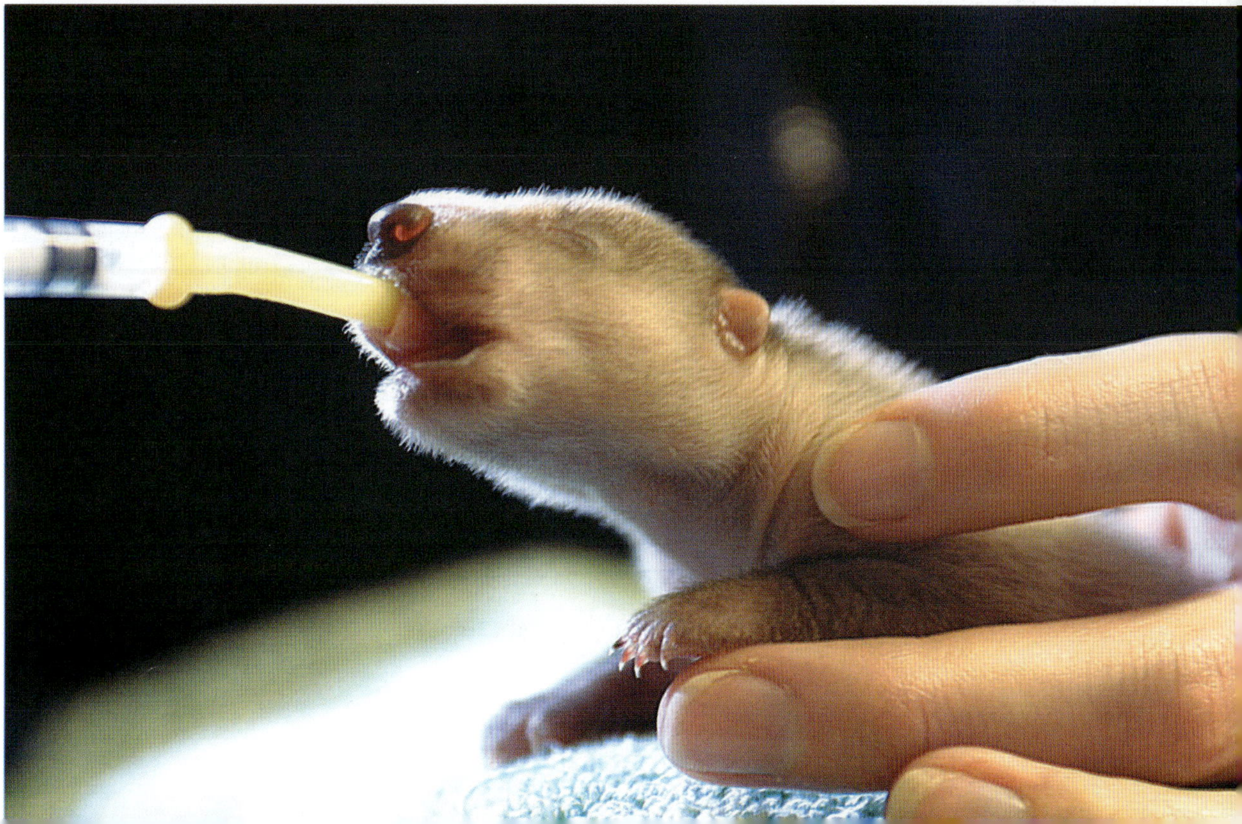

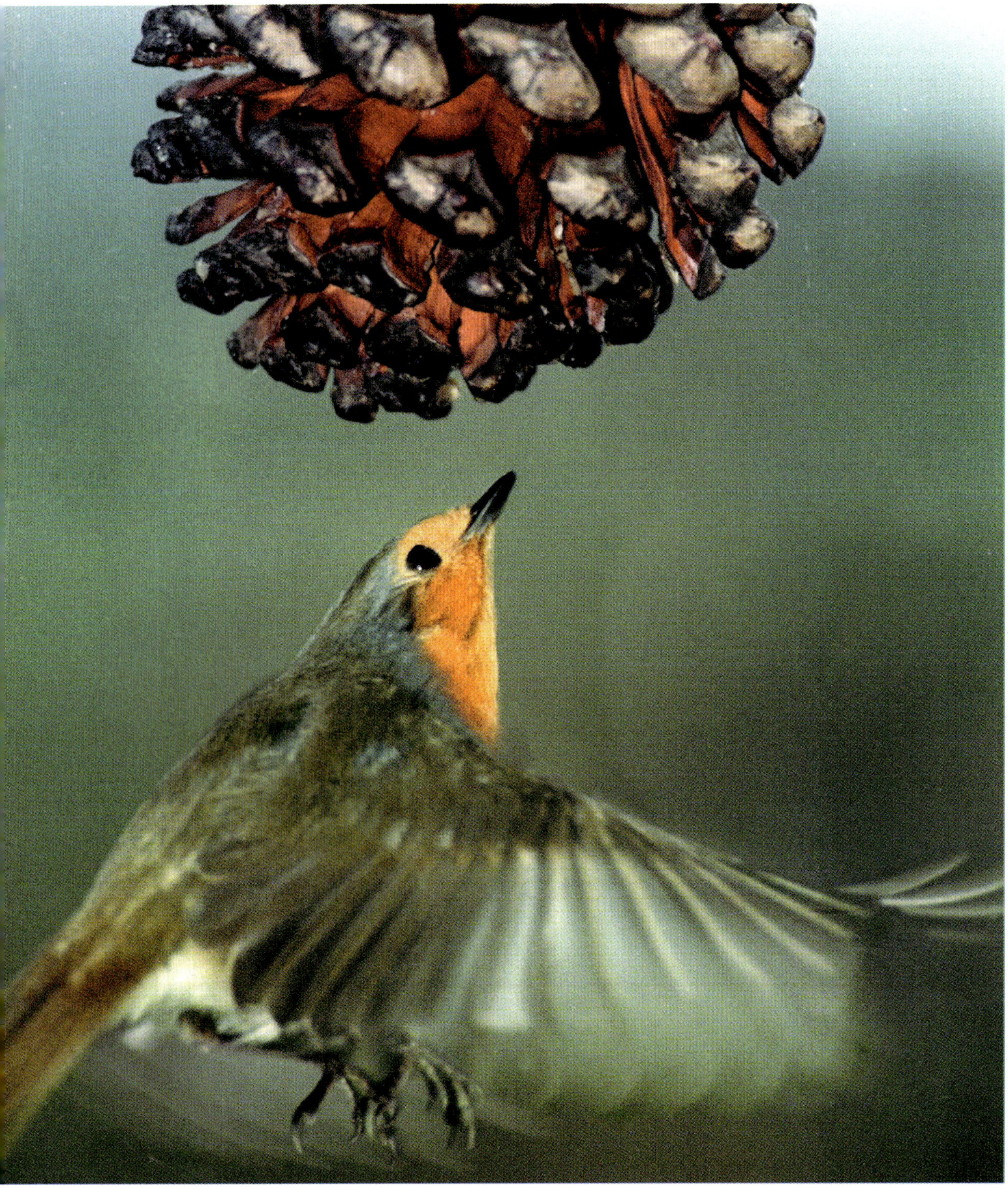

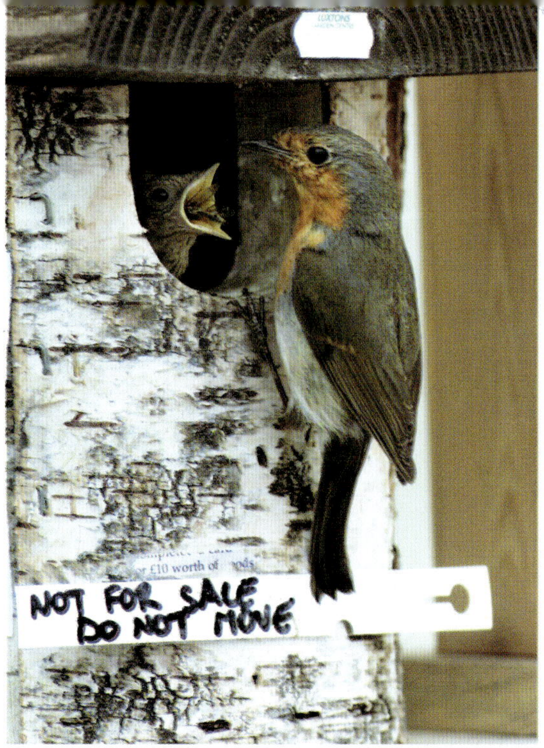


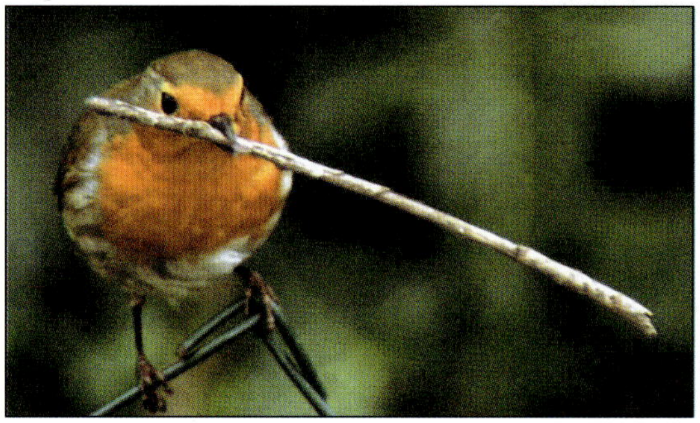

Robins, don't you just love them, from the cheeky pair who built a home in a nesting box that was still on the shelf in the shop to the humming-bird impersonator feeding on peanut butter wedged inside a fir cone to the robin who looked like he was building a log cabin rather than a moss-lined nest.

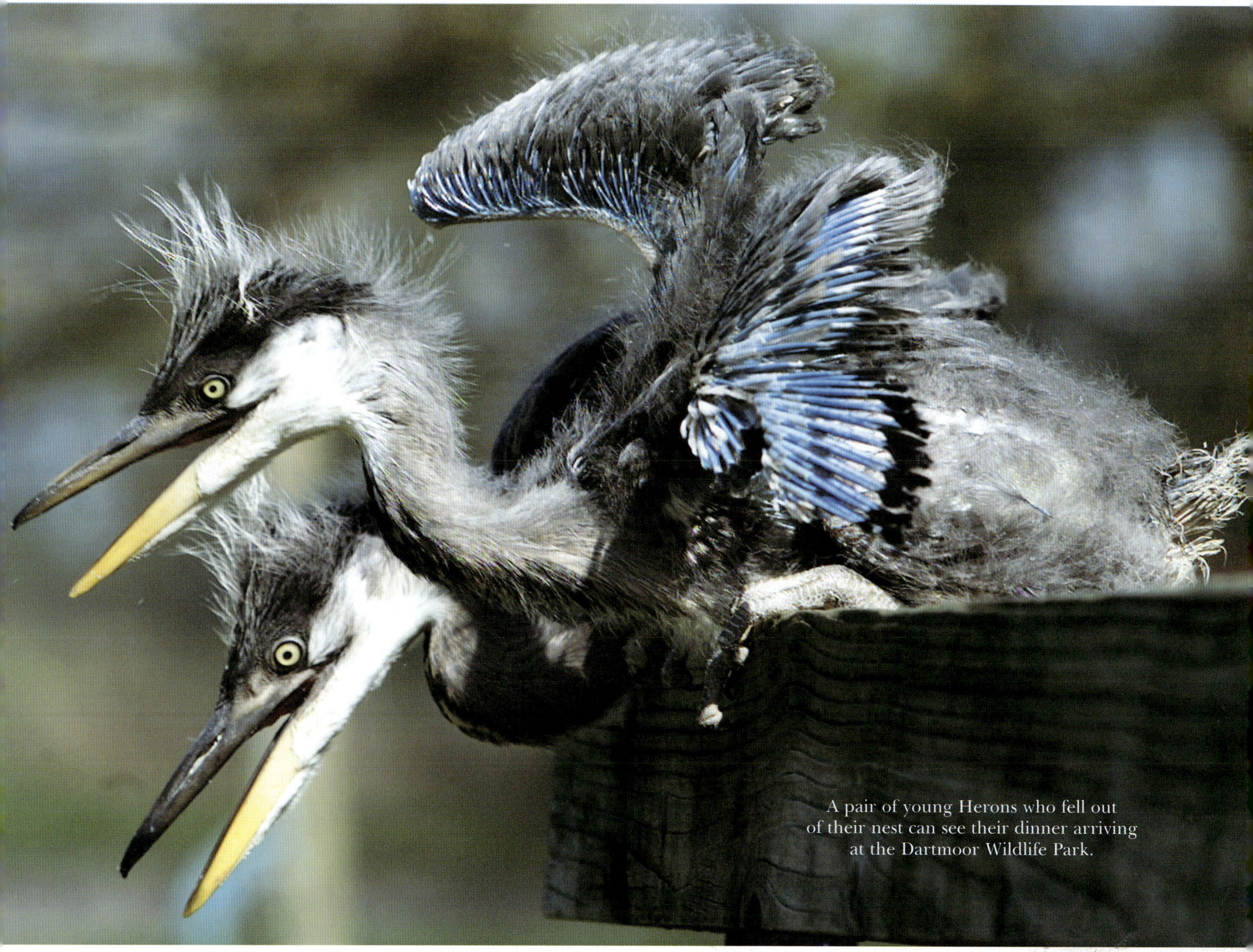

A pair of young Herons who fell out of their nest can see their dinner arriving at the Dartmoor Wildlife Park.

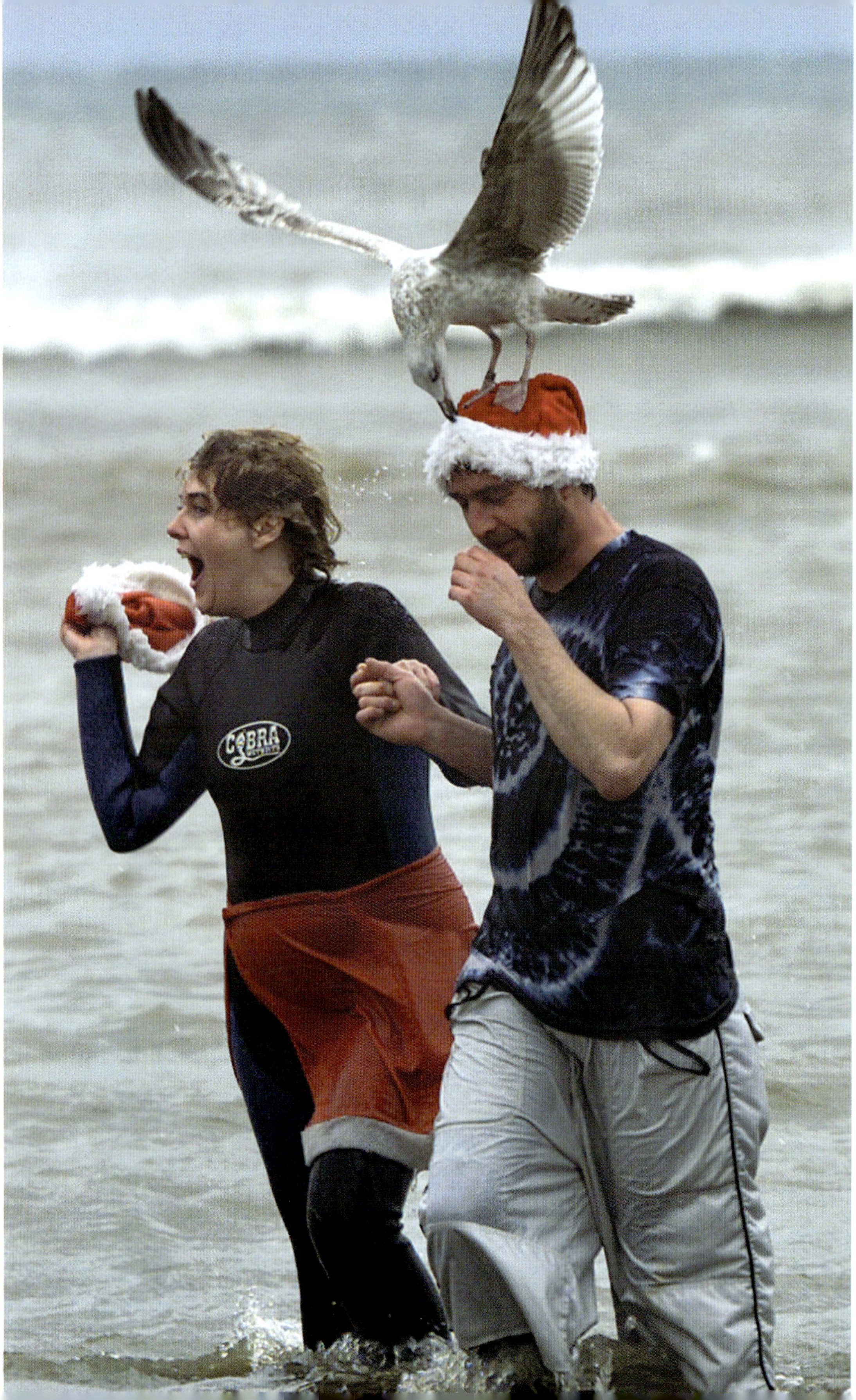


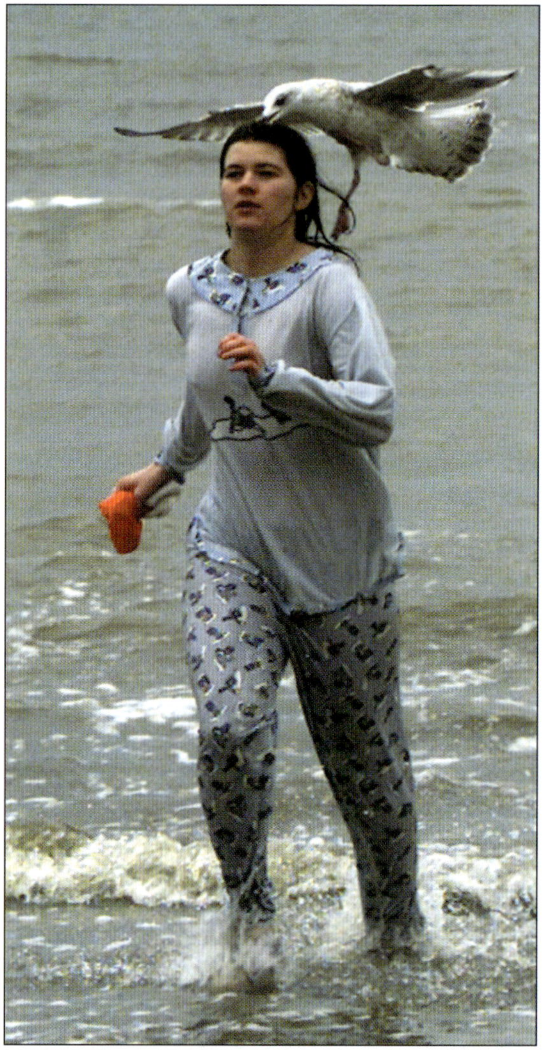

Not much Christmas cheer from this bad tempered Herring Gull as it attacked swimmers in Dorset. It was Christmas Day and the people of Charmouth were enjoying the annual Christmas Day swim when I noticed the young seagull homing in on the swimmers as they came out of the sea. Fortunately nobody was injured in the attack but they do have razor-sharp bills and could have inflicted a nasty cut on the head.

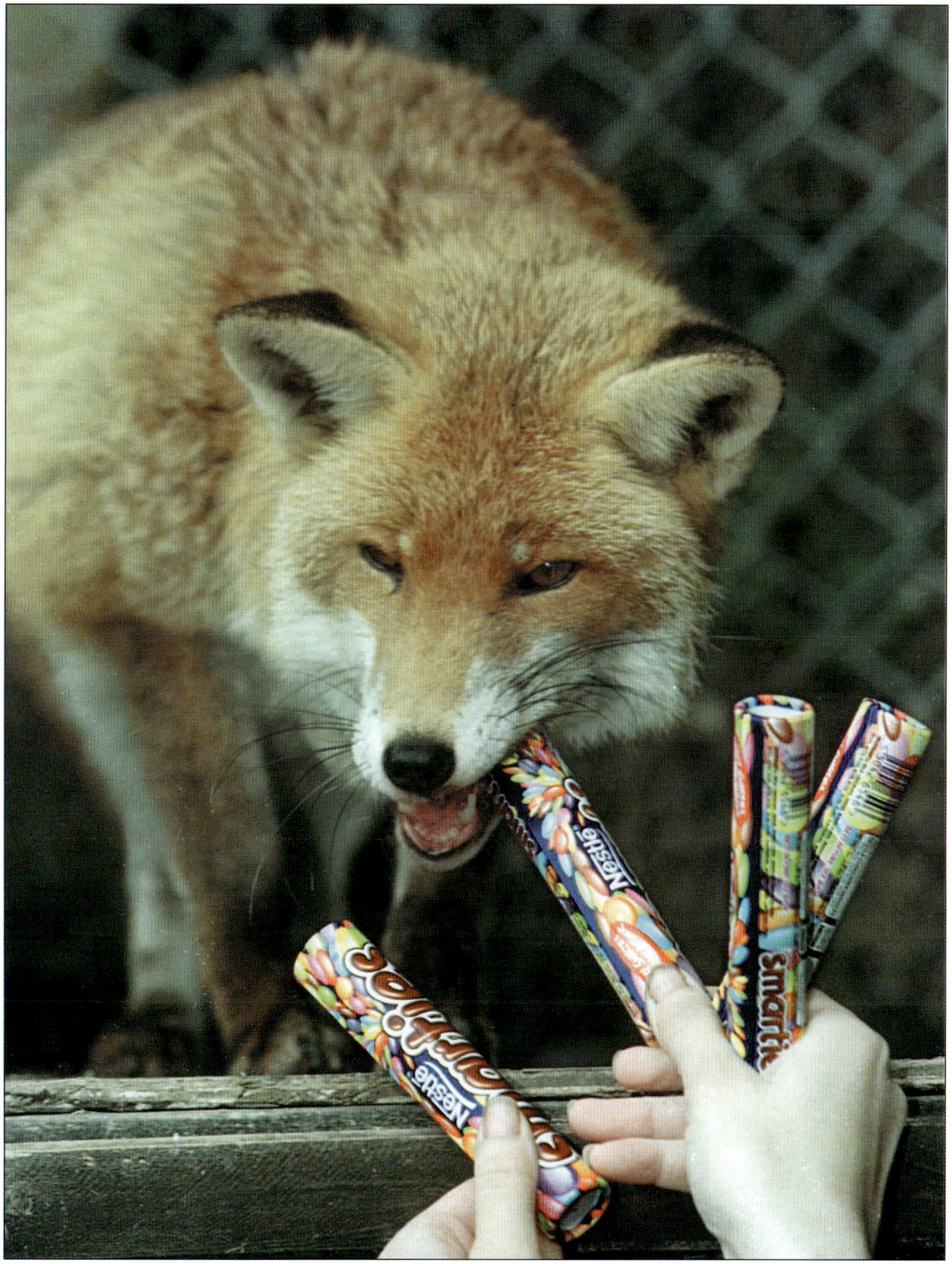


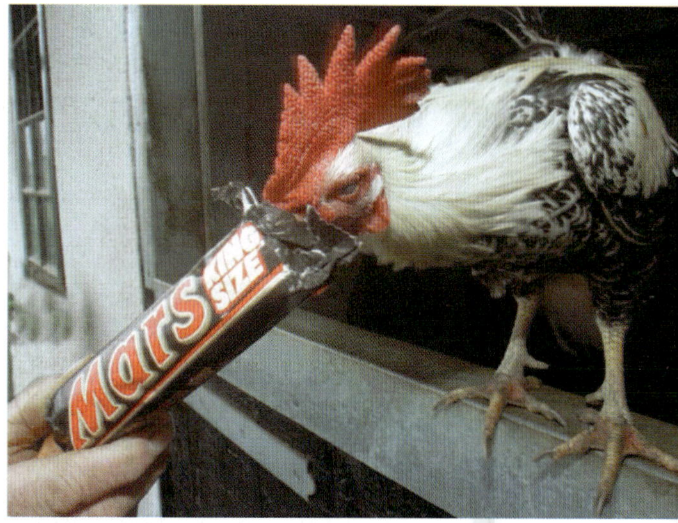


Amusing pictures of the fox who loved Smarties and the cockerel who was very close to being a chocaholic.

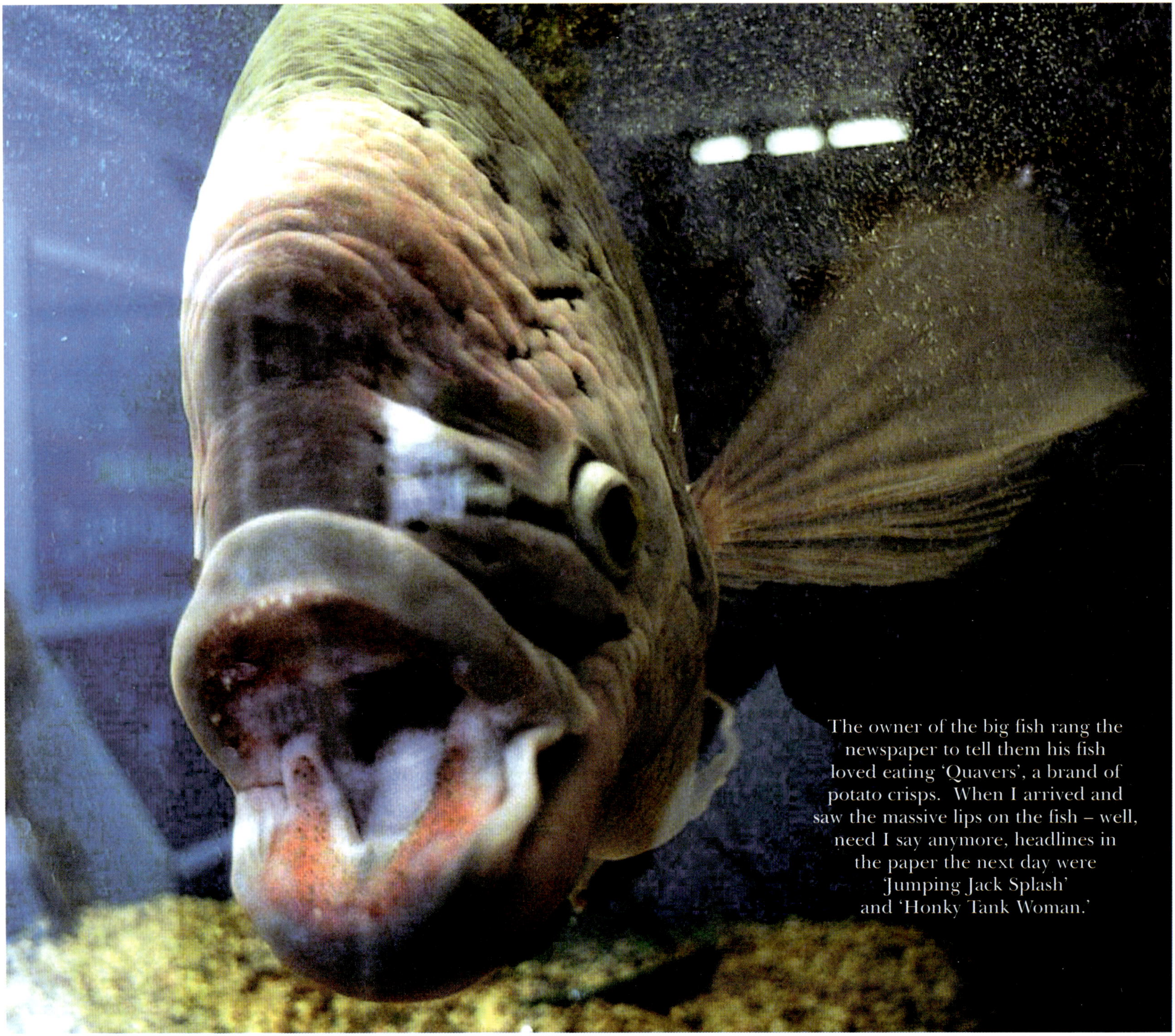

The owner of the big fish rang the newspaper to tell them his fish loved eating 'Quavers', a brand of potato crisps. When I arrived and saw the massive lips on the fish – well, need I say anymore, headlines in the paper the next day were 'Jumping Jack Splash' and 'Honky Tank Woman.'

With the unlikely name of Mr Woo the skinny and almost transparent little albino wallaby with bright red eyes became a media favourite in the months following his national debut in the newspapers.

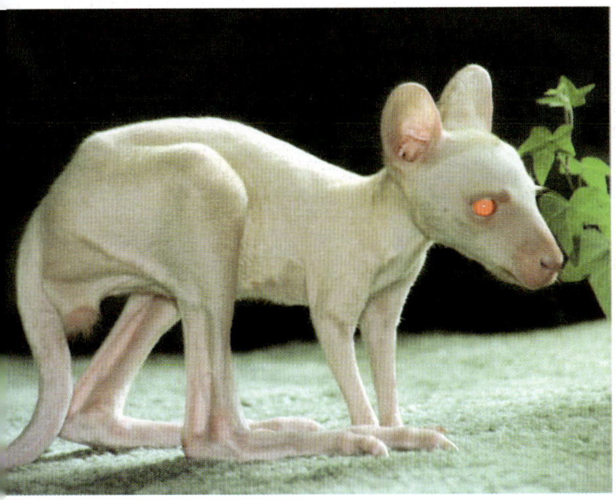

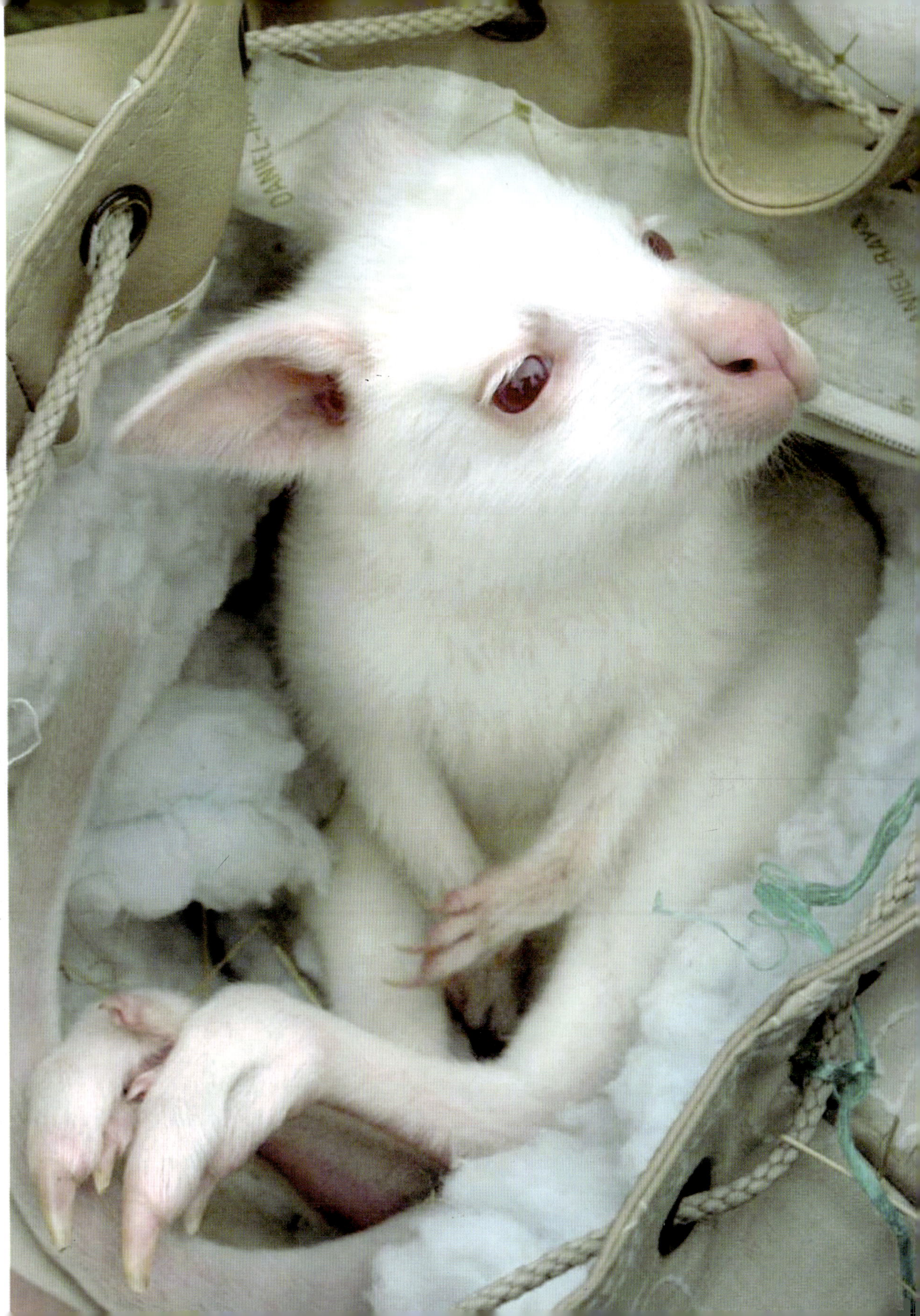

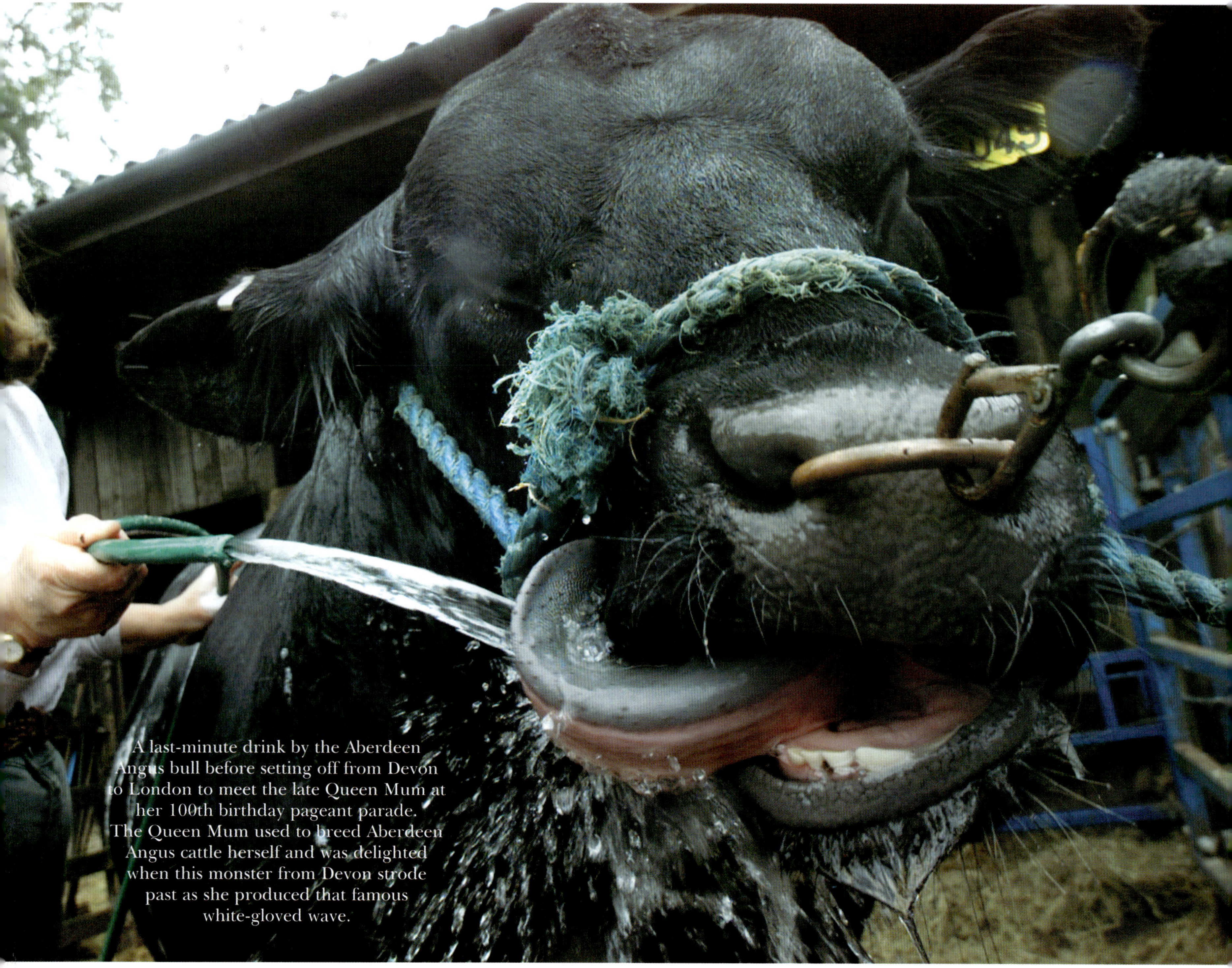

A last-minute drink by the Aberdeen Angus bull before setting off from Devon to London to meet the late Queen Mum at her 100th birthday pageant parade. The Queen Mum used to breed Aberdeen Angus cattle herself and was delighted when this monster from Devon strode past as she produced that famous white-gloved wave.

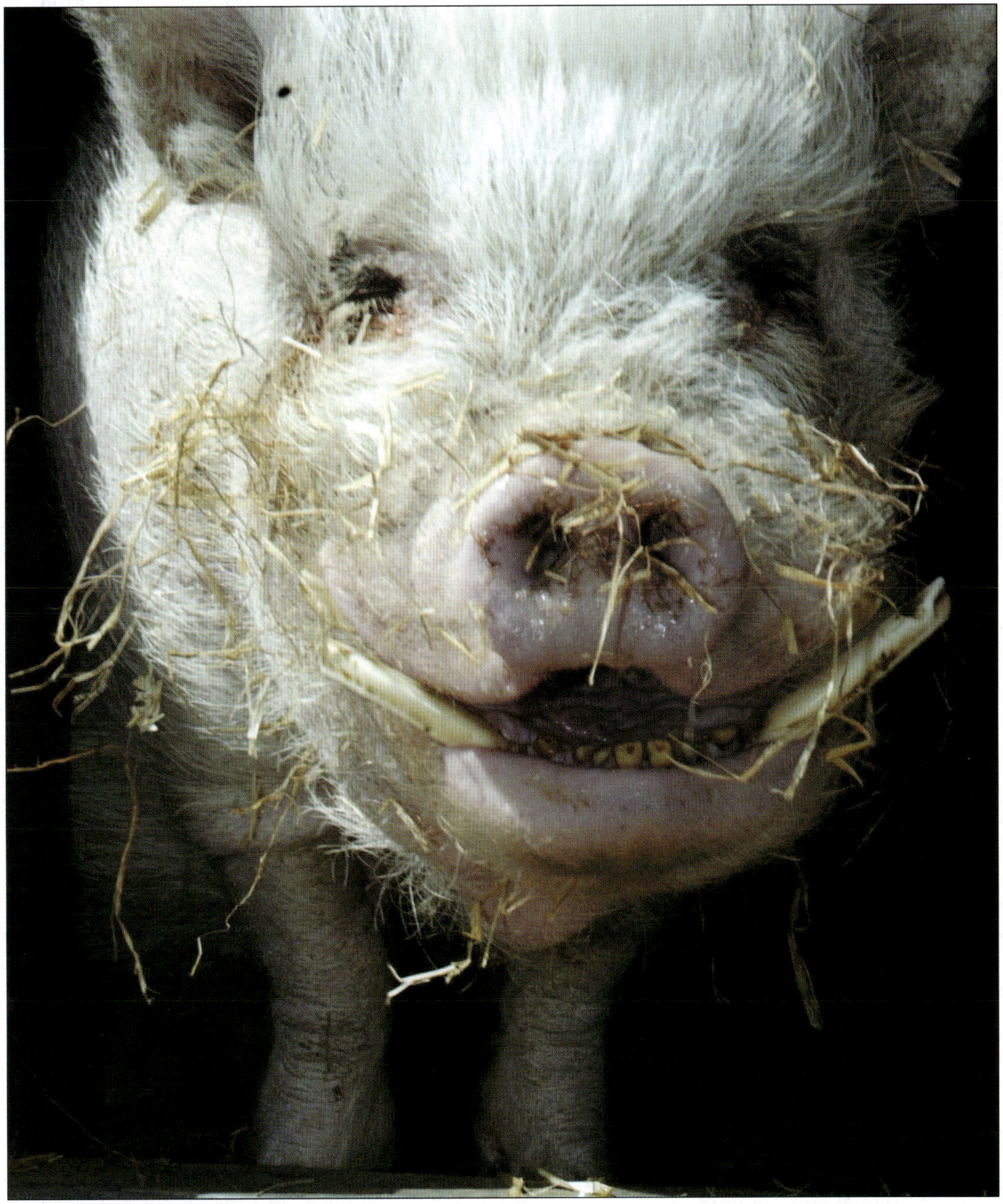

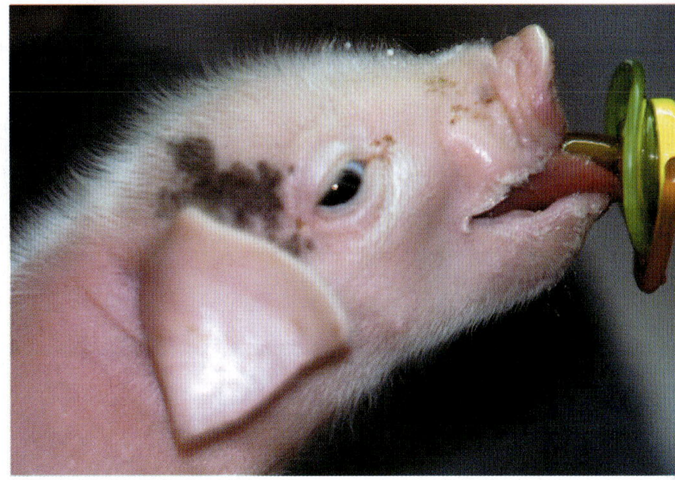

Yes the little piglet really did have a baby's dummy to keep her quiet between feeds and could grow up to be as beautiful as Peter the pig who doesn't look his best first thing. OK, his looks are on the wain, he makes a right mess of eating his shreaded wheat in the mornings, and his breath could strip paint off a wall from 5 yards, his dental hygene isn't all it could be, but this Casanova of the pig world – a cross between a Yucatan and Vietnamese pot-bellied pig – has sired well over 100 little porkers before he gave up his days as a lady's man due to old age and arthritis. He is now retired at the Dartmoor Miniature Pony Centre near Moretonhampstead on Dartmoor.

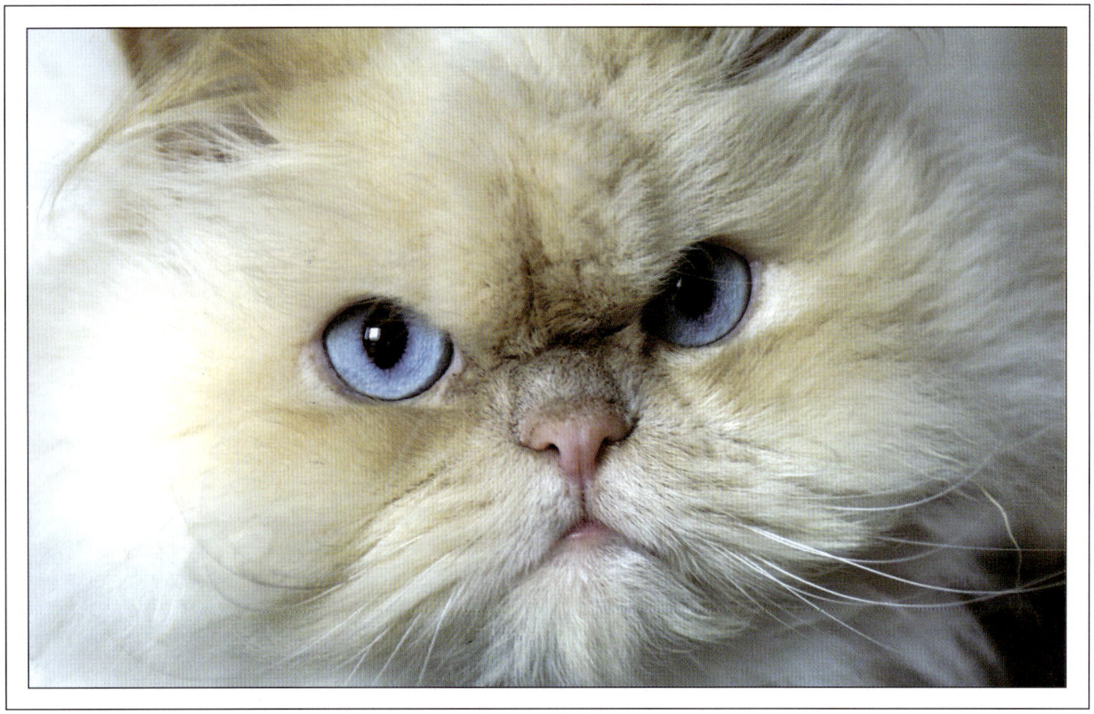

It was the eyes that did it. I couldn't resist a quick picture of the pretty face with the baby blue eyes.

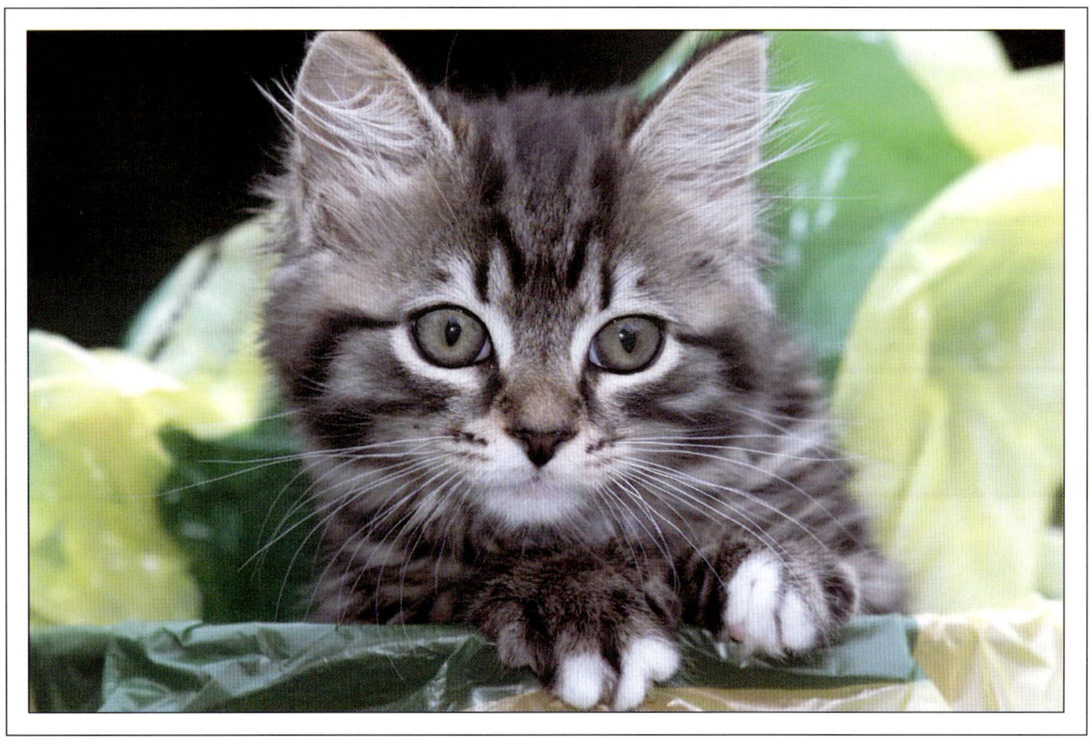

One life down with eight to go… It was hard to imagine just what sort of person would place a small kitten inside a plastic bag and dump her on a refuse tip, I photographed her with the original bag in the remote hope that somebody would recognise the bag and turn in the culprit.

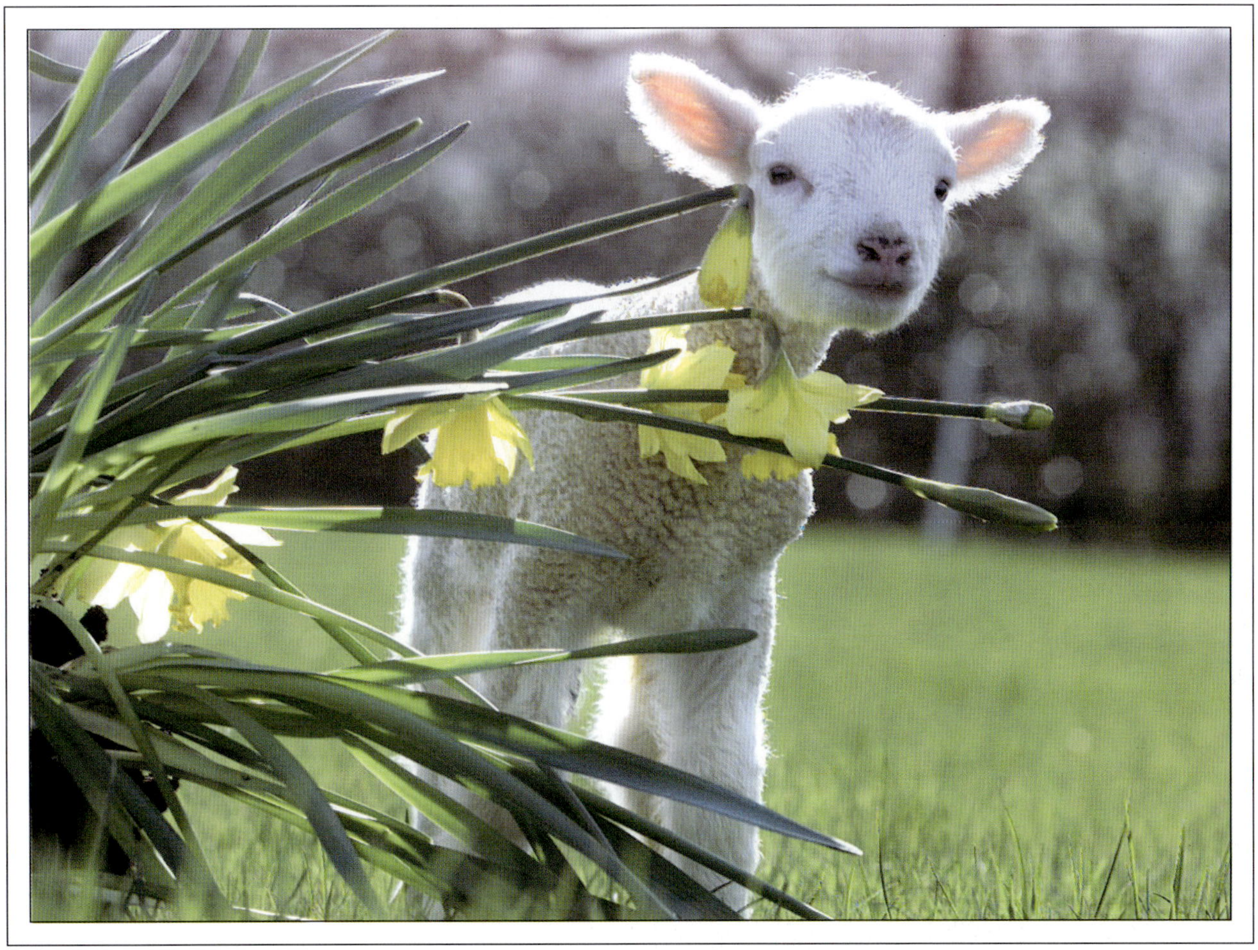

One year after the devastation of foot and mouth disease and what a change from the carnage in the countryside of twelve months before.

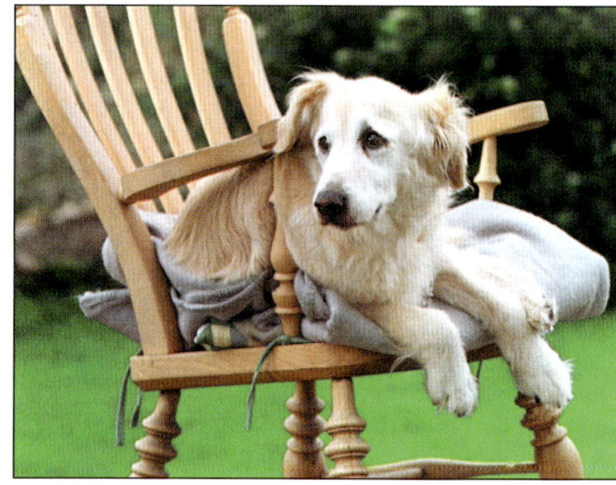

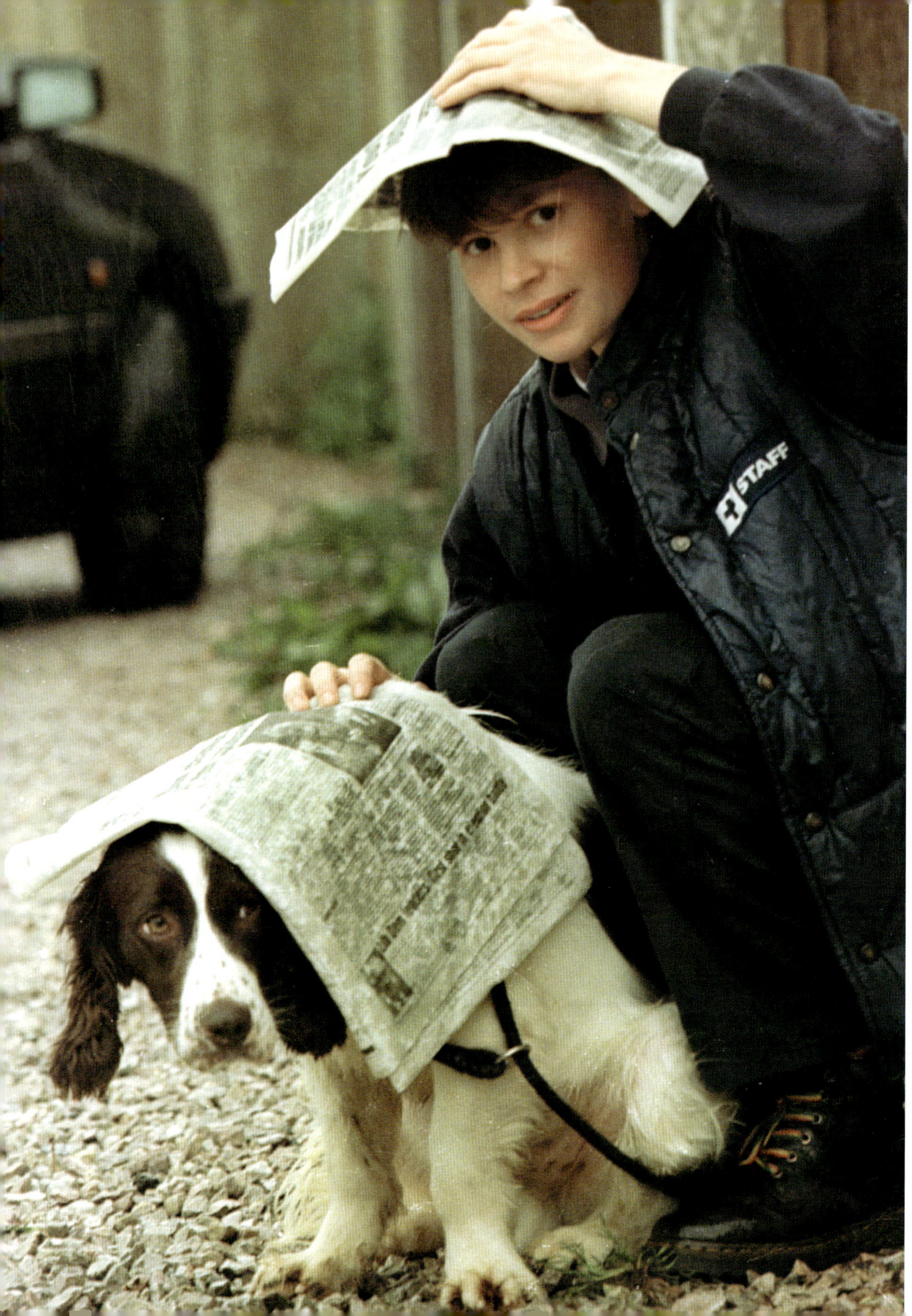


Sheltering from the rain at the Blue Cross Kennels in Bickleigh and taking it easy in the rocking chair in East Devon the Golden Retriever was deaf and a little blind but still had that special bond with his lifetime owner.

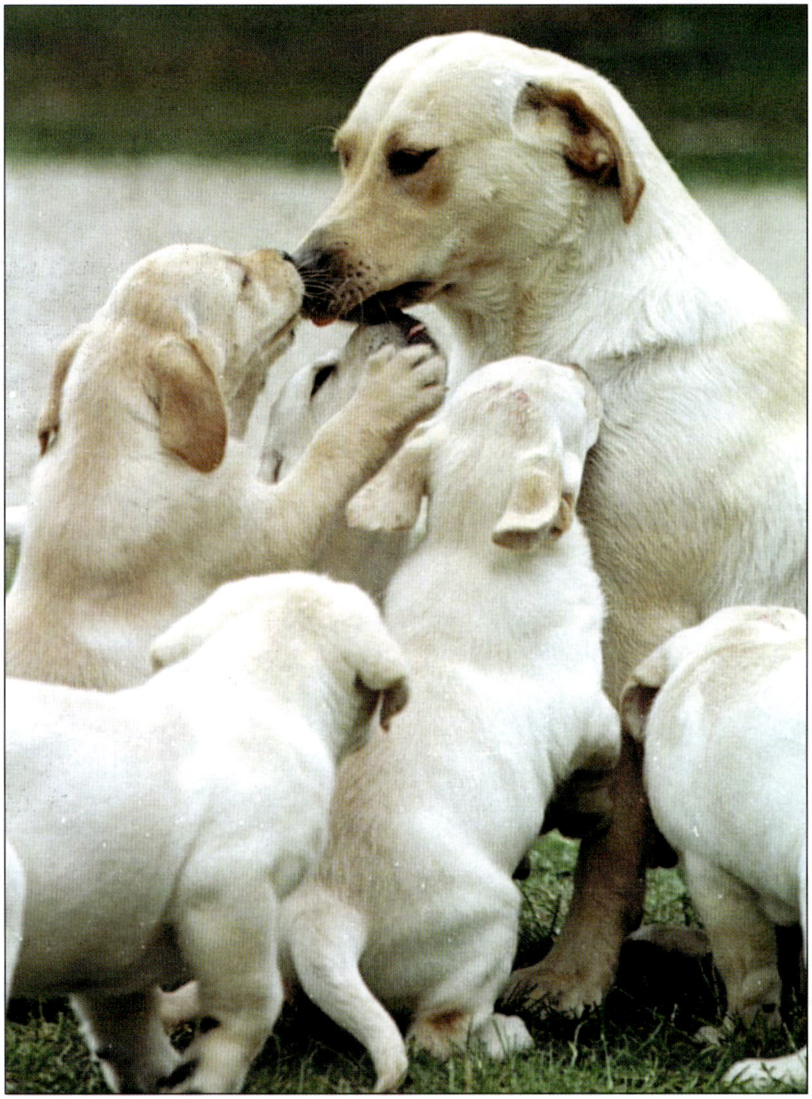

More milk mum – the ever hungry pups demanding that their mother roll over and feed them.

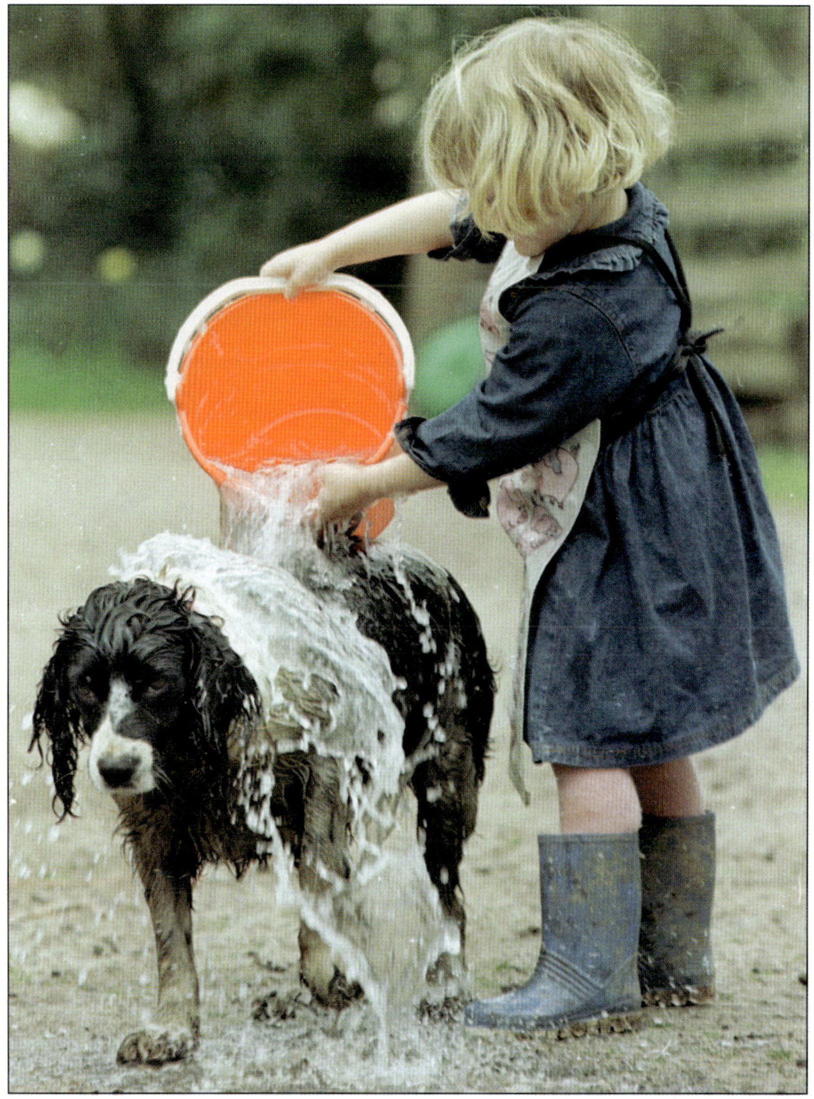

One way or another the family dog had become covered in sump oil and the finger of suspicion was pointing at the twin girls who agreed to give the old boy a soapy bath and promised to keep him away from any naked flames.

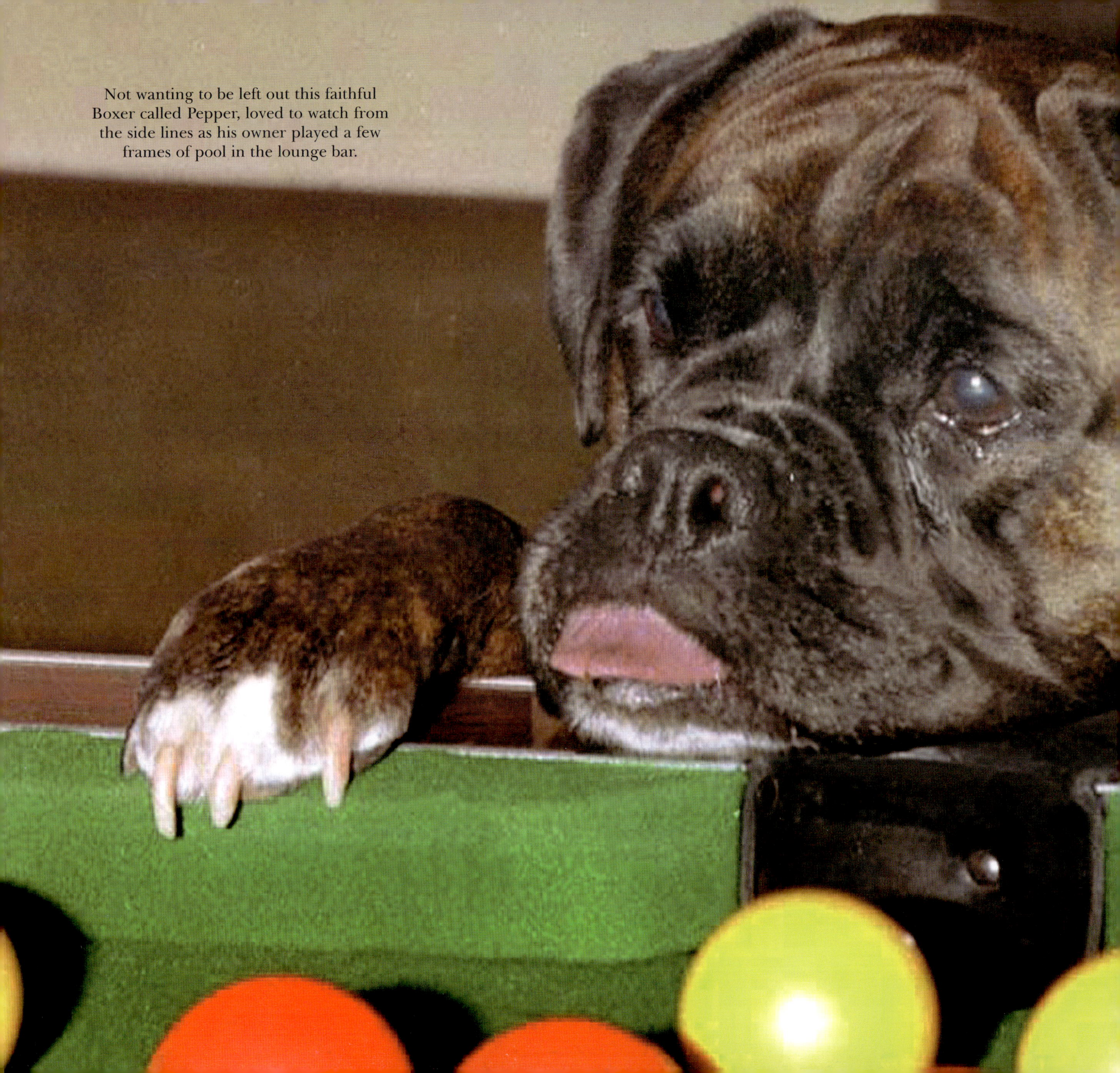

Not wanting to be left out this faithful Boxer called Pepper, loved to watch from the side lines as his owner played a few frames of pool in the lounge bar.

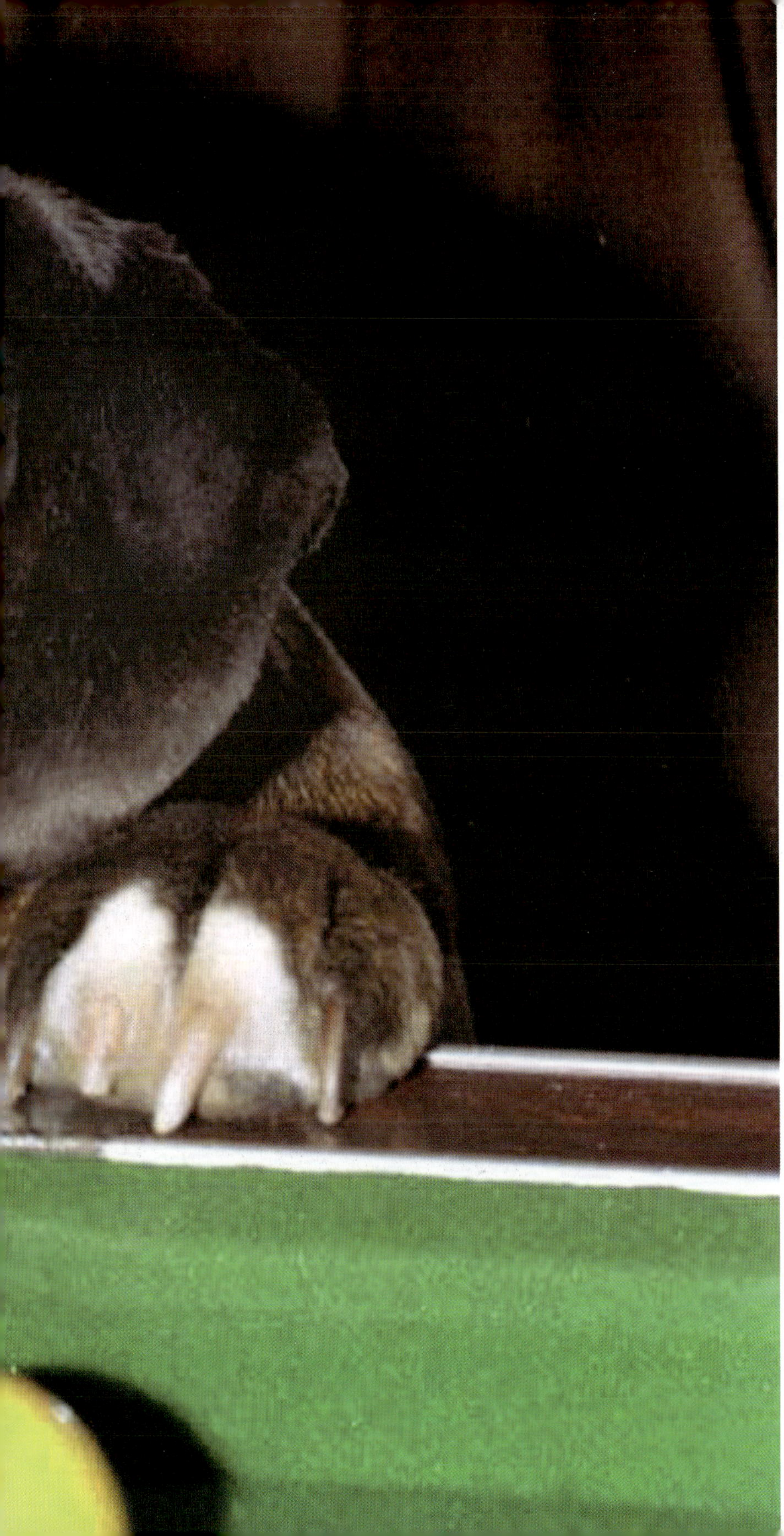

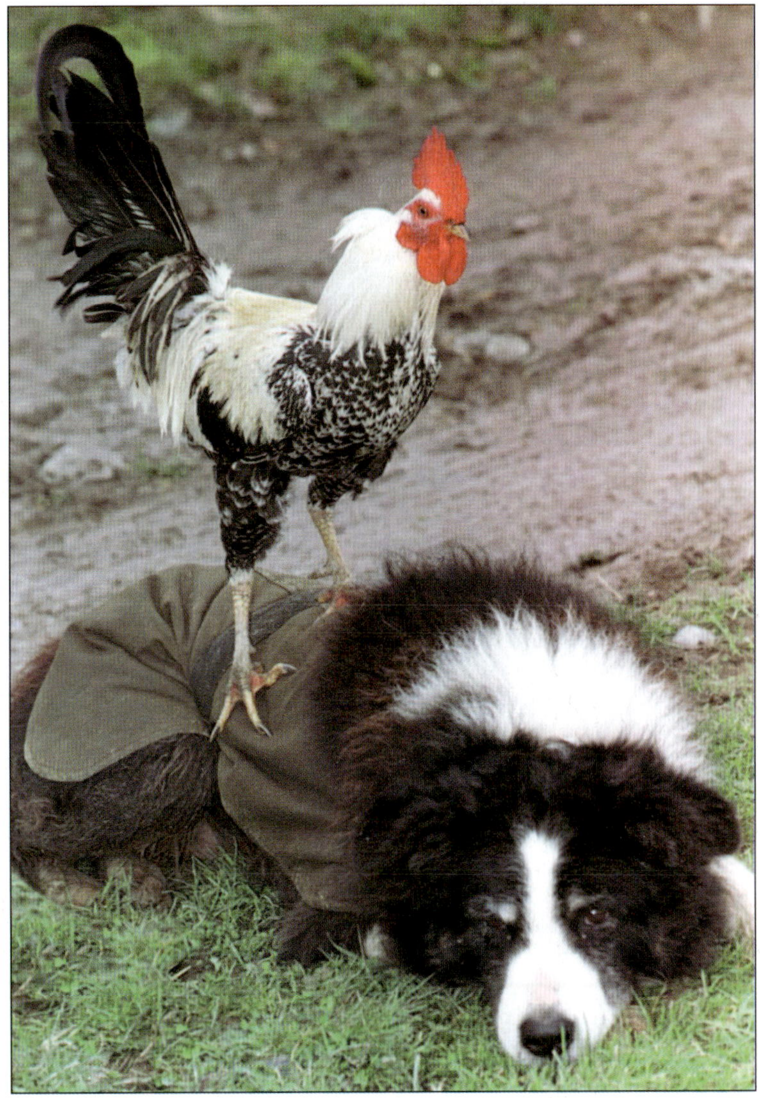

Some Border Collies are used as a doormat.
This tame old bird called Chirpy was inseparable
from the old sheepdog.

Border Collies are as bright as a button and some of them like nothing better than riding on the Grand Western Canal barge horses in Tiverton.

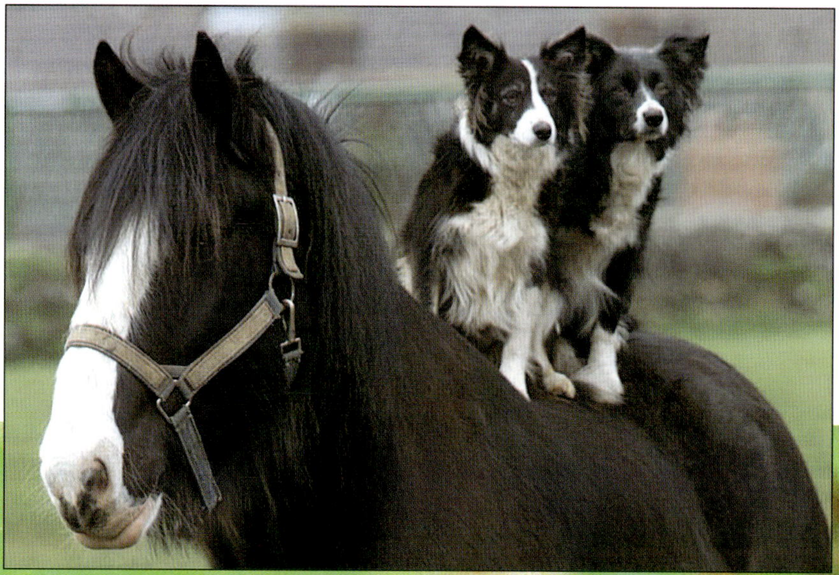

The playful Labrador pup hadn't a clue that his life as a working dog had been decided by his owners, The Guide Dogs for The Blind. Playing in the autumn leaves it was clear to me that he had the perfect temperament.

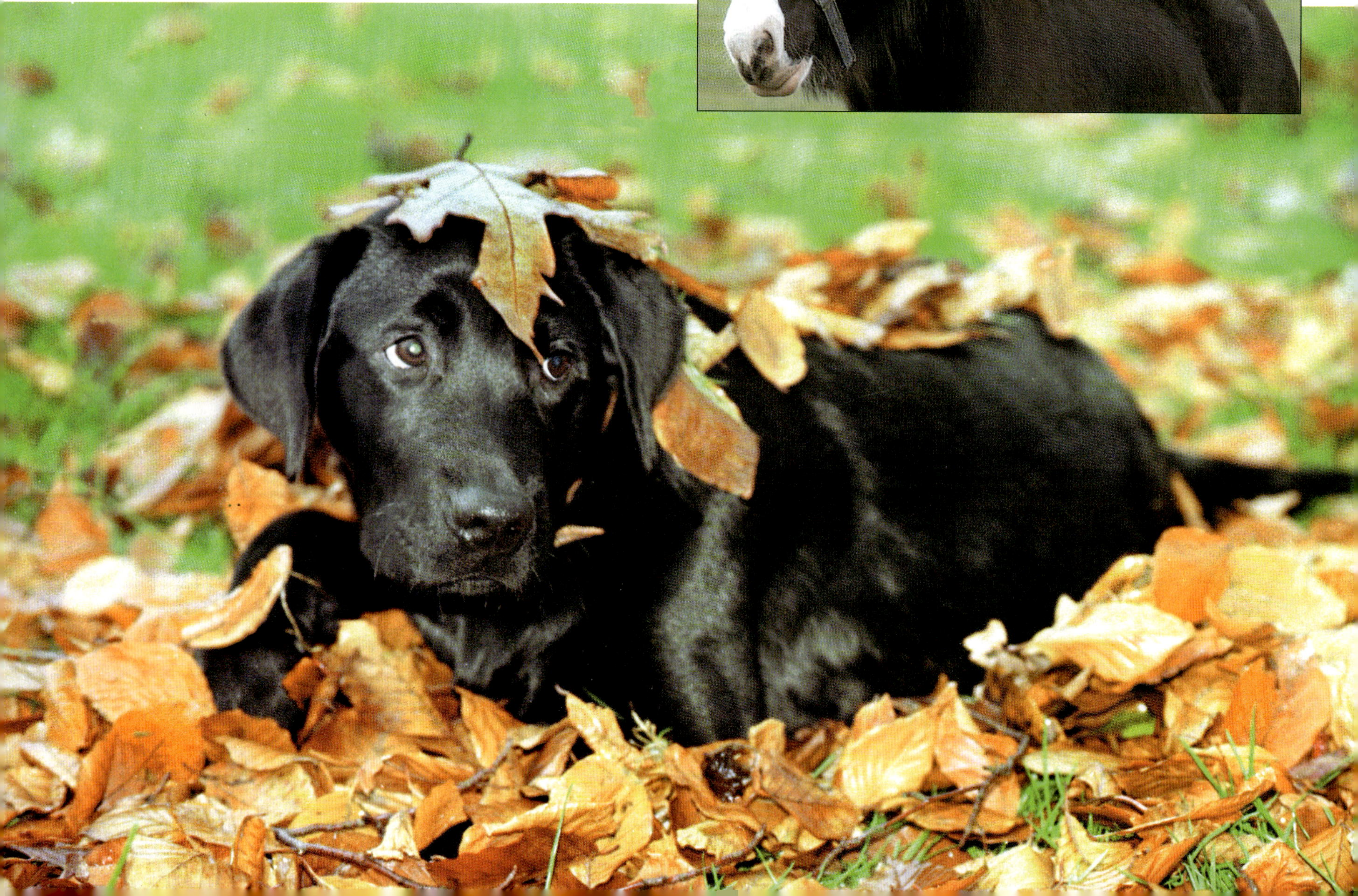

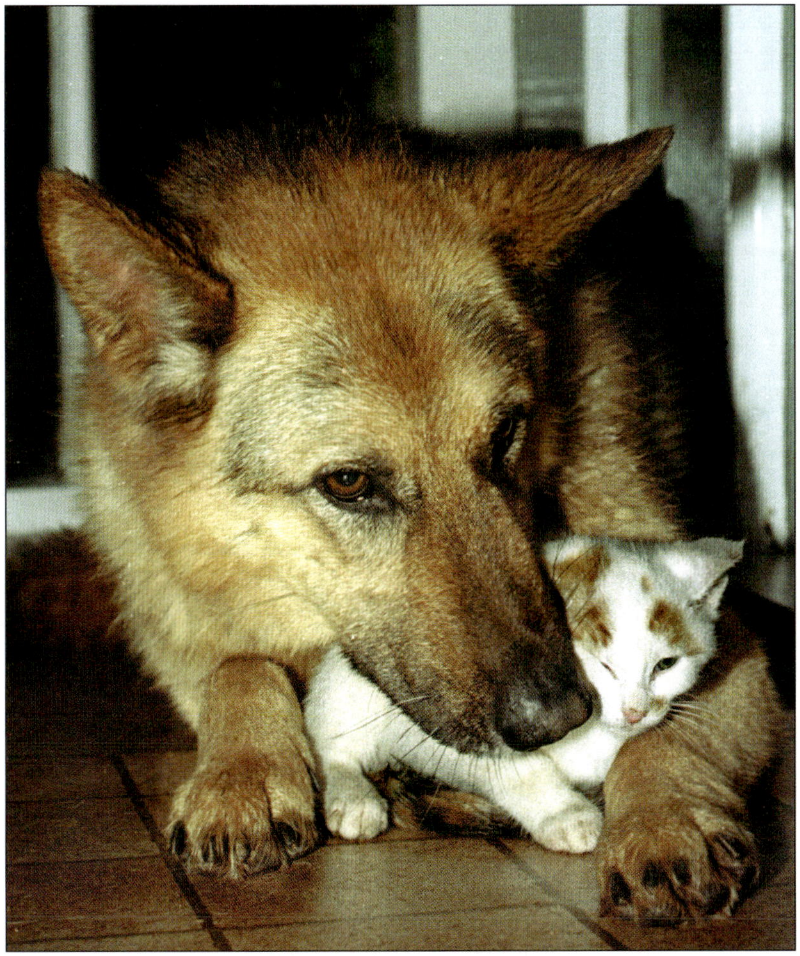

Just a big softie really, the Alsation dog  loved playing with the kittens at a Somerset cat and dog home.

The Harris Hawk perched on the hound dog as part of a display at at Country Game Fair caught my eye, the old dog had seen it all before and took all in his stride.

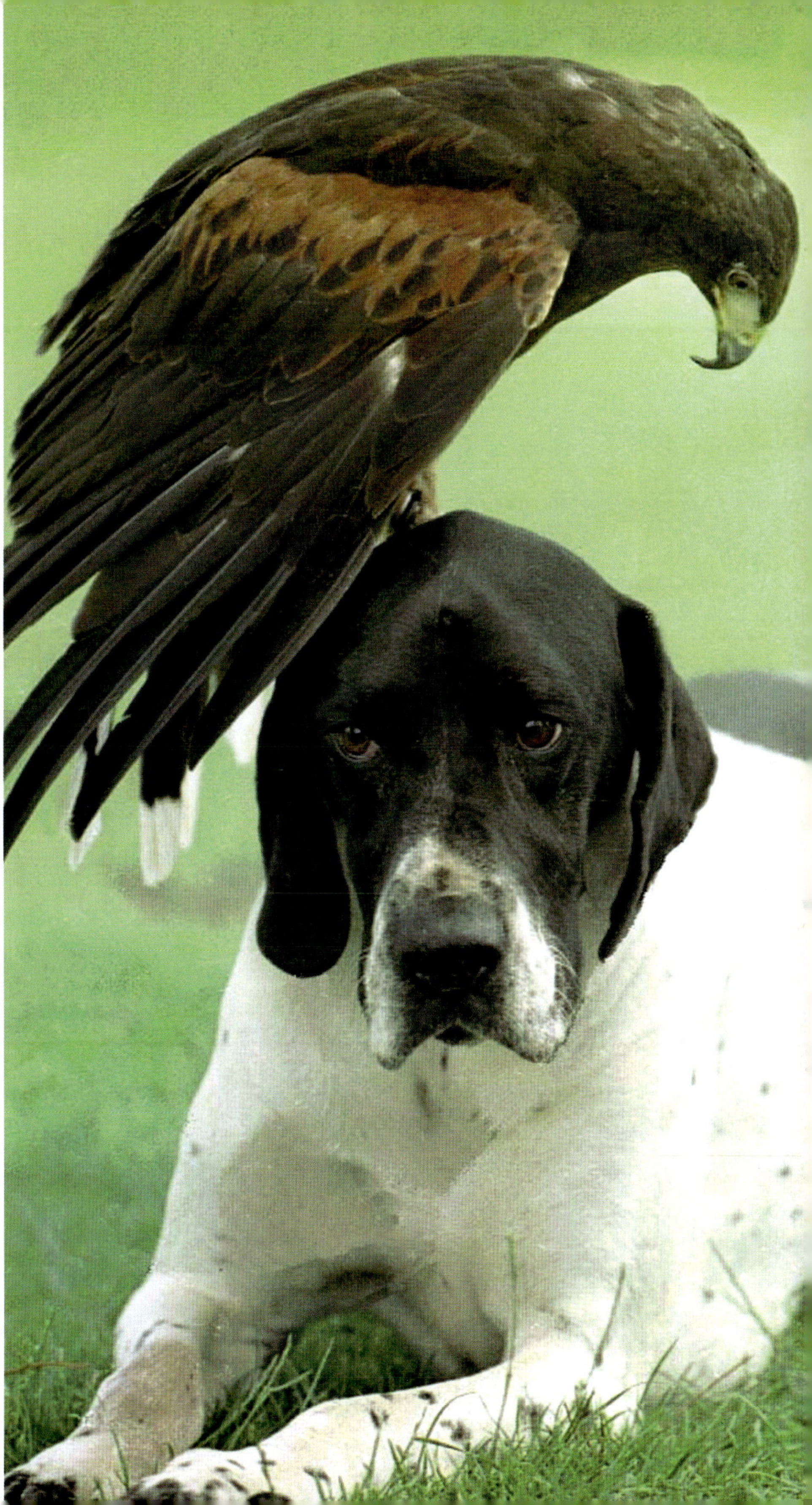

It's always a fascinating occasion when two different animals meet for the first time, the gosling and the ginger tom were sharing the warm spot by the fire when it seemed that the young goose wanted the cat to move out of the way... not a chance.

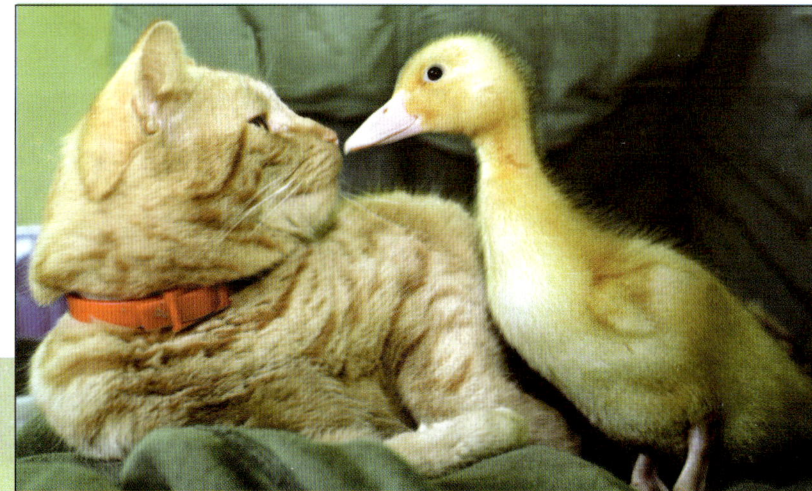

A classic moment when in the animal hospital the kitten met the baby hedgehog for the first time in either of their lives, shortly afterwards the kitten started to get a little playful and pawed the hedgehog, needless to say he didn't do it twice.

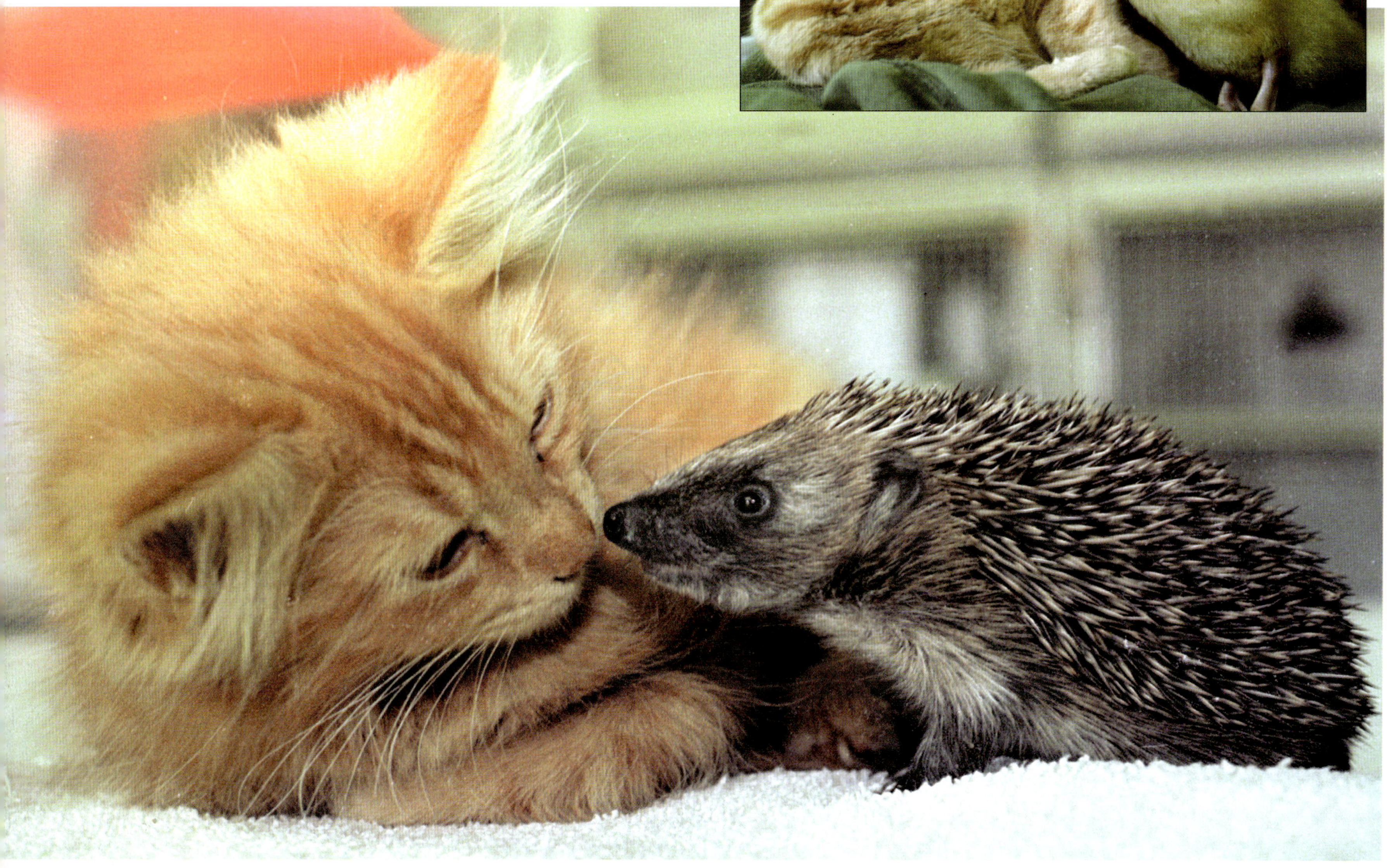

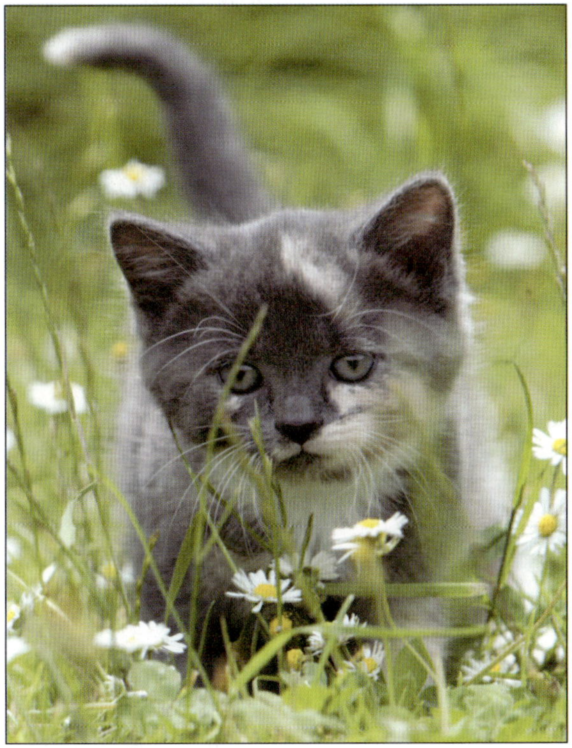

The young cat always on the lookout
for something to stalk in the long grass
as the dandelions tower above him.

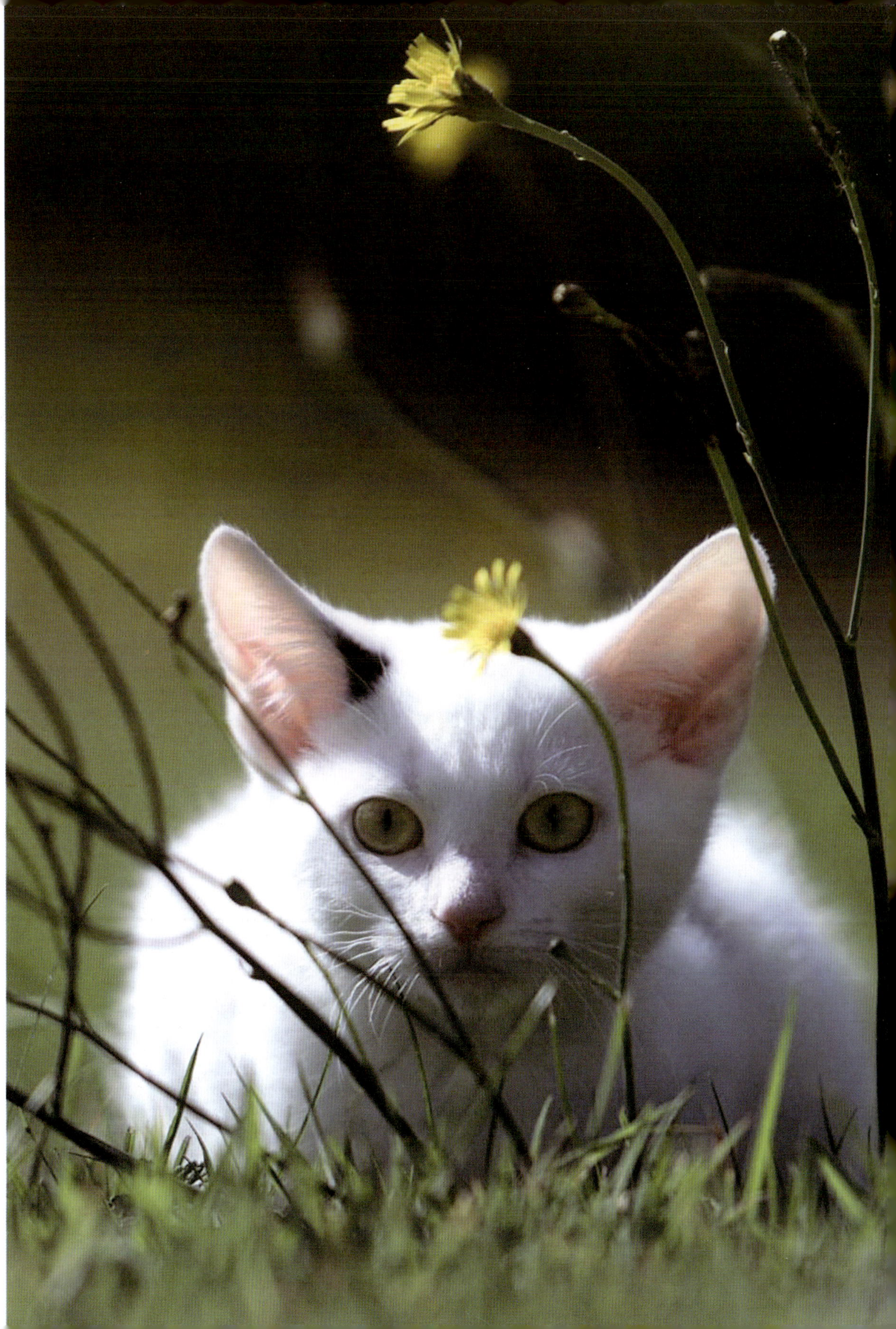

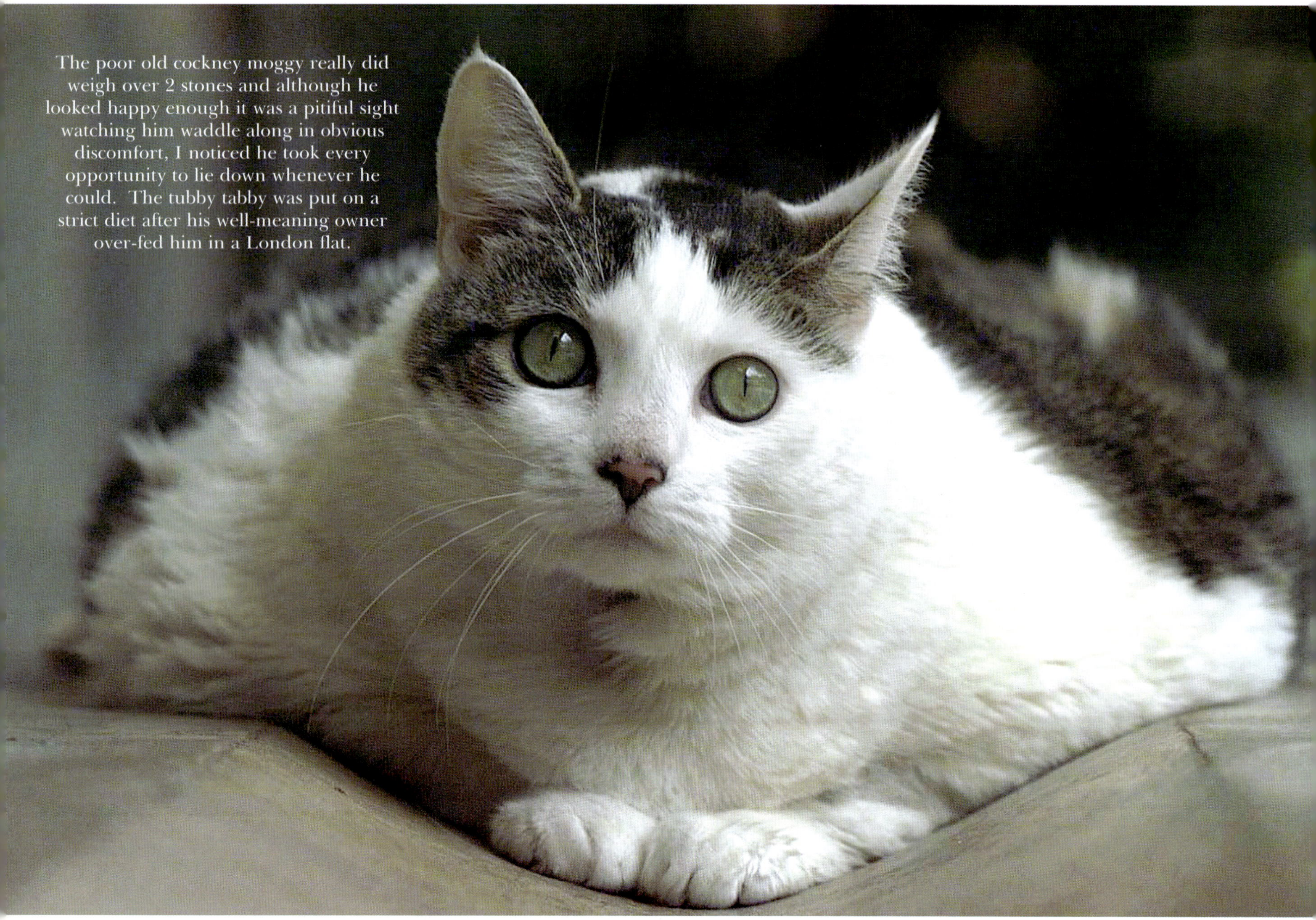

The poor old cockney moggy really did weigh over 2 stones and although he looked happy enough it was a pitiful sight watching him waddle along in obvious discomfort, I noticed he took every opportunity to lie down whenever he could. The tubby tabby was put on a strict diet after his well-meaning owner over-fed him in a London flat.

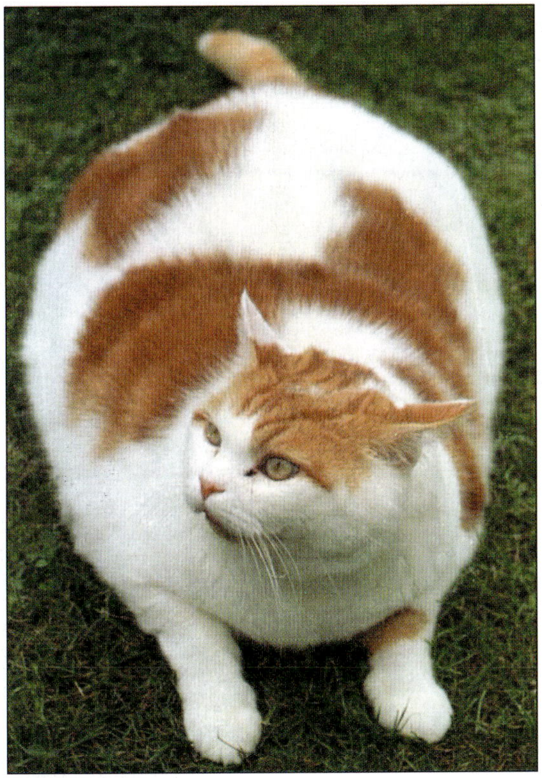

Another fat cat in the county of Devon.

Pups in shoes are perhaps a little old hat but I couldn't resist the picture of the Yorkshire Terrier as he seemed to enjoy himself playing around the old boot.

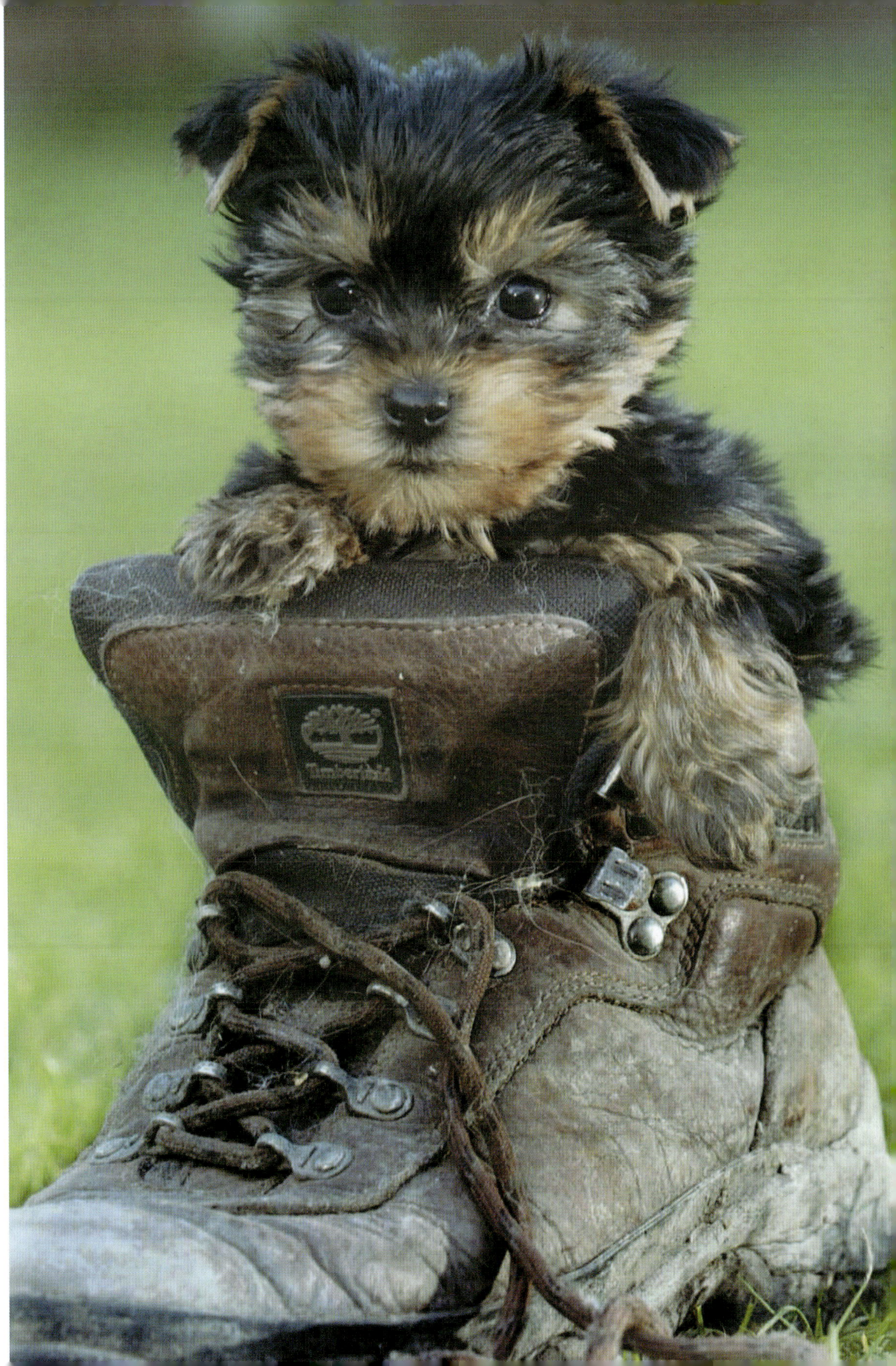

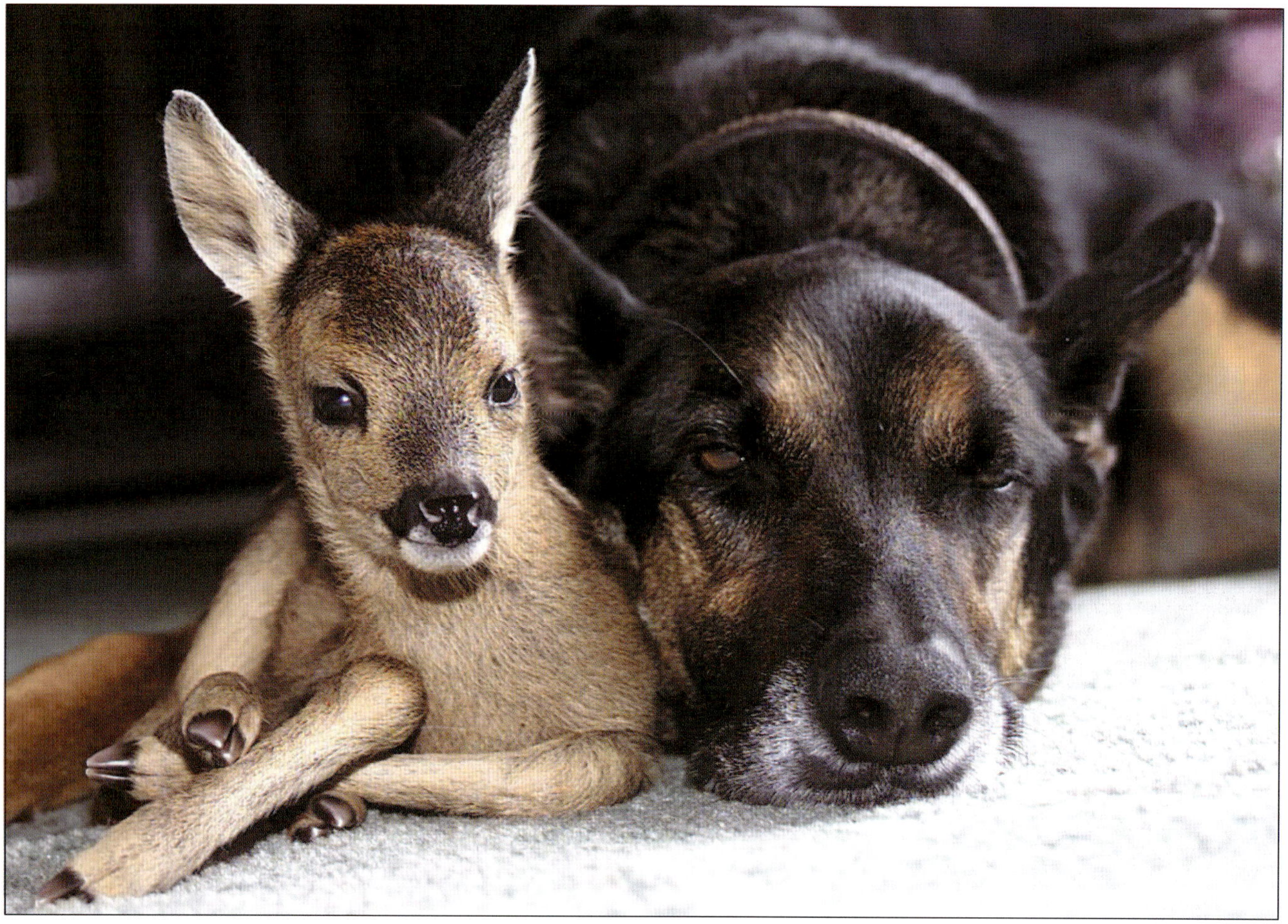

Murray the family dog at Secret World has seen it all before… badgers, foxes, roe deer, lambs, piglets and even a mink are just some of the young orphaned animals he curls up with in his unofficial role as surrogate dad on the odd occasions.

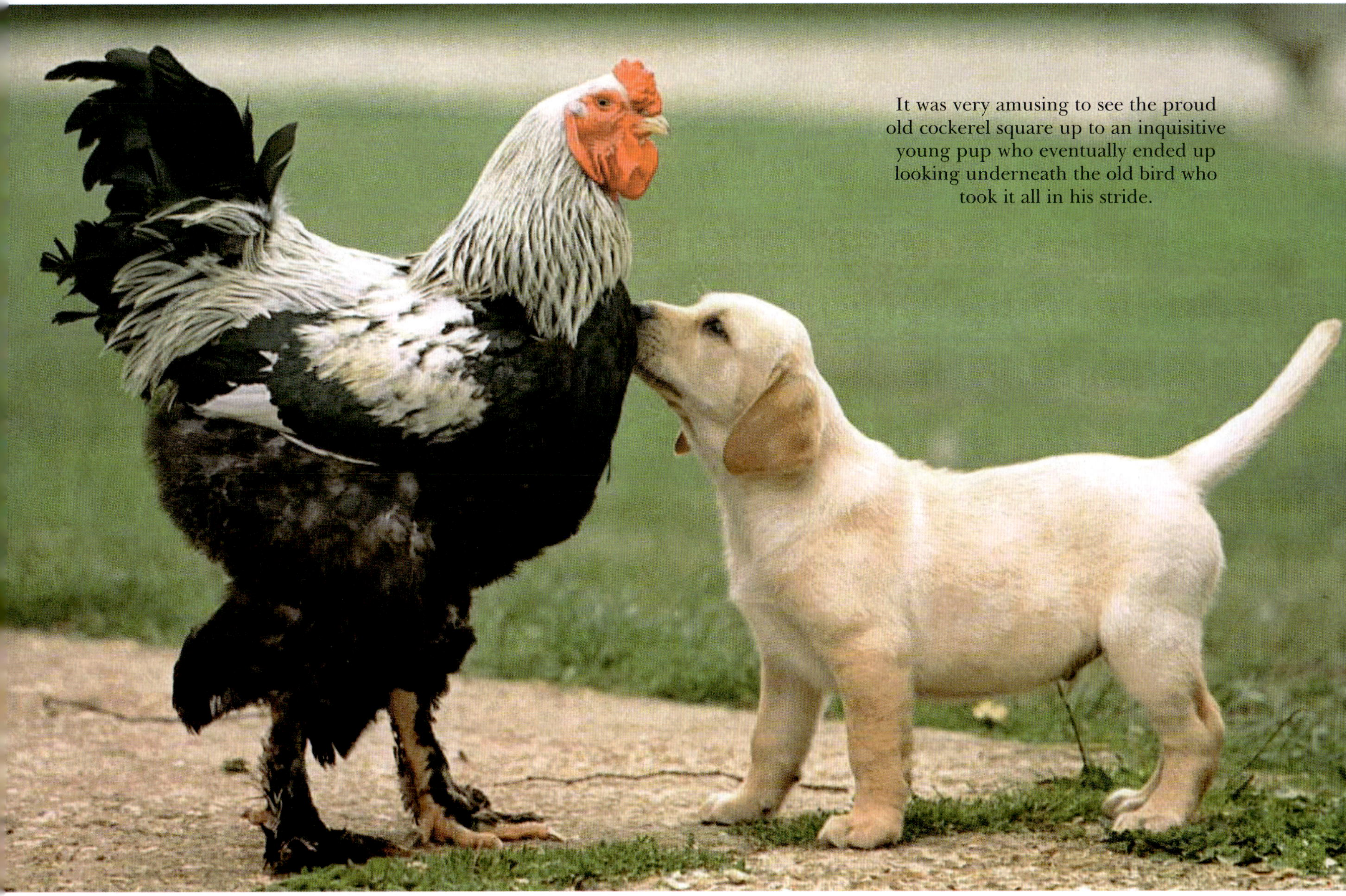

It was very amusing to see the proud old cockerel square up to an inquisitive young pup who eventually ended up looking underneath the old bird who took it all in his stride.

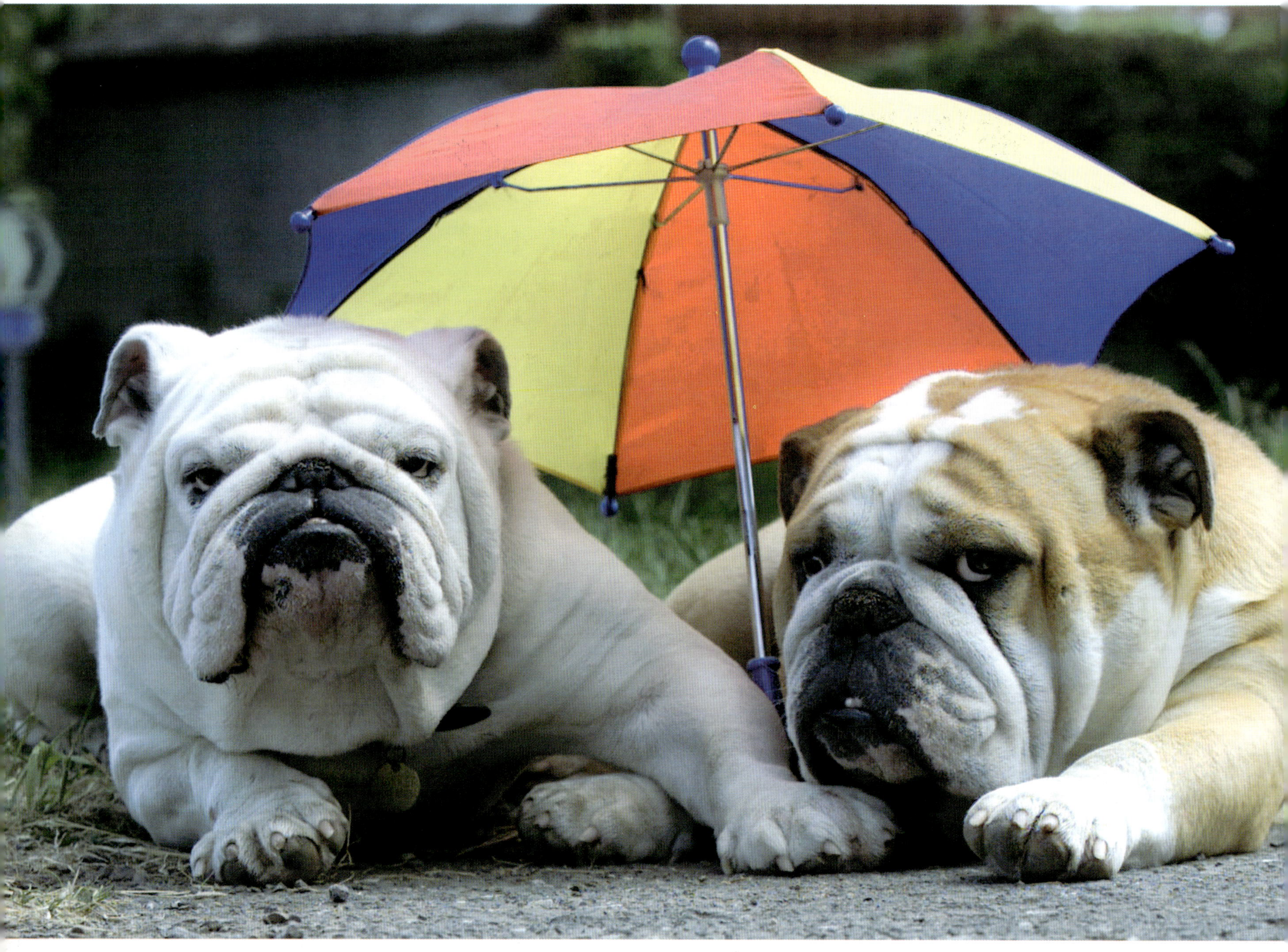

Driving through a North Devon village I spotted the two Bulldogs asleep on the pavement. Keeping them out of the sunshine I lent them my umbrella for the picture and neither of them bothered to get up as I introduced myself.

The story at the time was that the old spaniel had fallen off his first-floor veranda and nearly died from his many injuries. He was a super old dog and the fall had caused a stroke, but he was getting better and trotted towards the camera to prove the point. Sadly his injuries took a hold and a few months later he died.

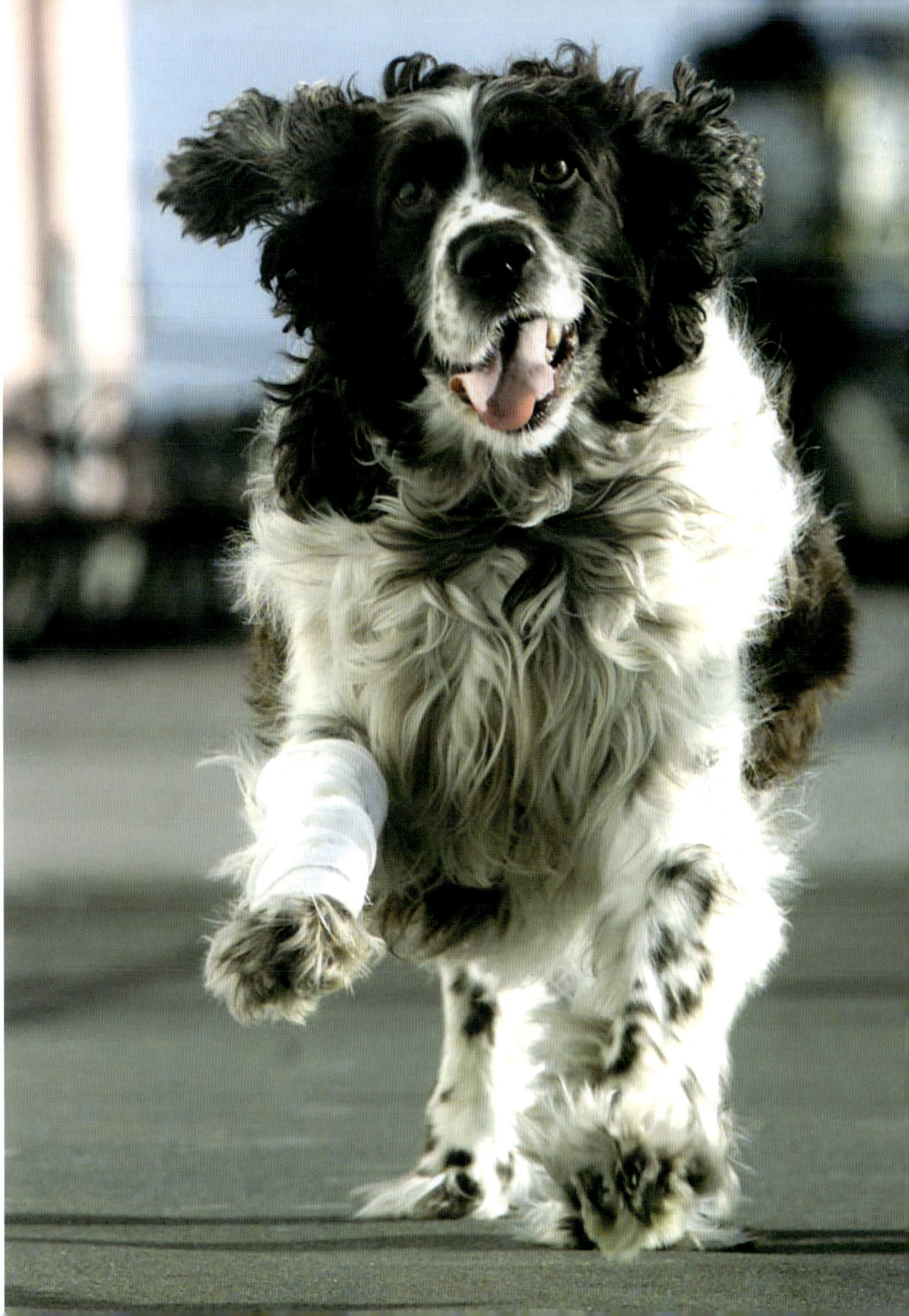

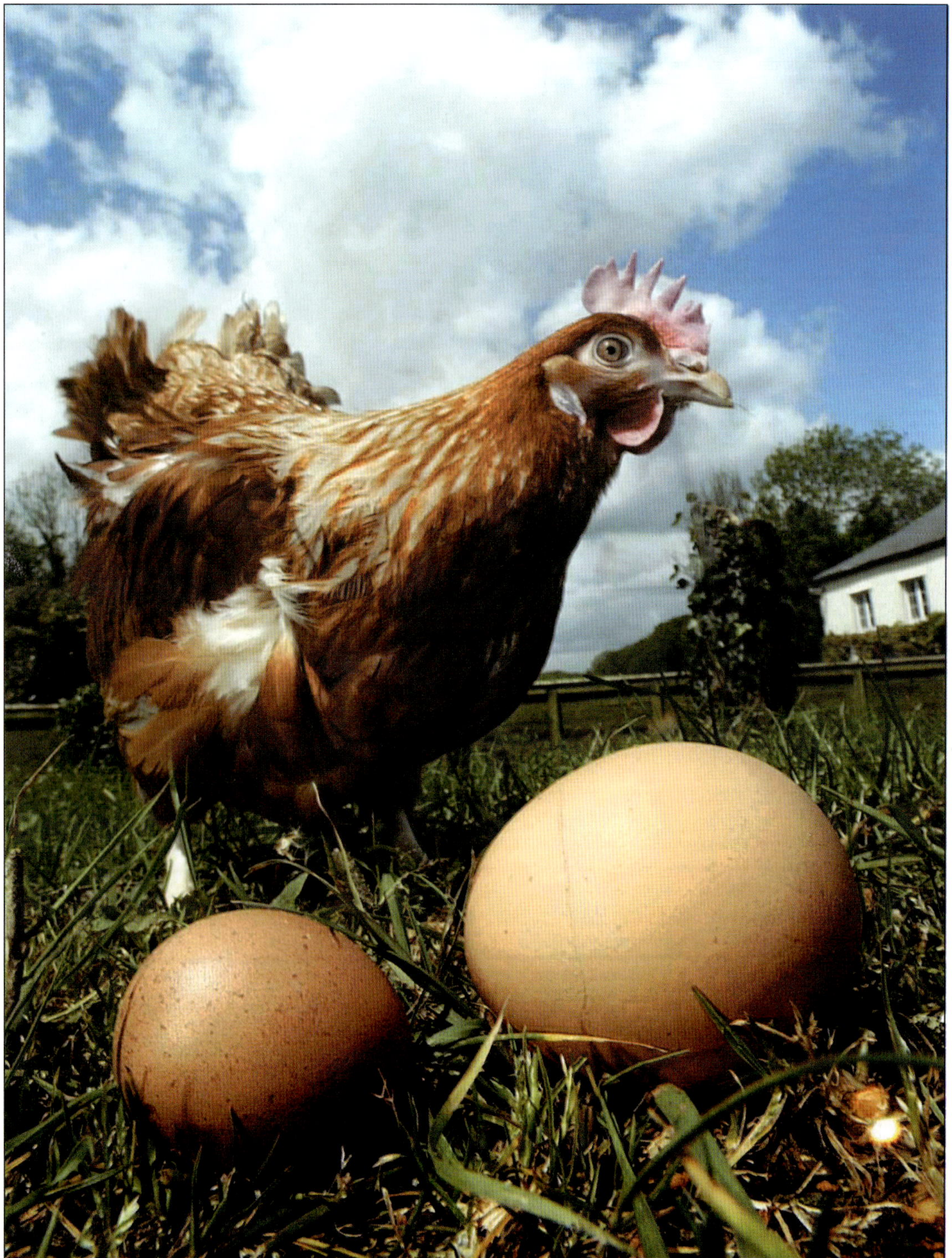

What a whopper, the old hen excelled herself with a double-yoked egg twice the size of her normal eggs.

Three young abandoned fox cubs unsure of themselves in the Somerset meadow all pulling a different face on their last day with humans before total isolation in readiness for an eventual release.

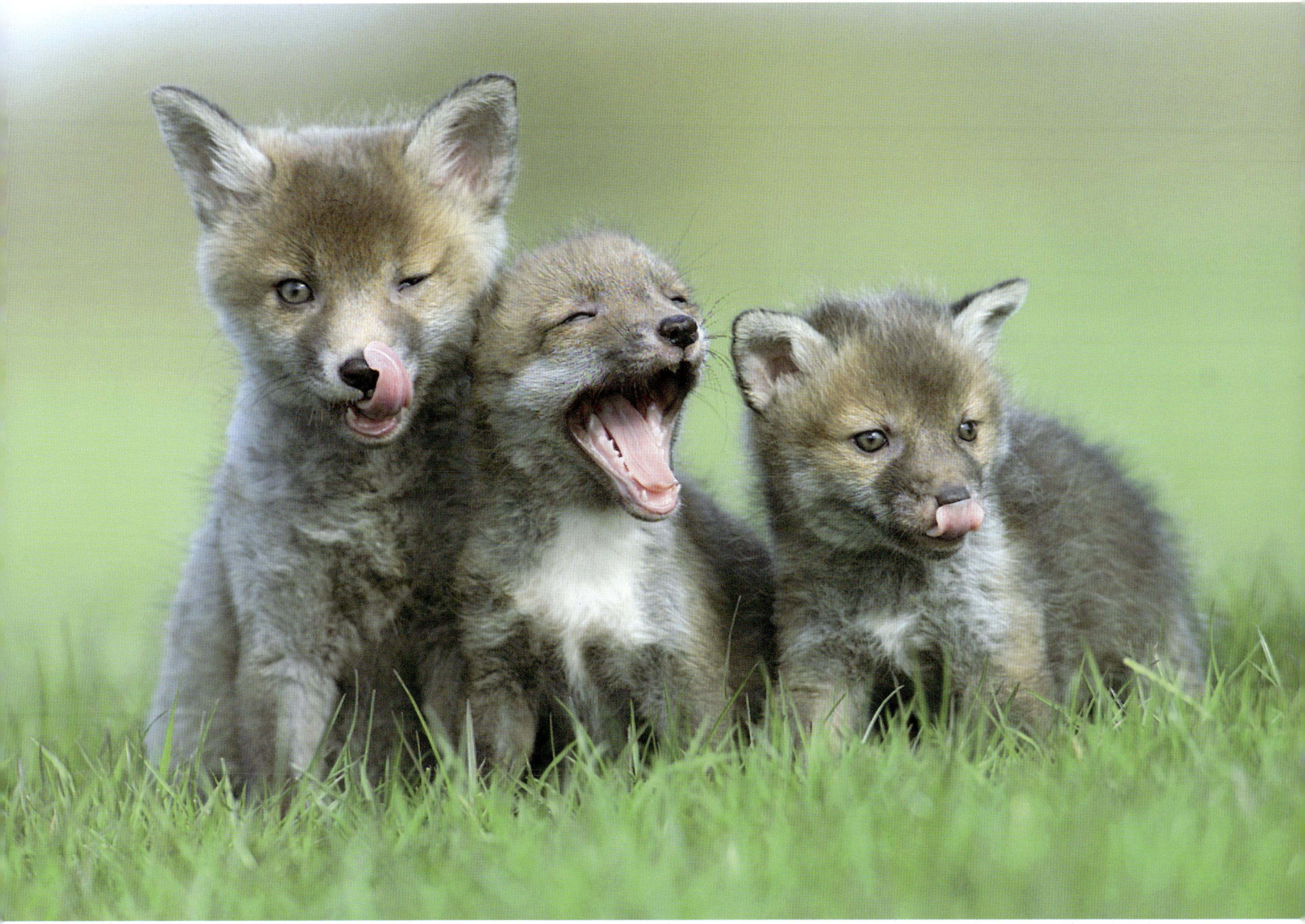

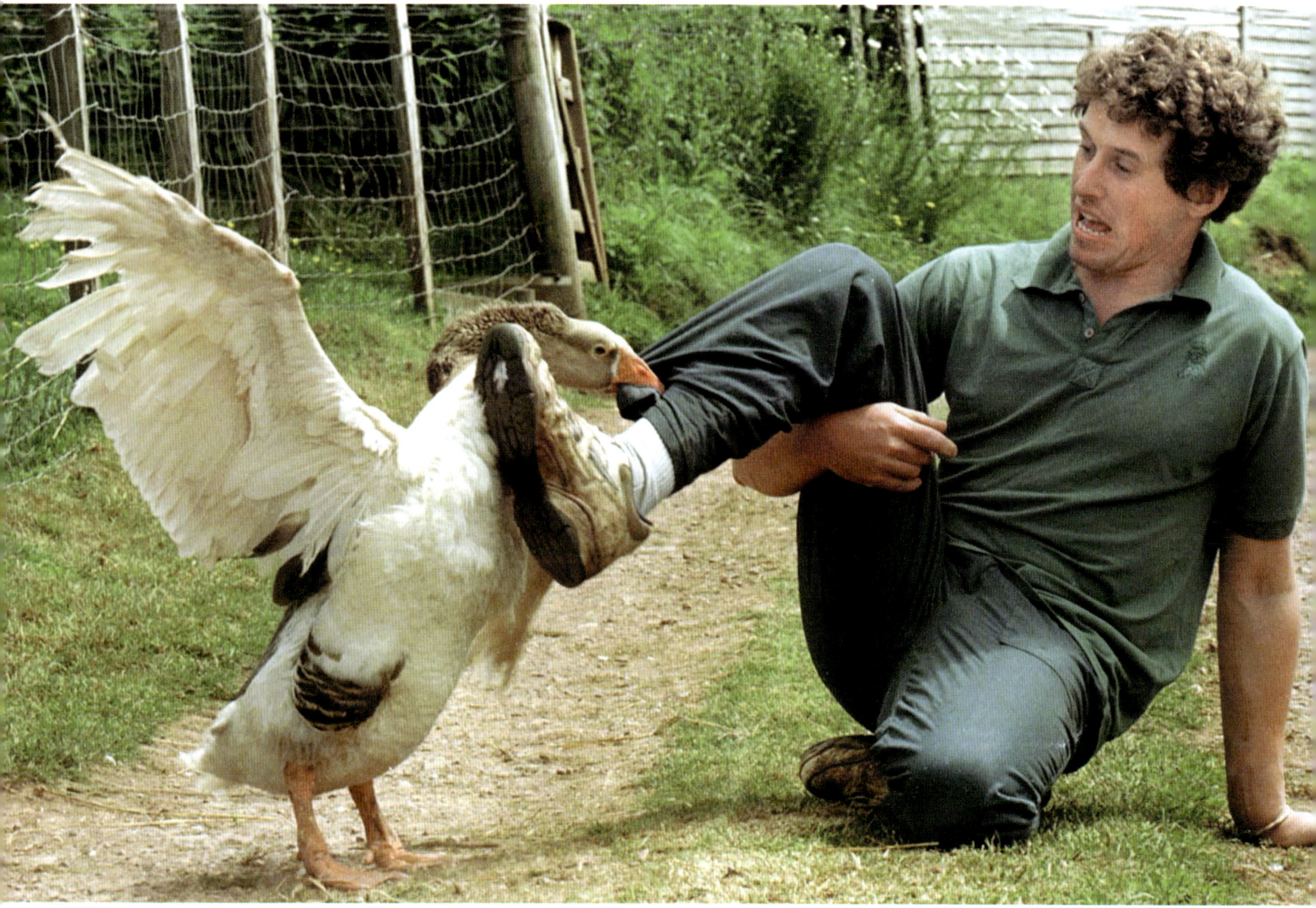

His name was Gazza the ankle-biting gander who loved nothing better than a daily tangle with his owner Simon Boulton in Somerset.

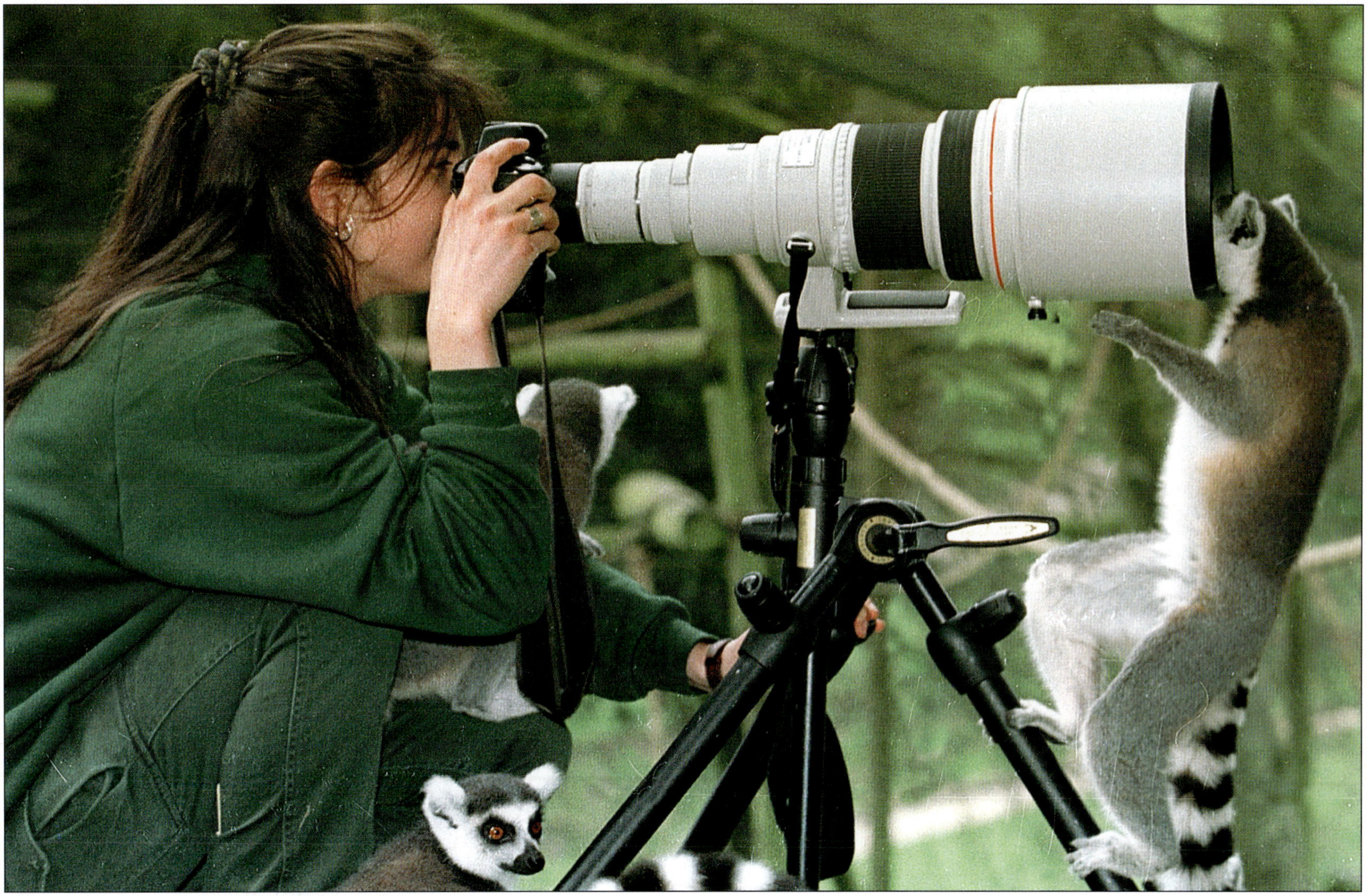

Yes, I admit it, I did hide a small piece of banana inside the lens hood, but it made a good picture.

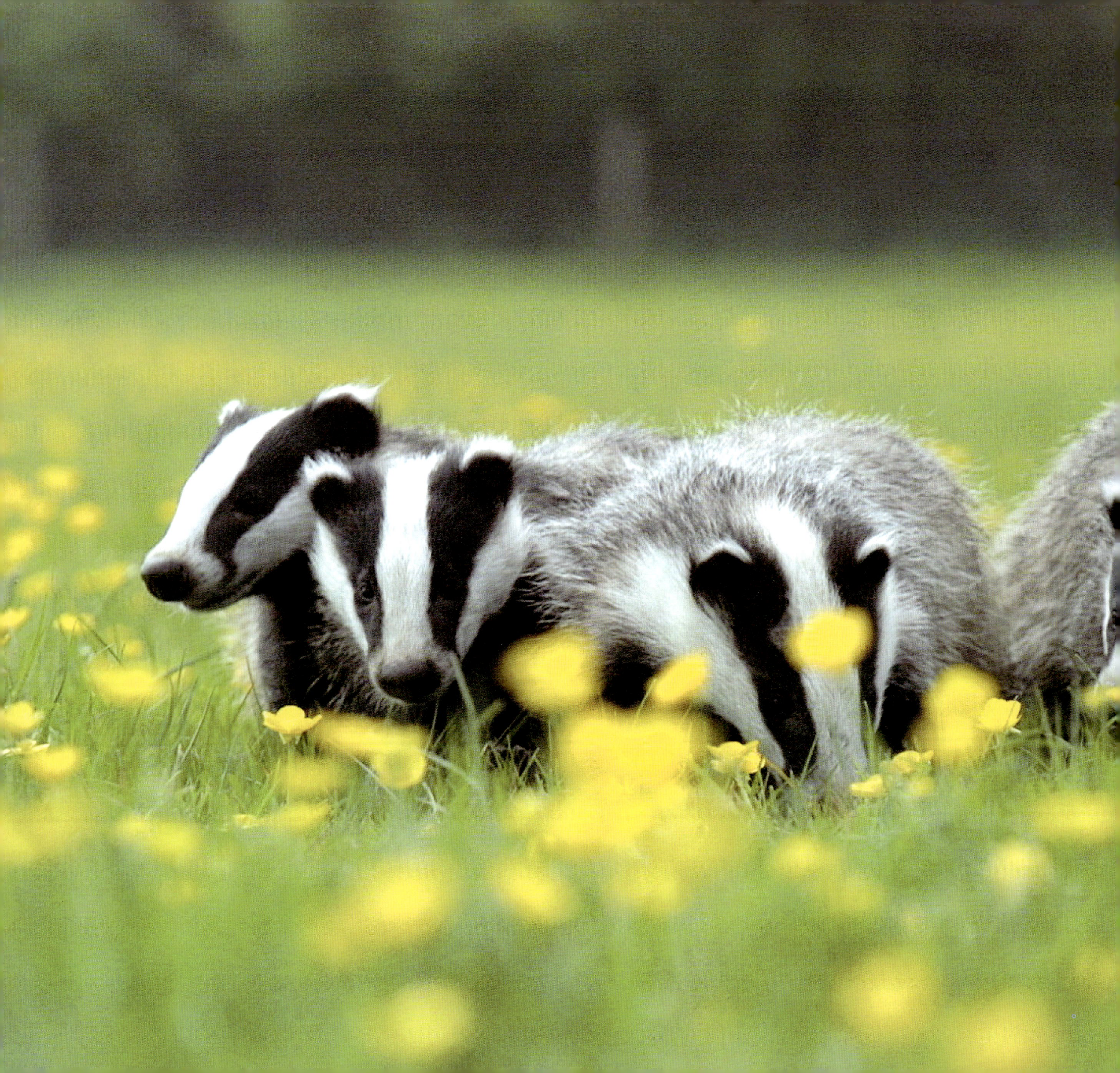

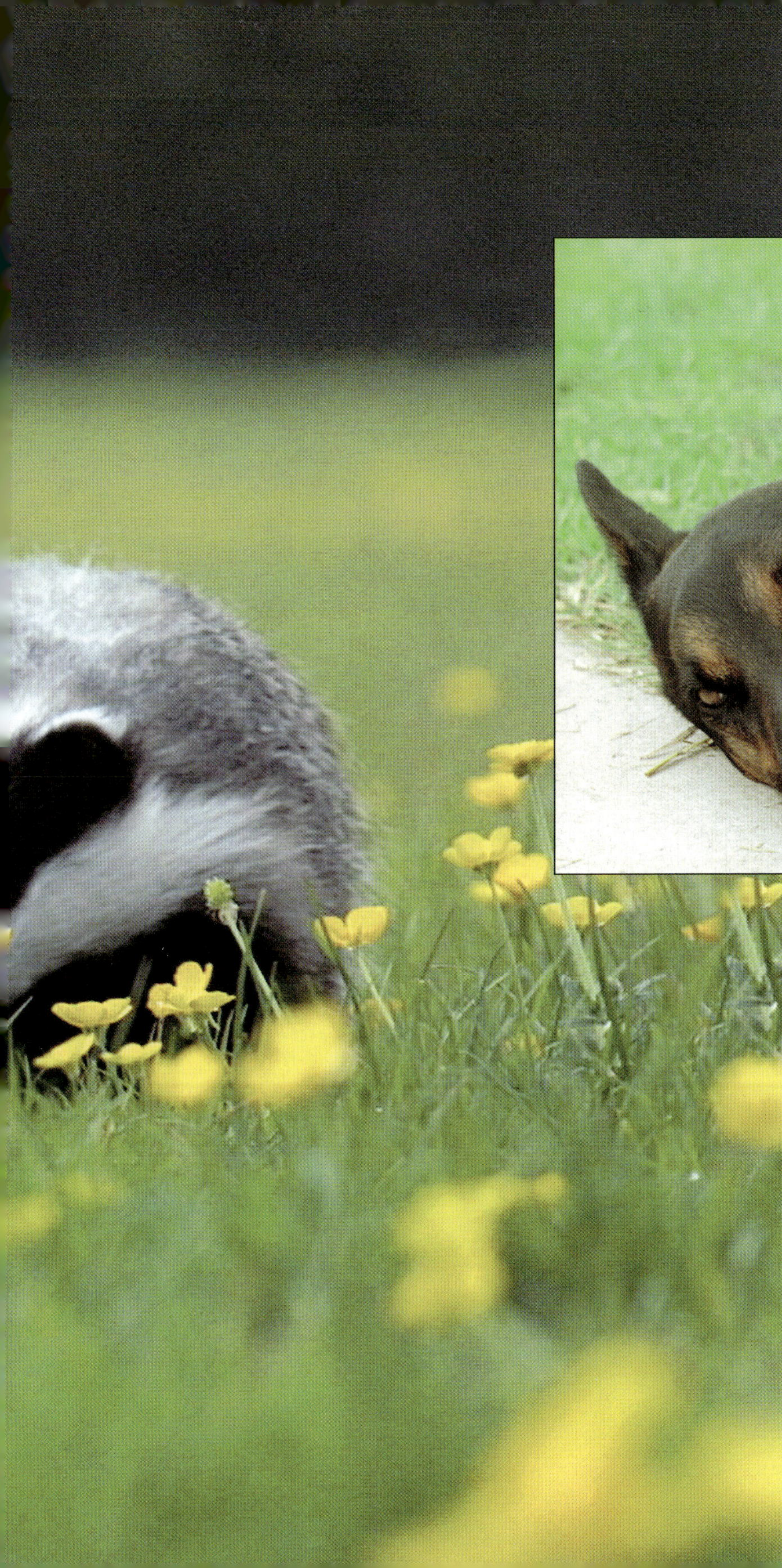

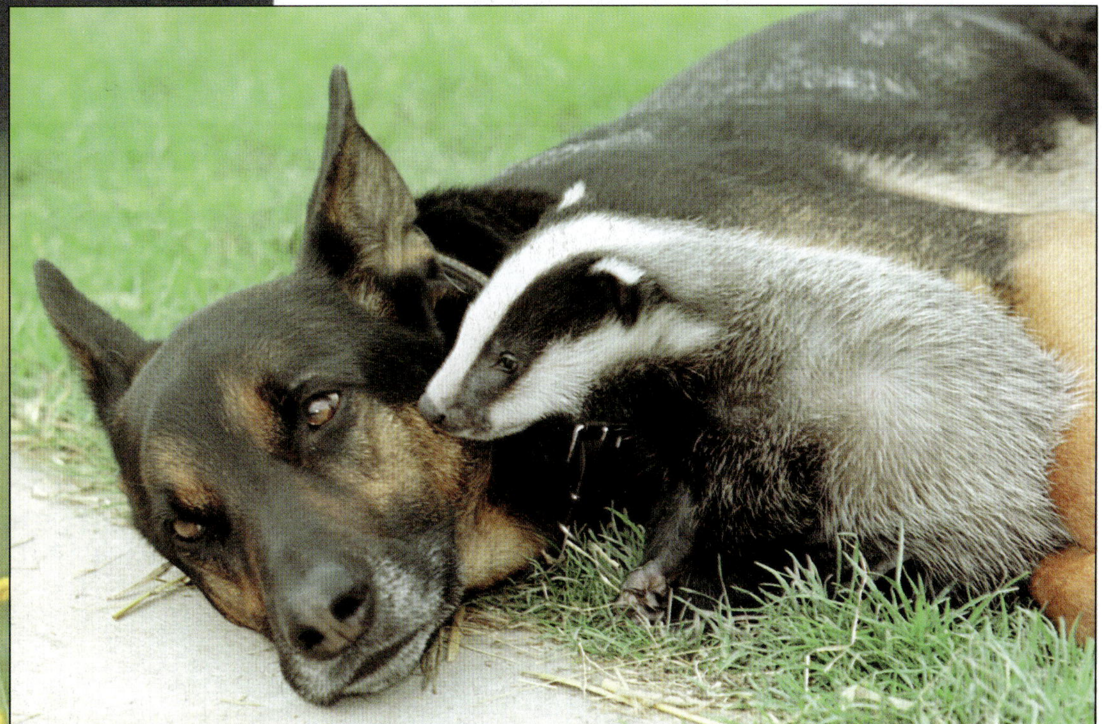

Badgers amongst the buttercups as
Murray the dog looks after the
smallest of the group.

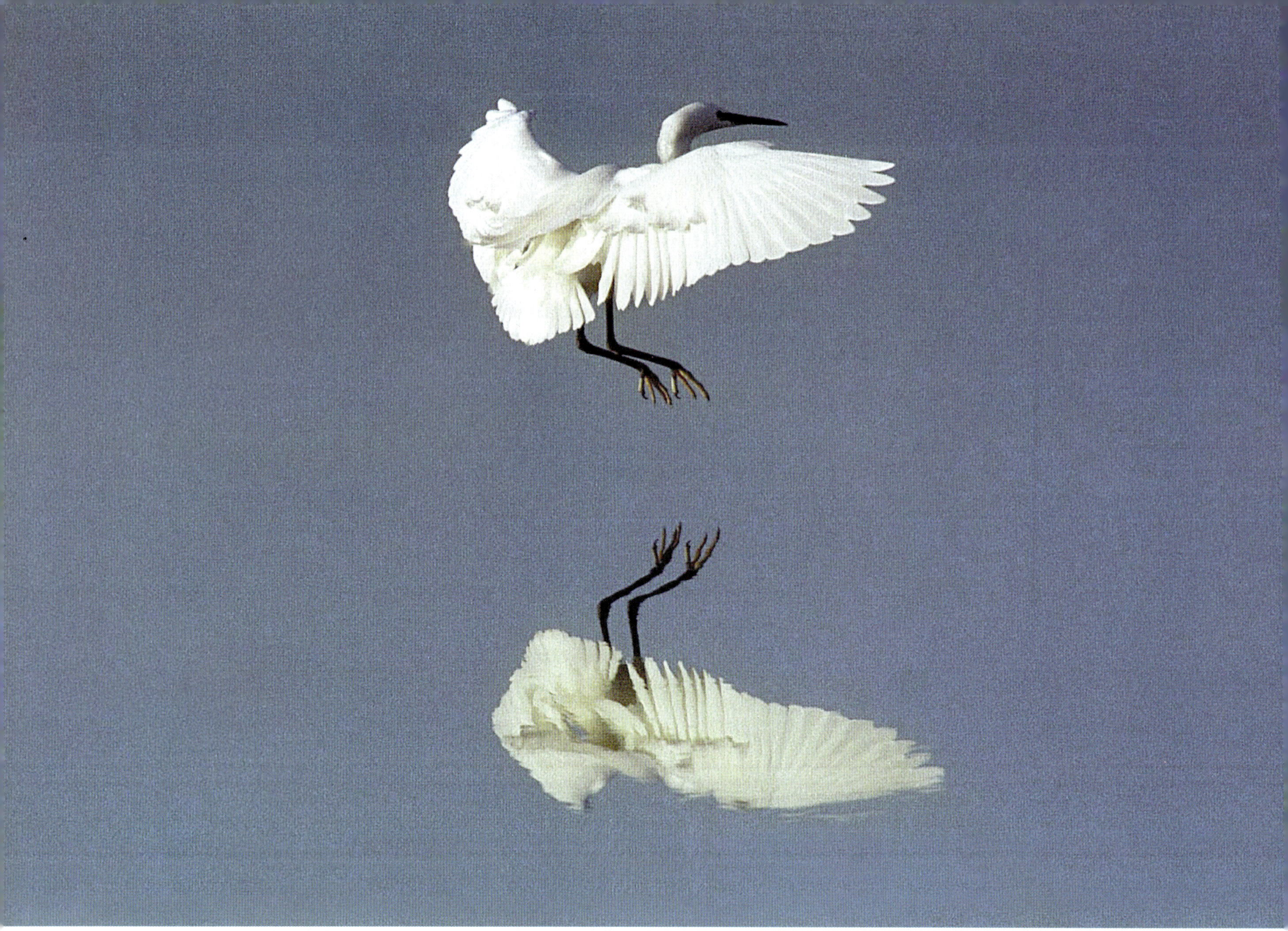

My favourite picture of the Egret taken on the perfectly still River Axe in East Devon. As the Egret waded along the river's edge I purposely disturbed the bird to photograph it in flight, he only flew a few yards and dropped into the water presenting me with the picture.

Little and large of the horse world, the two unlikely friends were inseparable with the Shetland pony possibly the shortest horse in the country, it was amusing to see the Shire horse gently kick his little friend in the backside to make him move forward.

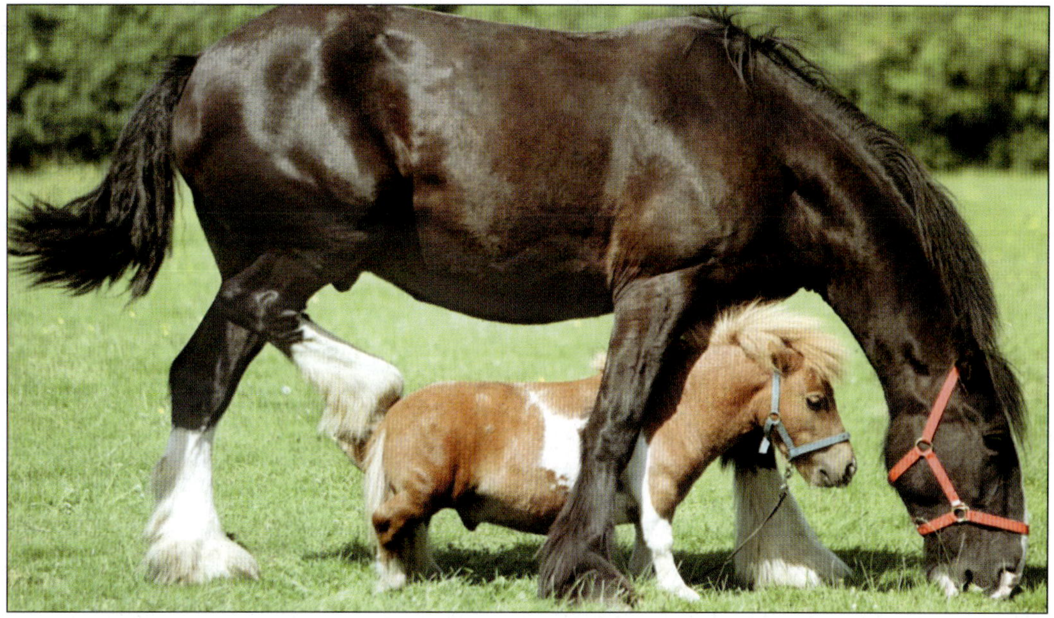

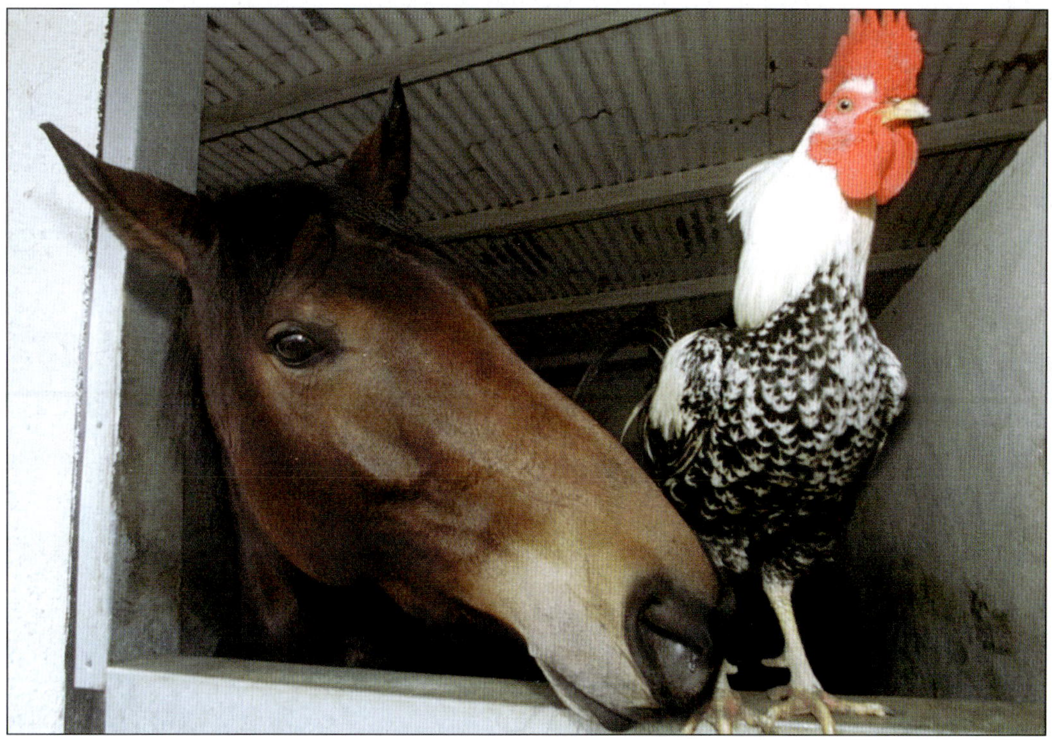

Chirpy the cockerel is not fussy with whom he spends the night, his favourite trick in the cold winter nights was to roost on the back of the lovely warm horse.

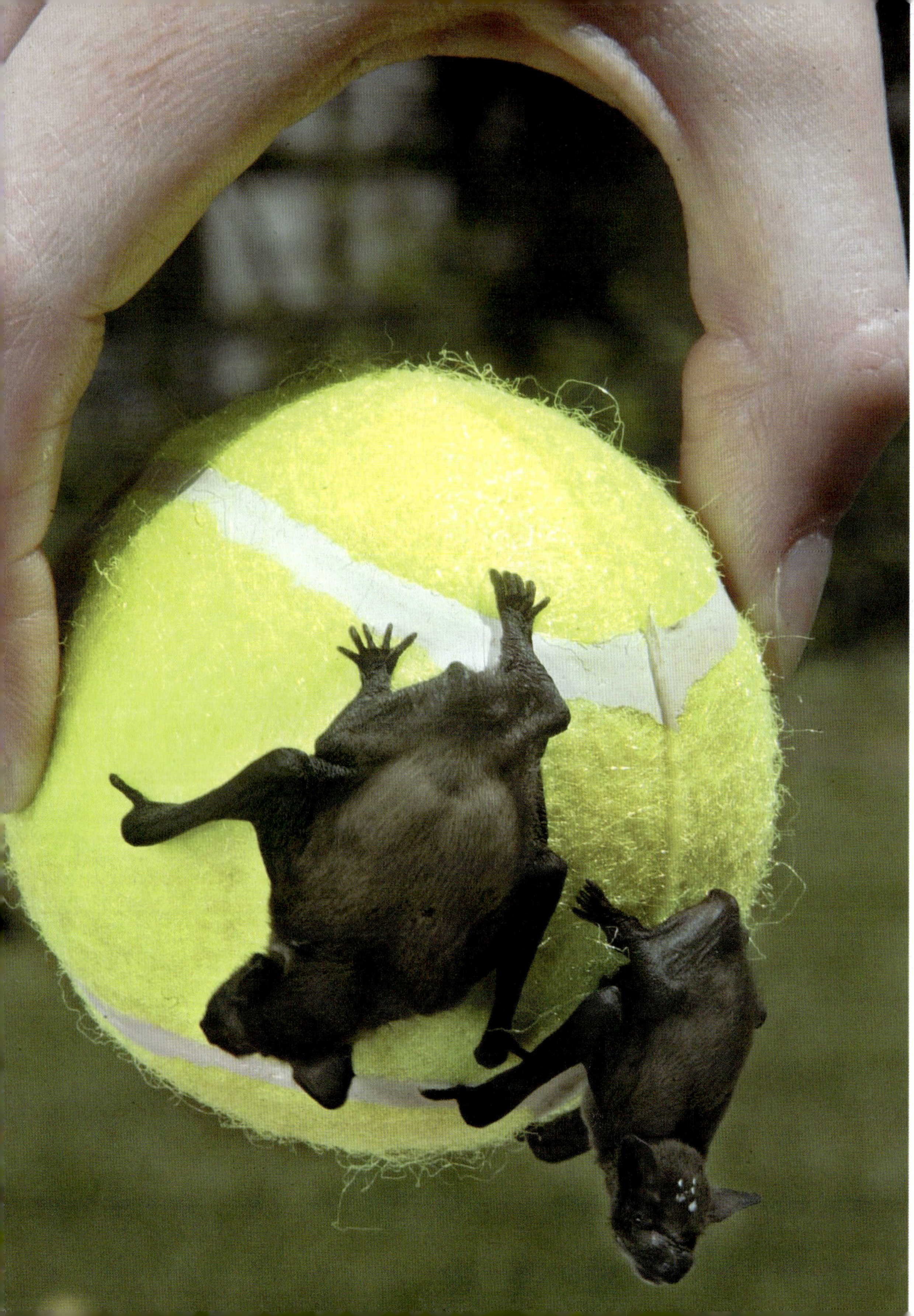

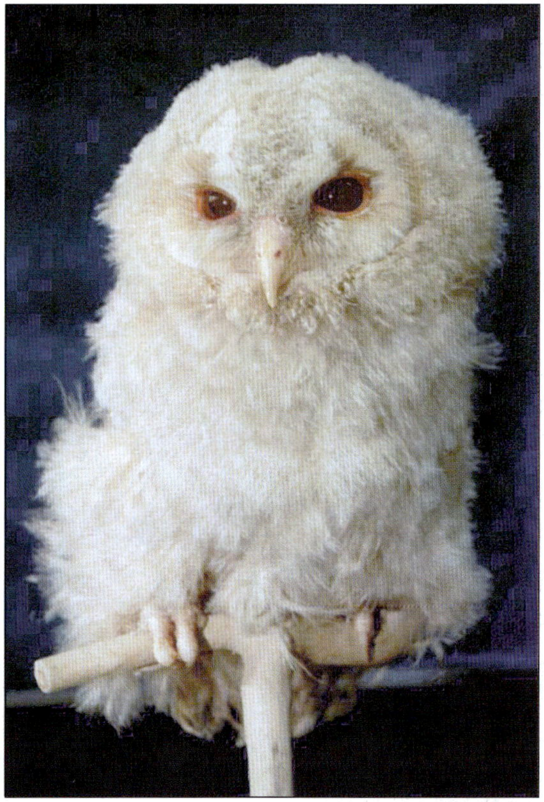

Albinos are rare in any species, so the bundle of almost white fluff with red eyes who was in fact a Tawny Owl made quite a number of newspapers as the story spread far and wide.

A tennis ball turned out to be the ideal fabric for baby Pipistrelle bats to cling to during Wimbledon week and highlighted the work done by Secret World Wildlife Sanctuary in Somerset.

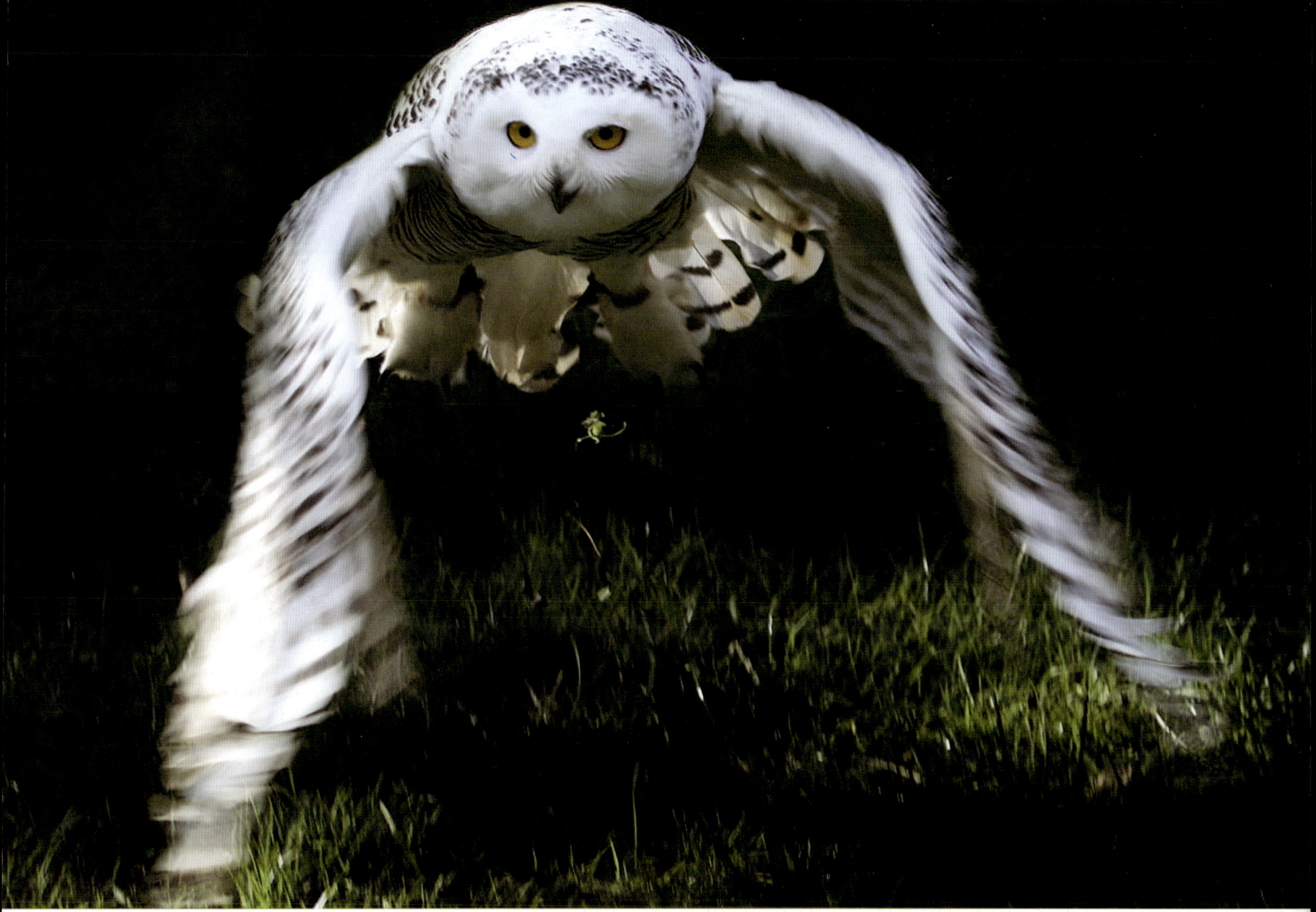

Harry Potter books created a new public interest in owls, especially Snowy Owls and I must admit that I hadn't paid particular attention to this beautiful bird of prey until I came across this female at Saker Falconry. One of the most noticeable features of the owl for me was the length of the bird's wings and the size of its talons.

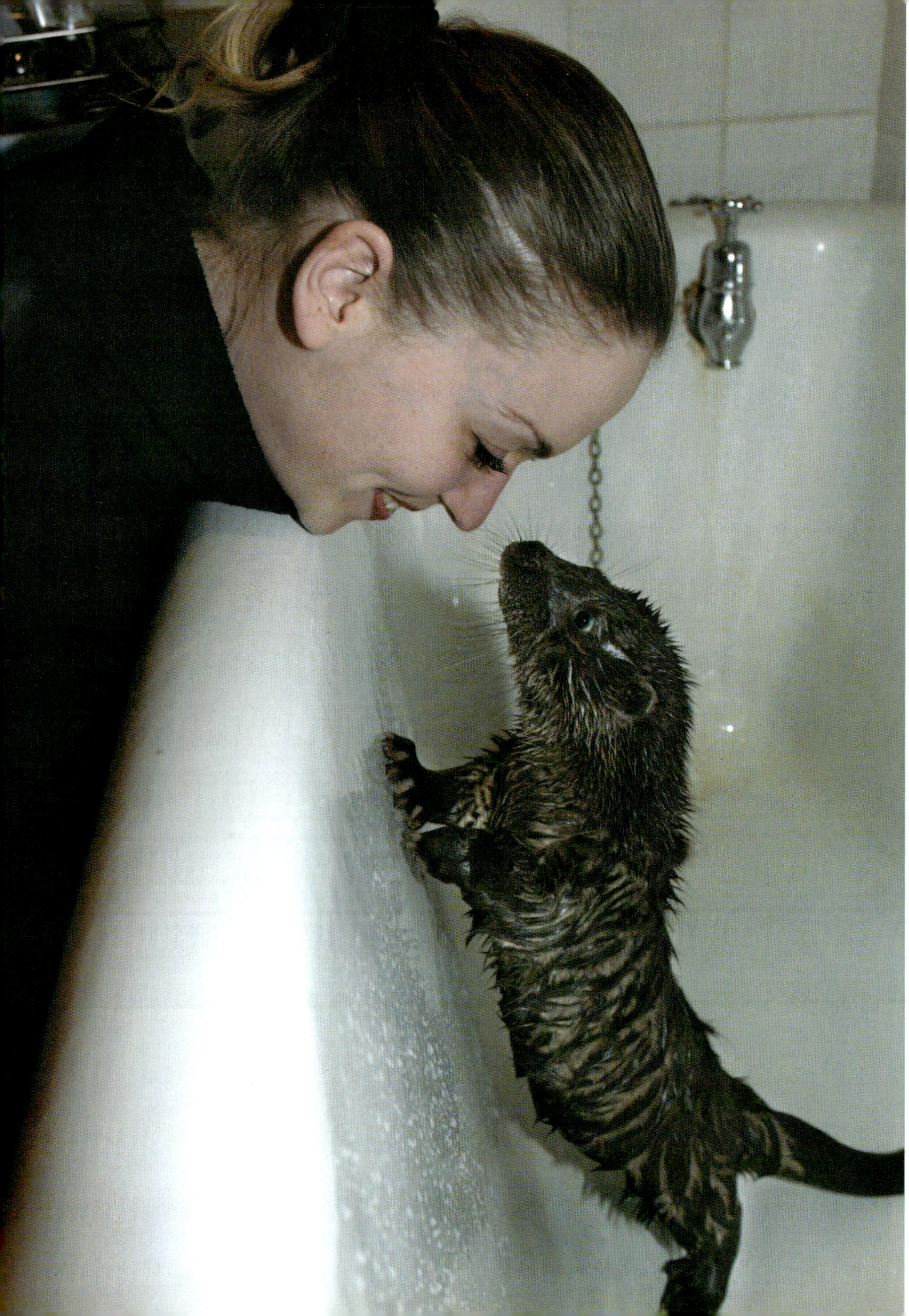

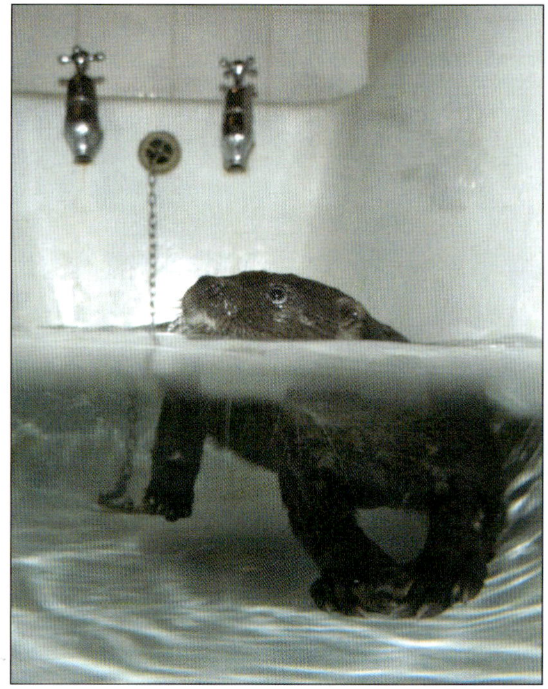

Otter cubs do not like the initial plunge into cold water and in the wild their mother will drag them from the holt and dump them into the water and force them to swim. This was the task for surrogate mum Nikki Hawkins from Secret World who introduced her baby otter to the bath twice a day until the otter loved every minute of his time in the bath.

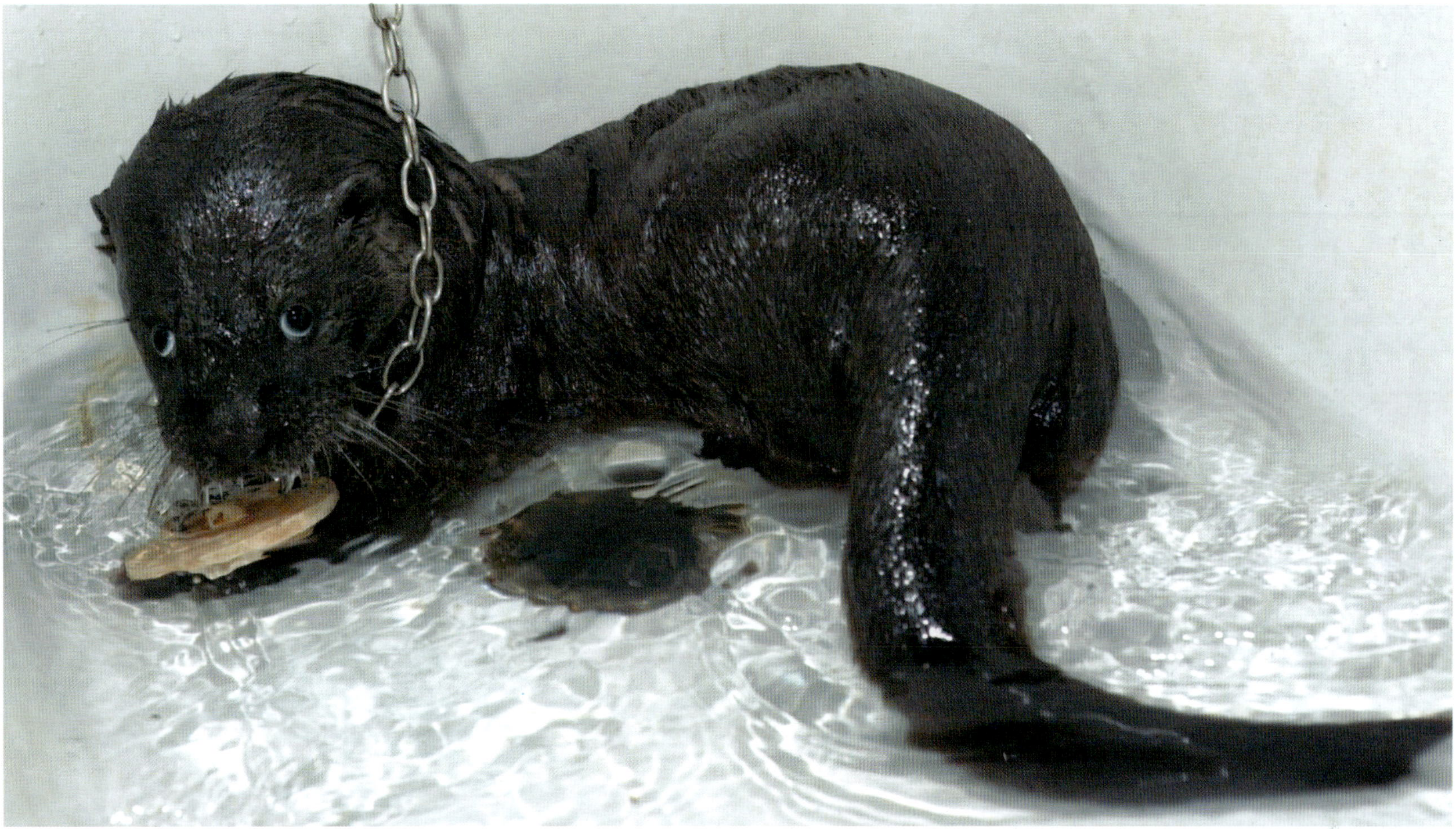

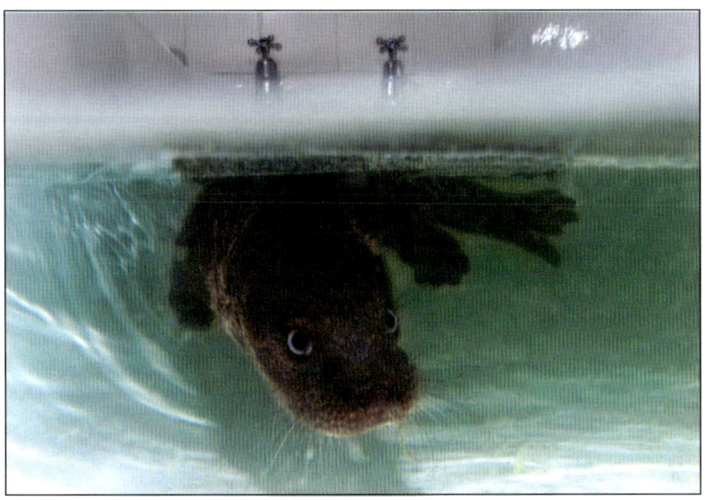

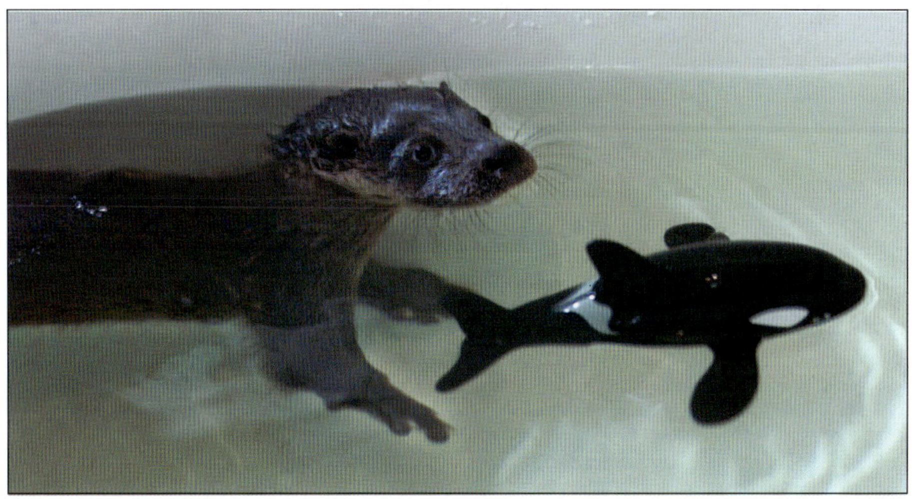

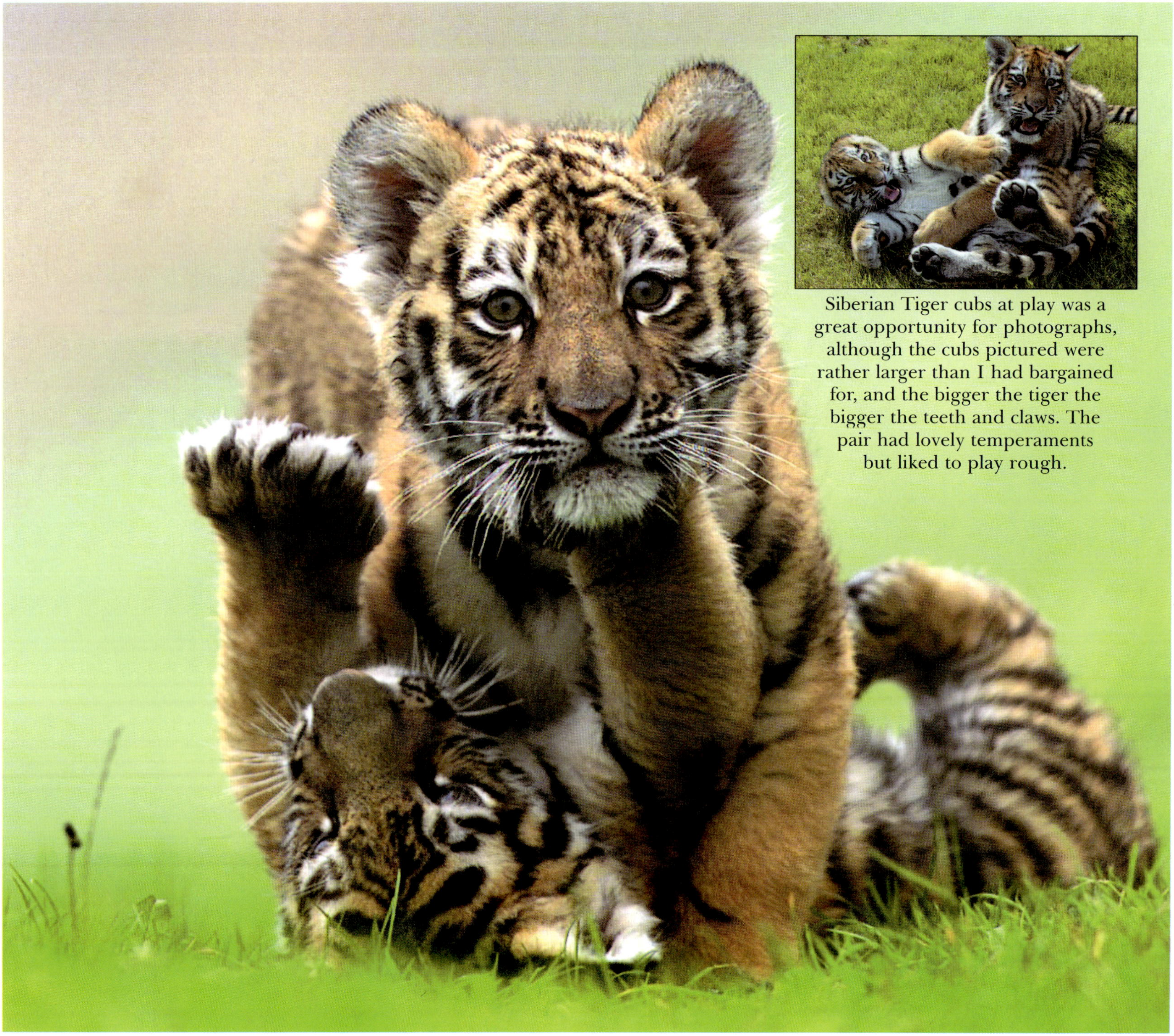

Siberian Tiger cubs at play was a great opportunity for photographs, although the cubs pictured were rather larger than I had bargained for, and the bigger the tiger the bigger the teeth and claws. The pair had lovely temperaments but liked to play rough.

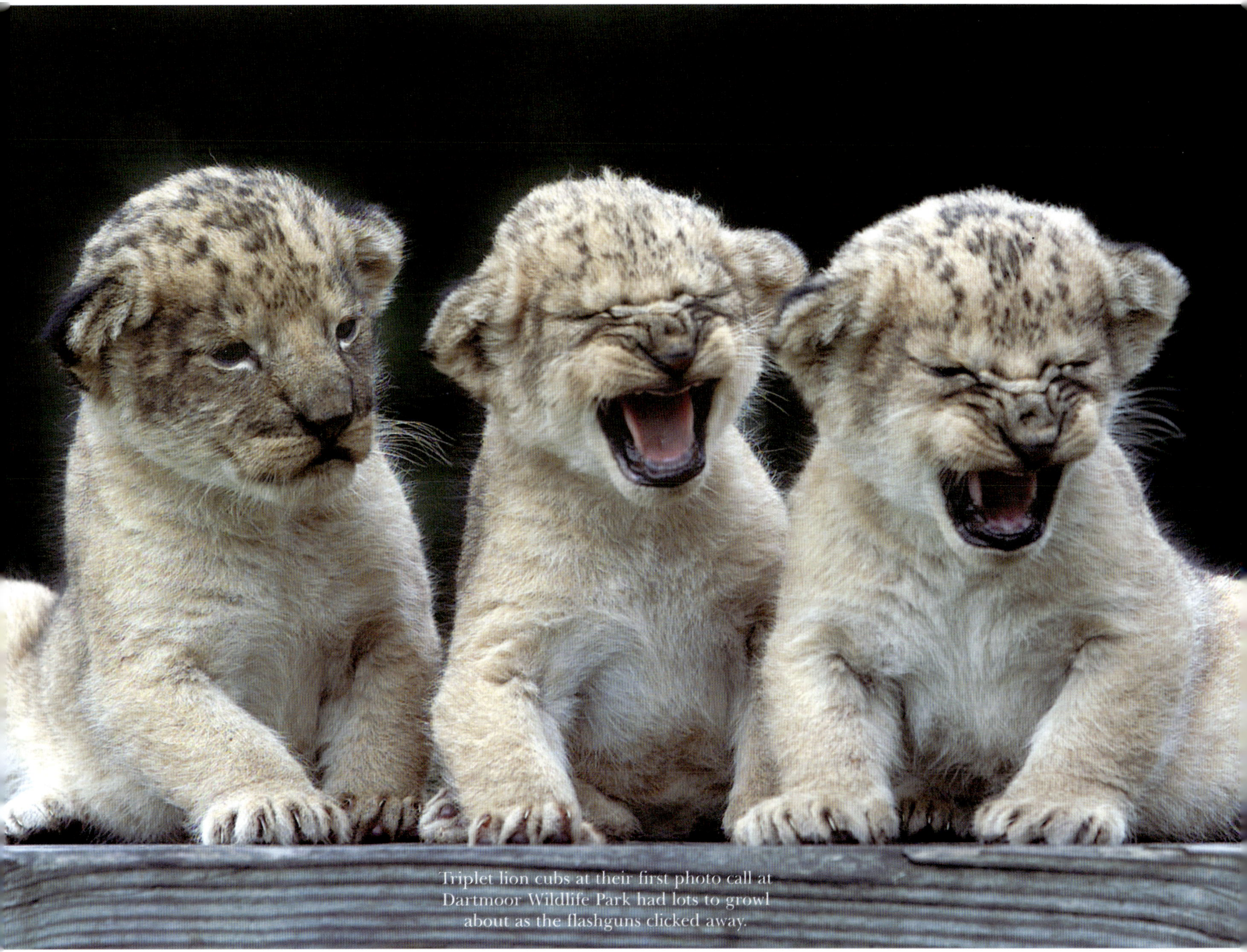

Triplet lion cubs at their first photo call at Dartmoor Wildlife Park had lots to growl about as the flashguns clicked away.

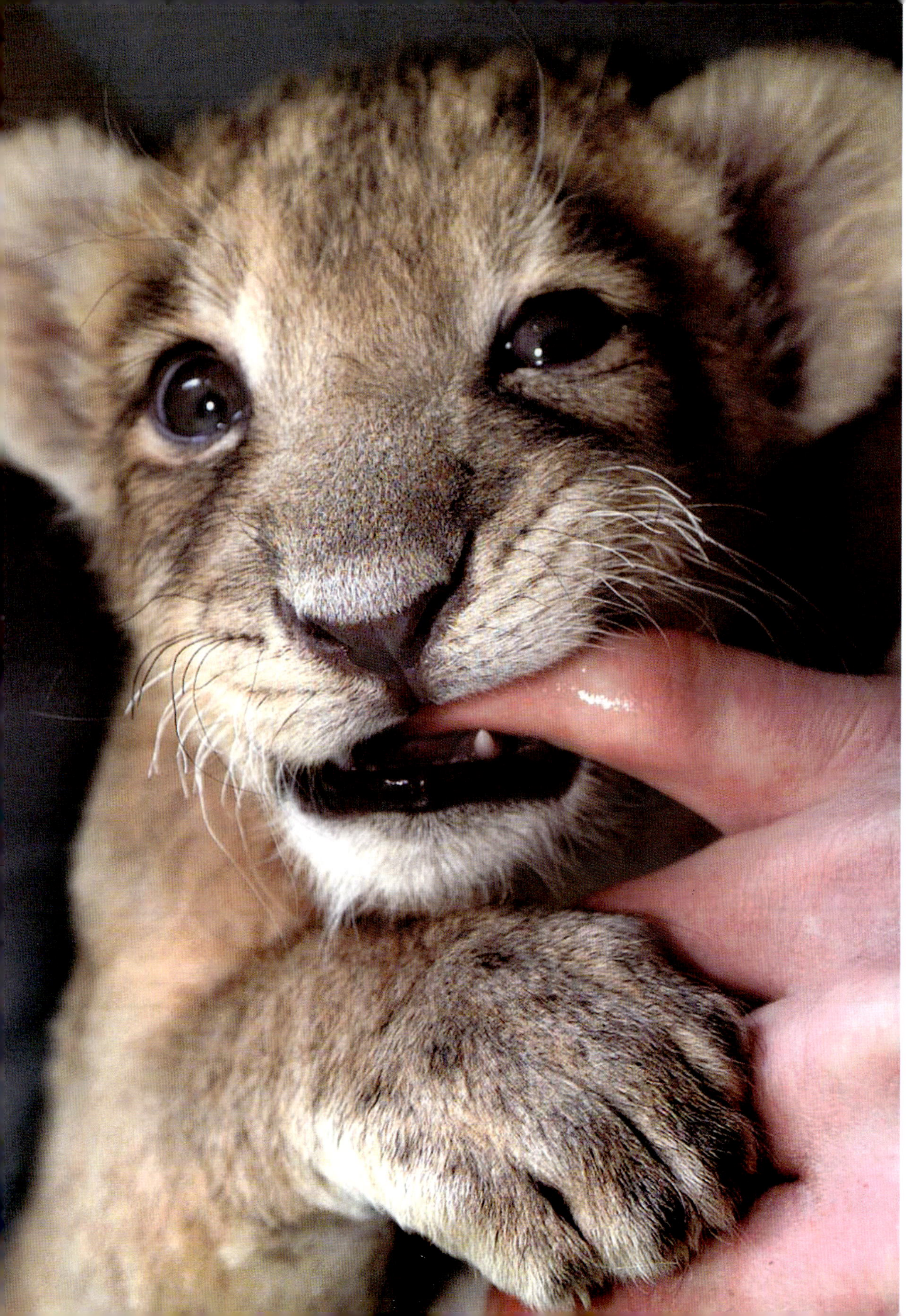

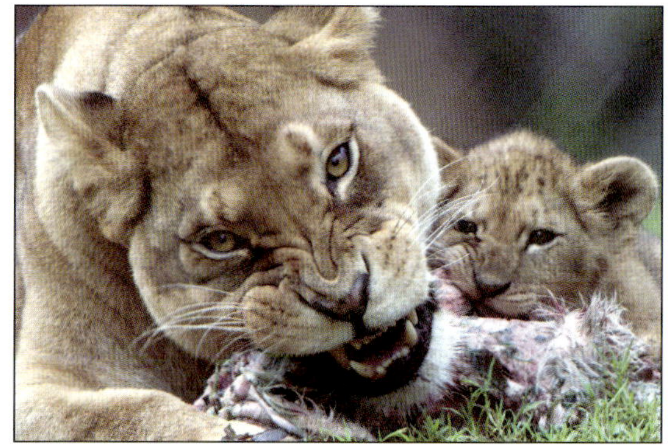

The abandoned lion cub at Paignton Zoo loved to chew on his minder's fingers whilst the full-grown lioness at Dartmoor Wildlife Park tucked into something a little larger.

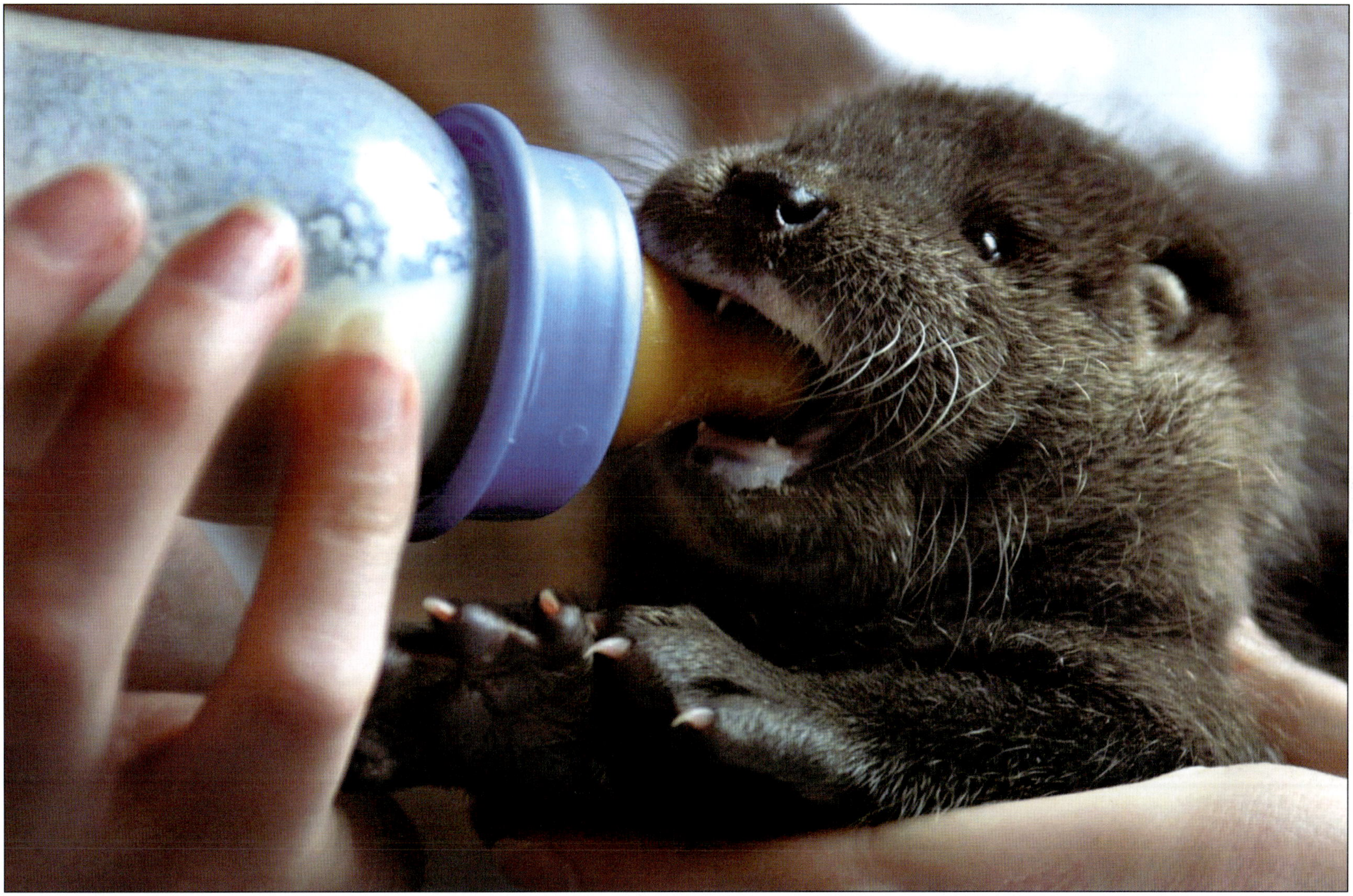

Just like all little babies, the otter cub likes a bottle at bed time.

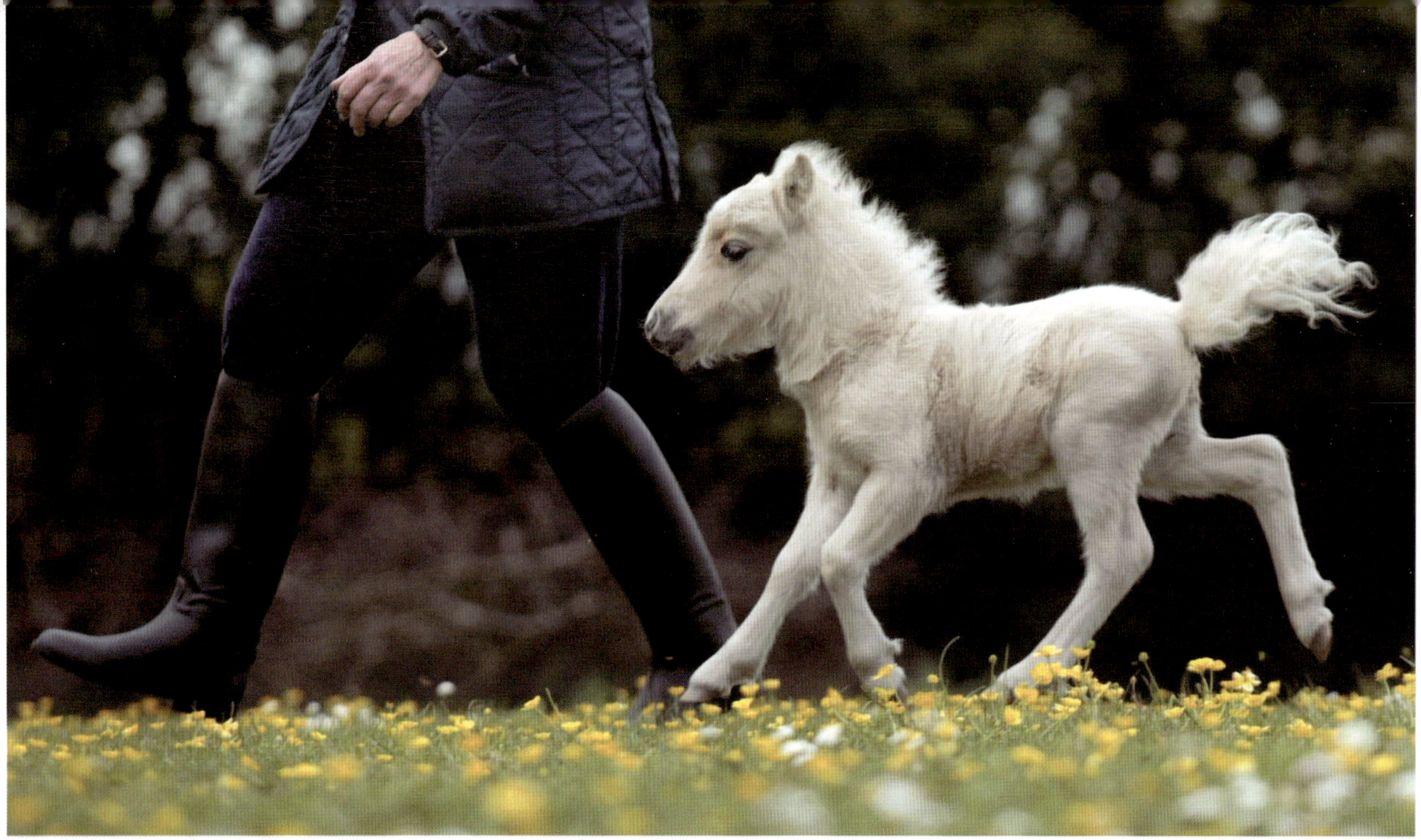

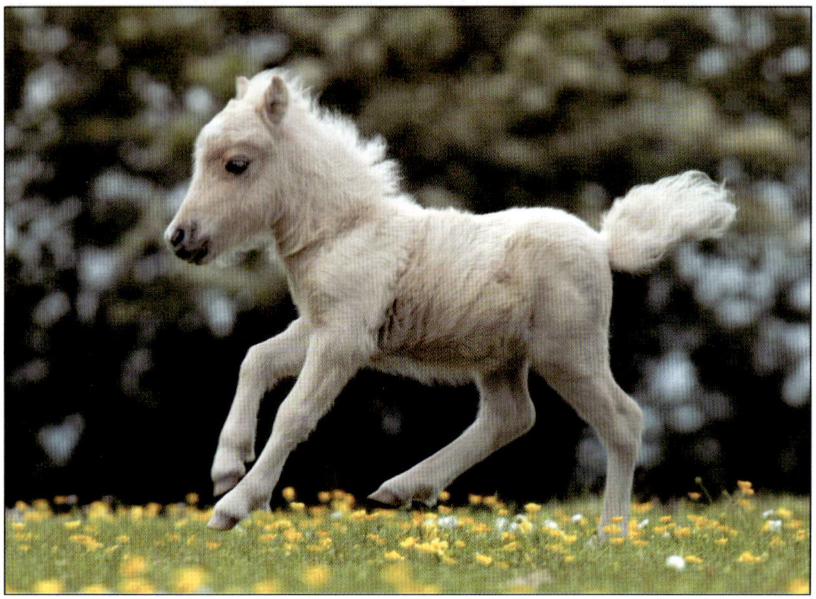

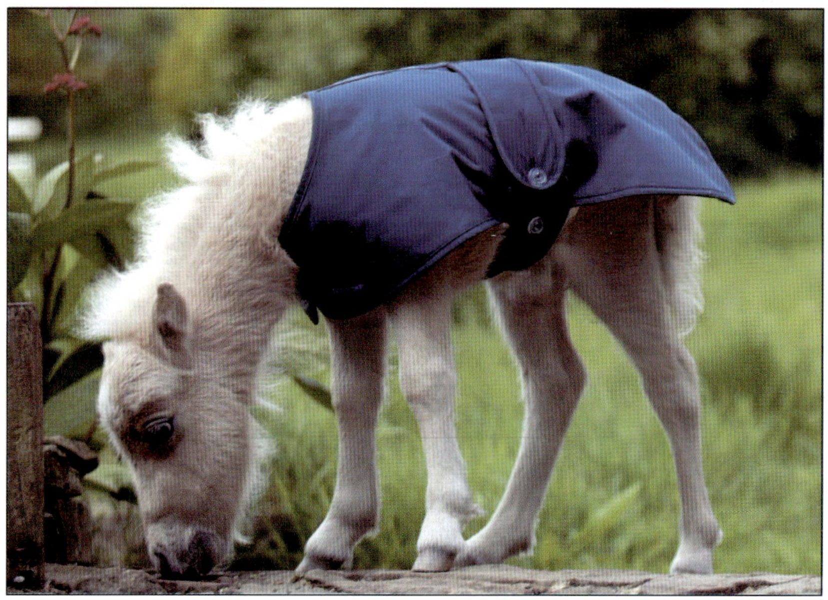

Rejected by his mother and kept alive by human kindness, the pure white Shetland foal had to be hand-reared before being allowed to join the rest of the horses in the paddock.

I waited for ages for the female Mute Swan with her babies riding on her back to turn her head one way or the other, the light and reflection in the water was perfect but the picture didn't work unless I had the side profile of her head. The feather hiding the cygnet's eye was frustrating but in the reflection he can be seen clearly beneath the feather.

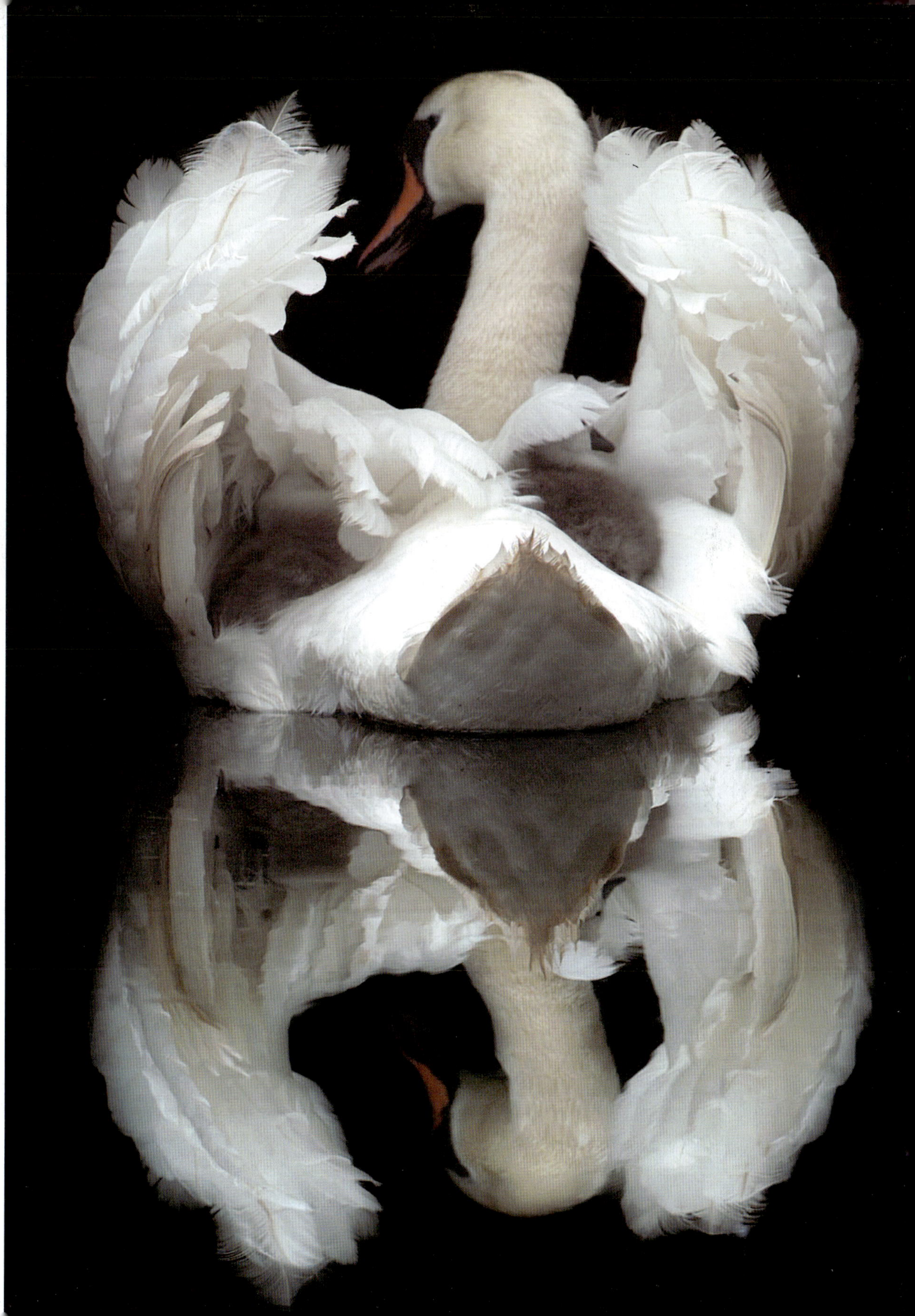

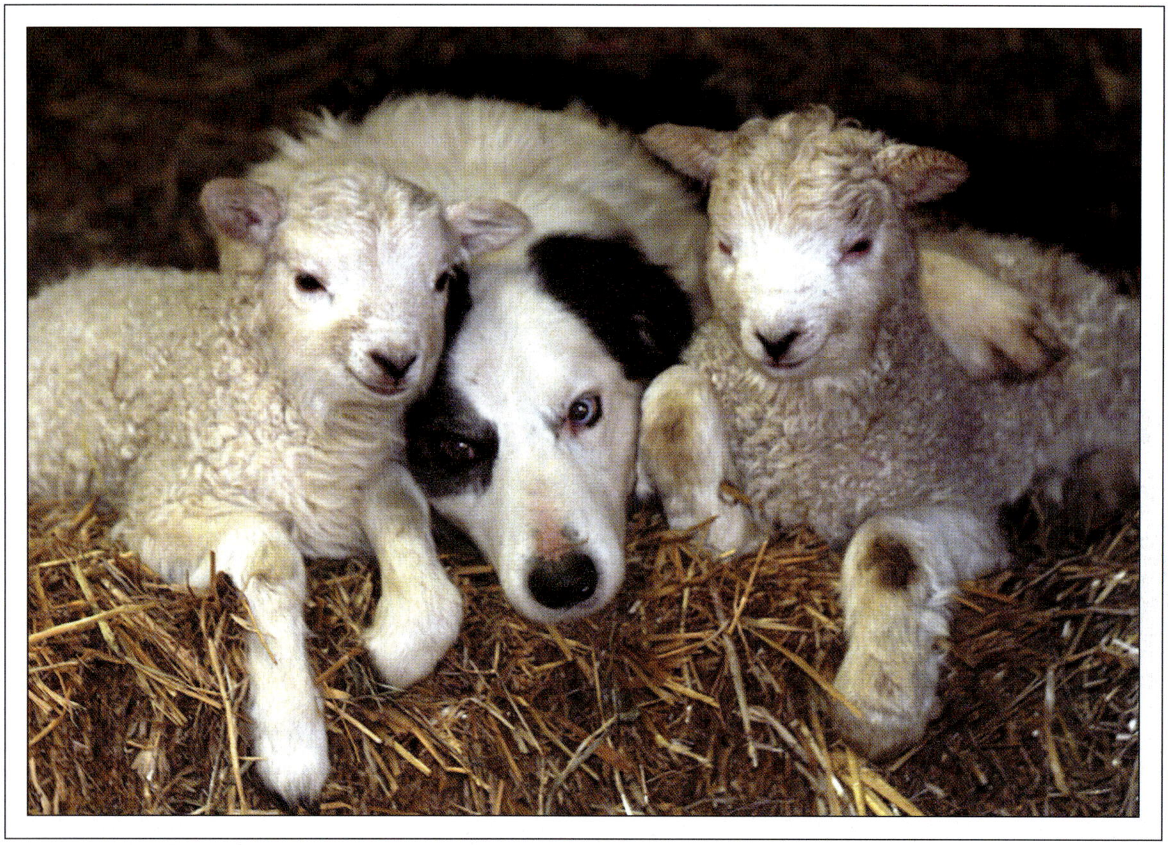

Spot the sheep dog has seen it all before and lambing season? well he takes it all in his stride even if he is left holding the babies at Pennywell Adventure Park in Buckfastleigh, Devon.

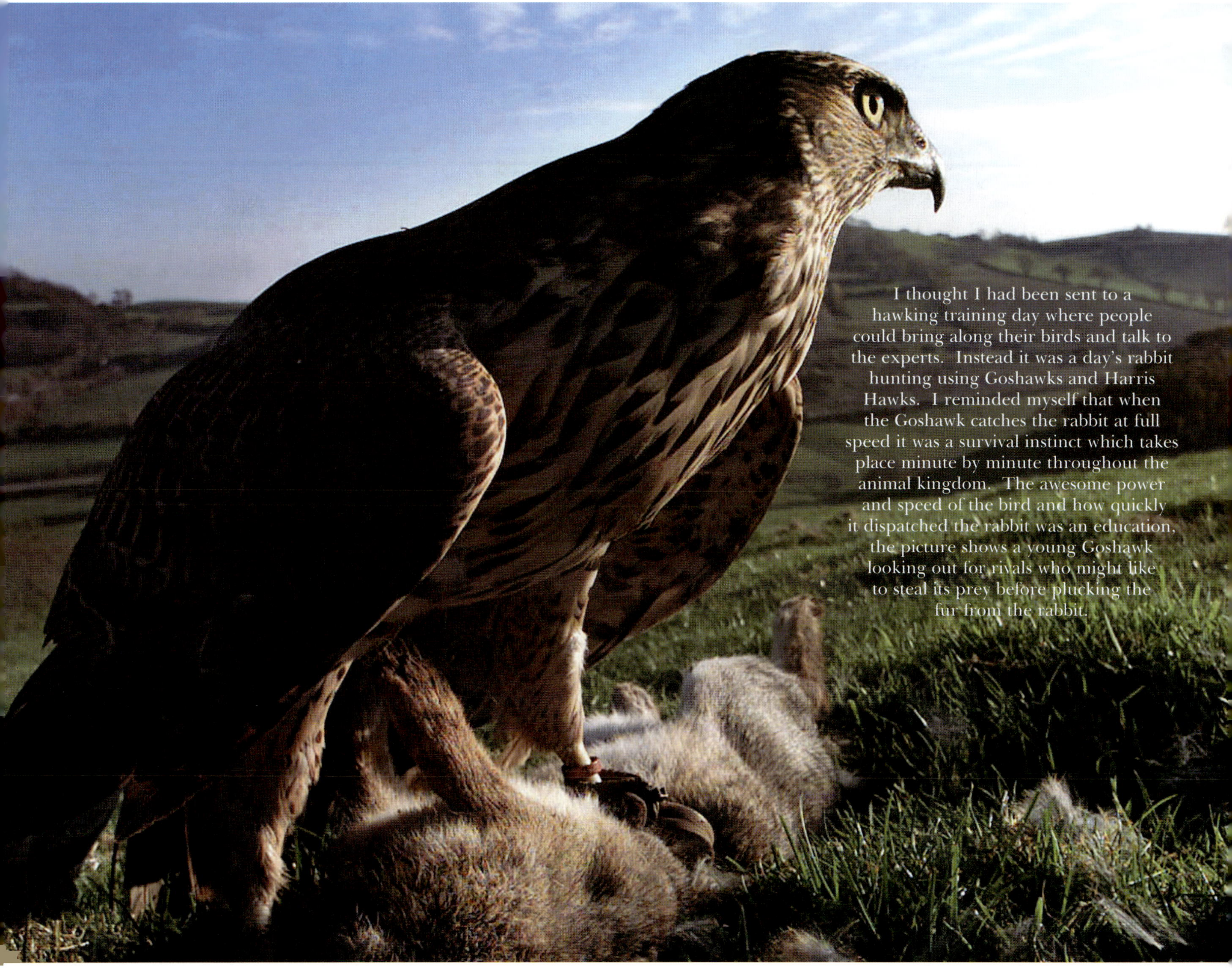

I thought I had been sent to a hawking training day where people could bring along their birds and talk to the experts. Instead it was a day's rabbit hunting using Goshawks and Harris Hawks. I reminded myself that when the Goshawk catches the rabbit at full speed it was a survival instinct which takes place minute by minute throughout the animal kingdom. The awesome power and speed of the bird and how quickly it dispatched the rabbit was an education, the picture shows a young Goshawk looking out for rivals who might like to steal its prey before plucking the fur from the rabbit.

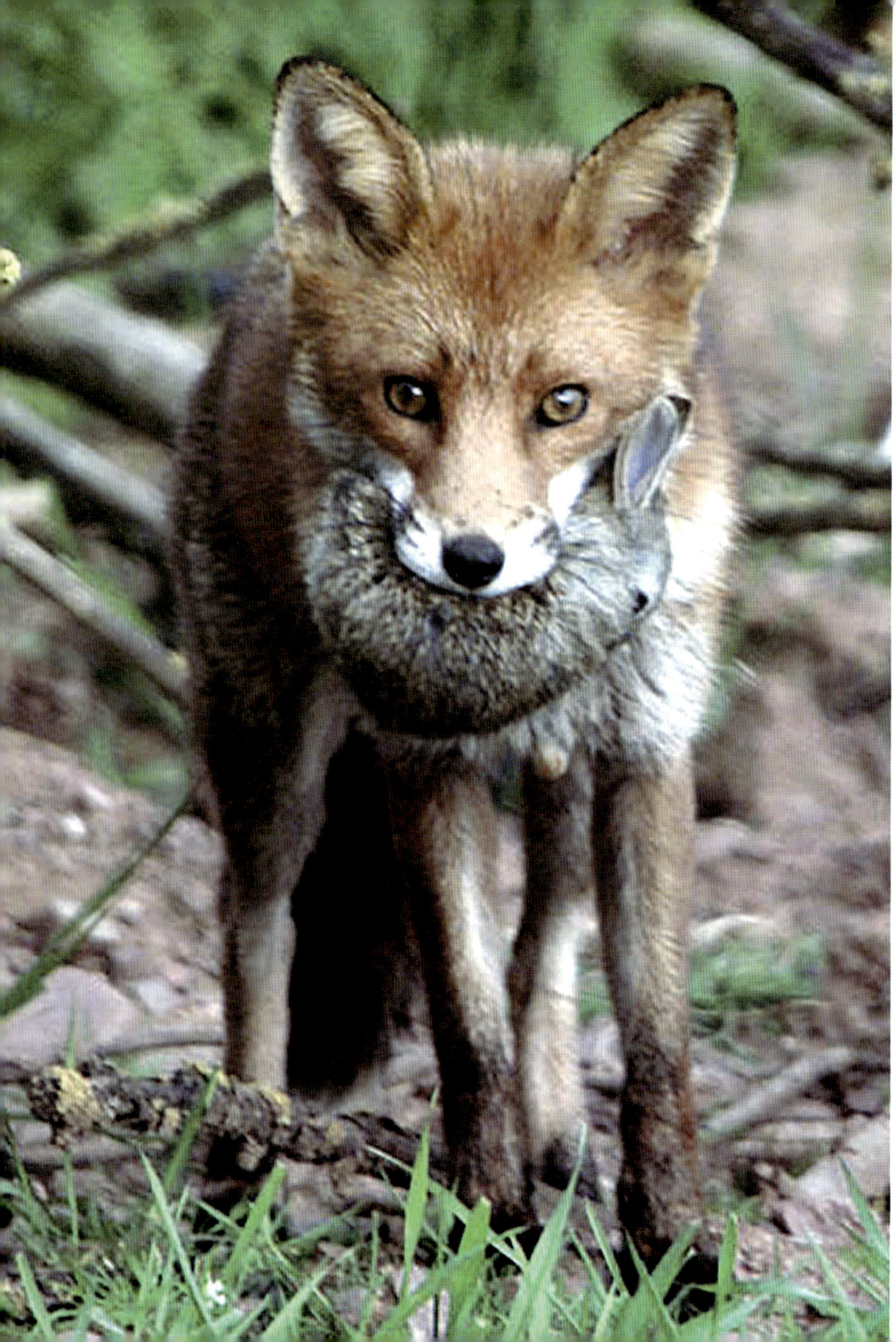

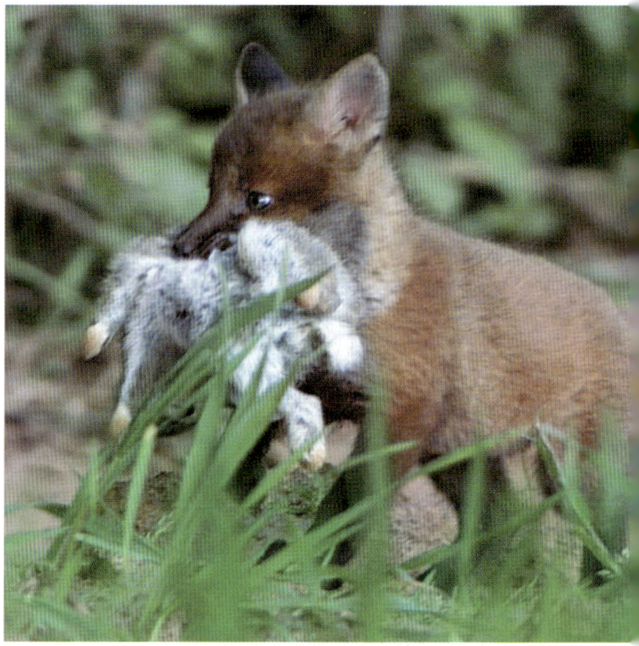

The vixen brings home one of dozens of rabbits which have fattened up her seven cubs in a field near Bradninch. No sooner had she taken the evening meal inside the earth, a cub came rushing out with the rabbit in his mouth obviously not wishing to share it with his brothers and sisters.

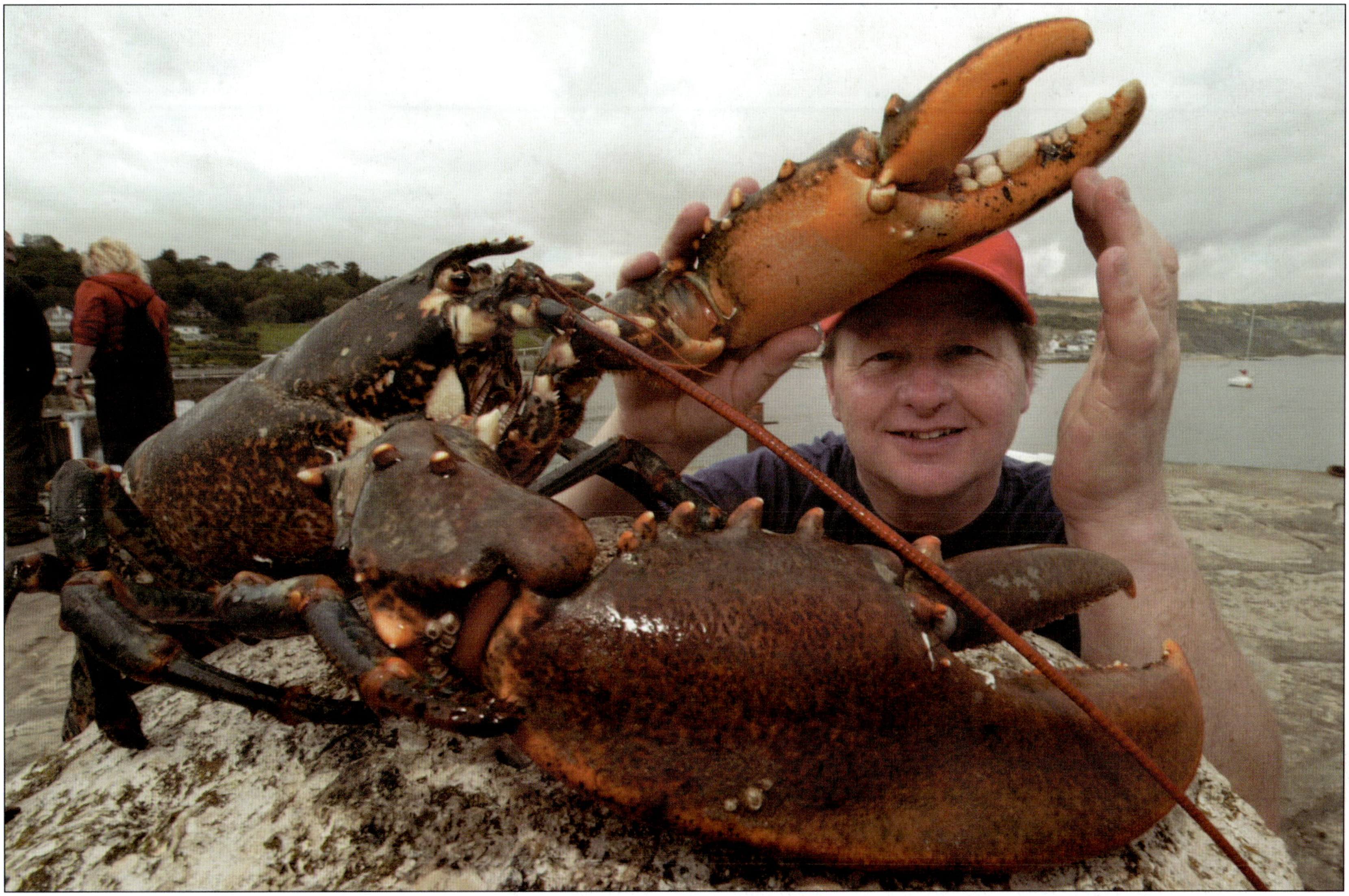

The theory is that when a lobster living on a wreck manages throughout its life to avoid lobster pots, he eventually becomes too big for them anyway. So this is why Claws, the huge lobster living on the wreck of an old German U-boat, managed to grow so big and ended up being caught by diver Norman Whitehead. He spent his summer as an exhibit in the local Marine Aquarium at Lyme Regis before being released back onto his wreck.

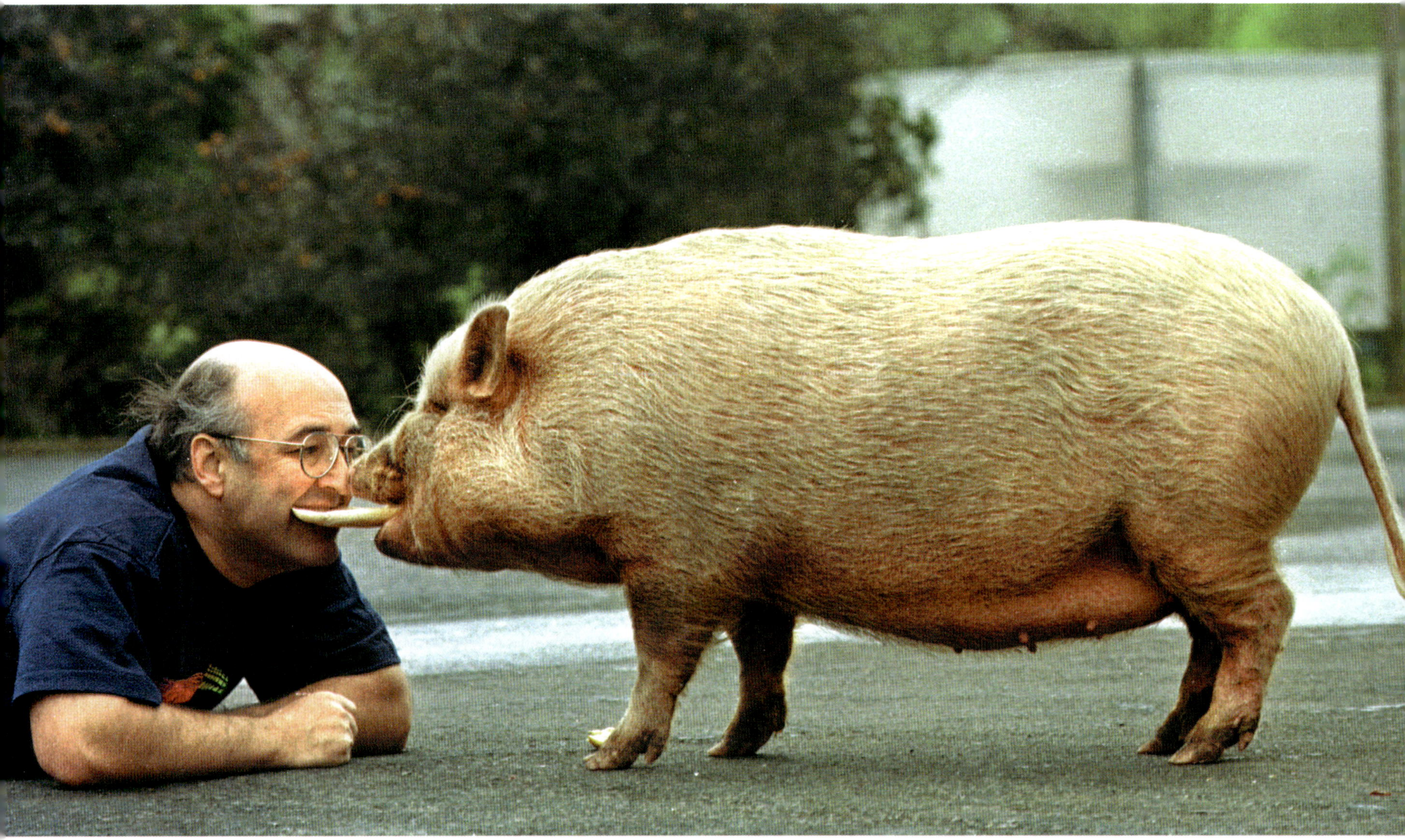

Steve Smith of Tropiquaria near Minehead likes to get close to his animals and the early-morning squabble over who had the last piece of breakfast toast was soon resolved – the pig won!

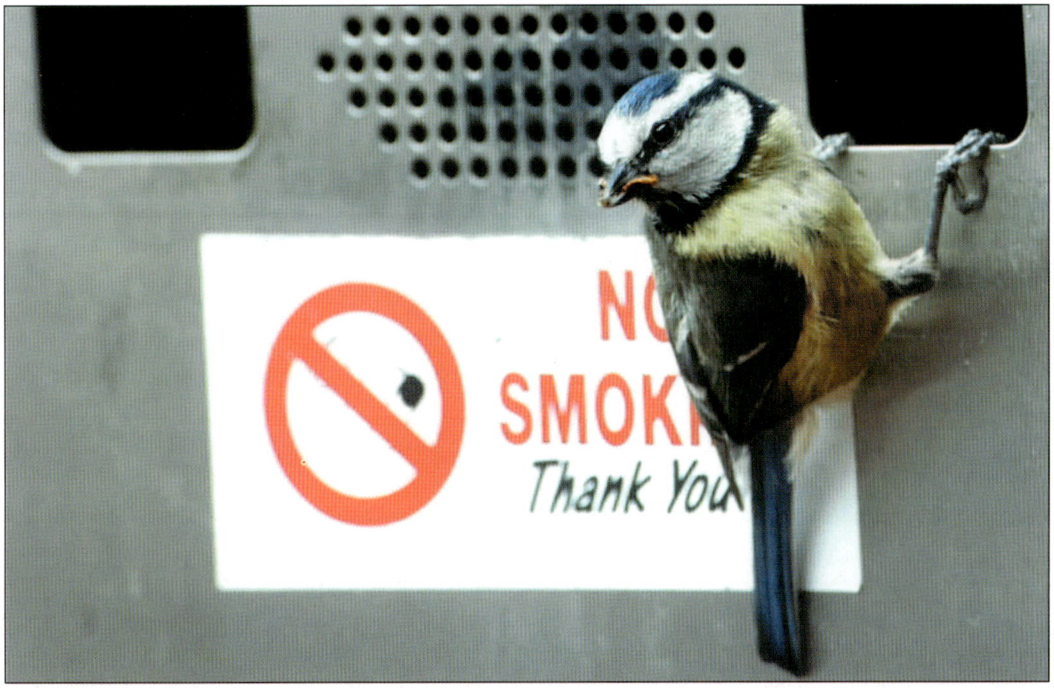


Not often the butt end of bird jokes, but the pair of Blue Tits who nested in the outside ashtray in Exeter raised more than a titter as the babies were brought up on a pile of dog ends.

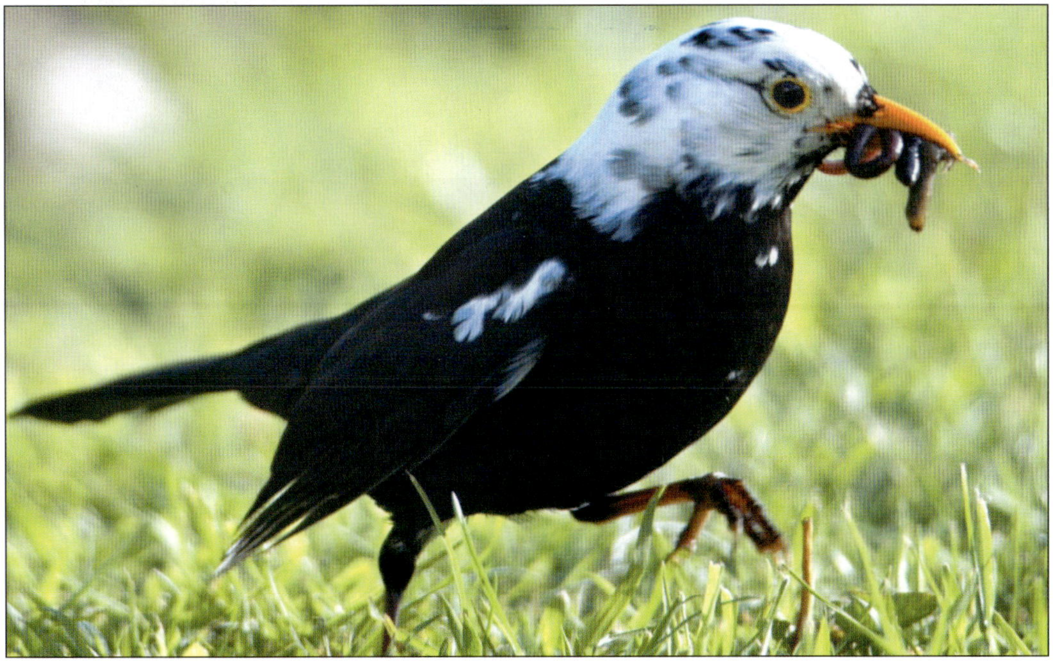

A call from a friend alerted me to this strange looking blackbird who looked as if he had been flying beneath a seagull, his strange markings made him stand out in a flock as he went about collecting worms for his babies nearby.

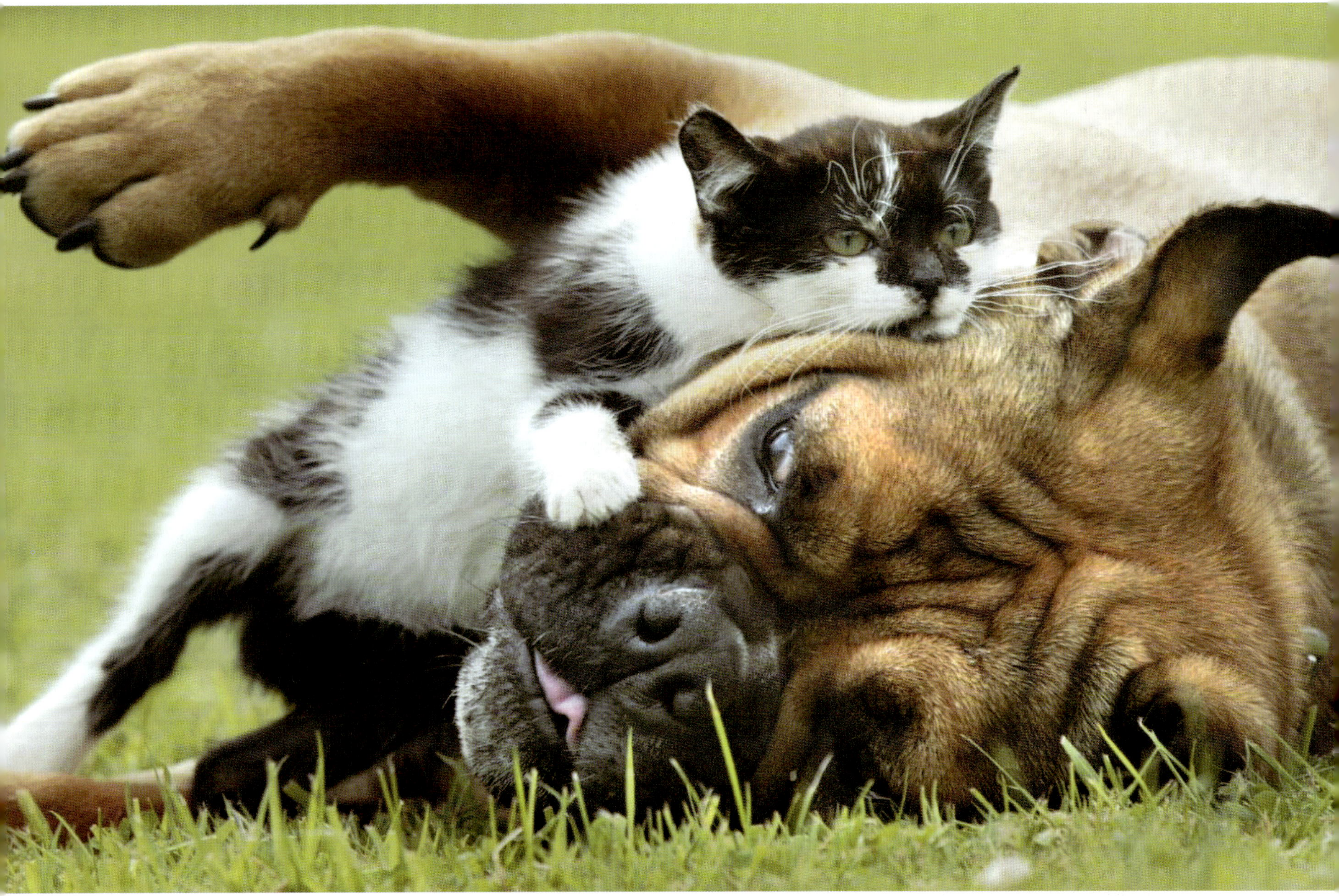

Tentative love at first sight… lucky for Tish the kitten that Rosie the Victorian Bulldog lives with four cats at home after the initial sniff a cuddle was the order of the day at the Axhayes Cats Protection Shelter near Exeter.

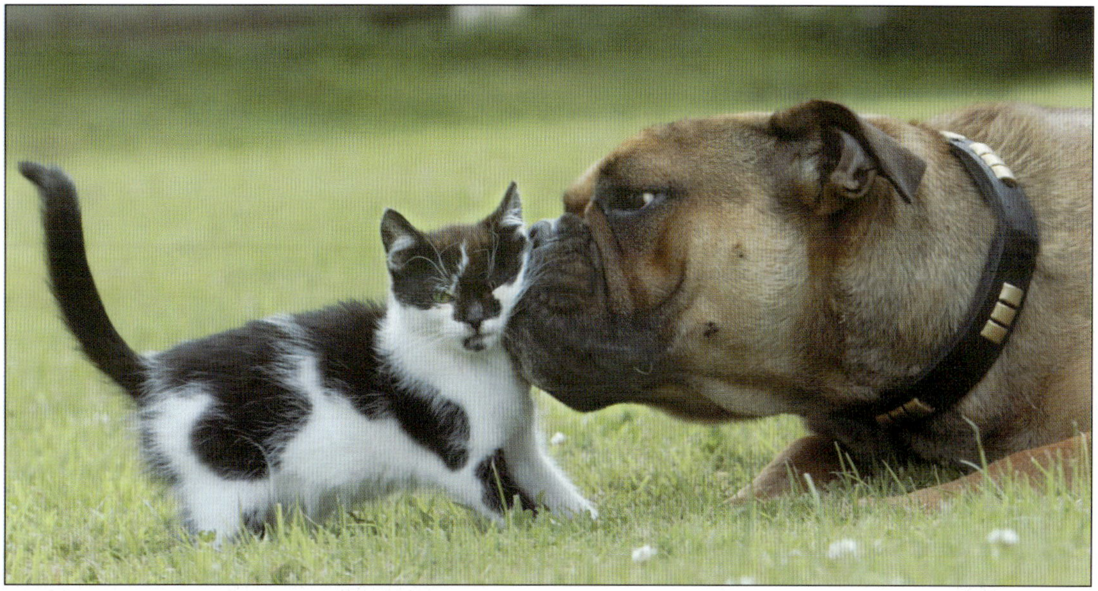

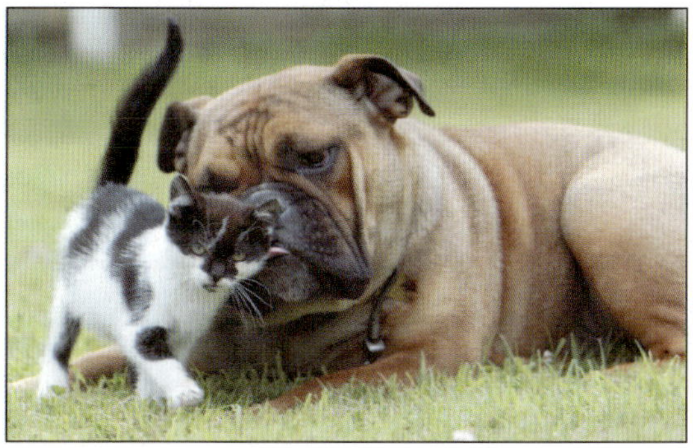

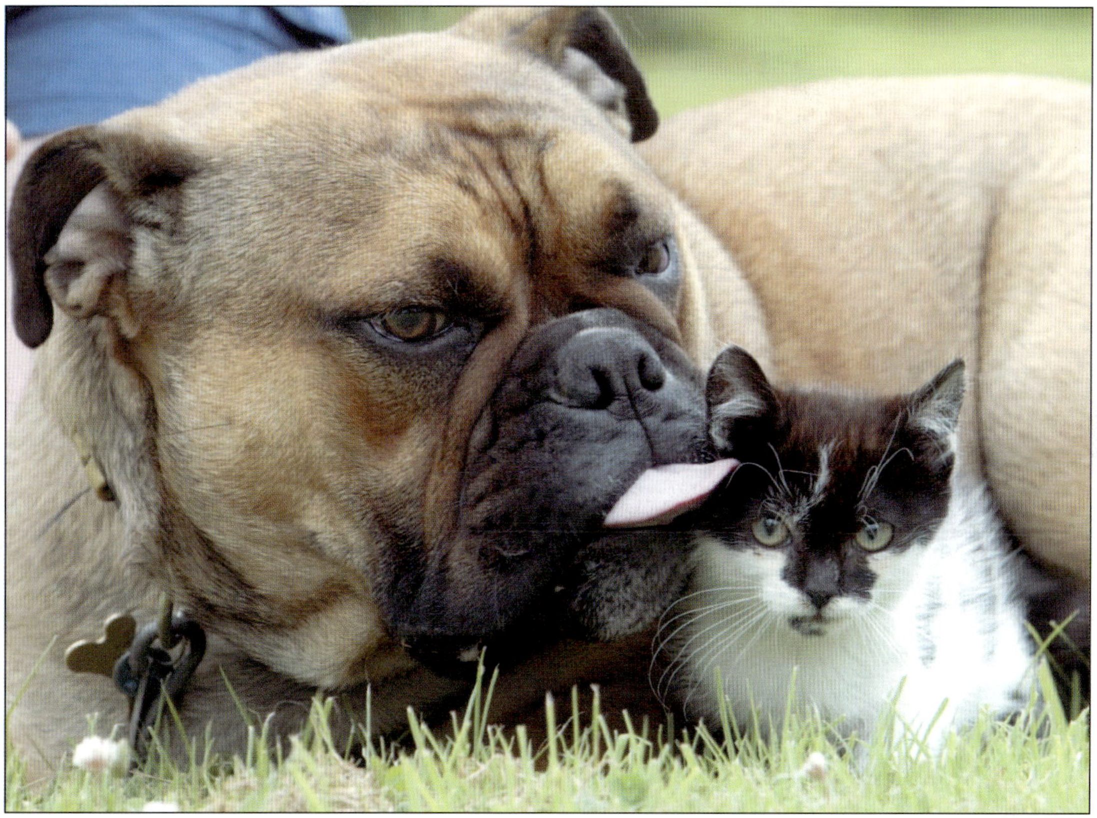

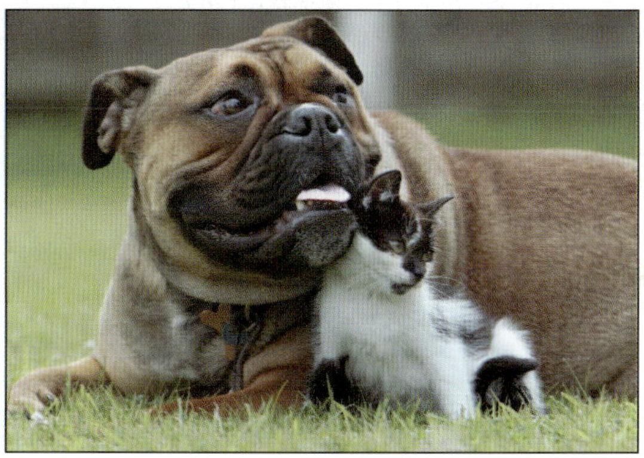

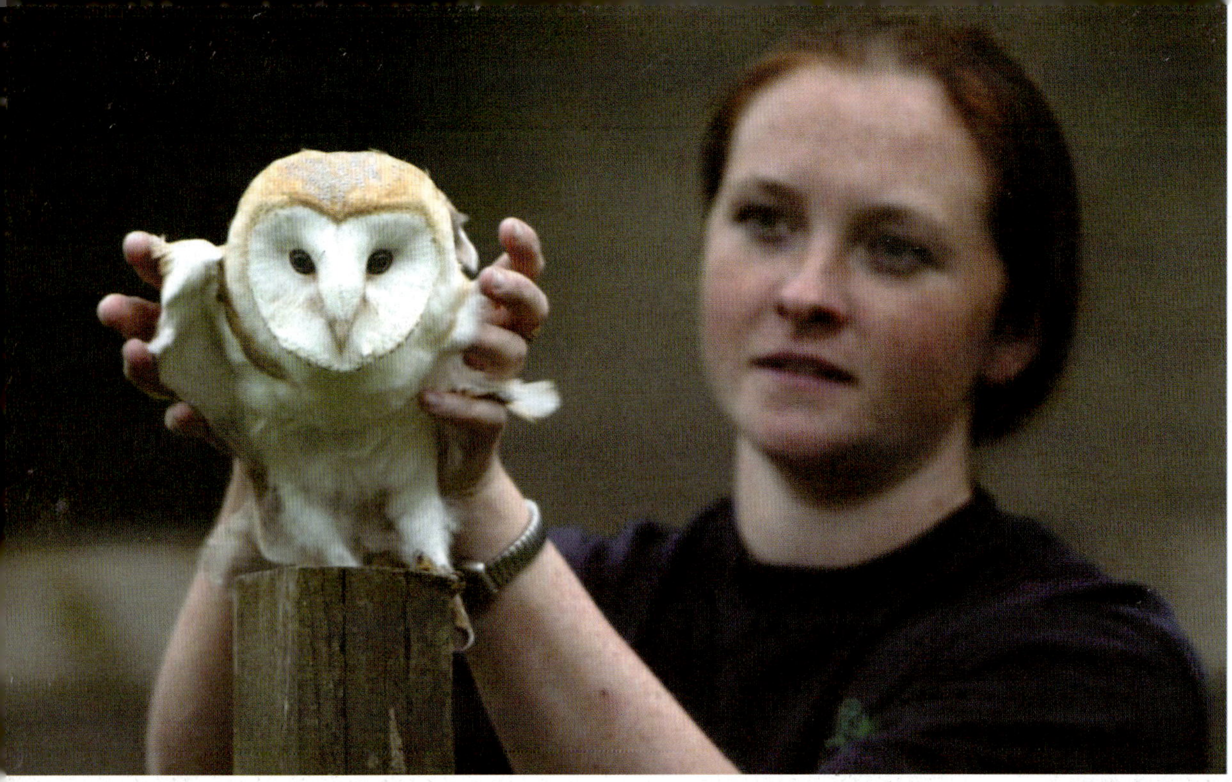

The delight on Ellie West's face says it all as she releases her recovered Barn Owl back into the Somerset countryside. The owl had been nursed by Ellie after a road traffic accident.

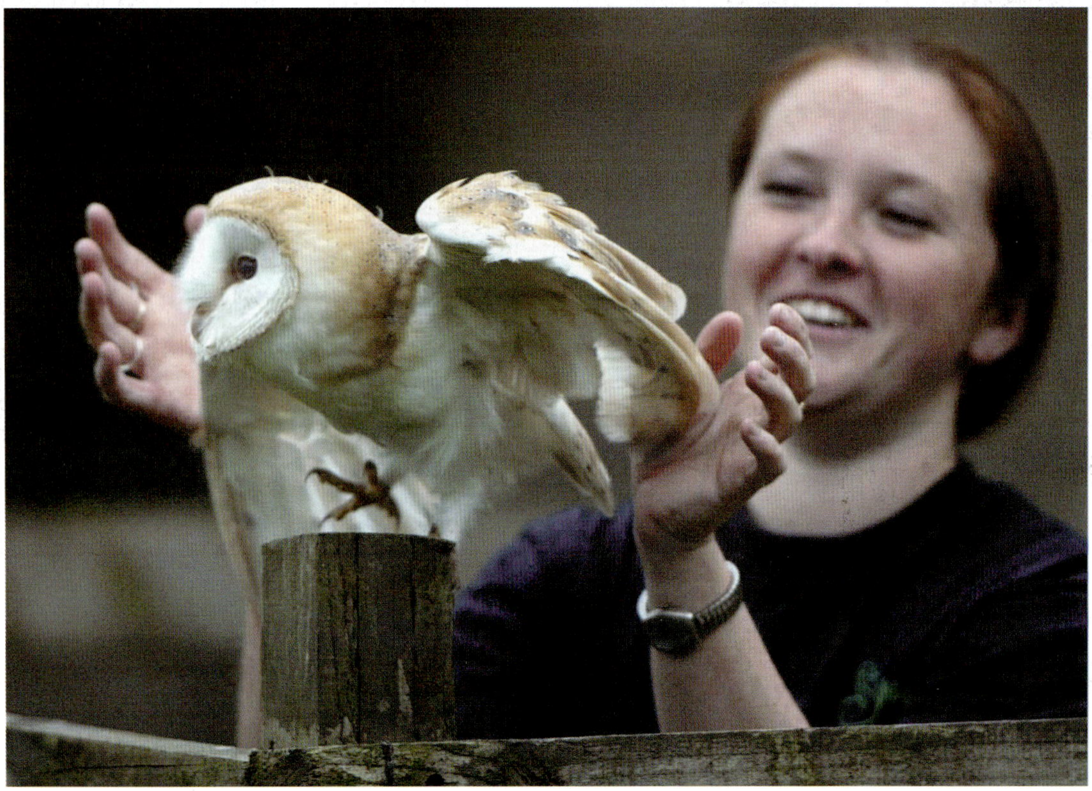

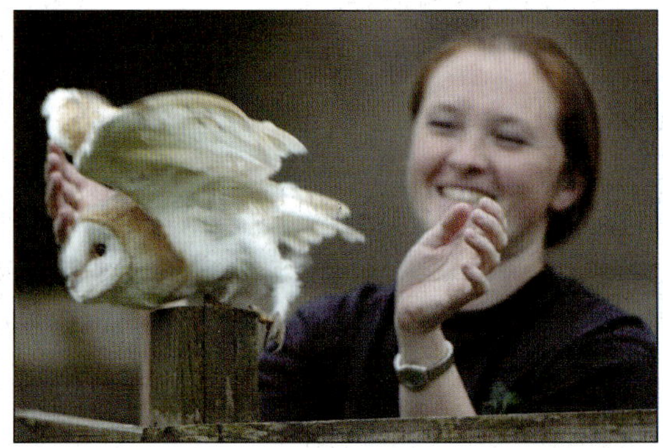

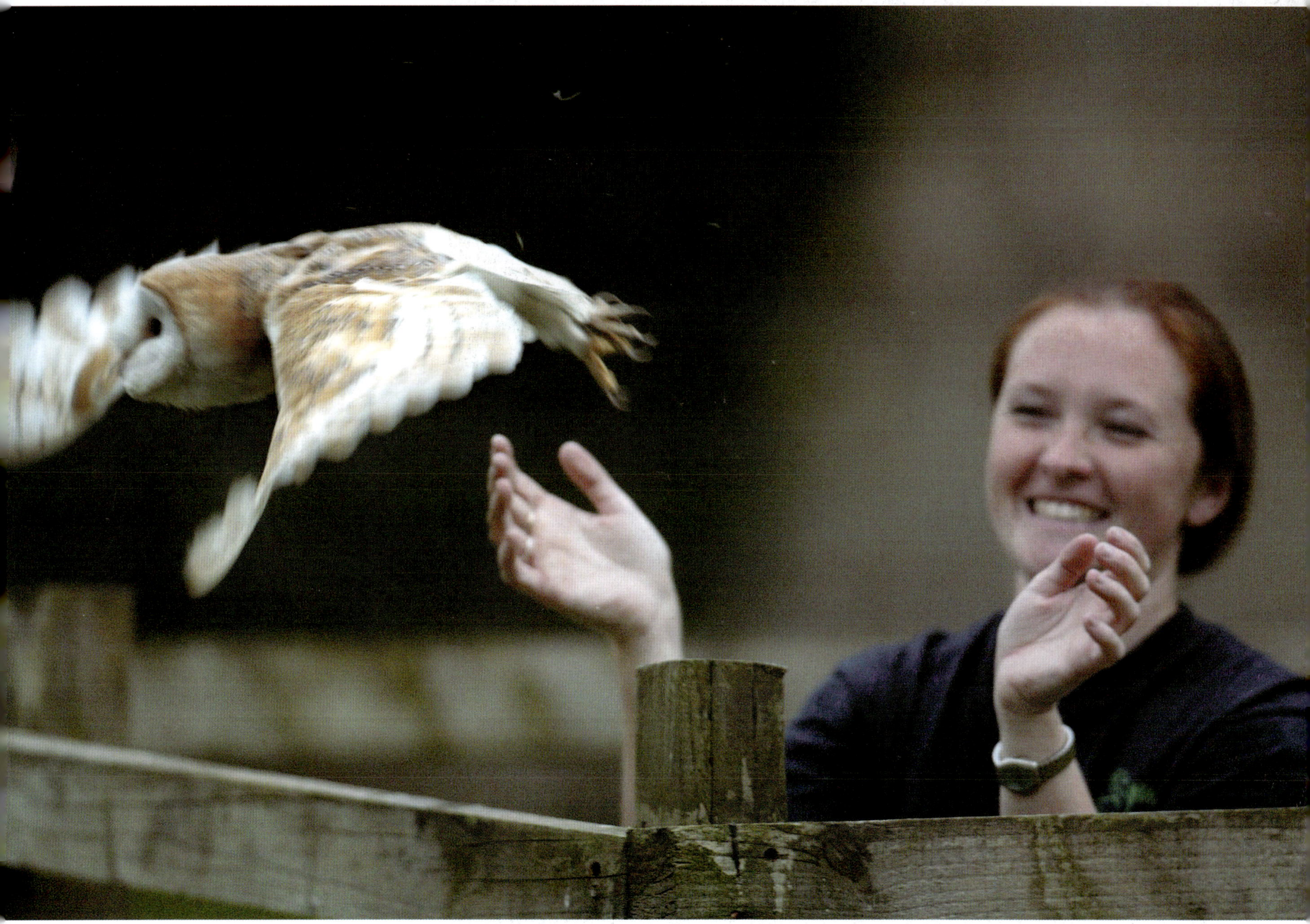

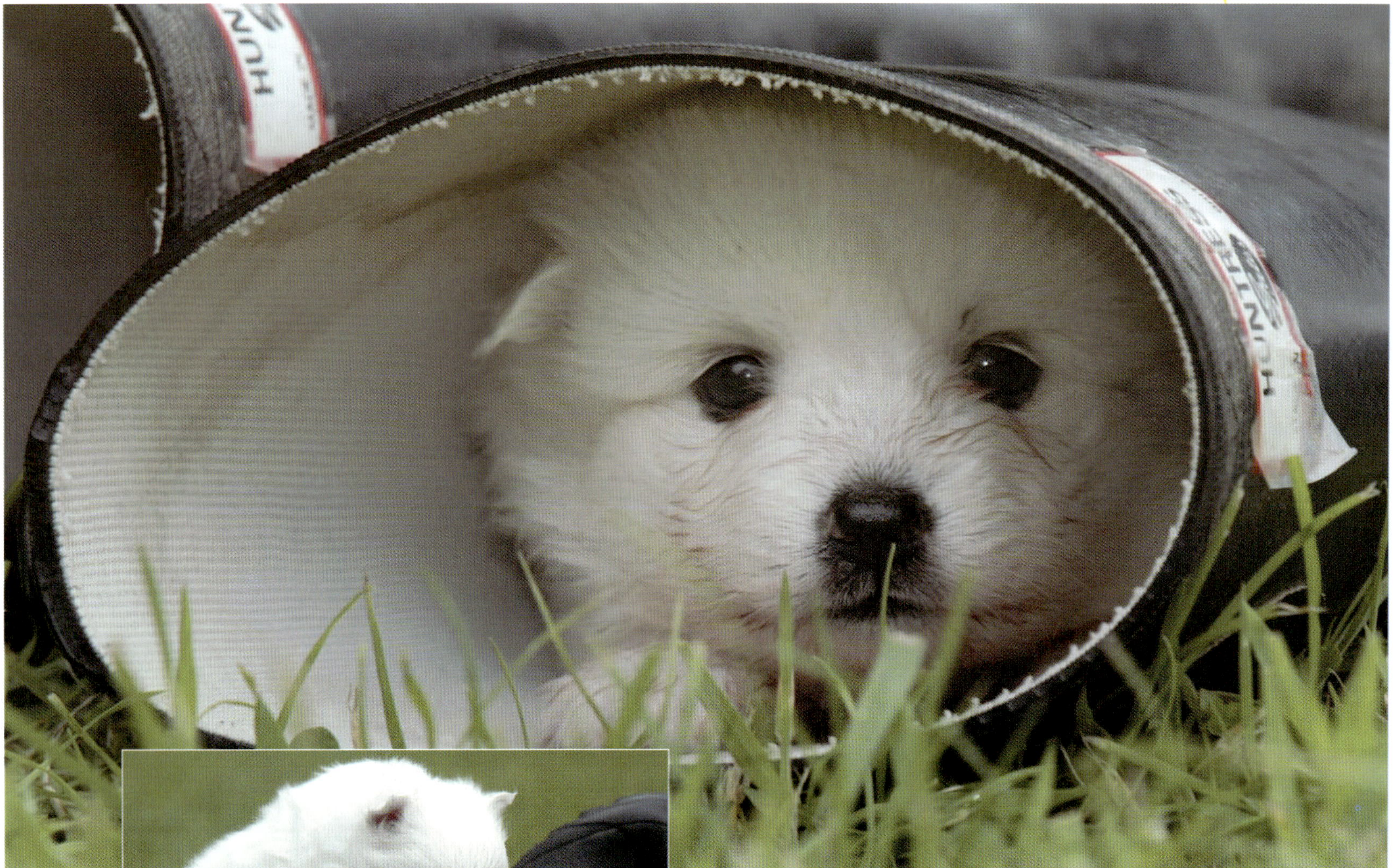

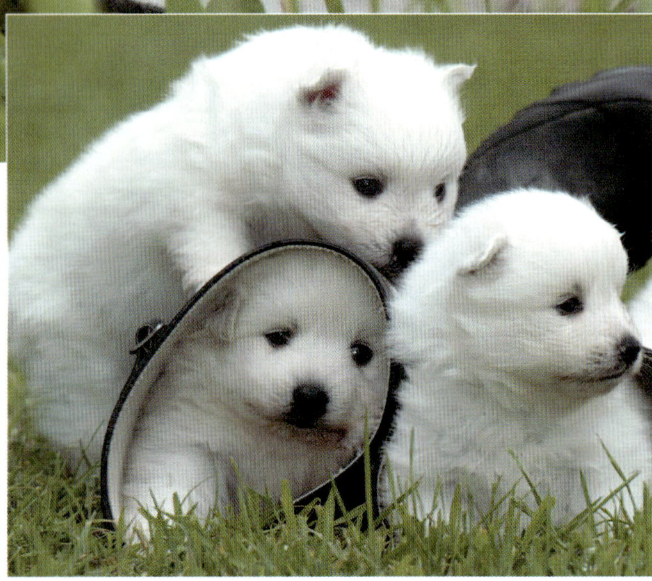

Japanese Spitz puppies playing in a pair of Wellington boots.